Peasant Rebellion and
Communist Revolution in Asia

## CONTRIBUTORS

John Badgley
Kathleen J. Hartford
Ying-mao Kau
John Wilson Lewis
Maurice Meisner
Rex Mortimer
Jeffrey Race
Michael Stenson
Charles Tilly
Christine Pelzer White
Se Hee Yoo
Donald S. Zagoria

# Peasant Rebellion and Communist Revolution in Asia

EDITED BY John Wilson Lewis

Stanford University Press, Stanford, California    1974

Stanford University Press
Stanford, California
© 1974 by the Board of Trustees of the
Leland Stanford Junior University
Printed in the United States of America
ISBN 0-8047-0856-8
LC 73-89860

*To Gordon B. Turner*

# Preface

The purpose of this book is to explain the relationship of peasant rebellions, historically considered, and the Communist-led revolutionary movements that became rooted in parts of Asia in this century. Any adequate explanation seemed to require a detailed examination of that relationship in specific revolutionary situations and an analysis comparing the encounter between peasant and revolutionary in different Asian cultures and with varying outcomes. These requirements, which obviously meant drawing on many sources of information and ideas, inevitably led to a research conference and to this collection.

The ideas that underlay this effort were long in maturing. The process was initiated by the Planning Group on Comparative Communist Studies of the American Council of Learned Societies (ACLS) through a grant from the Carnegie Corporation of New York. The Group was formed in the mid-1960's, and its membership during the years that I participated included Donald L. M. Blackmer, R. V. Burks, Frederic J. Fleron, Jr., Nicolas Spulber, Robert C. Tucker, Mark G. Field, and Ezra F. Vogel. Beyond my intellectual debt to these scholars—and that debt is substantial—I wish to acknowledge with thanks the generous support of Gordon B. Turner, vice-president of the ACLS, to whom this volume is dedicated.

The Group's concerns developed in periodic discussions over its seven-year life span and became concentrated on a number of specific problem areas and themes. The first book published as a result of the Group's activities was *Change in Communist Systems* (1970), edited by Chalmers Johnson. Others in press with other publishers are a volume on the social consequences of modernization in socialist countries edited by Mark Field, and one on the French and Italian Communist parties edited by Donald Blackmer and Sidney Tarrow.

The papers in this book were first presented at a research conference held in St. Croix, Virgin Islands, in January 1973. For help in the planning stages for the conference, I should like especially to thank Alexander Dallin, Shmuel Eisenstadt, William E. Griffith, Samuel P. Huntington, Alex Inkeles, Chalmers Johnson, Andrzej Korbonski, Leopold Labedz, Ruth T. McVey, Alfred G. Meyer, Michel Oksenberg, and Jan F. Triska. Seven scholars, in addition to the authors represented herein, participated in the St. Croix sessions: Frederic J. Fleron, Jr., Thomas T. Hammond, James P. Harrison, Robert N. Kearney, Robert W. McColl, Lucian W. Pye, and George O. Totten. The burden of organizing and running much of the conference fell to Gerry Bowman and to Kathleen Hartford, who acted as rapporteur.

My own interest in the theme of Communist revolutions in Asia began in my study of urban development on the North China Plain. As so often happens in studies that are meant to dig deeply into the data on a single place or subject, the questions inexorably became broader and more comparative. What intrigued me most about the origins of the city I was studying was the way the peasants reacted to urban and industrial development. They were organized, politically conscious, and highly active right from the start. What puzzled me was the response to Communism of the peasants who stayed in the surrounding villages. Steeped in the historical memory of resistance and rebellion, these peasants greeted Communist organizers with aloofness and hostility. My curiosity was further piqued by a trip that I made to the North China area immediately before the St. Croix conference and by interviews shortly afterward with former Chinese Communist agents who had attempted to build the revolution in that area.

My research on the problems of peasantries in revolution has been generously supported by grants from the Ford Foundation and the National Endowment for the Humanities, and I acknowledge their support with gratitude. I am deeply indebted as well to Jeanne Szeto and Charles W. Loomis for their able assistance during the years of my research. I would also like to express my appreciation to J. G. Bell and Barbara E. Mnookin of Stanford University Press and to Gerry Bowman and Kathleen Hartford for their work on the manuscript.

In editing this book I have tried to organize the papers in such a way that our hypotheses, findings, differences, and unanswered questions stand out. In the final analysis a conference volume should, in breaking new ground, challenge and provoke. The success of this volume will be measured more by the research that follows than by these pages themselves.

J.W.L.

May 1, 1974

# Contents

# Contributors

JOHN BADGLEY is President of the Institute of the Rockies at Missoula, Montana. He taught at Miami (Ohio) University from 1962 to 1966 and at Johns Hopkins University from 1967 to 1973. His publications include *Asian Development* (1971) and *The Red Peacocks* (forthcoming).

KATHLEEN J. HARTFORD is obtaining her Ph.D. in political science from Stanford University. She is currently completing a dissertation on the origins of peasant participation in the Chinese Communist Revolution. In the fall of 1974 she will join the political science faculty of Amherst College.

YING-MAO KAU, Associate Professor of Political Science at Brown University, is the editor of the journal *Chinese Law and Government* and the author of *The Political Work System of the Chinese Communist Military* (1971) and *The People's Liberation Army and China's Nation-Building* (1973). He is completing a book on China's organizations and political development.

JOHN WILSON LEWIS is the William Haas Professor of Chinese Politics at Stanford University. He is the author of *Leadership in Communist China* (1963), *Major Doctrines of Communist China* (1964), and (with George McT. Kahin) *The United States in Vietnam* (1967); and he has edited *Party Leadership and Revolutionary Power in China* (1970) and *The City in Communist China* (1971).

MAURICE MEISNER, Professor of History at the University of Wisconsin, Madison, is the author of *Li Ta-chao and the Origins of Chinese Marxism* (1967) and *The Chinese People's Republic, 1949–1974: An Interpretive History* (1974). He is the editor of a forthcoming book, *The Mozart-*

*ian Historian: Joseph Levenson on China and the World*, and is now at work on a study of the social and intellectual sources of Maoist utopianism.

REX MORTIMER, Professor of Political Studies at the University of Papua New Guinea, is the author of *The Indonesian Communist Party and Land Reform* (1973) and *Indonesian Communism Under Sukarno: Ideology and Politics, 1959–1965* (1974) ; and he is the editor of *Showcase State: The Illusion of Indonesia's "Accelerated Modernization"* (1973).

JEFFREY RACE received his Ph.D. in political science from Harvard University in 1973. He is the author of *War Comes to Long An: Revolutionary Conflict in a Vietnamese Province* (1972) and is currently preparing a comparative study of the impact of institutional development on social and economic inequality in Southeast Asia.

MICHAEL STENSON studied for his M.A. at the University of Auckland and for his Ph.D. at the University of Malaya. He has been teaching Southeast Asian history at the University of Auckland since 1968. He is the author of *Industrial Conflict in Malaya: Prelude to the Communist Revolt of 1948* (1970).

CHARLES TILLY is Professor of History, Professor of Sociology, and Director of the Center for Research on Social Organization at the University of Michigan. Among the works he has authored or co-authored are *The Vendée* (1964), *Race and Residence in Wilmington* (1965), *History as Social Science* (1971), *Subsidizing the Poor* (1972), *Strikes in France* (1974), and *An Urban World* (1974).

CHRISTINE PELZER WHITE is completing a Ph.D. dissertation for Cornell University on land reform in the Democratic Republic of Vietnam. She is the translator of a work by Truong Chinh and Vo Nguyen Giap, *The Peasant Question (1937–1938)*.

SE HEE YOO is Assistant Professor of Political Science at Hanyang University, Seoul. He earned his M.A. at Seoul National University in 1965 and studied at Columbia University, where he obtained his Ph.D. in the spring of 1974. His doctoral dissertation was on the Korean peasant and the Communist movement under Japanese rule.

DONALD S. ZAGORIA, Professor of Government at City University of New York/Hunter College, is the author of *The Sino-Soviet Conflict, 1956–1961* (1962) and *Vietnam Triangle: Moscow, Peking, Hanoi* (1967). In recent years he has been exploring the relationship between Communism and the peasantry in the prerevolutionary state.

# *Abbreviations*

ACLF   All-China Labor Federation
AEBUS   Anti-Enemy Backing-Up Societies (Malaya)
AFPFL   Anti-Fascist People's Freedom League (Burma)
AMCJA   All-Malayan Council of Joint Action
BCP   Burmese Communist Party; White Flag
CCP   Chinese Communist Party
CPB   Communist Party of Burma; Red Flag
CPI   Communist Party of India
CPT   Communist Party of Thailand
DRV   Democratic Republic of Vietnam; North Vietnam
KCP   Korean Communist Party
KMT   Kuomintang; Nationalist Party (China)
MCP   Malayan Communist Party
MPAJA   Malayan People's Anti-Japanese Army
MPAJU   Malayan People's Anti-Japanese Union
PKI   Partai Komunis Indonesia; Communist Party of Indonesia
PMFTU   Pan-Malayan Federation of Trade Unions
PNI   Partai Nasionalis Indonesia
PRP   People's Revolutionary Party (Burma)
PUTERA   Pusat Tenaga Ra'ayat (Malaya)
PVO   People's Volunteer Organization (Burma)
SOBSI   All-Indonesian Trade Union Organization

Peasant Rebellion and
Communist Revolution in Asia

# Introduction

JOHN WILSON LEWIS & KATHLEEN J. HARTFORD

This volume inquires into the causes of Communist-led revolutions in Asia and the relationship between those revolutions and the societies in which they occur. Its purpose is to bring contemporary Asian experience more directly within the purview of the comparative study of revolutions. Three central questions have guided our efforts: In what social settings do Communist revolutions take root or fail? How do Communist organizations arise and, once created, respond to the social pressures for rebellion or order? To what extent do the structures of revolt correspond to society-wide structures and processes?

The essays that follow will explore what rebels and Communist revolutionaries have discovered in action. Most early revolutionaries, with dissidence and breakdown all around them, began with the view that their societies were ripe for revolt. In places as diverse as Korea, China, Vietnam, Malaya, Indonesia, Burma, and India almost all Party leaders would have agreed with Mao Tse-tung that the single spark of a peasant uprising could start the prairie fire of the "proletarian revolution." Yet almost universally they feared the fire's burning uncontrolled and eventually put their faith in Leninist organization and military operations.

The answers that these men and women sought are among those we seek. Can the proletarian revolution begin as a mass peasant insurrection? Under what conditions can Communist revolutionaries operating in scattered guerrilla bands create a governing system that can rival the official one in legitimacy and power? Can this process be thought out in such a way that the moves or stages remain consistent with and are reinforced by the dominant processes and structures of the society itself?

Comparison appears to offer a promising approach to these questions on Asia's revolutions. Over the past decade a number of scholars have undertaken the kind of field studies that allow them to reach solid conclusions on a country-by-country basis; the problem is how to place these conclusions within frameworks where comparison might be facilitated. The quest for such analytical tools seems particularly timely because theorists of revolution have grown too dependent on frameworks developed largely from the evidence of Western revolutions.

The comparative approach raises both general problems and problems peculiar to Asia. As a general issue, we must decide on what analytical level and over what time period to study revolutions. More specifically with regard to Asia, we face some serious data problems. It has proved difficult to generalize on the reasons for the emergence of revolutions there because of the opaqueness and variety of each country's cultures and political processes. Revolutionaries themselves have found the thickets of social life dense and have seldom comprehended fully the likely consequences of their actions. Their problem, like ours, has been to penetrate the communities of peasants, astonishingly well versed in the art of detection and deception of strangers trying to pass unnoticed among themselves. Peasant groups long ago mastered the technique of masking their beliefs and actions from the prying eyes of Western social scientists, local officials, Communist organizers, or other "outsiders." Only through itinerant storytellers and word-of-mouth legends could traces of the peasant's true feelings be found.

For government officials as well there was little to be gained by honesty and openness. A mere hint of disharmony or unrest could spell the end of a career. Moreover, one would expect the writings of an official establishment to reflect or magnify only those conditions of order and stability that could substantiate the ruling elite's claim to be operating in the interest of the society as a whole. In surveying these documents one gleans only a biased view of a wise rulership, legitimate and in harmony with the natural ordering of the universe. The official literature, historical and contemporary alike, has an obvious self-serving intent and far outweighs the scattered writings of "bandits and riffraff." In a setting where few can write, we would not expect the literati to play devil's advocate for the powerless.

What has emerged from the new generation of scholarly work on Asian peasantries is a view of two communities, only one of which is in relatively clear focus. One is dominated by an official elite, the other by the peasantry. Throughout Asia these two communities in varying degrees have been in conflict—with intermittent periods of exhaustion and disengagement—over the long centuries. Conflict and unrest, not harmony and order, have been the norm. For the peasants, struggle has been a way of life, not an impulsive departure. Conflict, equated with chaos, prompted repression and an imposed discipline.

Most often neglected is the conditioning of revolutionary responses by the peasants' memory of past conflict. For the Asian peasant during the several hundred years before the advent of the West, rebellion was a common occurrence. The aftermath of uprisings, however, was often so devastating, the memory of failure so poignant, that the modern-day heirs of the tradition of revolt would not lightly feel moved to raise their battle flag again, let alone follow behind the banner of others. Yet for some the haunting memories of past failures had faded; with a hero, a sect, an incident, rebellion's time had come again. The Communist movement did not come to a continent or even a country at a single level of development or state of mind. In some villages peasants remembered and were quiet. Other communities were "ripe" for rebellion or revolution. The only way to distinguish them, Lenin once remarked, was to start the battle and see who joined.

Yet in a setting as chaotic as twentieth-century Asia, there are many battles to join, and we cannot satisfy ourselves by taking a strictly linear view of revolutionary progress. Conditions that might suit the formative period of a movement may abruptly turn sour. It may be no accident that the leaders of a number of successful revolutions were able to shift location or social targets, while those labeled failures remained tied to a single region or part of society. The military repression of a fixed zone of rebellion often marked only the final stage of failure in that zone. An earlier chain of apparently successful compromises necessary for attracting supporters and achieving security within such an area had already blocked further, more radical stages of revolution. Revolutionaries to succeed had to control the issues. Otherwise they could be left with a choice of *immobilisme* or compromising coalition. The Asian revolutions that finally prevailed had to break out from the prison of parochial interests. Such breakthroughs could be geographical or social, sometimes moving closer to mass support, sometimes away from it.

We must therefore take great care in interpreting the revolutionary

phenomena we are studying. Viewed in a wider geographical or historical context, a fact or event may take on quite different meanings
from those it has when examined in narrower perspective. However,
we still must choose the analytical frameworks within which to place
the revolutionary phenomenon. Social psychologists, historians, and
other social scientists are currently caught up in a debate on the study
of revolutions. Are they psychological phenomena, organized movements, manifestations of societal dysfunctions, symptoms or agents
of modernization, or unique history-changing events in which one
class replaces another in power? Even a cursory study of the literature
taking the different approaches evokes sharp reminiscences of the
parable about blind men defining an elephant.

A focus on the psychology of revolutionaries follows two possible
tracks. The scholar may assume that the revolutionary is a social
deviant and, in searching for the sources of deviance, rely on personal
data on participants; yet, as Dankwart Rustow has suggested for one
country,[1] participants may share their "peculiar characteristics" with
vast numbers of their non-revolutionary countrymen. Or, the scholar
may look for a psychology of revolutionary situations and find himself
relying on untestable hypotheses in extrapolating conclusions on psychological states from economic, political, or social statistics.[2] A focus
on the movement obscures the entire societal and governmental context that, at least in part, gives the movement its raison d'être, sustains
its momentum, and limits its ends. A focus on revolution as a societal
dysfunction implies a prejudice on the side of societal order, and
often leads the scholar into an examination of such diverse phenomena as suicides, felonies, mental illness, and various forms of collective violence, assuming that all have something in common with
revolutions. The emphasis can then shift to the violent aspect of revolution, overlooking the possibility that violence may be only periph-
erally related to what is happening in the revolution. A focus on
revolution as a species of modernization runs a risk in seeing modernization as the revolutionary phenomenon and political revolution
as simply the vehicle moving a society along the path of modernization; this approach too often neglects the significance of the revolution
as a response to the very question of what modernization does or
should entail.

Even when the focus is on the event of revolution, the perspective
can vary, as Charles Tilly suggests in the final essay in this volume.
Noting that the "largest disparities in definitions of revolution come
from the time spans the definers want to consider," he writes:

In a short time span, we have definitions that concentrate on a central event: a certain kind of bid for power, a temporary dissolution of government, a transfer of power. In a medium time span, we have definitions that examine the population or government before, during, and after such a crucial event, and ask whether any significant change occurred; a coup d'état that substituted one military faction for another might qualify as a revolution under the short-run definition, but not under the medium-run definition. In a long time span, finally, we have definitions that relate the crucial event and the changes (if any) surrounding it to a reading of broad historical trends—for example, by restricting the name of revolution solely to those transfers of power that produce the durable substitution of one whole class for another.

While agreeing with Tilly on the disparity in definitions, we believe that the diverse time spans and approaches in the essays that follow reflect the fact that rebellions and revolutions, especially in the Asian context, are the convergences of many processes or groups of processes. These may be going on at the same time, but both their points of origin and their logical destinations often differ.

## The Roots of Revolution

Confronting the evidence on the causes of history's great revolutions, some scholars have claimed the ability to identify certain elements that make revolution probable. Others, impressed with the idiosyncrasies of each case and its outcome, have asserted the impossibility of determining any general causes leading inexorably to revolution. These differences remain unresolved after so much scholarly endeavor because of the complexity of the questions involved.

Quite often analyses of revolution have been fettered by reductionist approaches that attempt to isolate a single ultimate cause. This cause has been variously defined as either economic, social, or political. But although economic, social, or political variables may be correlated with instability, the path from correlation to causation is unclear. What translates rural instability into insurrection and insurrection into an effective revolutionary movement is an unsolved problem in most studies of revolutions and a matter of considerable dispute among social scientists and revolutionary theorists alike.

In the study of Asian revolutions attempted in the twentieth century the complexity of the problem is especially evident. All these revolutions have arisen in countries whose peasant populations were exploited, wretched, and illiterate. What forces would be sufficient to cause a mass upheaval of these populations? Would these same forces help the rebellious populace coalesce into a revolutionary movement and would they produce the processes that could result in a modernizing regime of Communist bent? To date, this problem has been a Gordian knot, sliced by would-be Alexanders but never fully understood. If each condition or event led directly and inevitably to the next, the problem would be simple. But in the glare of comparative analysis, determinism is revealed as a dead end. As the experience of the Philippines, Malaya, and Indonesia shows, conditions can be selectively manipulated, misunderstood, or misperceived. The prediction of revolution itself can change the possibility of revolution. Moreover, both the necessary and the sufficient "causes" of revolution, identified in some countries, are conditions that are apparently prevalent in places where revolutions have not been launched or have failed. The task of devising a viable theory of causes of revolutions has scarcely begun.

The task has not been simplified by those scholars who have adopted the systemic view of the changes wrought by revolutions.[3] One problem with that view is the limitation imposed by the way it defines revolution. When one takes a before-and-after approach to the study of revolutions, judging them in terms of the magnitude or the quality of the changes wrought, it is easy to slip into a definition of revolutions that makes each outcome inevitable. Theorists of the "total systems change" school would probably object to the implied charge of determinism. Yet the fact remains that such theories give the determining role to systemic collapse brought about by forces beyond human control, and cannot account for chance or for conscious, planned action.

A second problem with the systemic approach is its assumption that revolution stems from the disintegration of a formerly integrated system. The difficulties of this approach for Asian revolutions have already been mentioned. To get around that problem, to fit revolutions in these societies into a viable theoretical framework, must we limit the membership of a society to those in harmony with it, to the peaceful and well behaved? "Society" so restricted becomes integrated by terminological fiat.

Samuel Huntington has to some extent confronted both problems.[4] Revolution, he concludes, results from the inability of the institutions of an existing political system to absorb increased participation or accommodate demands for participation from groups within the society previously excluded from such participation.[5] Huntington shows that the collapse of the old order does not invariably mean the rise of a new one. A society may well totter along indefinitely, subject to confusion and instability but unable to develop a solution. To Huntington, the crucial factor is the rise of a party that can use the new participatory demands to reorganize the society. Resolution of the conflict is not then simply the reconstitution of the system according to new principles, but the rise of a new "system" whose boundaries as well as basic principles are unlike the old one's.

There is a third serious problem in the systemic view and in several other approaches to the causes of revolution. That is their omission of deliberate human action from the preconditions or necessary conditions for revolution. The causation of revolutions is widely seen by social scientists as a two-part scenario: objective factors first develop that disrupt the old order by the very logic of their development (the necessary conditions), and then human actors take advantage of this situation and of chance events (the sufficient conditions) to bring about revolutionary change. The systemic view sees the first step as the collapse of the old system under the weight of its internal contradictions. Others point to concrete factors such as land hunger, foreign invasion, or weakness of the old elite as crucial preconditions. But if the two-step scenario of necessary and sufficient conditions is set aside, the analysis of revolutionary causation becomes at the same time richer and more tuned to actual revolutions; for then we can come to terms with the possibility that revolutionaries themselves create some of the "preconditions" for their own success: they organize new social groupings, break up old ones, and through their actions kindle the new demands for participation. And this in turn leads us to inquire into the possibility that the revolutionary, acting intelligently, may discover opportunities for successful revolution in many different settings.

Similar problems arise for Marxist theorists in analyzing the causes of revolutions, especially in the Asian context—for first, was not Marx's view of why and how revolutions arise basically deterministic; and second, did he not think that socialist revolution could only come about in a country that was already industrialized? One classic statement of Marx's is commonly cited in support of the first interpretation:

> At a certain stage of their development, the material productive forces of society come in conflict with the existing relations of production,

or—what is but a legal expression for the same thing—with the property relations within which they have been at work hitherto. From forms of development of the productive forces these relations turn into their fetters. Then begins an epoch of social revolution. . . . No social order ever perishes before all the productive forces for which there is room in it have developed; and new, higher relations of production never appear before the material conditions of their existence have matured in the womb of the old society itself.[6]

Such a statement smacks of technological determinism; the forces of production apparently must change first, unbalancing the mutually supportive relationships of economic base and society's institutions, and thus necessitating at some point a change in the social and political superstructure.

Yet at times Marx brought man's conscious action back into his theory and softened the apparent determinism. In his "Theses on Feuerbach," for example, he adopted a more voluntarist position on human action: "The materialist doctrine that men are products of circumstances and upbringing, and that, therefore, changed men are products of other circumstances and changed upbringing, forgets that it is men that change circumstances and that the educator himself needs educating."[7] The modification is clear enough, but it does not help a potential revolutionary know how much circumstances will change him and how much he can change circumstances.

The options for an Asian revolutionary here seem extremely limited. For Marx, too, set out certain necessary conditions that could not be bypassed. He expected the socialist revolution to succeed only in industrially advanced capitalist countries. There alone was to be found the class capable of seizing and operating the means of production. Marx did not envision a spontaneous upsurge among urban workers; their revolutionary consciousness had first to develop. And this in turn depended on their acquiring habits of cooperation in production. Eventually, cooperation would enable proletarians to view themselves as a class with common goals, and to unite to achieve those goals.

As Maurice Meisner notes elsewhere in this volume, Marx saw little revolutionary potential in the peasants. They could never achieve a truly revolutionary consciousness, enmeshed as they were in the rural "idiocy" of individualistic production. The question is, why was he wrong? It would appear that Marx misread the role of peasants in socialist revolution, not because of a mistaken determinism of technological development, but because of his assumptions on how peasants organized their lives and how this organization affected the limits of their consciousness.

The perspectives offered by later Marxist theorists of revolution raise several questions on the relationship between revolutionary consciousness and the societal context, or what Marx called objective conditions. Consciousness cannot be an important factor in and of itself unless it is to some degree independent of these conditions. This very independence, however, could thwart relevant and effective actions. Among twentieth-century Marxists, both Lenin and the Italian Antonio Gramsci noted such difficulties in the development of a revolutionary movement among the proletariat. Lenin held that proletarians, if left to themselves, would work primarily for economist ends. A revolutionary vanguard party had to counteract this tendency by working to instill a revolutionary consciousness in workers, but it could as well win intellectuals and peasants over to the ideology.[8] Gramsci argued that since a "hegemony" of bourgeois institutions and ideas held sway over all in capitalist society, a vanguard had to build a new proletarian hegemony among workers before taking the path of revolution.[9] Both, obviously, believed with Marx that objective conditions alone could not breed a revolutionary class consciousness, and that this consciousness had to develop before revolution would occur.

But there are two ways in which this consciousness may be independent of objective conditions. One is seen in Gramsci's argument that a false consciousness, some illusion about the world, intrudes to prevent a class from realizing what its true situation is and what to do about it. Lenin's viewpoint, though encompassing this perspective on consciousness, lends itself to a broader possibility, that consciousness may develop to a point beyond what is indicated by the objective situation and especially beyond what a particular class's situation might seem to allow. Examples of such a possibility can be seen in the efforts of the Chinese Communists to instruct peasants and urban intellectuals in the principles of Marxism and to inculcate in them a "proletarian viewpoint" having nothing to do with their actual involvement with the urban working class. We might question the utility of the very term class consciousness when used so loosely. Yet at least one root of such usage can be seen in Marx's view of revolutionary proletarian consciousness: the aim of ideological training lay in transforming the motivation of peasant or intellectual into the same collective, self-sacrificing spirit that Marx expected to arise from cooperative production in the workplace. For the Asian peasant nations, the protracted guerrilla war could serve the same collectivizing function.

In addition to the question of how far consciousness depends on objective conditions, there is a second aspect of the issue of revolutionary consciousness that must concern us. That is, how important a role does outlook or consciousness play in the rise of revolution? Must potential revolutionary actors know what they are doing? How much is revolutionary action intended for definite ends by those who engage in it, and how much is it simply a reflex that has consequences unforeseen by the mass of those involved in it? We might pose the question in terms of the contrast between those who deliberately murder a king so as to succeed him and those who are able to step into a throne that has been emptied by spontaneous mob action. Most likely we can never come down completely on one side or the other of the question.

The essays in Part I, "The Roots of Revolution," address this question in its many aspects. What prompts peasants, workers, or intellectuals to revolt? Do we trace a revolutionary response to the peasantry's desire for land, to nationalism, to a generalized reaction to oppression, to a desire for a particular reorganization of their world, or to a combination of some or all of these? Each question raises others. We need to know more about the conditions that move acts of defiance toward revolution and away from ritualistic escapism. Frustration and discontent, of course, play a part in revolution, but these have been with mankind throughout history. The critical change comes in the conditions for action. The chemistry of revolution adds new ingredients to individual and mass response. The first ingredient is the combination of a collective mood of resistance and a willingness to entrust the fate of the community to a new, radical leadership.

It is this ingredient that is investigated by Donald Zagoria. His essay begins by identifying the peasantry living in commercialized rural systems as the critical population for revolution. Within this population, the peasants most likely to become revolutionary are those in a family-size tenancy system experiencing severe pressures on the land. In itself this finding is already an advance over theories that treat the peasantry as an undifferentiated mass, but this is just the starting point. Zagoria's analysis consists of two parts. The first sets forth the conditions most likely to result in a family-size tenancy system. Arguing that, globally, these are most prevalent in the monsoon areas of Asia, he then examines the elements of such systems that tend to produce radical movements or to help such movements survive. Monsoon Asia, he suggests, "has a unique combination of very heavy pressure on the land, an unusually heavy concentration of landless and land poor, an increasing trend toward pauperization of the peasantry, and a high degree of parasitic landlordism—all within the framework of a family-size tenancy system."

Using the hypotheses for Monsoon Asia, the essay then draws on data concerning voting statistics and support for radical agrarian movements. The evidence, on balance, supports the initial hypotheses, Zagoria holds. Where it does not, it is possible to single out the intervening variables that explain the apparent failure of conditions conducive to peasant mobilization to lead to the emergence of a peasantry's radical consciousness.

Se Hee Yoo's researches into the relationship between Korea's peasants and the Communist movement yield findings in apparent contradiction to Zagoria's. The most successfully sustained Communist-led peasant movements flourished precisely in those areas with the lowest incidence of land tenancy. Yet Korean radical history by no means contradicts Zagoria's hypothesis, for Korea's traditional peasant rebellions were provoked by basic land grievances. This was true even as late as the 1920's, which saw increasing numbers of tenancy disputes, particularly in the south. Yet when, in the late 1920's, the Korean Communists belatedly recognized the revolutionary potential of the peasantry, they had their greatest success in the northeast, which had the lowest rates of tenancy and landlessness in the country. Accordingly, Yoo concludes that in the Korean case, economic factors alone do not sufficiently account for revolutionary activity.

The contrast between Zagoria's and Yoo's findings highlights the general problem of relating the peasants' situation to the conditions for mobilizing a peasant population. Zagoria suggests that two factors are necessary for the successful mobilization of peasants into Communist-style movements: the weakness of the landed elite and the decay of state control. What Yoo's case demonstrates is that these two factors, in varying degrees, are often the most difficult to obtain in areas with the highest incidence of family-size tenancy. Societies seem to have a way of complicating social transformations by simultaneously strengthening the mechanisms of resistance to change and the conditions crying out for change. As a result, the most likely revolutionary class as measured by the land-tenancy issue may be prevented from acting. It may "give way" to the next most potentially active class when it comes down to fighting a revolutionary war. Such findings correspond to Eric Wolf's suggestion that the freeholding middle peasant is more likely to participate in insurrection than the poor peasant tenant because of his greater "internal leverage" and independence from landlord control.[10]

This does not gainsay the poor peasant's revolutionary potential but rather underscores the requirements for realizing that potential. Hamza Alavi, focusing on this same problem, notes that, though revolutionary struggle by the middle peasant is necessary at the outset in order to weaken the established order, the poor peasant must ultimately participate if the revolutionary movement is to succeed. Once the opening created by middle peasants' actions becomes apparent and shows the potential for success through combat, the poorer must join, or agrarian radicalism will be dissipated.[11] There can be rebellion, but not revolution, without the poor peasantry.

Zagoria contends that, in order for this class to act, not only objective grievances and absence of control, but also mass revolutionary consciousness must exist. This "revolutionary consciousness" consists of the peasants' belief that revolutionary change is both necessary and possible, even inevitable. But the change envisioned could be of many sorts. Generally, the peasant casts his view of the ideal future in terms already familiar to him, longing for a return to some legendary era of harmony, equality, peace—and the absence of outsiders. Obviously such an outlook alone cannot lead the peasant into a Communist-style movement. Something must first be added or changed. Christine White in her essay on the origins of the Vietnamese revolution illustrates one way this can occur. The rebelliousness of the Vietnamese peasantry was by and large backward-looking, revealing a yearning for the return to a lost golden age. Only the intellectuals and workers possessed a forward-looking revolutionary consciousness, and a way had to be found to transmit this to the peasants before a revolutionary movement could succeed. Otherwise, another peasant rebellion would have aimed simply at a return to a pre-modern era, a manifest impossibility once the French had entered on the scene.

White locates the origins of this forward-looking consciousness among intellectuals and workers in the growth and development of the Vietnamese nationalist movement. The more active elements of these two classes wanted Vietnam to become a part of the modern world that the French had, quite unwittingly, revealed to them. But in agitating for the realization of nationalist demands they soon discovered that the only support for Vietnamese self-determination came from the Soviet Union and the Communist parties in the Third International. Thus the worker-intellectual radicalism that was later to influence the peasant took first a nationalist and then a pro-Communist turn.

The transmission of revolutionary propaganda to the peasantry, White argues, was facilitated both by a fluidity of class lines—workers were almost always former peasants, numbers of peasants were former or part-time workers, many of those with technical training were intellectuals in the sense that they were literate in a largely illiterate society—and by the common antipathy of a majority in all three groups toward the French colonialists. The peasants, protesting against worsening economic conditions in the depression years of the 1930's, were ready to ally with workers and intellectuals who began entering the villages during the 1930 uprising and explaining Communism's program for revolution. The Leninist analysis of imperialism inspired all three groups to strike for independence rather than for accommodation, for Lenin had predicted the inevitability of imperialism's collapse under the weight of its own internal contradictions.

White's essay on the formation of the revolutionary coalition, the first of several dealing with this important problem, provides a missing piece to the puzzle of how mass revolutionary action originates. It is in the formation of this coalition that revolution becomes distinguished from rebellion. Both types of political upheaval among the peasantry are grounded in economic grievances, and especially, as White and Zagoria note, drastically worsening economic circumstances. Agitation on economic issues alone, however, cannot mold the peasant into a complete revolutionary. A way must be opened for peasant and urbanite to combine forces. It is through this alliance that a rebellion over land issues can become a national revolt and thence a revolutionary movement toward modern statehood and all that that implies. These two "revolutions" are not totally distinct; neither are they inextricable. It is the combination of the two that the word revolution so often calls to mind.

We have, from the essays in this section, a view of the sources of the land revolution and its consequences. We have as well at least an inkling of some of the forces that presage the national revolution and link it to the land revolution. There emerges a mixed picture of social causation. As far as we can tell from the Asian data, the results of revolution are neither totally foreseen nor totally unpredictable. Each rebel or Party group can grasp only a part of the future. In the process of acting together against common enemies, the rebels start to fit the pieces together and understand a little more of the reality they seek to change. How that fitting process takes place is a subject to which we now turn.

## Organization-Building and Leadership Strategies

The search for explanations begins, not ends, with conditions for revolt. There is no simple, either-or approach to the comparative study of Communism or revolution. The study of the preconditions of revolution and the study of its leadership and organization must proceed hand in hand. Concentration on revolutionary organization and leadership alone would simply beg the question. How did these organizations arise in the first place? Why did they arise in some parts of a country and not in others, and why did some individuals or groups join them and others refuse to do so? Why do the organizations appear to take root in a society at one time and not at others? We seek to explain the interrelationships of organization-building, leadership strategies, and peasant responses. Thus the essays in Part II are closely related to those of Part I.

A central dilemma confounding the work of Communist organizers becomes apparent in the essays of this section. Should a Communist Party, in its attempts to gain peasant support, direct itself to the interests and aims of existing groups in the society and devote its organizational skills to mobilizing them to achieve those aims? Or should it bypass those groups and try to create its own organizations from scratch, drawing in individuals on its own terms? If we look to those cases in which a Party has chosen to rely on existing groups and issues, we find that the objective conditions of group life tend to overwhelm the revolution. If, on the other hand, we look at cases where Communist leaders have created their own organizations, the question remains open how far objective conditions still limit revolutionary possibilities.

The alternatives that confront Party organizers are never posed in black-and-white terms, and the best choice is by no means an obvious one. Communist leaders usually juggle their efforts at combining the old and the new. The emphasis varies from country to country, and within countries from region to region and from one time to the next.

But we can identify cases in Asia in which the Parties over time came down on one side of the choice or the other. The perspectives on Indonesian Communism in Rex Mortimer's essay illustrate the way the choice may be predetermined for Communist leaders. For Indonesia colonialism was especially important in this regard.

The colonial experience and the Japanese occupation were to alter the course of the revolution everywhere they touched in Asia. We have already noted this for Vietnam. There both the French and the Japanese proved so oppressive that the peasants reached out for a new leadership, not so much from rational calculation but because they simply had no other choice if their communities were to survive. The Dutch in Indonesia, for their part, enlisted traditional village and other rural elites into the colonial administrative apparatus, rendering them less capable of acting as mediators for peasant interests.

Communist organization appeared to fill the leadership gap. Mortimer's conclusions in this regard appear to sustain the findings of David McClelland concerning the "two faces of power."[12] McClelland notes that revolutionaries typically offer potential followers the one thing they seem to need most: an escape from their powerlessness. In the patron-client or landlord-tenant relationships so common throughout Asia the peasant has found himself increasingly helpless. Whether his impotence is real or imagined does not really matter, for the effect is the same. As McClelland explains it, the effective leader is one who arouses confidence in his followers and inspires them to accomplish the goals they share in common. Mortimer's essay, as well as others in this volume, describes a kind of power in Communist movements that is characterized by a concern for group goals and the empowering of the socially weak.

The problem, however, is that the creation of effective relationships between leader and follower under these conditions may force the revolutionaries in the early stages of organization-building to concede too much. They may accommodate for immediate support or momentary advantage in such a way as to make themselves vulnerable to repression if government policy changes. More specifically, as in this case, revolutionary strategy may become so finely tuned to the values and demands of a single ethnic-religious group that the Party may be susceptible to easy isolation when times and issues change.

In Indonesia, PKI leaders in urban areas pursued a purely modernizing and class-based strategy that contradicted the more traditionalist strategy adopted among the non-Islamic peasantry. From the point of view of its peasant supporters the PKI was acceptable to the degree that it defended communal customs and rights against foreigners, urbanites, and Islam. This orientation not only foreclosed the emergence of a worker-peasant class coalition, but had somehow to be reconciled with the views of the Party's other principal supporters, the radical nationalist youth. The Communist movement right down to its virtual destruction in 1965 was caught up by the contradictions inherent in its base of support and torn apart by the effectiveness of its opposition. Either way the Communists could not have won a majority. They were thus in the position of being weak yet threatening at the same time. To the extent that they had to act, Party cadres found themselves in the unenviable position of catering to the very forces of peasant conservatism and provoking those of Islamic radicalism that were later virtually to obliterate Communism in Indonesia.

Mortimer's findings demonstrate the weakness of the class model for understanding the sources and structure of revolution in Asia. It was the multiplicity of ethnic and religious divisions in Indonesia that undermined the growth of nationwide or even Java-wide class allegiances. In no Asian revolution, including the Chinese, has it been possible to develop a strictly class-based movement. This is particularly the case for those revolutions that draw heavily on peasant support. Regional, ethnic, religious, and other cleavages have simply been too strong. The result in the Indonesian case was to propel the Party to ally with groups it could not control and to accommodate in ways that were to prove its undoing. Eventually the PKI attempted to offset these weaknesses by joining forces with Sukarno; even this failed as a way to turn defensiveness into a positive strategy for taking power.

Michael Stenson, in his discussion of the ethnic and urban bases of the Communist revolt in Malaya, further illuminates the problem of the ethnic and communal divisions that exercise so powerful an influence on Asian political life. This was particularly a problem for the Malayan Communist Party in the late 1930's and early 1940's because ethnic divisions not only reduced the Party to a permanent minority position, but also, as Stenson points out, limited their "revolutionary space." The Chinese, virtually the sole base of MCP support, were concentrated in the urban areas of Malaya, and thus the Party was more vulnerable to repression.

The Malayan case illustrates the weakness of a revolution originating out of sentiments that have little root among the dominant population. In large measure, the MCP recruits to the cause were drawn by a spirit reflecting attitudes in China, not Malaya. It was only after joining the Party that they read the Marxist-Maoist classics and settled, somewhat arbitrarily, on a strategy. Seeing the world through Chinese or Marxist lenses, the MCP cadres were scornful of the Malay peasants and did almost nothing to try to overcome that bias.

Perhaps more than any other in Asia, the Malayan experience indicates that revolt need not be precipitated by what Chalmers Johnson calls societal dysfunctions—unless the only evidence of dysfunction is the revolt itself. According to Stenson, popular mobilization at the time the armed revolt began was at a minimum, economic circumstances had improved, the leadership capacities of the ethnic communities were being restored, and even the aspirations of the youth for a better future in an independent state seemed about to be realized. The decision to launch the revolution came, then, not from pressures within the society, but from pressures within the Communist elite itself. When the MCP did take to the countryside to conduct armed operations in the late 1940's, its rural base had only geographical, not social, dimensions. Malayan Communism became a rural revolution lacking both peasants and effective links back to the city.

Burma offers an example of the reverse side of the problem. In his study of Burmese Communism, John Badgley shows that unlike their comrades in Indonesia and Malaya, the Burmese Party cadres were never able to bridge the gap between Marxism-Leninism and the native culture of any considerable segment of the population. In Indonesia and Malaya, the Party was damned because it made the linkage; in Burma its fate was the same because it did not make the linkage and relied instead on an external "fountain" of legitimacy. The precise pattern of the rise and fall of the Burmese Party may have been different, but the outcome was about the same.

The Party's experiences with the British and the collegial ties between Indian and Burmese intellectuals generated a climate of doctrinaire debate divorced from practice. Marxism and Maoism were too abstract and too easy to cite in support of all opposing courses of action. The tendency, as Badgley shows, was for strategic debates to become irreconcilable and bitter to the point of organizational rupture. Those with Leninist or Maoist leanings tended to split off or engage in purges in order to pursue a more militant line.

It was after such a struggle and purge in 1948 that one Party group decided to cast its lot with China. Finding insufficient support among colleagues and countrymen, some of the Burmese revolutionaries, much like their Korean counterparts, moved across the border. It was only under Chinese tutelage in the 1950's that the BCP gained a degree of unity and clear direction. But the result of this reliance on an outside force—as the Lin Piao thesis on self-reliance would have predicted—was continued isolation from the populace and a debating-society atmosphere within the Central Committee. To top it off, a conflict erupted in the BCP's special college set up by returnees from China and ended finally in numerous defections and murders.

The Party in such circumstances is a ready target for governmental countermoves. As in the Philippines under Magsaysay, a combination of amnesty, relatively restrained military and police action, and credible nationalistic appeals by the government undercut Communist recruitment and propaganda. The Rangoon Government now pursues a strategy of socialism and nationalism that opposes outside interference as well as indigenous Communism. Thus preempted, the BCP has become a faction-ridden movement uniquely dependent on outside (i.e., Chinese) assistance and able to survive precariously only among Burma's hill tribes.

The records of Burma, Malaya, and Indonesia reveal that Communist leaderships, despite external appearances, are often ill-prepared for the very revolutions they seek. Their perspective is frequently a limited one, demanding strikes in the name of social transformation, and calling demonstrations revolution. Their internal communications can be surprisingly primitive, the one hand of the movement blind to what the other is doing. Thus it is not surprising that the revolutionaries often not only are off in their timing but also are easy targets for the repressive reactions that they provoke. What the first three essays in Part II show is that good rebels are not necessarily good revolutionaries. Revolutionary organization, to succeed, must consist of more than old groups or institutions with a new coat of ideological paint. The problem then is how to build something new.

Jeffrey Race's essay addresses this question in examining why men and women join the revolutionary movement, how and why the organization emerges in the first place. Using social exchange theory he seeks to explain the emergence of new authoritative structures. Essential to the growth of organization are cooperative agreements between the current revolutionaries and their potential recruits or followers that not only bring to both benefits they could not achieve independently, but also create political powers where none may have existed before. Men and women join because they have something to gain— not because they have little or nothing to lose. Moreover, repression may fail to forestall the process in three ways: first, by forcing the revolutionary leadership to respond more directly and quickly to mass demands; second, by adding to the value of the exchange; and third, by sparking the memory of exchanges made long ago and thought forgotten. Should the organization be hard hit and driven underground, the remembrance of cooperation may linger on and facilitate the rapid reemergence of rebellious organizations when the time once again becomes opportune.

In examining the prospects for organization-building, it is important to distinguish the initial stage of creating the basic Communist organization from the later stages, when organized Communist functionaries attempt to build bases of support among the peasantry. These two stages are sometimes categorized as elite mobilization and mass mobilization, or the urban and the rural phases. But the shift from recruiting urban intellectuals into the Party to enlisting rural peasants to support the movement, though important, may not be as critical as the shift within the Party from establishing an organization to using it as a leadership tool. In the first stage, potential revolutionaries may create something out of nothing by joining ranks, but later the very existence of the Party institutions may offer the peasant something of value. The exchange made with the peasant, as contrasted to that with the initial recruits, is thus more tangible and more immediately reciprocal. It depends not so much on a promise as on a present reality.

Collective action resulting from such networks of exchange looms larger and more powerful than the sum of actions of the persons involved. Organizations empower the weak and give individual actions multiple impact and staying power when the going gets rough. The tendency in the Vietcong, for example, was to build three-man cells that have been described by three different members as "very helpful to me . . . when I was tired or sick"; "When I quarreled with someone, the other two men helped me to calm down and explained to me what the problem was"; "I think human beings have the tendency to work with friends rather than working alone. Three heads are better than one, as you know."[13]

Much of the revolutionary group's solidarity seems to depend on the government's moves. The government might attempt to co-opt most potential joiners, thus to a degree controlling the buildup of revolutionary organs by its own actions—by changing the supply as well as the demand for the new "exchange." What Race shows for southern Vietnam and northern Thailand is that the government can effectively compete in this "exchange war" only if it resists the temptation to insulate itself from the people's demands. As with Ngo Dinh Diem's regime in Saigon, the government may forsake truly national self-reliance by becoming isolated in its forts, by substituting force for cooperation, or by turning outward for support from foreign countries. What is often viewed as the collapse of government under these circumstances is most often the result of a series of choices by the government. These choices demonstrate the government's failure to remember that it too was once the beneficiary of exchange relations and to appreciate that, though now formalized in institutions, these exchanges cannot survive without periodic renewal.

To a certain extent, as Race indicates, the government may be at a decisive disadvantage in competition at both stages of revolutionary development, creation of the organization and expansion of mass support, if the society is undergoing rapid social change. Rapid commercialization, urbanization, and general social change may so alter the definition of center-to-village relations and so proliferate the number of potential and alternate leaders that the government cannot hope to compete with the revolutionaries without forsaking its principal values and becoming a revolutionary force itself. For a time it may be difficult for officials in the capital to distinguish between changes that are "manageable" as before and those that are radically new. The prevailing norms concerning who has legitimate influence tend to erode in these circumstances, and all sides—Communist, government, and neutral—may find it difficult to measure and predict influence.

### Revolution: Town and Countryside

The competition between the government and the revolutionary organization is conditioned both by the existing structures of the society at large and by the forces of change to which the government as well as the revolutionaries must respond. The essays of Part II provide examples of how well or intelligently revolutionaries react, how much they understand or can control of the social context within which they act. But in order to evaluate their actions within that larger setting we must determine to what extent Party actions and organizations respond to and are influenced by it. To do so we must proceed to examine the basic relationship characterizing a peasant society and a peasant nation: that between town and countryside.

In examining the Marxist and Maoist analyses of revolution, Maurice Meisner notes that both theories emphasize the separation of town and countryside and consider the ultimate goal the abolition of the distinction between them. But when it comes to the means of attaining that goal, Meisner finds Mao much closer to Marx's ideological opponents, the utopian socialists and the Russian Populists, than to Marx himself. Like the utopians, Mao tends to regard the city and its institutions as unnatural and evil. His anti-urban biases, according to Meisner, led him in the first instance to justify the concentration of the revolution in the countryside, and finally to work toward the combination of agriculture and industrial production as a way of turning away from the modern industrialized city.

Essential to Mao's view is his repudiation of the necessity of the "stage" of bourgeois capitalism as a precondition for socialist revolution. This rejection stems from his equation of capitalism with imperialism and imperialism with what is foreign and reactionary. The revolution could not center in the Chinese city, the very symbol of capitalism, foreignism, and conservatism. It must arise in concert with "natural" forces of development, and these could be found primarily in the village.

Increasingly after the debacle of the first period of attempted revolution in the late 1920's Mao came to regard the peasants as the "real motive force of historical development in Chinese feudal society."[14] Yet he took pains to point out that it was the leadership of the Party and the army that gave the peasantry its revolutionary potential, that was alone capable of transforming its actions from rebellion into revolution. Moreover, Mao recognized that the cities held the ultimate power, and the final target of his revolution was always their conquest. The lack of purity in his view is seen in this quote:

> The slogan, "the poor peasants and farm labourers conquer the country and should rule the country," is wrong. In the villages, it is the farm labourers, poor peasants, middle peasants and other working people, united together under the leadership of the Chinese Communist Party, who conquer the country and should rule the country, and it is not the poor peasants and farm labourers alone who conquer the country and should rule the country. In the country as a whole, it is the workers, peasants (including the new rich peasants), small independent crafts-

men and traders, middle and small capitalists oppressed and injured by the reactionary forces, the students, teachers, professors and ordinary intellectuals, professionals, enlightened gentry, ordinary government employees, oppressed minority nationalities and overseas Chinese, all united together under the leadership of the working class (through the Communist Party), who conquer the country and should rule the country.[15]

Similarly in the 1940's Mao time and again had to emphasize the need to contain the peasantry and to keep it from doing chaotic and impetuously rebellious things, mostly in regard to the land reform.[16]

The vision of the Communists is thus a varied one. Throughout Asia one finds tension within the Communist parties between essentially peasant and essentially urban points of view. The polarized types that Meisner sets out as Marxist and Maoist are reflected from Party to Party, although almost never in their pure form. In the end no simple, either-or view would work in Asia because, as we noted earlier, the transformation from rebellion to revolution requires that groups from both town and country ally in a revolutionary coalition.

There are a great many factors affecting the ability of Communist leaders to mobilize groups within urban and rural locales, and to link them in this coalition. We have already pointed out the possibility that the impact of modernization on peasant nations may create circumstances that alter the relationship between town and country, and thus by extension provide previously nonexistent opportunities for Communist movements to grow. Race, for example, notes that the mechanisms which traditionally ensured mutually beneficial exchange relationships between village and town had begun to break down in Vietnam, to the acute disadvantage of both traditional local elites and villagers. The French colonial policy of forced modernization undermined the power of local councils and created new socioeconomic demands that the peasants found ever harder to meet and to accept. This, in conjunction with the expansion of literacy and the resulting wider exposure to new ideas, including revolutionary ideologies, paralyzed the traditional mechanisms of social control and increased the degree to which anti-establishment leaders could take matters into their own hands. Most governments have proved inept in handling such situations, and have intensified the centrifugal forces in their societies. The tendency of governments faced with the rise of counterelites demanding a greater say in and share of the allocation of society's resources is to shut the door. Typically, officials translate programs for social reform and the technologies meant to achieve them into programs for social order and the technologies for repression, actions that because of new social arrangements are both ineffective and illegitimate so far as the population is concerned.[17]

Ying-mao Kau's essay suggests, however, a way in which some of the advantages fall to government. The effects of modernization favorable to revolutionary movements are concentrated in cities, the sites, as well, of easiest government control. The Communists must respond to the rise in number and complexity of urban social organizations by themselves becoming more specialized, complex, and centralized, and thus an easier target for repression. In the opening section of his historical review of the Chinese Revolution, Kau asks why, in the urban phase of Chinese Communism between 1921 and 1927, the movement at first appeared so strong but finally proved so fragile. Initial successes had depended on effective leadership by urban intellectuals, tutored and assisted by Comintern agents, in molding an alliance between Party operatives and city workers. The alliance was shaky internally because the two partners in the coalition had very different aims, but more important, the social base of the movement was too limited and too ready a target. Party intellectuals and workers were never able to work out a common agenda before the White Terror struck, and the Communist organizations in the cities were destroyed.

The subsequent Party-army coalition with the peasants proved more stable and dependable than the urban alliance, but was still probably not sufficient to have captured the entire country. What the Communists could do in the countryside was to build large "base area" social systems combining villages, towns, and small cities, and eventually to use the many different base areas from which they were operating to launch the final rural-to-urban phase after World War II. In this final phase another coalition emerged, uniting peasants and workers as well as a number of other class elements.*

The central importance of the linkage between rural and urban areas is given special emphasis in the essay by Tilly. He begins by examining Antonio Gramsci's distinction between industrial "generative" and nonindustrial "parasitic" cities. Each type affects differently the prospects for rural-urban coalition. The parasitic city feeds

---

* The Chinese case demonstrates the method for achieving a revolutionary rural-urban alliance via organizations that absorb members from both locales. The alliance is more than a partnership of two distinct groups; it is an entity in itself.

on the countryside, generating a class division between city and countryside. In cases of urban parasitism violent conflict is most likely to develop into rebellion and further division, since workers and peasants never ally. The industrial city, in contrast, serves as a generator of rural activity, and the resulting close relationship between the two locales facilitates worker-peasant collaboration. The revolutionary movement in such a setting brings city and countryside closer together. Thus, it is the social structure, not grievances or popular mobilization, that in the final analysis explains the possibility of revolution.

What Tilly styles revolution begins when "a government previously under the control of a single, sovereign polity becomes the object of effective, competing, mutually exclusive claims on the part of two or more distinct polities." For any situation to become revolutionary, significant segments of the populace must commit themselves to the claims of an alternative polity, and the existing government must fail to suppress that polity and its claims.

Since so much depends on the government it then becomes important to know whether the instruments of government are concentrated in cities and if so, cities of what type. In Asia most of the government's coercive power is typically located in "parasitic" cities, so that the challenging guerrillas are doubly isolated: physically and by the sharp class divisions. Thus excluded from the urban areas the rebels must, if they are to succeed, overcome the antipathies Gramsci noted between urban and rural populations in such settings. As in Malaya and Indonesia, ethnic and religious differences can widen the rural-urban gap and further complicate the rebels' task. Unless they can forge a coalition despite the gross disparities in outlook and goals, the challengers usually fail or their actions dissipate in sporadic peasant revolts. It is here that Communist cadres play a decisive role. On them falls the burden of attracting both workers and peasants to the cause.

Even the most heroic efforts, however, will fail if the local elites maintain their power. Most often the landowning elites hold the key, as Zagoria too has noted. They have traditionally been the crucial link between the rural areas and the national structures of power. For an alternative coalition to be created, it is necessary to erode and replace that link. As we point out in the discussion of Race's essay, modernizing processes may themselves dissolve that link. Evidence presented by Kau and Tilly, however, indicates that the course of modernization may in the long run work against revolution. The weakening of local institutions that accompanies industrialization may provide central authorities more direct access to the peasantry, to the disadvantage of potential revolutionaries. The government can fashion new rural-urban linkages more to its liking and can use them to limite further the options of the rebels.

The success of the entire process of coalition-building depends on what Tilly identifies as the basic conditions for resistance: a focused threat to peasant survival, a significant local framework for collective action, and the availability of urban-based allies. The triggering mechanism is the focused threat. It is then the existence of the framework for collective action and of potential allies that allows the rebellion to be transformed into revolution. These conditions are most likely to coincide when the traditional rural-urban links have been broken and before (or until) the government has forged new ones—that is, during the early phases of rapid urbanization and especially where the rural population is predominant and dispersed.

Thus we see that much more than the peasantry goes into the "peasant revolutions" of Asia, which has provided the principal testing ground for violent group conflict in the past century. This volume treats the social setting of the Asian peasant, the degree to which his situation affects the possibilities for Communist action and successful revolution, and the degree to which revolution pushes him ahead. The metamorphosis from peasant rebellion to Communist revolution is a process only now becoming clear. These essays examine that process in depth.

## PART ONE

# The Roots of Revolution

# Asian Tenancy Systems and
# Communist Mobilization of the Peasantry

DONALD S. ZAGORIA

In the growing literature on rural social movements, one of the most persistent weaknesses is the failure to distinguish such movements according to the agrarian class structures in which they arise and according to the rural classes and strata on which they are based. This failure is rooted in a general underdevelopment of theory relevant to rural property and class structures. As a result, the "peasantry" is often treated as an undifferentiated whole.

In this paper, using and extending a model developed by Arthur Stinchcombe,[1] one of the few writers who have sought to develop a typology of rural property structures, I want to argue that one particular type of rural class structure—family-size tenancy in conditions of heavy pressure on the land—is particularly conducive to rural instability. In such a system, the tenants, laborers, and poor peasants are particularly susceptible to organization by any radical movement pressing for land reform and redistribution.

Recognizing that precommercial agrarian systems are too complex and varied to classify, Stinchcombe has concentrated on a typology of commercialized rural systems, that is, rural systems that produce for the market. He distinguishes five such rural enterprises, each with differing class structures—manorial, family-size tenancy, family smallholding, plantation, and ranch.

According to Stinchcombe, in three of these five agrarian systems —the manorial, plantation, and ranch—the lower classes tend to be politically incompetent, apathetic, or dispersed, and, therefore, in all three cases, difficult to organize. In the manorial, or hacienda, system, the poor peasantry is apathetic because it usually does not have the basic tools of political organization, such as freedom of association, voting power, experienced leadership, and education. Moreover, its pattern of life is not dependent on market prices of goods and therefore it is not sensitized politically. The plantation proletariat is apathetic not only because workers are often imported from more economically backward areas or recruited from an economically backward native population, but also because the system itself tends to induce in the labor force a poverty of associational life. In the ranch-type enterprise, the labor force is free-floating, mobile, and often has few family ties, and is therefore socially undisciplined.[2]

In the fourth type system—family smallholding—even when there are disparities in size of holdings between larger and smaller owners, the common opposition to urban interests and the common interest in maintaining prices of agricultural commodities often unify all owners, rich and poor alike, and thus deflect the possibilities for redistributive movements based on the small owners alone.

In sum, in four of these agrarian systems, the potential for political organization of the lower classes is very limited. In the family-size tenancy system, by contrast, there is a large potential for such organization. There are a number of reasons why this is so. Some have to do with the way in which the system tends to sensitize the lower classes politically. Some have to do with the unusual and highly visible exploitative aspects of the system. Some have to do with the intense competition for land between the landowning class, on the one hand, and the tenants, wage laborers, and poor peasants, on the other. Finally, some have to do with the political competence of the lower classes in a system in which they have a minimum amount of independence and considerable intraclass communication.

First, in a tenancy system, the issue between owner and renter is clear. The lower the rent charged by the landlord, the higher the income of the sharecropper or tenant. The issue itself thus contributes to the political sensitizing of the renter.[3]

Second, the landowner shifts as much of the risk of the crop failure as possible to the tenant. This makes the income of the renter highly variable and also contributes to his political sensitivity.

Third, the landowner does not have the protection of the peasant's ignorance about the nature of the enterprise, as does the large-scale capitalist farmer or the plantation owner. It is perfectly clear to the tenant farmer that he could raise and sell his crops just as well with the landlord gone as with him there.

Fourth, conditions of tenancy are generally insecure. Tenants usually have no heritable rights and landowners can reoccupy the property at will.

Fifth, the tenancy system, for reasons we shall come to shortly, is often associated with heavy pressure on the land and increasing fragmentation of the land into uneconomic parcels. In such circumstances, the tenant is more aptly described as a "hunger renter." He is forced to lease land on whatever terms are available in order to feed his family. Characteristic of such a system, too, is downward social mobility for large numbers of poor peasants because of growing scarcity of land and population pressures.

Sixth, under such conditions, where there is a concentration of poor tenants, holders of uneconomic parcels, and rural proletarians, it is easier for class organization and for class consciousness to emerge than in conditions of an isolated and atomized peasantry scattered throughout the countryside.

Finally, in the family-size tenancy system, the poor peasantry has much more independence than it does on the hacienda, plantation, or ranch. The poor tenant or tenant-laborer often owns his hut and lives apart from the landlord. He is not subject to the "beck-and-call" relationship characteristic of the hacienda. He is freer from economic and social obligations than is the laborer or poor peasant in "feudal" conditions.*

Taken together, these factors mean that in conditions of family-size tenancy, particularly when it is accompanied, as it often is, by heavy pressure on the land, the landowning class appears alien, superfluous, grasping, and exploitative; at the same time, the lower classes are able to develop a relatively high degree of independence, political sensitivity, and organization.

### The Emergence of the Family-Size Tenancy System

What, then, are the conditions under which the family-size tenancy system is likely to emerge? Stinchcombe contends that this type of

---

* Daniel Thorner has argued that the most important distinction to be made in employer-laborer relationships in agriculture is between arrangements in which the laborer contracts freely and those in which his bargaining power is abridged. Working with Indian data, he identifies four subgroups of free labor relationships and three types of unfree labor. See Thorner, *Land and Labour in India* (New York: Asia Publishing House, 1962), chap. 3, "Employer-Labourer Relationships in Agriculture."

system occurs most frequently when five conditions are met: land has very high productivity and high market price; the crop is highly labor intensive and mechanization of agriculture is little developed; labor is cheap; there are no appreciable economies of scale in factors other than labor; and the period of production of the crop is one year or less.[4] To Stinchcombe's five conditions for tenancy, however, a sixth must be added: population pressure. On a worldwide basis, these six conditions are most fully met in the densely populated, wet-rice areas of Asia.

The correlation between tenancy and high land valuation is confirmed by a variety of evidence. In many Asian countries, the highly valued wet-rice land is in tenancy and the less valuable dry land is owner-operated. Moreover, the relationship seems to be direct. As Stinchcombe points out, up to World War II, whenever the price of land went up in Japan, so also did the proportion of land in tenancy. The correlation between tenancy and population pressure has also been established. Colin Clark has found a direct relationship between population density and high rents in a number of countries, both in the past and in the contemporary world. He concludes that rents are highest on the most crowded land provided tenants have nowhere else to go, that is, either to more favorably situated agricultural land or to industry.[5]

Tenancy serves a useful function when the landowning class has no interest in maximizing agricultural production but merely wants to maximize its own surplus. Leasing out land enables a landlord to collect rent without any effort on his part, frees him from the tedious chore of supervising a hired labor force, and allows him to reap the surplus product quietly and unostentatiously.[6] Where there is heavy pressure on the land, the parasitic landlord can take advantage of the competition for land by extracting onerous rents from the renter. "Tenancy" under such conditions is thus a means whereby a landlord can in effect hire labor at below subsistence wages.

Several writers have sought to distinguish such an agrarian system, in which landowners have no interest in increasing production, from one in which owners do have such an interest. Hans Bobek has called the first type of system "rent capitalism."[7] The second might be called "entrepreneurial capitalism." The argument to be advanced here is that the first type of system, rent capitalism, is especially conducive to rural instability, and that this system is particularly widespread in Asia.

*Family-size Tenancy and Its Concomitants in Asia*

The family-size tenancy system is much more widespread in Asia than in any other area of the world. To understand why this is so and to understand the pervasive rural instability that the system has produced, it is necessary to appreciate some of the basic geographic, climatological, and ecological factors that distinguish South Asia and the Far East from other underdeveloped areas of the world. These include the great fertility of the soil; the enormous population pressures on the land; the intensification of agriculture; the concentration of a large landless proletariat or semiproletariat of tenants, sharecroppers, and landless laborers; and the widespread existence of parasitic landlordism.

Geographers call the area extending from Pakistan to Manchuria, together with the arc of offshore islands from Ceylon to Japan, Monsoon Asia.[8] One distinctive characteristic of this area of the world is its extraordinary fertility. The monsoon ensures a seasonal rainfall. In addition, the area contains some of the mightiest rivers in the world: the Yellow, Yangtze, Irrawaddy, Mekong, Indus, Ganges, and Red. It contains many smaller rivers as well. The small state of Kerala in India alone has 23 rivers. Thus, to supplement the regular—but occasionally erratic—rainfall, there is a source of irrigation. Monsoon Asia contains 70 per cent of the world's total irrigated area. In addition, these rivers overflow their banks during the monsoon and deposit substantial quantities of silt in the great river plains and deltas, thus rejuvenating the soil and enabling cultivation to continue for centuries without danger of soil exhaustion. These vast areas of alluvial soil constitute the "rice-bowls" of Asia—the Indo-Gangetic Plain in northern and eastern India, the Cauvery and Godavari deltas in southern and eastern India, the lower and middle Yangtze plains in South and Central China, the Canton Delta in South China, the Irrawaddy Delta in Burma, the Mekong Delta in South Vietnam, the Red River Delta in North Vietnam, and the lower range of the Menam in central Thailand. It is these basic facts that explain why Monsoon Asia is able to accommodate approximately half the world's population—some one and a half billion people on a mere 15 per cent of the earth's land area.

The rural population of Monsoon Asia is largely concentrated in these fertile wet-rice areas. Thus, in French Indochina in the 1930's, an area of 740,000 square kilometers, some 7,500,000 people, or one-third of the total population, lived on 15,000 square kilometers of the Red River Delta.[9] The same concentrated and lopsided distribution of rural inhabitants is characteristic of prewar China, contemporary India, and many other countries in the area.

This concentrated population can sustain itself only because farmers have continually intensified their techniques over the years to the point where they now get two or even three crops of wet-rice per year on a virtually inexhaustible soil. Moreover, their crop is ideally suited for intensive agriculture. Wet-rice requires vast amounts of labor input, particularly at crucial parts of the crop cycle, for weeding, leveling, transplanting seedlings, water control, and harvesting. Most important, it has an ability to absorb an almost limitless number of cultivators on a unit of cultivated land so long as it is given loving care and attention.[10]

In sum, wet-rice cultivation in areas with good soil can resist famine and sustain rising populations in an almost undamageable habitat. It is no wonder that these wet-rice lands are the most crowded of any rural areas on the earth.

In these populous river valleys, deltas, and coastal plains, where peasants have concentrated for centuries, there are many features of life conducive to rural unrest. First of all, there is land hunger caused by an intolerable pressure on the land at existing low levels of productivity. The causes of "pressure on the land" are varied. It is not simply a demographic matter. Nor is it simply a matter of insufficient land. Institutional arrangements, cropping patterns, and crop yields all play an important role.[11]

The principal indication of pressure on the land is the density of the agricultural population in relation to the arable land—what demographers and geographers call "agrarian" or sometimes "physiological" density, as distinguished from the cruder index of overall population density. But this man-land ratio by itself is an insufficient index of pressure on the land. If high agrarian density is accompanied by high per capita productivity, as in the case of the Netherlands or Belgium, even large numbers of agriculturalists can obtain decent livelihoods from the crowded soil. As Colin Clark points out, the density of the agricultural population is as high in Italy as it is in India, but the average Italian cultivator produces twice as much as the average Indian.[12] Thus, the average Indian cultivator is much worse off than the average Italian despite the comparable levels of density. Indeed, as Gunnar Myrdal has demonstrated, in terms of man-land ratio alone, South Asia is not more "overpopulated" than Europe.

Therefore, it is the combination of high agrarian density and low per capita output that generates land hunger. Where yields per unit of agricultural land are abysmally low, as they are in most of Asia, and where there are large numbers of cultivators per unit of arable land, as there are in the fertile areas of Monsoon Asia, the level of life is bound to be poor. In more technical terms, the output per capita $(C)$, which ultimately determines the level of existence, is equivalent to the yield per unit of area $(Y)$ divided by the density of the agricultural population $(D)$, or $C = Y \div D$.[13]

Even the combination of low productivity and high agrarian density, however, can be offset by a more or less equitable sharing of the available produce. In some countries where there is little private ownership of land, traditional communal patterns of landownership ensure more or less equitable distribution. The pre-1917 Russian village commune, or *mir*, sought to serve this purpose by periodic redistribution of the land. Indeed, Nicholas Georgescu-Roegen argues that traditional peasant societies are all characterized by ideologies and institutions designed to provide equal access to the land for those willing to toil.[14]

Moreover, in some agrarian societies with both high agrarian densities and low per capita output, land reform measures have offset the inequities of private ownership and land concentration by putting ceilings on ownership, improving terms of tenancy, reducing rents, and even redistributing land. Such measures have, to one degree or another, reduced inequities in distribution.

The worst cases of pressure on the land and land hunger, then, are found in those countries, or parts of countries, where there is a combination of high agrarian density, low per capita output, and inequitable distribution of land.

As Table 1 suggests, large parts of Latin America, Africa, and the Middle East, as well as some parts of the Far East, do not fall in this category. Neither Africa nor Latin America has as many agriculturalists per unit of land as South, Southeast, and East Asia. Indeed, in many parts of Latin America, the number of people per unit of cultivated land is less than it was in pre-Columbian times.[15] In Africa, too, pressure on the land is not a serious problem, both because agrarian

TABLE 1

*Countries with Over 40 Per Cent of the Population in Agriculture*
*Ranked According to Agrarian Density*

| Country | No. of people per sq. mile of cropland | Country | No. of people per sq. mile of cropland |
|---|---|---|---|
| South Korea | 3,148 | Philippines | 975 |
| Taiwan | 3,130 | Pakistan | 906 |
| North Vietnam | 3,044 | Brazil | 892 |
| Egypt | 2,536 | Colombia | 756 |
| Peru | 1,625 | India | 673 |
| China | 1,584 | Thailand | 668 |
| Indonesia | 1,356 | Burma | 621 |
| South Vietnam | 1,233 | | |

SOURCE: *Production Yearbook, 1960* (New York: United Nations, 1961); *Demographic Yearbook, 1960* (New York: United Nations, 1961).

density is relatively light and because communal patterns of land tenure prevail in much of the continent, particularly in sub-Saharan Africa. As Table 1 indicates, of the 15 underdeveloped countries with an agrarian density higher than 600 persons per square mile of cropland, 11 are in Asia.

Within Asia, there are wide variations. Although Japan has the highest level of agrarian density in the world, its productivity per hectare of cultivated land is five times that of South Asia, four times that of the United States, and double that of Europe.[16] Moreover, both in Japan and in Taiwan, land reform has greatly reduced rural inequities. In addition, in some parts of Asia where extensive agriculture predominates, there is not as much crowding as where there is intensive cultivation. Finally, plantation agriculture in Ceylon, Malaya, Java, Sumatra, and the Philippines, though associated with high levels of agrarian density, is much more productive than peasant farming. According to Myrdal: "In [Ceylon and Malaya] agricultural output per head of population is between two and a half and three and a half times that of either the Indian subcontinent or the rest of Southeast Asia. Highly productive plantations in those two countries are, of course, mainly responsible for their high ratings."[17]

In short, the worst cases of pressure on the land and land hunger exist in those countries, largely but not exclusively in Monsoon Asia, where there is a combination of heavy agrarian density, low per capita output, and inequitable distribution of land. Conditions with respect to these three factors vary considerably from one region of the world to another and within regions. But by far the largest number of countries in which all three factors are found are in Asia, and particularly in the most fertile and therefore most crowded parts of Asia.

In addition to pressure on the land, the second notable characteristic of Monsoon Asia is its vast concentration of landless, land-poor, and sharecropping peasants. In some parts of Monsoon Asia, such as India, landlessness (in which term I comprehend the land poor) is reflected in the existence of a huge class of agricultural laborers who own no land at all. They work for wages whenever work is available, usually at the parts of the crop cycle requiring heavy labor inputs. By one estimate in 1953, of 140,000,000 landless laborers in the world, 60,000,000, or almost half, could be found in Monsoon Asia.[18] According to Myrdal's careful study of South Asia, landless laborers account for at least a third of the agricultural population in most countries of the area, and in some regions the figure rises to as high as 60 per cent.[19]

In some countries of Monsoon Asia, landlessness is reflected in a very large concentration of tenant farmers and sharecroppers. In India, sharecroppers and laborers are often difficult to disentangle; but in other countries of the region they form a more distinct class. R. H. Tawney estimates that in prewar China more than half of the peasants in the southern rice areas were tenants, and in some districts, such as Hunan, the center of the peasant movement in the 1920's, the figure was as high as 80 per cent.[20] In Indonesia in 1960, by the estimate of the Ministry of Agrarian Affairs, 60 per cent of all peasants were sharecroppers;[21] in some surveyed villages "no less than 92% of the families in the village were compelled to work full or part time as tenant farmers or agricultural laborers."[22] In the Philippines, share tenants and share-cash tenants accounted for 27.1 per cent of all farm operators, according to the 1948 census, but in certain parts of the most crowded rice-sugar areas of central Luzon, such as Tarlac and Pampanga, tenancy ranged from 60 per cent to 90 per cent of all farms operated.[23]

Agricultural laborers and sharecroppers represent two kinds of predominantly landless peasants in Monsoon Asia. A third pattern of landlessness is reflected in what Tawney refers to in prewar China as "the propertied proletariat." These are peasants who own land but in such small quantities that they cannot produce enough to feed their families at acceptable levels of nutrition. According to figures he cites for 1917, 36 per cent of all Chinese farms were smaller than 1.5 acres and an additional 26 per cent ranged from 1.5 to 4.3 acres; the average holding for the country as a whole was 3.6 acres. These figures varied widely from one part of China to another, however. Typically, the largest concentration of very tiny holders was in the most densely populated southern rice areas. According to Tawney, the largest holdings in prewar China were in the northeast, where land was "still abundant"; the next largest in the northern provinces of China proper; and the smallest in the south, "where climate, soil, irrigation, and the double cropping facilitated by them, make it possible for a morsel of land to yield a living."[24] The causes of this *morcellement* of land, says Tawney, were first of all population pressure ("the natural consequence of the relation existing between resources and population"), and second, the rule prescribing equal partition of property among heirs.

The "dwarf holder" is also a typical figure in southern and eastern India, as well as in Java. In Kerala, land is measured in "cents," which is equivalent to one-tenth of an acre. Many "landowners" have only 50 or 60 cents of land. The average per capita holding in Kerala is about an acre. In Java, the distinction between "owner cultivators" is between the "just enoughs" and the "not enoughs." Almost all of the dwarf holders in Java, in India, and in prewar China are, or were, hovering on the brink of subsistence.

Monsoon Asia, then, has the highest concentration of landless agricultural laborers, sharecroppers, and dwarf holders of any region in the world. Moreover, this landless and semi-landless class is not distributed evenly. Within Monsoon Asia, the most fertile, most densely populated coastal plains and river valleys have the largest concentration of landless and land poor.

The third characteristic of much of Monsoon Asia is an increasing trend toward landlessness, or the "proletarianization" of the peasantry. The theoretical explanation for this development appears to be that mounting population pressures lead inexorably to subdivision and to fragmented farms that are no longer capable of sustaining a family. Small owners are thus reduced within a generation or two to tenancy or agricultural labor. Myrdal confirms this trend toward landlessness in South Asia as a whole: "The population increase, which contributes to the fragmentation and subdivision of holdings, also produces impoverishment of the peasantry. As the economic circumstances of smallholders worsen, they become more vulnerable to complete loss of their lands. A weeding-out of the smallest holdings thus tends to occur, leaving an increasing proportion of the population landless."[25]

The result of this trend toward landlessness is downward social mobility for the great majority of rural inhabitants. A study conducted in 1955 by a University of Ceylon team in the densely populated district of Kandy showed that the average size of a holding in Ceylon could be halved in a single generation.[26] In one careful study done in Madhya Pradesh in India, a state that is not particularly "overpopulated," the number of small holdings under 10 acres increased by one-third in the two decades between 1930 and 1949.[27]

The precise degree to which such pauperization is taking place varies, of course, from country to country and within countries of the area. Although the necessary data to support an area-wide generalization are lacking, it seems likely that the process is particularly intense in the most crowded areas.

One of the few economists to have studied this process in some detail over a long period of time is Robert Sansom. Sansom studied the economic history of the Mekong Delta between the middle of the nineteenth century and the early twentieth century—that is, before the Communists took hold in the Delta. His study provides detailed evidence on the relationship between population pressure and declining living standards for the great majority of the peasantry.

Settlement in the Delta was relatively negligible until the French began to encourage it in the 1860's. In the years from 1868 to 1930 the Delta developed at a rate unmatched anywhere, anytime. From 1868 to 1930 the area cultivated rose from 215,000 to 2,214,000 hectares, and the population grew from 1,679,000 in 1880 to 4,484,000 in 1931. By the early 1960's the population reached 9,000,000.

Although Delta economic conditions improved during the initial period of settlement, "by the early 1930s, the overall economic picture in the Delta was one of a fixed land frontier, static techniques of production, unchanging market opportunities, and a high rate of population growth."[28] What is most significant from our point of view is the careful accumulation of evidence by Sansom that, beginning in the late 1920's and early 1930's, the real income of the majority of the peasantry, now forced off their land into tenancy or into work as laborers, declined significantly. Too many people were chasing too little land in a static situation. Rigid institutions accelerated the process. Landlords, profiting from a Malthusian situation, bought out an increasing number of small landholders and forced them into tenancy; similarly, by playing off one tenant against another and driving up rents, they forced small tenants off the land into a rural proletarian class. This class grew rapidly. "By 1945 the institutions of tenancy had become rigid and elite-serving; they were economically unproductive for, and socially unacceptable to, the vast majority of the Delta's inhabitants."[29] In a later passage, Sansom concludes:

> It could hardly be a coincidence that the evidence presented . . . on residual rice consumption, wages and production techniques—gathered from diverse sources and analyzed from different viewpoints, using pessimistic assumptions with regard to the expected outcome—has given compatible results. In every case the results indicate that the economic conditions of the rural Delta declined in the post-1930 period after having risen sharply during the preceding period of settlement. It seems clear that economic conditions were deteriorating; furthermore, this development was the expected outcome from the prevailing institutional conditions. As the population grew, landlords were able to prevent the rural population's near-subsistence needs from supplanting production going to the export market; therefore, economic conditions became progressively worse.[30]

Sansom's study points to the fourth characteristic of Monsoon Asia —the widespread existence of parasitic landlordism within a family-size tenancy system. The enormous population pressure raises land values, and high land values make it more profitable for landowners to lease land, usually at exorbitant rates of interest in cash or kind, than to work it themselves. Sharecroppers in Monsoon Asia are not uncommonly asked to pay 60 or 70 per cent of their harvest (or its market value) to landowners who make virtually no contribution in capital or labor to the production of the crop.

To sum up the socioeconomic side of the argument, it seems likely that Monsoon Asia has a unique combination of very heavy pressure on the land, an unusually heavy concentration of landless and land poor, an increasing trend toward pauperization of the peasantry, and a high degree of parasitic landlordism—all within the framework of a family-size tenancy system.

## The Development of Peasant Revolutionary Consciousness

The existence of a large, concentrated class of landless and semi-landless peasants in a family-size tenancy system does not by itself produce a revolutionary situation. The proclivity, or lack of procliv-

ity, of the peasantry for radical movements depends in large part on
its socioeconomic status. But it also depends on the peasantry's perceptions of its own situation. That is, even when most of the "objective" conditions conducive to peasant mobilization are present, there
are "subjective" conditions—the ideas and values peasants have—
that may either facilitate or inhibit the development of "mass revolutionary consciousness."

Unfortunately, there has been little systematic research on the conditions that facilitate or inhibit the development of a revolutionary
consciousness among the peasantry. Marx looked into the question,
but he never developed a theory. The point of departure for such a
theory has been well stated by H. Wolpe: "Radical changes in attitudes and action cannot simply be ascribed to relatively unchanged
structural conditions. What needs to be examined is the way in which
objective reality comes to be subjectively perceived and this entails
more than an analysis of objective conditions coupled with a description of subjective reactions."[31]

As Wolpe points out, the peasantry, or a substantial portion of the
peasantry, may have a feeling of overwhelming dissatisfaction with
the status quo. But such a feeling is not sufficient to produce a revolutionary response. A given peasant may believe that the status quo
is immutable, a view that would almost always be reinforced by traditional religious belief.

According to Wolpe, the two requirements for the development of
revolutionary consciousness are first, a belief that revolution is necessary, and second, a perception that change is possible in two different senses. He says: "Institutions which have assumed a natural,
reified and immutable appearance must come to be seen as man-made
and changeable. This implies the dereification of the institutional
structure in men's consciousness. In the second sense, [there must
be], above all, a conception of the assailability of the structure of
power."[32]

Wolpe has put his finger on one crucial aspect of our problem. How
does the rural proletariat chained to a traditional culture come to
believe that change is possible?

One answer to this question is the answer provided by the Lenin-
ists: that revolutionary consciousness must be transmitted to the
worker or peasant from the outside by a revolutionary party. Although I do not wish to deny the importance of a revolutionary party
in stimulating revolutionary consciousness among the peasantry, I do

want to argue that certain objective conditions facilitate the receptivity to change among the peasantry, most notably the breaking of its traditional isolation and its increased communication with the larger society.

Up to this century, one of the most important social-psychological facts of traditional peasant life in most parts of the world was the degree of peasant isolation. This point was first emphasized by Marx and provided the basis of his explanation for the political impotence of the French peasantry in the nineteenth century. Peasant isolation, according to him, is the combined result of a self-sufficient mode of production involving little social interaction, dispersal throughout the countryside, poverty, and poor communications. It is, in fact, a triple isolation: physical, social, and mental. The effect of this isolation is to make it extremely difficult for peasants to achieve class consciousness, that is, to form political parties, to develop a sense of community, or to develop any kind of national associations.[33]

Along similar lines, Pitirim Sorokin and Carle Zimmerman argue that the distinctive characteristics of the countryside—isolation, limited mobility, greater homogeneity, slower rates of social change—combine to reinforce a tendency toward provincialism, traditionalism, and resistance to change in the peasantry.[34]

One of the most potent forces in overcoming peasant isolation in the modern world is education. The importance of literacy as a radicalizing force in the countryside was impressed upon me by the data I gathered on the rural base of Indian Communism. If India is divided into districts of low, medium, and high literacy, landlessness "explains" 64 per cent of the Communist vote in the high literacy districts, but only 8 per cent and 9.6 per cent, respectively, in the low and medium literacy districts.[35]

Thus, in India, even when pressure on the land is disregarded, the combination of landlessness and literacy is correlated to an extraordinarily high degree with the Communist vote. This does not mean that pressure on the land is insignificant. As one might expect, the combination of landlessness, high literacy, and heavy pressure on the land produces the highest variance in the Communist vote. In the 25 districts of India that are high both in literacy and in density, landlessness "explains" 71.4 per cent of the Communist vote, that is, almost three-fourths of the variance.[36]

It is scarcely surprising, therefore, that the Kerala Communists have the strongest, most consistent, most reliable base among the rural poor of any Communist Party in the world. Kerala ranks first in all of India in terms of literacy, pressure on the land, and landlessness. Nor is it surprising that the landless laborers and land-poor peasants in Kerala are much more politically conscious than the landless anywhere else in India. My recent comparison of the Communist voters of Kerala and West Bengal shows that Communist voters in Kerala, many of whom are literate, are more loyal to the Communist Party, more aware of the importance of voting, and much more decisive in their political opinions than their more illiterate Communist counterparts in West Bengal. To take but one example, Communist voters in West Bengal consistently responded "don't know" or "incorrectly" to questions on which the Communist Party has a very clear position, such as, does the Congress Party represent the rich or the poor? In Kerala, by contrast, the percentage of "don't know" or "incorrect" answers on any given question was considerably lower.[37]

Unfortunately, there are few empirical studies on the effects of literacy on peasants in underdeveloped countries and fewer still on the effects of literacy on a landless or semi-landless rural proletariat. The few available studies all indicate that literacy makes men more open to change and to new information, and greatly increases imaginativeness about alternatives to existing conditions of life.[38] Thus, where the actual daily experiences of life have a potentially radicalizing effect, it is the awareness of the possibility of change that can trigger this effect.

It is not only literacy that opens up landless peasants to change or helps overcome their isolation. It seems quite likely that poor peasants in densely populated rural areas are more receptive to change than poor peasants in sparsely settled areas because the populous areas usually are closer to cities, markets, and transportation, and have better communications. In the more crowded rural areas, generally speaking, there is more trade, more economic and political organization, a greater division of labor, more urbanization, and higher levels of communication.[39] For all of these reasons, peasants in crowded areas may be more ripe psychologically for change—and for organization—than peasants in isolated, sparsely settled areas.

There are probably other social-psychological factors at work in the more crowded areas of family-size tenancy that help to radicalize the poor peasants. It is relatively easy for the rural elite to keep the landless peasants isolated and atomized in an area where they make up only 5 or 10 per cent of the total agricultural population. But where the landless and land poor comprise 40 per cent or more of the total agricultural population, they become aware of the power of their numbers and it is much more difficult for the richer peasants to keep them "in place." And, finally, an important psychological fact alienating many of the landless in densely populated areas may well be the sheer difficulty of the work. Ester Boserup has emphasized the much harder work required in densely settled, labor-intensive peasant communities; in more sparsely settled areas, where cultivable land is relatively abundant, a surplus of subsistence crops can be produced "without great effort" by the ordinary household.[40] In fact, minimal amounts of peasant labor are characteristic both historically and contemporaneously in areas of sparse population and extensive land use. By contrast, in densely settled, intensively cultivated areas, the amount of work is both greater and more onerous. This is particularly true of wet-rice cultivation. As one Indian sociologist with considerable firsthand experience of Indian villages points out: "Wet paddy cultivation requires long hours of backbreaking work which might have to be performed for weeks in mud or standing water with the rain beating down. Those who work in the fields through the day are sometimes too exhausted to take the filth off their bodies at night and such people frequently suffer from recurring skin ailments."[41] It is understandable why, in such conditions, even small landowners prefer to have their work done by sharecroppers or hired laborers. In the areas of Kerala I investigated in the summer of 1972, it is not uncommon for an owner of even half an acre of land to hire labor at those parts of the crop cycle that demand the most difficult work.

These, then, are some of the social-psychological factors at work in crowded areas of Monsoon Asia that can help the landless and land poor to overcome their isolation, to develop "class consciousness," and to undermine the legitimacy of the landed elite even before the revolutionary party emerges on the scene.

## Land Tenure and Rural Radicalism

If the most fertile, densely populated parts of Monsoon Asia with family-size tenancy systems do, indeed, have so many of the characteristics I hold to be conducive to rural instability, what is the evidence that it is exactly those areas that have shown a high potential for rural radicalism?

The connection between landlessness, rural instability, and Com-

TABLE 2
## Districts of India in Which Agricultural Laborers Represent 40 Per Cent or More of Peasant Cultivators, 1961

| Area[a] | Crop[b] | % agricultural laborers | Cultivators per 100 acres | % total tenancy | % dwarf holdings | % CP vote |
|---|---|---|---|---|---|---|
| India | | 19.3% | 38 | 18.0% | 5.0% | 8.9% |
| Cannanore | R | 71.8 | 43 | 86.1 | 37.4 | 38.5 |
| Amravati | C | 65.1 | 25 | 19.0 | 1.0 | 7.2 |
| Palghat | R | 60.8 | 58 | 90.6 | 21.8 | 46.0 |
| West Godavari | R | 60.75 | 64 | 31.9 | 13.4 | 29.8 |
| East Godavari | R | 60.3 | 73 | 38.1 | 18.2 | 21.9 |
| Yeotmai | C | 59.9 | 27 | 24.7 | 0.1 | 4.3 |
| Akola | C | 59.1 | 24 | 18.1 | 0.6 | 2.0 |
| Krishna | R | 58.4 | 50 | 18.6 | 11.2 | 35.8 |
| Wardha | C | 56.2 | 23 | 12.8 | 0.4 | 6.95 |
| Alleppey | R | 51.6 | 55 | 27.1 | 61.4 | 38.2 |
| Buldhana | C | 49.7 | 26 | 13.4 | 0.9 | — |
| Kurnool | J | 48.9 | 24 | 20.1 | 2.9 | 13.45 |
| Parbhani | J | 48.3 | 21 | 23.2 | 0.1 | 6.5 |
| Trichur | R | 47.9 | 54 | 81.8 | 33.0 | 38.2 |
| Thanjaour | R | 47.4 | 63 | 52.7 | 15.5 | 16.6 |
| Guntur | R | 47.2 | 43 | 25.3 | 12.0 | 29.6 |
| Calicut | R | 46.9 | 30 | 84.9 | 35.0 | 19.9 |
| Jalgaon | C | 46.1 | 30 | 13.4 | 2.0 | 5.3 |
| Bidar | J–GR | 45.4 | 26 | 14.9 | 1.9 | 7.65 |
| Darbhanga | R | 45.3 | 80 | 39.0 | 39.0 | 7.85 |
| Nanded | C | 44.9 | 26 | 17.4 | 0.4 | 9.75 |
| Dhulia | J–C | 44.2 | 31 | 13.1 | 0.6 | 6.8 |
| Osmanabad | J | 44.1 | 24 | 18.1 | 0.3 | 3.7 |
| Broach | C | 43.7 | 29 | 28.6 | 1.4 | — |
| Nellore | R | 43.1 | 45 | — | 17.6 | 25.15 |
| Kottayam | R | 43.1 | 28 | 23.4 | 50.4 | 36.3 |
| Champaran | R | 43.0 | 71 | 45.0 | 25.7 | 10.75 |
| Khamman | R | 42.0 | 52 | 18.5 | 4.5 | 40.5 |
| Chingleput | R | 41.9 | 69 | 32.6 | 18.9 | 1.7 |
| Birbhum | R | 41.2 | 40 | 23.5 | 9.3 | 12.0 |
| Ernakulam | R | 40.6 | 42 | 55.2 | 45.4 | 34.0 |
| Nalgonda | J–R | 40.6 | 37 | 16.3 | 8.7 | 48.5 |
| Trivandrum | R | 40.5 | 51 | 19.2 | 60.7 | 38.1 |
| Nagpur | J | 40.45 | 27 | 9.6 | 0.9 | 2.0 |
| Howrah | R | 40.05 | 61 | 31.6 | 41.6 | 23.6 |

SOURCE: Donald Zagoria, "The Ecology of Peasant Communism in India," *American Political Science Review*, 65.1 (Mar. 1971) : 144–60.

[a] Districts in italics have both above-average tenancy and above-average dwarf holdings.

[b] R stands for rice, C for cotton, J for jowar, and GR for gram.

TABLE 3

*Ordered Cumulative Multiple Regression of Per Cent of the Vote of the Communist Parties in India by District with More than 45 Cultivators per 100 Acres*

| Step number | Independent variable | Cumulative $R^2$ | Contribution of $R^2$ | Area |
|---|---|---|---|---|
| 1 | Landless labor | .416 | .416 | Total India |
| 2 | Less than 1 acre | .489 | .073 | $N = 103$ |
| 3 | Tenancy | .512 | .023 | Total variance explained: 51.2% |
| 1 | Landless labor | .589 | .589 | Southern zone |
| 2 | Less than 1 acre | .615 | .026 | $N = 38$ |
| 3 | Tenancy | .621 | .006 | Total variance explained: 62.1% |
| 1 | Tenancy | .473 | .473 | Northern zone |
| 2 | Less than 1 acre | .559 | .086 | $N = 7$ |
| 3 | Landless labor | .559 | .000 | Total variance explained: 55.9% |
| 1 | Tenancy | .029 | .029 | Central zone |
| 2 | Less than 1 acre | .060 | .031 | $N = 27$ |
| 3 | Landless labor | .060 | .000 | Total variance explained: 6.0% |
| 1 | Less than 1 acre | .255 | .255 | Eastern zone |
| 2 | Landless labor | .284 | .029 | $N = 28$ |
| 3 | Tenancy | .301 | .017 | Total variance explained: 30.1% |
| 1 | Landless labor | .225 | .225 | Western zone |
| 2 | Tenancy | .386 | .161 | $N = 3$ |
| 3 | Less than 1 acre | .392 | .006 | Total variance explained: 39.2% |

SOURCE: Same as Table 2.

NOTE: The figure for the Communist vote is the average vote in three general elections—1957, 1962, and 1967. It includes the combined vote in 1967 of the CPI and the CPM, the two Communist parties that compete in elections.

munism in Monsoon Asia can be demonstrated most precisely in the case of India. India is the one country in the area that has a considerable amount of landlessness spread unevenly throughout the country, that has fairly accurate census data pinpointing those districts with the highest incidence of landlessness, and that has had free elections over the past 20 years in which the Communists have participated. There are more than 300 districts in India. In only 35 of them do agricultural laborers represent 40 per cent or more of all peasant cultivators. As Table 2 indicates, the Communists receive a higher than average vote in 21 of the 35. If one takes those 18 districts that have above-average tenancy and dwarf holdings, the Communists receive an above-average vote in 16 of them. In most of the 18 districts, the vote is usually two or three times the average for all of India. All 18, moreover, are districts in which wet-rice is the principal crop. Of the two exceptions to this pattern, one, Darbhanga in Bihar, is an area of growing Communist strength, and the other, Chingleput in Madras, is an area in which a regional movement has preempted the Communists by appealing to the landless and land-poor peasants with a mixture of populism and linguistic nationalism.

Another reflection of the relationship between landlessness and Communism can be found in Table 3. If one takes the 103 districts of India in which there are the greatest number of cultivators per unit of land (more than 45), landlessness "explains" a variance of 51.2 per cent of the Communist vote. Moreover, this combination of land-lessness and agrarian density "explains" a variance of at least 30 per cent of the Communist vote in four of five geographic regions of India.[42]

Indonesia and the Philippines also provide clear-cut evidence of a high correlation between landlessness and density, on the one hand, and Communism, on the other. The strength of the Indonesian PKI lies not in the sparsely populated parts of west Java, but in the densely populated parts of central and east Java. Moreover, there are sta-tistical data available to demonstrate a very high correlation between tenancy in the most densely populated areas of Java and PKI strength (Table 4). Similarly, the traditional base of the Huks, and of the Sakdalistas before them, is central Luzon, the area of the Philippines with the highest rates of tenancy and the densest rural populations.[43]

Thus, in three cases where statistical techniques and data can be employed to measure the distribution of Communist strength within

TABLE 4

*PKI Vote, Tenancy, and Population Density in the 1957 Kabupaten Elections in Indonesia*

| Population density per square km | Number of kabupatens | Gamma[a] |
|---|---|---|
| 0–99 | 11 | −.158 |
| 100–399 | 22 | .186 |
| 400–550 | 32 | .115 |
| 551–1,154 | 20 | .630 |

SOURCE: Based on data gathered by Mavis Taintor for use in her forthcoming Ph.D. dissertation, State University of New York, Buffalo.

[a] The gamma value expresses the correlation between PKI vote, tenancy, and population density.

the rural areas of a country, it is clear that those parts in which landlessness and heavy population pressures combine are the "reddest."

The case of pre-Communist China is more complex. Roy Hofheinz,
Jr., who has analyzed what data there are most carefully, argues that
there is no perfect correlation between land tenure patterns in southern China during the 1920's and 1930's and areas of Communist
strength.[44] Hofheinz has demonstrated convincingly that there were
several areas of South China with high tenancy rates—notably the
Canton Delta—in which the peasant movement led by the Communists in the 1920's and 1930's had relatively little strength. Yet he
himself has elsewhere provided the explanation why the Communists
had great difficulty in penetrating the Delta: the gentry forces in the
Canton area were much more powerful than were the gentry in those
parts of South China where the peasant movement was able to establish itself.[45] From this fact, Hofheinz has generalized that

> there was no single factor which provided both the necessary and the
> sufficient conditions for peasant movement success. While it may well
> have been that economic grievances were necessary to provide a spring-
> board for the earliest penetration they alone were not sufficient to put
> the movement across. . . . The other necessary condition appears to
> have been a sufficiently low level of potential local opposition, whether
> in the form of political resistance through the KMT, organized gentry
> forces or . . . "illegal" elements such as bandit bands or secret socie-
> ties.[46]

Clearly, to state the argument in this fashion is to underline the
limitations of an exclusively socioeconomic approach to peasant radicalism. Economic grievances arising from land tenure patterns are
necessary but not sufficient to explain the success of a peasant movement. This does not invalidate the general argument being advanced
here. Nowhere in Monsoon Asia, or anywhere else for that matter, is
there a perfect correlation between economic grievances and peasant
unrest. More specifically, even in areas where there is acute peasant
unrest that can be traced to socioeconomic grievances, there are always countervailing factors. In the Philippines, as Edward J. Mitchell
has demonstrated, despite favorable "ecological conditions," the Huks
have been unable to penetrate those parts of central Luzon in which
the peasants speak Tagalog. They have been most successful in Pam-
pangan-speaking areas of central Luzon. This can be traced to historic antipathies between the Pampangan- and Tagalog-speaking
peasants.[47] In India, as I have indicated, in 1961 the Communists

were heavily entrenched in 16 of the 18 districts with the highest percentage of landless and land poor. In one of those districts, however, they had been preempted by a populist regional movement based on the Tamil-speaking peasantry. In the case of South China, it may well be that the crucial intervening variable inhibiting peasant mobilization in one or another densely populated, high-tenancy area was the strength of the gentry or the secret societies. But, again, this in no way invalidates the general point being made here—that "economic" grievances making the peasantry susceptible to a revolutionary movement are likely to be greater in areas with a high proportion of landless peasants and very great pressure on the land. What all this does point to is the need to consider carefully those factors in such areas that can either inhibit or accelerate peasant mobilization by a revolutionary movement.

Still another argument sometimes used to invalidate the "ecological" approach in China is that the Communist movement had no difficulty in taking hold in North China, though South China was more densely populated and had a higher incidence of tenancy. Although the south undoubtedly did have a higher degree of tenancy, dwarf holding, and pressure on the land than the north, North China was hardly a rural paradise: one 1945 study estimated that 62 per cent of the population there consisted of poor peasants who held only 27 per cent of the land; and a recent study suggests that war, inflation, and famine may have severely debilitated large segments of the peasantry in northern China during and after the war with Japan.[48] Jane Price, who has made the most thorough study of the situation in North China between 1946 and 1949—the decisive phase of the Communist struggle with the Nationalists—concludes: "Although assessments of tenancy patterns may differ, it is probable that during and after the anti-Japanese war there emerged a sizable number of impoverished peasants in North China for whom agrarian reform had an enormous appeal."[49]

One can only add to this statement that if this was not the case, the entire course of the civil war and the enormous success the Chinese Communists had in recruiting peasants into their armies after redistributing land would be largely inexplicable.

Somewhat different objections have been raised by some writers to correlations between inequality of land tenure and Communist strength in South Vietnam. In a 1967 article Mitchell argued that the areas of greatest inequality in South Vietnam were dominated by the government, whereas the Vietcong was strongest in areas with more equitable patterns of land distribution.[50] Jeffrey Paige has since shown that Mitchell achieved his results by lumping together four regions of South Vietnam with quite different patterns of tenure and agricultural organization: the northern coastal lowlands, the southern coastal lowlands, the southern plateau, and the Mekong Delta.[51] Of these four regions, it is the Delta that has the longest, most sustained record of agrarian instability. As Paige puts it: "Almost all social movements have been concentrated in the Mekong Delta proper. In the period between the consolidation of French administrative and colonial power after the defeat of the last major primary resistance movement in 1917 and the outbreak of World War II, there were two major millennial religious movements promising liberation from the French, and two violent agrarian uprisings."[52] The Sansom study I cited earlier establishes clearly the link between the Communists and the socioeconomic grievances of the Delta peasantry.

The Mekong Delta, as I have said, is one of the two most densely populated regions of South Vietnam; some 85 per cent of the population of South Vietnam live either in that area or in the other major rice-growing area—the northern coastal zone. The Delta has a higher rate of tenancy than the northern coastal zone, indeed the highest rate in the country. It also differs from the northern zone in two other ways: it is much more commercialized and has much larger holdings than the rice area of the north. But as Paige makes clear, the northern coastal region, an area of even greater pressure on the land than the Delta, also has a history of agrarian unrest in the 1930's and was the weakest of the four regions in terms of government control as of 1945.[53]

In other words, the evidence from South Vietnam lends further weight to the general argument I am advancing: that there is a strong correlation within Monsoon Asia between wet-rice areas with heavy pressure on the land and family-size tenancy on the one hand, and agrarian instability and Communism on the other. That this correlation is not perfect is obvious; there is no straight line between socioeconomic conditions and politics. That the correlation is strong throughout Monsoon Asia should by now, however, also be obvious.

### Opportunity for Rebellion: Elite Weakness and State Breakdown

I have singled out the concentration in densely populated areas of a rural proletariat and semiproletariat as one of the conditions that facilitates the development of a revolutionary movement in the countryside. The weakening of the traditional rural elite is another. Wherever that elite is strong and maintains its legitimacy, the entry of any revolutionary movement is problematic. Thus, as Hofheinz has noted, the peasant movement in China in the 1920's was unable to penetrate those areas of the south where the gentry, clans, or secret societies dominated the countryside. In central Java, Mavis Taintor has found a strong inverse correlation between the strength of the Communists and the strength of the orthodox Islamic party, the NU.

In my own research in India in 1972, I found much the same pattern. Communist leaders told me that they have had the greatest difficulty penetrating those rural areas in Kerala in which the authority and legitimacy of the traditional rural elite remain intact. They referred to such areas as feudal or semifeudal. Similarly, in France, Juan Linz found that the areas of the countryside most unlikely to vote for the Communists were those where the Church was strong or where there was a strong aristocratic class.[54] Exactly what factors account for the stability of traditional rural elites in many parts of the world, even in areas penetrated by the forces of modernization, is a question that has not yet been adequately answered. What does seem apparent is that there are various objective economic or political factors that can contribute to the weakening of such an elite. These include change in agricultural technology, penetration of the market, and war.

Typically, a traditional elite is first weakened by such factors and subsequently loses the will and the ability to govern. Henry Landsberger, Barrington Moore, and Chalmers Johnson have all pointed to this sequence and its importance. Johnson calls it "power deflation," Moore calls it the loss of the "natural basis of respect for the landlord," and Landsberger has formulated a general proposition: "Peasant movements are most likely to occur in societies where traditional elites have lost ground relative to newer elites through objective economic changes in the importance and structure of agriculture or objective political changes, such as war."[55]

There is considerable empirical evidence to support such a proposition in Latin America. In Brazil a peasant movement developed in Pernambuco as the traditional sugar growers were being displaced by competition from the new, more modern plantations and mills of São Paulo. The landed oligarchy of Mexico lost ground under Porfirio Díaz, and on the eve of the Revolution the landowners could no longer depend on traditional forms of social control. Bolivia was bled by a series of wars with Paraguay that ended in defeat in 1935 and demoralized the landed elite; the result was a power vacuum filled by peasant unions and other new groups. Peasant movements began to appear in Venezuela when the rural oligarchy of that country began to decline with the loss of German coffee markets during World War I.[56]

The evidence from other parts of the world points in the same direction. The Russian nobles, never well integrated into village society, were falling deeper and deeper in debt on the eve of the Emancipation in 1861, were further weakened in the Revolution of 1905, and were virtually paralyzed during 1917, when the Tsarist autocracy crumbled. In China, the late nineteenth and early twentieth centuries saw a progressive alienation of the peasant masses from an ever more urbanized gentry. According to Joseph Esherick:

> In the nineteenth century, as commercial activity increased the size and attractiveness of the urban centers, the urbanization of the Chinese gentry accelerated. Specialized "landlord bursaries" (tsu-chan) were established to aid the city-based landlords to extract their rent from the countryside. Increasingly the landlord became totally divorced from production, providing neither seeds nor tools to the tenant, ceasing to personally supervise the post-harvest division of the crop, and ultimately accepting a fixed rent in either grain or money which required no knowledge of the harvest whatsoever. As landlord and tenant ceased to be part of a single, vertically integrated rural community, all sense of mutual trust was lost.[57]

This process increasingly exposed the Chinese gentry in the eyes of the peasant masses as a parasitic class, according to Esherick. As he goes on to say:

> Barrington Moore, in his brilliant comparative analysis of the relationship between peasants and their overlords, has suggested that the Chinese gentry was always basically parasitic and never performed any real function in the society. I would reject this view, which fails to explain to my satisfaction why the Chinese peasantry only succeeded in the twentieth century in terminating the centuries of gentry rule. In earlier centuries, rural gentry performed a variety of religious and ceremonial functions, advanced the economic well-being of the community by organizing irrigation and other public works and often represented the entire community in petitions to, or conflicts with, government authorities. It was only in the course of the nineteenth and twentieth centuries that the Chinese gentry ceased to be functional.

Once they became city-dwellers interested in Western-style urban and political modernization, their concern for the peasantry was limited to an interest in the prompt payment of rent and taxes.[58]

The Chinese gentry, already alienated from the masses of the peasantry as a result of this long process of urbanization, was further weakened by the Japanese invasion and the ensuing civil war. There was a vacuum of authority in the countryside that was filled by the Communists.

In India, too, there seems to be a general relationship between those areas where the authority of the dominant castes has been weakened and those areas where the Communists have been able to mobilize the poor peasantry.[59]

Where the weakening of the rural elite, always a long-term process, is accompanied by the breakdown of the state, the opportunity for a peasant rebellion greatly increases. As one observer has noted in reviewing Eric Wolf's *Peasant Wars in the Twentieth Century*:

> It is the breakdown of the state, caused by factors completely outside peasant control, which gives rise to rural violence and possibly to peasant war. If this is so, more attention should be given to the institutional crisis in Mexico in 1910, the impact of military defeat on the Russian state in 1917, the effects of the Japanese invasion on the Chinese and Vietnamese revolutions, the effects of the Second World War and Dien Bien Phu on the Algerian Revolution, and the collapse of the Cuban state under Castro's military-political offensive.[60]

Along similar lines, Hugh Seton-Watson observes: "The three victorious communist revolutions of the twentieth century—the Russian, Yugoslav and Chinese—depended in crucial stages of their struggle on peasant support. Yet in all three the communists became a force capable of seizing and maintaining power only when the old regime had been smashed by external force. It was only after defeat in war, and disintegration of the State machine, that the communists were able to mobilize the peasants for their purposes."[61] Seton-Watson overstates the case. The Chinese Communists were able to mobilize the peasants for their purposes well before the war with Japan.[62] But there can be little doubt that the war greatly facilitated the process.

By all evidence, then, the power and authority of the landed gentry can be undermined in several ways, most notably by a loss of markets, by commercialization of agriculture, or by war. But to relate this point to what has gone before in this paper, I would argue that the authority of the landed elites is very difficult to maintain in densely populated areas with large concentrations of landless and land-poor peasantry. In such situations of acute land hunger, there is a severe competition for land between peasants and "overlords."[63] And the temptations for a landed elite in a densely populated area to turn into a parasitic, rentier class are great.

## Communist Parties and Agrarian Revolution

Many of the conditions that help to radicalize the peasantry may be present in a given country, but the extent to which that revolutionary energy is focused, disciplined, and organized depends on the existence of a revolutionary movement. An intriguing question is why, in the modern world, it has been the Communist parties that have so often played the role of midwife to the revolution of the landless and land poor in Asia. In part, their preeminence is an accident of history. The product of the international Communist movement following the Russian Revolution in 1917, these parties have been in place for years in many underdeveloped countries and have been able to serve as "carrier groups" for any revolutionary forces. Such parties are "around," like Christianity in the age of Constantine.

But for the Communist parties of Asia to serve as the carriers of agrarian revolution has required an enormous change in ideology since 1917. The "peasantization" of Communist ideology has proceeded gradually from Marx to Lenin and finally to Mao. Lenin, virtually alone among the Bolshevik leaders, appreciated the importance of the agrarian question in Russia. After the Revolution, Lenin, Bukharin, and other Comintern leaders pointed out the crucial importance of the agrarian uprising in Russia in the fall and winter of 1917 to the victory of the Bolshevik enterprise. And they argued that the failure of the Hungarian Soviet in 1919 was largely due to Béla Kun's refusal to break up the large estates and redistribute the land.[64]

In the early years of the Comintern, the "peasantist" orientation was quite strong; it reached its height with the formation of the Krestintern in the mid-1920's. But there was always strong resistance from the "orthodox" Marxists to a revolutionary orientation based on the peasantry. Mao Tse-tung, in his early years, had to wage a continual fight against those in the Comintern who accused him of "populism," "empiricism," and other such sins because of his correct perception of the peasantry as the most consistently revolutionary force in the developing countries. Thus, not the least obstacle that Communist leaders in the developing countries had to overcome—if they were to lead agrarian revolutions—was a built-in classical Marxist bias against the peasantry as a backward, uncivilized class, destined in any case to disappear with the triumph of capitalism.[65]

There are several characteristics that seem to distinguish a Communist leadership successful in mobilizing the peasantry from one that is not successful. As "successful" Communist leaderships, I have specifically in mind those of China between 1927 and 1949, Indonesia between 1952 and 1965, and Kerala since 1957. As "unsuccessful" ones, I have in mind those of China before 1927, Indonesia before 1952, and West Bengal in India, as well as most of those in the Middle East and Latin America. My criterion for "success" is not necessarily success in gaining power but rather success in recruiting a substantial and loyal peasant following.

One characteristic of a successful Communist leadership has already been suggested. The leaders must be looking toward the countryside rather than toward the cities and the urban proletariat. Until the 1950's and 1960's, Communist leaders in many developing countries, perhaps even the majority, had a notable bias toward the cities and a scarcely veiled contempt for the peasantry. In Indonesia, it was not until the Aidit-Lukman leadership emerged in the early 1950's with an emphasis on agrarian revolution that the PKI began to look for, and to find, a peasant following. The Chinese Communists gained a peasant following only after Chiang Kai-shek drove them from the urban centers of China in 1927 and forced them into the hinterland.

A successful Communist leadership must also do its homework. The "rural surveys" conducted by Mao Tse-tung and the staff of the Chinese peasant institute he helped establish in the late 1920's provided a rich store of data on the countryside. The forms they used called for detailed reports on the wages, rent payments, and other conditions of life of the peasantry; on such sources of local authority as clans, kinship groups, and secret societies; on the strength and social composition of the peasant movement in the area; and so forth. Similar types of rural surveys were conducted by the Indonesian Communists after the Aidit-Lukman team took over in the early 1950's. As of the early 1970's, only one state Communist leadership in India—that of Kerala—had had the foresight and the determination to carry out such surveys. It can surely be no coincidence that these three leaderships, all of which have demonstrated an interest in gathering empirical data on the class structure in the countryside, have been among the most successful in Asia in mobilizing the peasantry for their purposes.

The Maoist approach to the countryside, which has been successfully used in China, Indonesia, and Kerala, is predicated upon the ability to divide the rural population into different classes: landlords, rich peasants, middle peasants, poor peasants, and hired farmhands. The distinctions between the various groups, it should be noted, are not made on the basis of size of plot—as they are in much Western literature on the subject—but on the basis of such factors as the source of income and the quantity and quality of the means of production.[66] Thus, a landlord does not engage in labor, whereas a rich peasant does. A rich peasant makes over 15 per cent of his annual income from "exploitation" (that is, rent), whereas a middle peasant does not. A poor peasant may own some land and implements, or he may own no land at all, but in general he has to rent land from others and is exploited by others through rent, loan interest, and the hiring out of part of his labor.[67] Political categories can also be included in the definitions. Thus, a "reactionary rich peasant" is a rich peasant who has engaged in serious counterrevolutionary activity before, and especially after, the "uprising."

It is quite likely that these Maoist categories are applicable for most of Monsoon Asia. They were being used in Kerala in the early 1970's with some adaptation to local conditions and with a considerable degree of success. Virtually the same categories were also used by the Indonesian Communists.

Another characteristic of a successful Communist leadership is the ability to develop links with the local rural intelligentsia—schoolteachers, lawyers, students, and the like—or with the "natural" leaders of the peasant movement in a given area. In Kerala, for example, I was impressed with the ability of the Communists to seek out and recruit those local people who already commanded the respect of large numbers of the landless. There was to some extent a certain friction between these "natural" or indigenous leaders and the more bureaucratically organized Communists, and each group eyed the other with a certain suspicion, but there was nevertheless a strong marriage of convenience and purpose. It seems likely that the Chinese and Vietnamese Communists were also particularly skillful in cultivating the natural leaders of the poor peasants and incorporating them into their own power structure.

It seems likely, too, that the social background of the Communist leaders plays some role in influencing their outlooks. A Communist leadership heavily dominated by an urbanized, upper class, Western-educated group is not as likely to empathize with the peasantry as a leadership with closer ties to the countryside. Only a handful of the Chinese Communist leaders in the 1930's came from the big urban centers of China. As Don Klein has pointed out to me, most of them came from areas like Kansas in the United States and, more particularly, from towns like Abilene, Kansas, that is, towns with a strong rural orientation. Similar generalizations can be made about the social background of the Kerala Communist leaders. Their "social distance" from the masses in the countryside was far less than that of most other state Communist leaderships in India. This is what separated them from the West Bengal Communist leaders who, despite favorable ecological conditions, did not begin making inroads into the countryside until the late 1960's.

Still another characteristic of a Communist leadership that is successful in mobilizing the peasantry is flexibility. In each of the various periods of the Chinese civil war, Mao and his colleagues carefully experimented with various tactics on the agrarian question. From the peasant movement period of the late 1920's, they learned the importance of establishing a Red Army. From the Kiangsi Soviet days of the early 1930's, they learned the importance of avoiding ultra-left policies of redistribution that would alienate the middle as well as the rich peasants. During the war with Japan, they learned how to appeal to "patriotic" landlords and rich peasants, that is, those elements of the rural elite who did not oppose them or who could be won over. And when it became clear in 1946 that they had to abandon the relatively moderate policy on redistribution pursued during the war with Japan and return to a more radical policy in order to win over the masses of poor peasants, they did so with considerable success.[68]

Throughout most of their history, Mao and his colleagues have been particularly flexible and realistic in the various land reform programs they have used to mobilize the peasantry. As early as the December 1, 1931, Land Law passed by the Kiangsi Soviet when Mao was chairman of the Central Executive Committee, Chinese Communist land reform legislation demonstrated considerable realism. That law, for example, confiscated without compensation all land belonging to feudal landlords, village bosses, gentry, warlords, bureaucrats, and other big private landowners. It redistributed confiscated land to poor and middle peasants. Rich peasants were to have their land confiscated but were entitled to allotments of poorer quality land on condition that they cultivated it with their own labor.

The law also provided for the confiscation and handing over to the peasants of land belonging to temples and shrines, but only with the approval of the peasants and only in a way that would not offend their religious feelings. The law left the choice of how to redistribute the land up to local authorities "in the light of local conditions in the different townships and villages," and taking into account the quality of the land as well as its quantity. It recognized nationalization as the ultimate goal but allowed the leasing and purchase of land to continue temporarily.[69]

One final element that needs to be considered is the Maoist emphasis on involving the landless and poor peasants themselves in the process of land reform and land redistribution. "Maoist" land reforms are never made by administrative fiat or passed down from above. After an investigation of local conditions and a determination that such and such land is surplus or owned by landlords or rich peasants, the actual redistribution is carried out by elected committees of the peasantry, including many poor peasants. In short, the redistribution is done not merely, or even mainly, to redistribute the land, but to politicize the poor peasantry and to mobilize them in support of Communist policies. In the process, a variety of meetings, "encounter sessions," and psychological techniques are employed to vent the hatred of the poor peasants against the landlords and rich peasants.

### Land Reform as Preemption of Agrarian Radicalism

There is one final element that I want to touch on briefly in this effort to understand what conditions facilitate successful Communist mobilization of the peasantry in Asia. Even assuming there are both favorable "objective" conditions tending to radicalize the peasantry and a good potential leadership for it, it seems probable that the forces upholding the status quo—the state apparatus and the local landed elite—play an important role in determining how the peasantry acts.

An intelligent land reform policy can almost always pacify, if not completely satisfy, a rebellious peasantry. If the Russian Provisional

Government had passed a land reform bill at any time in its tenure in 1917, the Bolsheviks may well not have succeeded in their October coup d'état or prevailed in the civil war that followed. Land reforms in the twentieth century in Japan, Taiwan, southern Italy, Iran, and Venezuela, to name a few, have undoubtedly all helped to deflect the forces of rural radicalism. On the other hand, the blindness of the Chinese Nationalist elite and the Diem government to the problems of the landless and land poor unquestionably contributed to their failure. Only time will tell whether the Indian government is willing and able to adopt a meaningful land reform.

Just why some states and some leaders have been able to appreciate the importance of land reform and to carry it out while others have not is an intriguing question. In the cases of Japan and Taiwan, the answer is not hard to find: the reform was carried out by an occupying army that had no ties to the indigenous landed elite. In both Iran and Venezuela, the state was able to draw on large oil revenues to buy out the landed elite on reasonably equitable terms. In southern Italy at the end of World War II and in South Vietnam in the late 1960's, the threat of a revolutionary movement forced the government to make some land redistribution as a means of undercutting the threat. It would seem, then, that only a rich or seriously threatened indigenous elite is likely to make a land reform.

In this article, I have attempted to sketch some of the conditions that facilitate or inhibit organization of the peasantry for revolutionary purposes. The main barrier to peasant mobilization is the one outlined by Marx: isolation in a triple sense, physical, social, and mental. It is this isolation that contributes to the provincialism of rural politics and reinforces the tendency toward traditionalism and resistance to change.

In pointing to the low organizational potential of the peasants because of their isolation, Marxists have identified the central challenge facing revolutionary movements hoping to mobilize the peasantry: how to overcome peasant isolation. In Marxist terms, the question is, under what circumstances can a "class in itself" be transformed into a class "for itself"? In contemporary social scientific terms, the question is, what are the prerequisites of conflict group formation?

For analytical purposes, the conditions for organization of the peasantry for revolutionary purposes can be divided into *social, psychological, political,* and *technical* conditions of organization.[70] *Social*

conditions of organization have to do with such factors as rural stratification patterns, the degree of urbanization, the extent of literacy,
and the density of rural population. The social conditions that I have
stressed are the existence of a large class of landless and land-poor
peasants in a tenancy system, heavy pressure on the land, and literacy.
*Psychological* conditions of organization have to do with the motivation of individual peasants. The psychological variable stressed here
is the awareness of the possibility of change and of the assailability
of the rural power structure. *Political* conditions of organization have
to do with such factors as the political permissibility of organization,
the strength of conservative landed elites, and the agrarian policies
of the state. The political condition I have stressed here is the decline
in power of the rural elite. Finally, *technical* conditions of organization have to do with the organizational skills of the revolutionary
movement seeking to mobilize the peasantry and with the organizational skills of the peasantry itself. I have discussed some of the organizational skills that distinguish "successful" Communist parties
from "unsuccessful" Communist parties.

Perhaps the major conclusion that emerges from this study, and
one that remains to be developed further, is that although Marx was
right in postulating isolation as the main factor inhibiting peasant
organization in the past, he did not foresee the possibility that, in the
modern world, peasant isolation could be ended under the impact of
forces such as population pressure, the revolution of communications
and education, and modern organization.

# The Communist Movement
## and the Peasants: The Case of Korea

Reexamination of the role of the peasantry as a major ally of the Communist movement has been a principal concern of contemporary social science. The Communists' achievements in China, and to some extent in South Asia and Latin America, which in many respects refute Marx's basic assumption about the conservative attributes and negative roles of peasants in a revolutionary situation, have raised certain fundamental questions, such as: Under what conditions do peasants rise? Which sector of the peasantry tends to take an initiative for anti-system insurrection? Which peasants—poor ones or middle ones—are most susceptible to Communist influence?

Most students of the peasant movement believe that unbearable economic difficulties and unjust social treatment of the peasantry are the most important causes of peasant revolt and peasant Communism. This seems to be a reasonable enough assumption, since such adverse conditions affecting a major sector of the population can be expected to lead eventually to social unrest, which in turn often leads to revolution. The weakness of this generalization, however, lies in its failure to make clear *how* unbearable and *how* unjust conditions must be to prompt peasant uprisings. With that in mind, it is my purpose to examine the relationship between the peasantry and the Communist movement in Korea in the 1920's and 1930's, and particularly the relationship between the peasantry's economic grievances and its susceptibility to Communism.

The Korean peasantry had a striking record of uprisings in the half century before the annexation of the country by Japan in 1910.

The preparation of this paper was supported by a grant from the East Asian Institute of Columbia University.

Small-scale rebellions erupted in more than 90 places in southern Korea in the late nineteenth century, culminating in a major revolt, the Tonghak Rebellion of 1894.[1] At first these uprisings centered mainly on socioeconomic grievances, such as the exploitation of the peasantry by the ruling class of the Yi dynasty, but later peasant anti-foreignism was also a factor. The peasants saw in foreign, i.e., Japanese, influence the basic cause of the corruption of the government officials, the factional struggles among the elite, and the financial bankruptcy of the central government, all of which, they thought, resulted in the endless exploitation of the peasantry. Indeed, the peasants came to feel that influence directly when Japanese troops were brought in at the request of the feeble Korean government to help quell the Tonghak Rebellion. Some of the peasants fought the Japanese again in the volunteer corps (ŭibyŏng) that were organized and led by the gentry in various areas on the eve of the formal annexation of Korea.

The March First Movement in 1919, the Korean response to the Wilsonian principle of self-determination, demonstrated the Korean people's eagerness to achieve national independence. This movement was initiated and led by urban elements—religious leaders, intellectuals, students, and small merchants—but once it was under way the rural masses responded enthusiastically. Indeed, that response was far beyond anything the leaders had anticipated—violent and bloody in many areas, despite their call for a peaceful protest based on non-resistance. Though the peasantry's role in the March First Movement has tended to be ignored or minimized, the fact is that this marked one of the most massive peasant mobilizations in modern Korean history, surpassed only by the peasant participation in the Tonghak Rebellion. One record shows that about 54 per cent of those prosecuted for their actions in the movement were peasants.[2]

The Korean people, urban dwellers and peasants alike, paid a heavy toll in 1919. One source puts the losses at 7,509 dead, 15,961 wounded, and 46,948 arrested.[3] But the affair had a broader impact on Korean society than just this, for with it came two significant developments: the emergence of organized social movements and the spread of socialist thought among the young.

### The Growth of Tenancy and of Tenancy Disputes

It was about this same time that tenancy disputes and numerous tenant associations began to emerge. The organization of these groups was given great impetus by the formation of the Korean Labor Mutual Aid Association (Chosŏn Nodong Kongje-hoe) in April 1920, which despite its name and clear labor emphasis was not a labor group in the strict sense, since it had many peasants and even "herb doctors in its branches."[4] In the beginning, many tenant associations accepted middle farmers and even rich farmers as well as peasant tenants. But more and more of them became class oriented as socialist theory took hold in Korean society, particularly among the young, who regarded the March First Movement as a complete failure of the nationalist approach to achieving Korean independence. This increasing class orientation was reflected in the uniting of 274 tenant and labor organizations into the All-Korean Labor-Peasant Federation (Chŏson Nonong Ch'ong-dongmaeng) in April 1924.

Two grievances above all brought tenants into conflict with their landlords: excessive rent and an arbitrary change of tenant. But these were only surface issues. The root problem was a scarcity of land. As Table 1 indicates, what land there was was spread thin, especially

TABLE 1

*Percentage of Korean Households Tilling One Chŏngbo or Less of Land, 1923*

| Area and province | 1 to .3 chongbo | .3 chongbo or less | Total |
|---|---|---|---|
| Southern Korea | 39.1% | 33.6% | 72.7% |
| South Cholla | 41.3 | 30.1 | 71.4 |
| North Cholla | 42.6 | 38.3 | 80.9 |
| South Kyongsang | 37.0 | 37.0 | 74.0 |
| North Kyongsang | 42.2 | 31.1 | 73.3 |
| South Chungchong | 32.6 | 34.7 | 67.3 |
| North Chungchong | 34.1 | 32.8 | 66.9 |
| Central Korea | 33.6 | 21.1 | 54.7 |
| Kyonggi | 36.2 | 25.5 | 61.7 |
| Hwanghae | 31.2 | 17.0 | 48.2 |
| Kangwon | 33.0 | 20.6 | 53.6 |
| Northern Korea | 24.9 | 10.8 | 35.7 |
| South Pyongan | 29.8 | 8.9 | 38.7 |
| North Pyongan | 23.5 | 15.0 | 38.5 |
| South Hamgyong | 23.5 | 10.2 | 33.7 |
| North Hamgyong | 23.7 | 4.9 | 28.6 |
| National average | 34.8% | 25.8% | 60.6% |

SOURCE: In Chong-sik, *Choson nongop kyongjeron* (Agricultural economy of Korea) (Seoul: Pangmun Ch'ulp'ansa, 1949), p. 181.

NOTE: 1 chongbo = 2.45 acres, or about 1 hectare.

in the south, Korea's major rice-growing area. It was in the southern region, with the highest density of population and the highest land prices, that the numerous peasant uprisings of the late nineteenth century occurred, and it was there, too, that the Tonghak Rebellion took place.

Though more and more acreage was added to the cultivable land after the annexation, the peasants failed to gain thereby. On the contrary, their situation worsened, for the population increased as well, and so did the monopolization of land by rich landlords and usurers. Beyond that, many peasants lost their holdings in the course of a land survey conducted by the Government-General of Korea from 1910 to 1918.

This survey, which the Japanese authorities initiated immediately after the annexation mainly for tax purposes, sought to determine who had legitimate claims to the land and how much it was worth. For the Korean peasants, however, the notion of landownership had little meaning. Theoretically, all land was owned by the state, but traditionally a son had always inherited the right to till the land his father had tilled; no one challenged anyone else's right in that regard. In a land survey based on the concept of private property and on a "report system," many illiterate peasants failed to report their land as their own property and lost it to the government through nationalization. In addition, a considerable amount of shared acreage, such as community or clan land, was nationalized for lack of proven ownership.[5] How much land was nationalized as a result of this survey is problematical; one Korean source puts the figure at some 177,500 chŏngbo (434,875 acres), or something over 4 per cent of the total arable land in 1919.[6]

The fact that land was much cheaper in Korea than in Japan had long been noted by the Japanese, who were firmly established on Korean soil well before the annexation.[7] By 1915, according to one study, more than 5 per cent of the total arable land in Korea was owned by some 6,900 Japanese landlords.[8] These holdings, moreover, were heavily concentrated in the most valuable and profitable region of the country, the rice-producing southern provinces.

Parallel with this rise in Japanese landlordism came a large influx of less affluent Japanese as the Japanese government sought to ease the lot of its own land-hungry peasantry by encouraging emigration to Korea. With financial aid provided not only for moving expenses and transportation, but also for the purchase of land, a flood of Japanese peasants poured into Korea. The massiveness of this movement can be judged by the fact that by 1931 the Orient Development Company alone had gathered and transported some 4,000 households of these so-called protected immigrants.[9]

Under the combined impact of Japanese investment and Japanese immigration Korea saw a major land boom in the 1910's, followed by an increasing monopolization of land by big landlords and usurers. Though it is impossible to say exactly how much land came under monopoly ownership (the pertinent statistics having never been released by the Japanese government), one study indicates that as early as 1918 about 50 per cent of the total arable land was in the hands of landlords, a group made up of both Koreans and Japanese and comprising about 3 per cent of the total agricultural population.[10]

Rising living expenses and farming costs, the systematic levy of taxes on land after the land survey, and the Great Depression in the late 1920's and early 1930's also contributed to the pauperization of the peasantry. Under the weight of these financial burdens, some once-independent peasants became agricultural workers in the space of a few years, and many others were forced into tenancy. By 1934, in fact, as Table 2 shows, there were over 1.5 million tenant farmers in Korea; that is to say, over half the total agricultural population had fallen into full tenancy.

As more and more peasants sold their small holdings to join the landless, the competition to lease land became increasingly severe, and rents rose accordingly, amounting in extreme cases to almost 90 per cent of the crop. The rents in the southern provinces were particularly exorbitant, but even in other areas a tenant could expect as a rule to turn over more than 60 per cent of his crop to his landlord. In this situation, thousands of peasants were caught in desperate straits. Some chose to move to urban areas—but there were too few industrial factories in those areas to absorb the floating rural population,[11] and most of the peasants were in any case unskilled and illiterate. Thousands more chose to emigrate to Manchuria as agricultural laborers. But the majority simply remained where they were, afraid to chance an uncertain future in strange surroundings.

The mounting competition for land was reflected in a shift in the main issues involved in tenancy disputes. At first the vast majority of the tenant-landlord conflicts centered on rent, with tenants demanding a reduction to 50 per cent of the harvest. Many such disputes were group actions, in which the members of a tenant associa-

TABLE 2

Composition of the Agricultural Population of Korea in Selected Years, 1914–1939

| Category | 1914 | 1919 | 1924 | 1930 | 1934 | 1939 |
|---|---|---|---|---|---|---|
| **Landlord** | | | | | | |
| No. of households | 46,754 | 90,386 | 102,183 | 104,004 | —[a] | — |
| Per cent of total | 1.8% | 3.4% | 3.8% | 3.6% | | |
| **Independent peasant** | | | | | | |
| No. of households | 569,517 | 525,830 | 525,689 | 504,009 | 542,637 | 539,629 |
| Per cent of total | 22.0% | 19.7% | 19.5% | 17.6% | 18.0% | 17.9% |
| **Semi-tenant peasant** | | | | | | |
| No. of households | 1,065,705 | 1,045,606 | 934,208 | 890,291 | 721,661 | 719,232 |
| Per cent of total | 41.1% | 39.3% | 34.5% | 31.0% | 24.0% | 23.7% |
| **Tenant peasant** | | | | | | |
| No. of households | 911,261 | 1,003,003 | 1,142,192 | 1,334,139 | 1,564,294 | 1,583,358 |
| Per cent of total | 35.1% | 37.6% | 42.2% | 46.5% | 51.9% | 52.4% |
| **Slash-and-burn farmer** | | | | | | |
| No. of households | — | — | — | 37,514 | 81,287 | 69,280 |
| Per cent of total | | | | 1.3% | 2.7% | 2.3% |
| **Agricultural laborer** | | | | | | |
| No. of households | — | — | — | — | 103,225 | 111,634 |
| Per cent of total | | | | | 3.4% | 3.7% |
| **Total agricultural households** | 2,593,237 | 2,664,825 | 2,704,272 | 2,869,957 | 3,013,104 | 3,023,133 |

SOURCE: *Chōsen no nōgyō* (Agriculture of Korea) (Seoul: Chōsen Sōtokufu, 1941), p. 46; *Tōkei nempō* (Annual statistical report) (Seoul: Chōsen Sōtokufu, 1938), p. 52.

[a] The Government-General seems to have lumped the landlords in with the independent peasants from 1934 on.

TABLE 3

*Issues Involved in Korean Tenancy Disputes, 1920's*

| Year | Amount of rent | Removal of tenant | Other | Total |
|------|------|------|------|------|
| **1920** | | | | |
| No. of incidents | 12 | 1 | 2 | 15 |
| Per cent of total | 80.0% | 6.7% | 13.3% | |
| **1921** | | | | |
| No. of incidents | 18 | 4 | 5 | 27 |
| Per cent of total | 66.7% | 14.8% | 18.5% | |
| **1922** | | | | |
| No. of incidents | 8 | 9 | 7 | 24 |
| Per cent of total | 33.3% | 37.5% | 29.9% | |
| **1923** | | | | |
| No. of incidents | 52 | 117 | 7 | 176 |
| Per cent of total | 29.5% | 66.5% | 4.0% | |
| **1924** | | | | |
| No. of incidents | 31 | 126 | 7 | 164 |
| Per cent of total | 18.8% | 76.9% | 4.3% | |
| **1929** | | | | |
| No. of incidents | 70 | 330 | 23 | 423 |
| Per cent of total | 16.5% | 78.0% | 5.5% | |

SOURCE: *Kōtō keisatsu hō* (High police report) (Seoul: Chōsen Sōtokufu Keimukyoku, 1933 [?]), 1, reprinted by Gannandō, Tokyo, in 1962, p. 65; *Chōsen nōchi nempō* (Annual report of Korean agricultural land) Seoul: Chōsen Sōtokufu Nōrinkyoku, 1940), 1: 21.

tion stood together to insist that they would not pay any rent at all unless the rate was reduced. But the main issue soon became, not whether the tenant would pay the required rent, but whether he would even be allowed to rent the land. In the face of peasant opposition to high rents, landlords simply began replacing "recalcitrant" tenants with other men who were willing to pay whatever the landlord asked (see Table 3).

To resist this practice, a threat that the landlords made good increasingly from 1923 on, the peasants in many areas again resorted to group action, the members of tenant associations either jointly working or jointly refusing to work a landlord's fields. As tenancy disputes developed in a radical direction and led to confrontations and even violence between landlords and peasants, the Japanese police began arresting the leaders of the tenant associations. A total of 344 leaders were arrested in South Cholla Province alone in 1924.[12]

The two most serious incidents triggered by tenancy disputes in the mid-1920's, in terms of both violence and the number of peasants involved, occurred at the southern islands of Am'tae (in 1924) and Chaŭn (in 1925). As a result of these and similar experiences in the first half of the decade, some of the tenant associations began to be reorganized into more systematic peasant unions after 1925.

## Relationship of Tenancy Disputes to the Communist Movement

Though the majority of the early Communist leaders of Korea were from the volatile southern provinces,* the Communists did not provide effective strategies for the peasantry. Ignoring a potential constituency of some 80 per cent of the population, they concentrated instead on establishing a sound central Party in Seoul and on organizing the relatively few industrial workers of the urban areas. To be sure, they believed that, like the peasant uprisings of the nineteenth century, the tenant disputes would lead to a major rebellion, but they made no serious attempts to take advantage of an increasingly inflammatory situation.

As Table 4 shows, what started as a relatively insignificant movement in the southern provinces in the 1920's spread gradually to other areas and became a problem of major proportions in the years 1933–39. However, though the turbulence in the countryside undoubtedly made the peasants more susceptible to Communist influence, the sharp rise in the number of conflicts in the 1930's is better ascribed to Japanese policy, and specifically to the banning of group appeals by peasants and mediation of disputes by peasant unions, than to Communist activity. Under this policy, instituted in 1933, all tenancy disputes had to be resolved by individual tenants and landlords with the mediation of a county tenancy committee; accordingly, the increase in disputes reflects by and large the prosecution of more and more individual cases as the power of the peasant unions waned, not the fruits of Communist agitation.

Another argument against the role of the Communists in this development is the fact that the area where true peasant radicalism emerged was the Hamgyong provinces of the northeast, which had

* According to official records, 171 of the 297 persons arrested and imprisoned in connection with the activities of the Korean Communist Party and the Korean Communist Youth Association in the 1920's had permanent addresses in the southern provinces. Kim Chŏng-myŏng, ed., *Chōsen dokuritsu undō* (The Korean independence movement) (Tokyo: Hara Shobō, 1967), 5: 342–43.

TABLE 4
*Incidence of Tenancy Disputes in Korea, 1920–1939*

| Area and province | 1920–25 | 1926–29 | 1930–32 | 1933–39 | Total no. of incidents |
|---|---|---|---|---|---|
| Southern Korea | | | | | |
| South Cholla | 197 | 193 | 326 | 23,780 | 24,796 |
| North Cholla | 21 | 1,471 | 248 | 19,990 | 21,730 |
| South Kyongsang | 174 | 169 | 299 | 17,141 | 17,783 |
| North Kyongsang | 28 | 7 | 82 | 15,039 | 15,156 |
| South Chungchong | 97 | 490 | 472 | 11,330 | 12,289 |
| North Chungchong | 20 | 48 | 44 | 13,970 | 14,082 |
| Central Korea | | | | | |
| Kyonggi | 10 | 81 | 173 | 6,899 | 7,163 |
| Hwanghae | 31 | 10 | 37 | 5,787 | 5,865 |
| Kangwon | 7 | 3 | 11 | 9,312 | 9,333 |
| Northern Korea | | | | | |
| South Pyongan | 16 | 1 | 2 | 6,955 | 6,974 |
| North Pyongan | 5 | 10 | 4 | 3,713 | 3,732 |
| South Hamgyong | 4 | 3 | 0 | 2,017 | 2,024 |
| North Hamgyong | 0 | 0 | 0 | 42 | 42 |
| National total | 610 | 2,446 | 1,688 | 136,215 | 140,969 |

SOURCE: *Chōsen nōchi nempō* (Annual report of Korean agricultural land) (Seoul: Chōsen Sōtokufu Nōrinkyoku, 1940), 1: 8–9.

the highest proportion of independent peasants relative to the total agricultural population and the fewest tenant disputes in the whole of the country.

## The Red Peasant Union Movement

Still, if the Communists played less than a major role in the growth of the tenancy movement, they did in fact begin working actively among the peasantry after 1928. This change of direction was brought about in part by the relentless pressure of the Japanese authorities in Seoul and other urban areas and in part by the will of the Comintern, expressed in the so-called December Theses adopted that year.

In the space of about three and a half years, from the founding of the Korean Communist Party (KCP) in April 1925 to the Fourth KCP Incident in October 1928, the alert Japanese police managed to arrest almost all of the important Party leaders,[13] and by late 1928 the tenacious attempt to maintain a Party based on the principle of "organization from above" seemed to have reached its limits. The

Communists came at last to appreciate that a Party without a grass-roots organization was not only difficult to maintain, but also difficult to rebuild, for each decimation of leadership by the police led to factional struggles and to competing claims of having refounded the true KCP.

It was in these circumstances that the Executive Committee of the Comintern adopted the December Theses, which called for the elimination of factional struggles among the Korean Communists and stressed the importance of establishing a mass base, particularly among the peasantry, which represented the bulk of the population. The Comintern also emphasized the desirability of changing the Party leadership from intellectuals to persons of the working class.[14]

In pursuit of this new policy, the KCP Reestablishment Preparation Association (Chosŏn Kongsandang Chaegŏn Chunbi Wiwŏnhoe), the Korean Communist Consultative Council (Chosŏn Kongsanjuŭija Hyŏbŭihoe), and other groups concerned with reestablishing the KCP worked with Comintern and Profintern agents to form underground peasant organizations. About 70 red peasant unions (chŏksaek nongmin chohap) are known to have been organized from 1930 to 1939.

As Table 5 indicates, this movement was much more successful in the eastern regions of Korea than in the western regions; the provinces of North and South Hamgyong, North and South Kyongsang, and Kangwon in the east had 46 of these unions, whereas the western provinces of Hwanghae, Kyonggi, and North and South Chungchong had only five. A partial explanation of the reasons for this east-west cleavage will be offered later.

Some of these unions were crushed by the police while in the process of organizing. Others managed to survive for a time and to attract a number of members. And still others gained substantial memberships and became fully organized, with a central headquarters at the county (kun) level, branches in the cantons (myŏn), and squads (pan) in the precincts (ri). Their leaders were local residents, though in many instances outside Communist agents advised them in organizing techniques, tactics, and the like. In line with one of the central goals—to develop mass organizations—members of other illegal groups, such as the Youth League and the Women's League, were recruited into the unions' youth and women's departments. Their main interest, however, was enlisting agricultural laborers, tenants, and semi-tenants, and to a lesser extent, poor independent peas-

TABLE 5
*Known Sites of Red Peasant Unions in Korea, 1930–1939*

| Area and province | Site |
| --- | --- |
| Southern Korea (32) | |
| South Cholla | Changsong, Cheju Island, Kangjin, Kwangju, Kwangyang, Muan, Naju, Sunchon, Yosu |
| North Cholla | Chongup, Okku, Puan |
| South Kyongsang | Changwon, Chinju, Haman, Kimhae, Kosong, Namhae, Samchonpo, Tongyong, Uiryong, Ulsan, Yangsan |
| North Kyongsang | Andong, Kimchon, Kyongju, Ponghwa, Uisong, Yechon, Yongju, Waegwan |
| South Chungchong | ——— |
| South Chungchong | Yongdong |
| Central Korea (9) | |
| Kyonggi | Pyongtaek, Suwon, Yangpyong |
| Hwanghae | Chaeryong |
| Kangwon | Kangnung, Kosong, Samchok, Ulchin, Yangyang |
| Northern Korea (28) | |
| South Pyongan | Anju, Kaechon, Kangso, Yonggang |
| North Pyongan | Sinuiju, Yongchon |
| South Hamgyong | Anbyon, Chongpyong, Hamju, Hamhung, Hongwon, Iwon, Kapsan, Kowon, Munchon, Pukchong, Pungsan, Tanchon, Togwon, Wonsan, Yonghung |
| North Hamgyong | Hoeryong, Kilchu, Kyongsong, Myongchon, Odaejin, Onsong, Songjin |

SOURCE: Kōtō keisatsu hō (High police report) (Seoul: Chōsen Sōtokufu Keimukyoku, 1933 [?]), 2: 16–21, 71–72; Kōtō Hōin Kenjikyoku (High Court Prosecutor's Bureau), *Shisō geppō* (Thought monthly), 3.4: 4–6, and *Shisō ihō* (Thought reports), 1: 3–11; 2: 5, 46–57; 3: 5; 5: 5–6, 77–78, 165–76; 6: 9–27; 7: 5; 8: 11–27; 9: 8–11; 10: 4–5, 271–77; 13: 9; *Kōtō keisatsu kankei tekiroku* (Summary related to high police) (Pusan: Keishō-nandō Keisatsubu, 1936), pp. 82–88, 92–103; Kim Chong-myong, ed., *Chōsen dokuritsu undō*, 5: 381–82.

ants. The unions' principal support came from the young, as is clear from the ages of those arrested in February 1936 in connection with the Second Myongchon Red Peasant Union Incident: 557 of the 578 activists taken in hand were under thirty years old, and 444 were under twenty-five.[15]

By the end of 1930 the Chongpyong Red Peasant Union, which seems to have been one of the largest, had branches in each of the nine cantons in the county and squads in 133 of the 216 precincts. It had a total membership of 4,147 persons, which meant that it had about one member for every three households in the county.[16] Other unions were of course far smaller.

All of the unions carried on roughly the same activities. Chiefly this meant the indoctrination of the peasantry by conducting night schools (for children as well as adults), by publishing pamphlets and newspapers, and by distributing various other Communist materials. Most unions made clear who their target audience was in the names they chose for their publications, e.g., *The Red Peasant* (Pulgŭn nongmin), *The Story of Peasant Fighters* (Nongmin chŏnt'u-gi), and *Peasant Newspaper* (Nongmin sinmun).[17] But it is doubtful that these had the impact the night schools had, for the peasants proved eager to learn and attended in large numbers. The Chongpyong union alone at one point had 37 schools with 1,203 students and 53 teachers (who were union cadres, not licensed personnel).[18] Police raids were a common occurrence, however, and with the hard evidence of Communist textbooks in hand, the police frequently closed the schools. In many cases this led to clashes between police and peasants.

This very belligerence in fact—toward landlords as well as the Japanese authorities—was one of the chief differences between the red peasant unions and the pre-1930 peasant unions. It manifested itself not only in widespread interference with the collection of taxes,[19] but also in direct and often violent action.

The red peasant unions in the Hamgyong provinces, that is, the northeastern provinces, were the most radical and best organized in the country, and those of Yonghung, Chongpyong, Myongchon, Songjin, and Kilchu were particularly so. In many places, these "reddest" of the red unions went so far as to lead mobs in attacks on police stations in order to rescue union leaders who had been arrested. Many also took steps to defend themselves against the violence of the police and other hostile elements. The Myongchon union, for example, organized a Martial Committee, which oversaw an Information Corps, an Investigation Corps, and a Sentry Corps. The union also had a Comrade Recapture Corps, which was charged with rescuing members held by the police.[20] On several occasions in 1935 and 1936 the union's Action Corps attacked the police and Korean collaborators with sticks, sickles, and hoes, and in some instances even convened people's courts.[21] Members of the equally militant Chongpyong union practiced mock attacks on police stations and trained groups for sentry duty and intelligence work. The leaders of one squad of the union even tried to collectivize the farming in their village, but they were forced to give up the attempt in the face of widespread dissent.[22]

Despite differences in degree and scale, extreme radicalism was the general trend in the northeast.

Yet no underground peasant organization could hope to survive very long under the eyes of the ever-vigilant authorities. In 1931 and 1932 alone the police reported rounding up and arresting 1,815 persons belonging to 31 red peasant unions.[23] As noted, numbers of groups, particularly in the western provinces of North and South Pyongan and North and South Cholla, were crushed by the police soon after they started up. But in many parts of the Hamgyong provinces the peasants showed themselves just as determined to maintain their unions as the police were to destroy them, and no sooner was an organization shattered than another emerged. Indeed, the unions of Myongchon, Songjin, and Kilchu counties in North Hamgyong were so difficult to wipe out that a special provincial government unit, the Three-County Thought Purification Committee, was established in 1936 precisely for that purpose.[24]

## Sources of Regional Support for the Red Peasant Unions

The key question that arises, then, is what made the Hamgyong peasant more radical, or at least more susceptible to Communism, than the peasants of other areas of the country?

It is safe to say that the answer does *not* lie in the hostility between tenants and landlords, for as was pointed out earlier the Hamgyong provinces had the lowest rate of tenancy in the country; and the number of tenant disputes there, before 1934 anyway, was negligible (see Table 4). In Myongchon County, for example, where one of the most radical peasant movements developed, there were only 1,824 tenant and 4,331 semi-tenant households in a total of 15,957 agricultural households in 1933; the two groups combined represented but 38.5 per cent of the rural population at a time when the national figure was something over 75 per cent.[25] Moreover, those peasants who were tenants had less reason for grievance against their landlords than peasants elsewhere, since their rents ranged from 30 to 60 per cent, the lowest rate in the country.[26] This does not necessarily mean that the peasants of the northeast did not have other cause for grievance; on the contrary, by reason of the unfavorable weather and the poor quality of the soil, their economic condition was hardly better than that of their counterparts in other areas. Nevertheless, it is clear that the most extreme movement did not develop in the areas where the tenant-landlord controversy raged most fiercely, as the Communists of the 1920's believed it would.

What the Communists overlooked, I think, is the fact that national consciousness might come to play a greater role than class consciousness. That is to say, as the Japanese acquired large chunks of land, particularly in the southern provinces, the focus of the peasants' hatred became not just the landlord as such, but rather the Japanese landlord (and ultimately the Japanese). In addition, as we have seen, the single most important issue in tenancy disputes was the landlord's replacement of one tenant with another. Consequently, these disputes to some extent spurred disunity among the peasants rather than unity: confrontation between tenants and landlords increased, but so did confrontation between former tenants and their successors.

Turning, then, to the question raised earlier, why peasant radicalism developed in the northeast, two factors appear to have played a decisive role: geographical location and topography. As immediate neighbors of the Soviet Union and China, these provinces furnished a large proportion of the peasants who emigrated to those countries. At the time Korea was formally annexed by Japan about 52,000 Koreans were residing in Russia, and an estimated 46,000 more crossed the border between 1910 and 1921; 62 per cent of this post-1910 wave were from the Hamgyong provinces.[27] A far greater number of Koreans went to Manchuria—as many as 377,807 in the years 1910–31 by one count—and again a high percentage of them (45.9) were from those provinces.[28] Many of these emigrants resided in areas close to their homeland (e.g., the Russian Maritime Province and Chientao, Manchuria) and maintained regular contact with those they had left behind. Thousands, moreover, eventually came back to Korea; close to a third of those who went to Manchuria between 1910 and 1931 are estimated to have returned to their homes.[29] It is easy to suppose that these migrants transmitted considerable information about the revolutionary practice in the Soviet Union and Manchuria to their relatives and friends in Korea.

Geographical location also played a role in the level of Communist activity in the northeastern provinces, for Korean activists could easily make good their escape to Manchuria or the Soviet Far East, just as infiltrators could move over the borders into Korea. In consequence, the Communists could risk more activity there than they could elsewhere. And they had the additional advantage of the mountainous terrain, which not only provided physical sanctuary, but also provided a certain political sanctuary: these provinces, effectively isolated from the central government by the north-south chain of mountains that traverses the country, were difficult to bring under strong administration. The fact that most of the other Korean red peasant unions were also in remote areas suggests a very intimate relationship between the degree of the central power's reach and peasant radicalism. This partially explains why Communist influence was not as strong in the Pyongan provinces of the west, though as northern border states they had some of the same advantages for the Communists as the eastern provinces.

By virtue of its physical characteristics, then, the northeast was a hospitable area for Communist activity. It was made even more so by the relative neglect of the Japanese authorities until 1930. Because of the deepening unrest among the peasants of the south during the 1920's, the Japanese authorities believed (as did the Korean Communist leaders themselves) that if a Communist revolution broke out in the countryside, it would erupt in the southern provinces. As a result, the government concentrated most of its attention on what was seen as the "Front Line of [Communist] Thought."[30]

The Korean case is instructive in pointing to the significant differences between traditional peasant radicalism and modern peasant radicalism. As we have seen, it was economic conditions above all that led to the numerous peasant uprisings of the late nineteenth century; rebellion was centered in the southern regions, where landlord-tenant relationships were at their worst. In the 1930's, however, economic hardship, though certainly a necessary condition for peasant radicalism, did not play the only or even the crucial role in the organization of the peasants' Communist movement. Rather, this development seems to fit Eric Wolf's hypothesis that two types of peasantry "possess sufficient internal leverage to enter into sustained rebellion": "(a) a land-owning 'middle peasantry' or (b) a peasantry located in a peripheral area outside the domains of landlord control" or "beyond the normal control of the central power."[31]

There are differences of form as well as of origin between traditional peasant radicalism and modern peasant radicalism. If traditional peasant uprisings can be characterized as unorganized, amorphous, and spontaneous, then modern peasant uprisings can be said to be more organized, systematic, and contrived. The traditional uprising was a more or less natural phenomenon arising in the face of possible starvation; economic factors played a decisive role. The modern peasant uprising, in contrast, possesses a relatively clear goal as well as calculated strategies; political factors, such as leadership and ideology, play a vital role. This type of uprising has the advantages of a better trained leadership and better means of organization and manipulation through modern communications, propaganda techniques, and the like. But it has a major disadvantage as well: with these same innovations, the government's counterinsurrectionary capability is also vastly improved.

# The Vietnamese Revolutionary Alliance:
## Intellectuals, Workers, and Peasants

CHRISTINE PELZER WHITE

The Vietnamese revolution has often been correctly described as a nationalist and peasant movement. But it cannot be fully understood unless a crucial third aspect, modernization, is taken into account. Were the Vietnamese revolution nothing more than a nationalist peasant uprising, it would be no different from the peasant rebellions and wars against foreign invaders that characterized hundreds of years of Vietnamese history. These, in fact, had not been revolutions in the strict sense of the term, for they had never led to a fundamental change in the social, political, or economic system.[1]

Although peasant wars had often succeeded in repulsing foreign invaders, they had never been able to overthrow the feudal system and replace it with another national system better suited to peasant interests.[2] In a recurrent pattern that could be called the cycle of Vietnamese history, land-poor peasants repeatedly revolted against the Vietnamese landed elite or rose up to expel Chinese or Mongol invaders and overthrow their landholding Vietnamese collaborators. If successful, the victorious leader would proclaim himself king and return most of the land of the supporters of the defeated regime to the peasantry as communal land, a traditional institution of peasant land tenure. However, the new king would also award large tracts of private land to his major lieutenants and members of his family, thereby forming a new landed elite and laying the basis of a new cycle

I am grateful to the following people for their valuable comments on earlier drafts of this paper: Benedict R. O'G. Anderson, David Elliott, Lynn Hunt, George McT. Kahin, David H. Penny, Nguyen Thi Thanh, and D. Gordon White. Although they, along with John W. Lewis and the other participants in the conference at which this paper was first presented, have helped me greatly, responsibility for any errors is mine alone.

of land concentration. Later, as the dynasty weakened, this elite would expand its holdings, causing a rebellion of the increasingly impoverished peasantry.[3]

It was French conquest that broke this cycle and created the final preconditions for revolution. Although the French ruled Vietnam for less than a hundred years, in this period the traditional Vietnamese social, political, and economic system was permanently destroyed. The French also sowed the seeds of a new order by creating new classes, introducing industry, and forcibly bringing Vietnam into the modern world.

However, colonial rule introduced only a truncated form of modernization. The French did not want Vietnam to become a fully industrialized nation: they wanted it to supply cheap raw materials and labor. They allowed only the development of industries that did not compete with French businesses. They tried to turn back the clock by restricting access to Western education and by maintaining the monarchy, the mandarinate, and the rule of village notables. But while the French tried to prop up the Confucian system, many Confucian scholars themselves rejected it and sought knowledge of Western systems.

Furthermore, in order to run their colony, the French had to introduce some Western education to Vietnam, for they needed interpreters, clerks, and administrators for the colonial bureaucracy and engineers and skilled workers for their mines and industries. Although some Westernized Vietnamese, especially the wealthier ones, remained loyal collaborators of the French, others, not willing to use their talents simply for French profit, applied them instead to the task of expelling the French. Thus, in a process that liberal historians tend to call "ironic" or "paradoxical" and Marxist historians call "dialectical," French colonialism played a major role in creating the forces that eventually overthrew it.

The perspective of the peasants was quite different, though their prescription was the same. They opposed the colonial rule not because they felt they were being deprived of the advantages of a modern economic system but for the simple reason that they were worse off under the French than they had been under the previous oppressive feudal regime.[4] Because the French ruled as much as possible through the intermediary of the existing elite, the peasants now had to toil for two masters. Peasant taxes were increased many times over in order to pay for a huge colonial budget that dwarfed the outlay of the traditional Vietnamese government.

Peasants had to pay the costs of modernization without receiving any of the benefits. Roads and railroads for which the peasants paid so dearly in both labor and taxes did nothing to improve agricultural production, but made it possible for merchants to accumulate and export the peasants' rice. To peasants, mines and plantations did not represent "modernization"; they were places where landless villagers had to go to slave and die because their land had been given to Frenchmen as concessions by the colonial government or stolen by mandarins or other collaborators.

As other papers in this book indicate, partial modernization accompanied by accelerating peasant poverty is hardly unique to the Vietnamese colonial experience. Suffering is far more widespread than revolution, let alone successful revolution. This paper will focus on one major factor in the unusual success of the Vietnamese revolution: the emergence of an alliance between a peasantry that wanted to throw off the burdens of both French colonialism and Vietnamese feudalism and anticolonial intellectuals and proletarians, new social groups that wished to create a new and progressive system. Since this coalition occurred under the banner of a Communist Party, this paper is also an account of the origins of the Vietnamese Communist movement.

Although for analytical purposes I have assigned people to the categories of revolutionary intellectuals, proletarians, and peasants, there was considerable overlapping among groups. Since the proletariat was recruited from the countryside, most workers were ex-peasants. Owing to the great turnover in the work force, a large number of peasants had been members of the proletariat at some point in their lives. Many peasants in the suburbs worked part-time in the cities, and many workers habitually returned to their villages to help with the harvest. Some sons of workers and peasants attended primary or technical schools; as literates in an illiterate society, they could be considered intellectuals in a certain sense. Social boundaries were thus fluid, and this very fluidity contributed to the forging of the revolutionary alliance.

## From Patriotic Scholars to Revolutionary Intellectuals

In traditional Vietnam the leadership of wars of resistance against foreign invaders and their Vietnamese elite collaborators was provided by Confucian scholars who had remained in their villages instead of accepting official posts as mandarins.[5]

Although in the second half of the nineteenth century the ruling

Nguyen court preferred to capitulate to the French rather than risk being overthrown in the process of mobilizing the peasantry to fight them, in time-honored fashion scholars led the first sustained resistance to the French, the Van Than (Scholars' Resistance) and Can Vuong (Loyalty to the King) movements of 1885–97.[6] Among the Vietnamese people, the heroic words and deeds of that period were added to tales of earlier scholar-led uprisings against Chinese and Mongol invaders, keeping alive the memory of active resistance.

Major centers of Can Vuong activity, especially central Vietnam, were the site of subsequent revolts against French rule and produced a disproportionate number of Vietnamese revolutionary leaders. This is particularly true of Nghe An province, where a Communist-led peasant uprising was to occur in 1930 and where Ho Chi Minh spent his boyhood nurtured on stories and ballads of peasant resistance to the Chinese and the French.[7]

Ho's father, an accomplished Confucian scholar reputed to have taken part in the Scholars' Resistance, accepted an appointment to the Ministry of Rites at the Imperial Palace in Hue in 1905. A few years later the French dismissed him from office as district magistrate in Binh Dinh province because of his nationalist sentiments. As a result, Ho had to end his studies, and his father spent the rest of his life in poverty, eking out a bare living as a wandering scribe and practitioner of traditional medicine.[8]

Many of Ho's close associates in the Vietnamese Communist movement also come from central Vietnam and have similar family histories. Thus the father of Vo Nguyen Giap, the DRV's noted military strategist, was a poor scholar in Quang Binh province, who participated in the Scholars' Resistance in the late 1880's.[9] The father of Pham Van Dong, the present DRV Premier, was a cabinet officer under Duy Tan, the patriotic young king who was deposed in 1916 for an attempted insurrection.[10] The father of Tran Phu, the first Secretary-General of the Indochinese Communist Party, was a mandarin, "poor because he was upright," who resisted French orders to suppress peasant protests and committed suicide in despair in 1908, the year of peasant tax revolts in central Vietnam. Tran Phu's mother died soon after, and the orphaned Tran Phu suddenly experienced extreme poverty.[11]

These family histories may help explain why some members of the elite of Vietnamese society, educated sons of Confucian scholars and mandarins, subsequently embraced Marxism, a doctrine of social revolution. In addition to their family socialization in anticolonialism, these sons of scholars and mandarins personally experienced poverty as a result of their fathers' patriotism. Furthermore, as in the case of Tran Phu, their fathers' concern for the poor may have served as a model. For example, when Ho was a boy his father harbored fellow villagers fleeing dangerous corvée road labor.[12]

On the other hand, mandarins who collaborated with the French were able to accumulate great wealth. One such example was Ngo Dinh Kha, a high court official and the father of Ngo Dinh Diem. This difference in family background is probably a significant factor in the differing political paths taken by two famous alumni of Quoc Hoc high school, Ho Chi Minh and Ngo Dinh Diem. Diem too was an anti-French nationalist, but he adamantly opposed social revolution.

These effects of the early division of the Confucian scholar class into rich collaborators and poor resisters were not, of course, to emerge for many decades. All that was obvious around the turn of the century, after the defeat of the Scholars' Resistance, was that seemingly invincible "Western barbarians" had conquered Vietnam, and that the range of possible responses was limited to heroic but hopeless struggle, passive resistance, suicide, or collaboration.

The year 1905 marked the beginning of a new era in the history of Vietnamese nationalism. The Japanese victory over Russia, the first defeat of a European power by an Asian nation, awakened patriotic Confucian scholars to the potential of modernization and infused them with new hope. The leading figures in the nationalist modernization movement were two ranking Confucian scholars, Phan Boi Chau and Phan Chu Trinh, who both advocated modern learning and industrialization for Vietnam. Unaware of the potential of organizing the population to expel the French and modernize Vietnam, they looked largely to outside forces to achieve their ends. Chau, while organizing secret-society-type networks and insurrectional conspiracies within Vietnam, spent much of his time trying to enlist foreign military aid for ousting the French. But Trinh, though his ultimate aim was independence, abhorred violent means and sometimes went so far as to say that he would prefer to live under an "enlightened" modernizing colonial regime than under a backward, feudal independent Vietnamese government. Although Chau's attempts to get foreign arms and military support and Trinh's petitions to the colonial government were without effect, these two men played a major role in rejecting the Confucian educational system and introducing and popularizing Western ideas in Vietnam.

Starting in 1905, Chau arranged for annual contingents of young

Vietnamese to go to Japan for a modern education in the hope that
Vietnam would be able to learn the secrets of Japan's success. This
so-called Dong Du (Eastern Study) movement began at a time when
there was no French-established university in Vietnam. Most of the
200 Vietnamese students who left the country secretly for Japan were
sons of scholars who had taken part in the Can Vuong movement.[13]
The Dong Du movement came to an end in 1909, when all Vietnamese students were expelled from Japan under the terms of a Franco-
Japanese agreement.

Meanwhile, in 1907, reformist scholars connected with Phan Chu
Trinh set up the Dong Kinh Nghia Thuc (Eastern Capital Free Tu-
ition School) in Hanoi, with classes in Vietnamese history of a
distinctly nationalist character as well as instruction in science, math-
ematics, and other Western subjects. An assault on old-fashioned
practices, symbolized as in China by a hair-cutting campaign, originated at the school and spead throughout Vietnam. Probably the
school's greatest contribution to the Vietnamese revolutionary movement was its advocacy of the use of *quoc ngu* (romanized Vietnamese
script) as a vehicle for popularizing modern ideas and techniques.
The school was shut down by the French authorities in January 1908,
after less than a year of operation. Several schools in other areas met
the same fate.

When peasant demonstrations against high French taxes and the
corvée began in Quang Nam province in March 1908 and quickly
spread to other areas of central Vietnam, the French used them as a
pretext to crack down on the reformist scholars, whose ideas, they
claimed, had stirred up the trouble. Several of the would-be modern-
izers were executed, and many more, including Phan Chu Trinh, were
arrested and spent several years on the prison island of Poulo Condore.

Ruthless French repression of Vietnamese nationalism, not just of
a violent character as embraced by Phan Boi Chau, but also of a
peaceful reformist nature as advocated by Phan Chu Trinh, led a
younger generation of Vietnamese intellectuals to seek a still more
radical solution to their country's dilemma. To the uncompromising
anticolonial activism of Phan Boi Chau and the modernism of Phan
Chu Trinh, they added a third objective—social revolution.[14]

The first Vietnamese who systematically combined these three aims
was Ho Chi Minh. Ho was personally acquainted with both Chau and
Trinh and was influenced by them in his early years. Chau, a native

of Nghe An and a frequent visitor at Ho's father's house, later wrote that his friend's nine-year-old son listened attentively to Chau reciting poetry and never forgot the lines he heard.[15] Although Chau urged Ho's father to send the boy to Japan to study, the father felt that a French education was more practical, and sent him to the first high school in Vietnam to combine Vietnamese and Western education.

In 1905, when Ho was fifteen years old and beginning his studies at Quoc Hoc high school in Hue, he was already engaged in underground work, serving as a "messenger for scholar patriots."[16] He left school after his father's dismissal from office and took a teaching job at a school in Phan Thiet connected with Phan Chu Trinh's modernization movement. After less than a year there he left for Saigon, where he enrolled briefly in a course on marine navigation. At the end of 1911 he signed on as a galley assistant on a French steamship in order to make his way to France—attracted to the West, according to an official biography, "by ideals of freedom, civil rights, democracy and modern science and technology."[17]

After a period of holding various menial jobs, in the course of which he visited many French colonies as well as England and the United States, Ho arrived in Paris during World War I. There he worked closely with other Vietnamese patriots, especially Phan Chu Trinh, recently freed from Poulo Condore prison, who taught him how to retouch photographs so he could earn his living as a photographer's assistant. In January 1919, with Trinh and another compatriot, Ho drafted an eight-point petition, which he sent to the secretariat of the Versailles Peace Conference. In this mild document, Ho did not ask for Vietnamese independence, but merely requested that such civil liberties enjoyed in France as freedom of the press, freedom of assembly, and freedom of travel be allowed in Vietnam. Very much a child of the modernization movement, he also asked for "freedom to study and the opening of technical and professional schools."[18] The petition was not considered, and an attempt by Ho to argue his country's case with President Wilson himself at Versailles was rebuffed.

His attempts to interest Western democracies in Vietnam's plight thwarted, Ho soon found concern for the colonial problem in another quarter. According to one of his few autobiographical writings, he joined the French Socialist Party because "these 'ladies and gentlemen,' as I called my comrades at that moment, had shown their sympathy toward me, toward the struggle of the oppressed peoples. But

I understood neither what was a party, a trade union, nor what was Socialism or Communism." It was Lenin's "Thesis on the National and Colonial Question" that finally turned him toward Communism. On first reading the work, he was "overjoyed to tears. Though sitting alone in my room, I shouted aloud as if addressing large crowds: 'Dead martyrs, compatriots! This is what we need, this is the path of our liberation!' " At the Socialist Party's Tours Conference in 1920, from which the French Communist Party emerged, Ho participated in the debates, arguing on behalf of the side that he felt to be the most anticolonialist. Then as always first and foremost a patriot, Ho became a member of the French Communist Party because of its support for the Vietnamese cause.[19]

During the next few years, many articles by Ho, most of them concerning colonialism, appeared in French Communist Party newspapers. He formed the Union Intercoloniale, an organization of French colonial subjects residing in France, in 1921, and founded and edited its newspaper, *Le Paria* (The Outcast), the following year.[20] Despite the stress in Marxist literature on proletarian revolution, Ho had not lost sight of the fact that the majority of the people in his native Vietnam were peasants, not workers. Several of his articles written in this period, and portions of his first long study, *French Colonialism on Trial*, are devoted to the plight of the peasantry in French colonies.[21] Nor was the Communist International then completely unaware of the importance of the peasant problem in the colonies. In October 1923 Ho attended the Congress of the Peasants' International in Moscow.[22]

In mid-December 1924, after a year in the Soviet Union, Ho arrived in Canton as part of M. M. Borodin's Comintern staff. There he contacted his father's old friend Phan Boi Chau, and apparently working with Chau's approval, chose members of the Tam Tam Xa (Union of Hearts) to form the nucleus of the first Vietnamese Marxist organization, the Viet Nam Thanh Nien Cach Menh Dong Chi Hoi (Vietnam Young Revolutionary Comrades Association), usually referred to simply as Thanh Nien (Youth). The young members of the Tam Tam Xa, most of them from Ho's and Chau's native Nghe An, had been brought to Canton by Phan Boi Chau's Viet Nam Quang Phuc Hoi (Vietnam Restoration Society), but finding that organization too conservative had formed their own group.[23] Their backgrounds were very similar to Ho's own. The biography of one of them, Pham Hong Thai, who died in an assassination attempt on the French

Governor-General of Indochina just before Ho's arrival in Canton, follows the familiar pattern: gentry father whose participation in the Can Vuong resistance brought economic hardship on the family; education in Franco-Vietnamese and technical schools; a series of manual jobs.[24]

In late 1925 Phan Boi Chau was betrayed, under obscure circumstances, to the Sûreté (the French political police) and condemned to death by a French court in Vietnam; but this news set off such a wave of strikes, demonstrations, and student protests that the French had to grant him amnesty. A year later Phan Chu Trinh died, and a mass funeral procession accompanied his remains to a memorial on the outskirts of Saigon. These two events sparked a nationalist upsurge in which, for the first time, students and Western-educated intellectuals played a leading role.[25] Many students expelled from school for participating in strikes made their way to Canton to enroll in Ho Chi Minh's course on revolution.* Ho wrote out his lectures on Communism and the techniques of mass organizing in a manual entitled *The Revolutionary Road*, which guided his students on their return to Vietnam.[26] According to a Sûreté report, by May 1929 at least 250 Vietnamese had received a revolutionary education abroad, and there were Thanh Nien cells in all three French colonial subdivisions of Vietnam: Tonkin, Annam, and Cochinchina.[27]

Though Ho and the revolutionary intellectuals he led to Communism in the 1920's were the natural successors of the anticolonialist and modernizing Confucian scholars, they added a new ingredient: social revolution and mass organization. In the words of Truong Chinh, one of the Communist Party's leading intellectuals:

> Vietnamese revolutionaries before President Ho's time considered that the revolution in our country was to be waged by outstanding heroes and scholars, who need only address a call to the masses for the latter to rise up as one man. . . . Before President Ho Chi Minh, many Vietnamese revolutionaries held that in order to overthrow the imperialists

---

* Participation in the student strike movement of 1925–26 was the first political activity of many leaders of the Indochinese Communist Party, including three members of the Lao Dong Party (as it has called itself since 1951) Politburo: Pham Van Dong, Vo Nguyen Giap, and Truong Chinh. Pham Van Dong and another Politburo member, Hoang Van Hoan, were among Ho Chi Minh's first students in Canton. On these men, see, respectively, Wilfred Burchett, *North of the Seventeenth Parallel*, 2d ed. (Hanoi: Red River Publishing House, 1957), pp. 64–65; *Vietnam Advances*, 7.9 (1962); Bernard B. Fall, Introduction to Truong Chinh, *Primer for Revolt* (New York: Praeger, 1963), p. xi; and *Vietnam Advances*, 8.3 (1963).

and feudalists one would only need to assassinate or poison the enemy's chief administrative officials or highest-ranking officers and the most wicked among the Vietnamese mandarins ... or one would only need to urge Vietnamese soldiers [in the colonial army] to rise up and turn their guns against the enemy: this would suffice to bring victory to the revolution and independence to the country.... Ho Chi Minh is the first Vietnamese revolutionary leader to have seen clearly the mistaken character of those methods of individual assassination and soldiers' insurrection. He became aware that patient work is needed to bring about the triumph of the revolution, that one must conduct propaganda work among the masses to enlighten them, organize and lead them to struggle for their daily interests.[28]

Ho Chi Minh's lessons on mass organizing were soon put into practice. During the years 1926–29, the Thanh Nien instructed its petty-bourgeois intellectual members to find jobs as manual workers in factories, mines, or plantations. This "proletarianization movement" had the dual aim of organizing the workers and forming experienced cadres.[29] Nguyen Luong Bang, son of a poor rural scholar and currently Vice President of the DRV,[30] has described his activities during this period. Since he had no technical training and so was unable to find a job in a factory, he joined a number of other comrades in becoming rickshaw-puller. "The decision on proletarianization had immediate effects. Our comrades organized the movement of struggle in all the factories where they worked. They did likewise among the rickshaw-pullers. In 1930 there was a general strike by rickshaw-pullers in Haiphong."[31]

At the same time some revolutionary intellectuals in the Thanh Nien took jobs as rural schoolteachers, thus spreading Marxist influence into the countryside. As General Le Quang Ba, from a poor peasant family in Cao Bang and now a member of the Lao Dong Party Central Committee, recalls: "Towards 1926–27, at a time when we were seeking to improve our [economic] condition, Hoang Dinh Rong, the first man in our province to become a communist, began his activities in our region under the guise of a private teacher."[32]

Thus revolutionary intellectuals had begun to make contact with workers and peasants even before the Indochinese Communist Party was founded in 1930, when it immediately assumed leadership of a mass movement of strikes and peasant demonstrations sparked by the depression. Before discussing the events of the "revolutionary high tide" of 1930–31, however, we must backtrack and examine the development of the Vietnamese working class and the Communist revolutionary movement among that class.

## The Proletariat

By introducing modern industry to Vietnam the French created the Vietnamese proletariat. By the turn of the century, several enterprises had been set up. The largest was the Société des Charbonnages du Tonkin, which as early as 1900 had 3,000 Vietnamese at work in the coal mines of Hong Hai, near Haiphong. Other industries then in operation included three cotton mills and a cement factory. These were soon followed by printing presses, ship and railway car construction yards, cigarette and match factories, tanneries, breweries, and distilleries. By 1906 there were 200 mechanized factories, employing 50,000 workers, in Vietnam.[33]

Since workers were recruited primarily from the peasantry rather than from the artisan class as in Europe or India, the lack of skilled workers was acute.[34] To deal with this problem, the French opened a technical school in Hanoi in 1899, which had 200 students in its first year. It is symbolic of the changes the French were causing in Vietnam that the site on which the school was built had previously been used for Confucian examinations.[35] Other technical schools were opened in Saigon, Haiphong, and Hue.[36]

During World War I, nearly 100,000 Vietnamese were sent to France. Most of them were peasants recruited in the Vietnamese countryside; only about 2,000 were skilled workers.[37] Half of these recruits were used in the army, mainly as support troops; the rest were employed as workers. Both as workers and as soldiers they drew high praise from their French supervisors. A letter of commendation to the commander of the 11th Indochinese battalion stated: "I was astonished at the rapidity with which they learned how to use our tools and the quality of their work, which quickly surpassed that of non-specialized European troops."[38] A report on Vietnamese truck drivers noted their skill in map reading and their endurance on the road, and added that expenses for the upkeep of the trucks they drove and serviced were less than one-fourth those required for trucks driven and maintained by Europeans.[39] Their skill as munitions workers and airplane mechanics was also commended. At one aviation school, where damage to planes on the ground had been high, losses dropped to zero after Vietnamese were put in charge of ground work.[40] A technical inspector reported: "Vietnamese are doing well at de-

manding, skilled labor; putting on airplane wings, assembling airplanes, forging. They are very interested in everything mechanical,
anything relating to machines."[41]

These favorable reports were culled from French archives in the
1920's by a Vietnamese candidate for a French doctorate intent on
proving that Vietnamese were loyal and capable French subjects.
It is clear, however, that the facility with which Vietnamese peasant
recruits learned the technical skills necessary for successful modern
warfare boded ill for continued French military domination of Vietnam. Like Prometheus stealing the fire of the gods, Vietnamese who
worked in France learned the secrets of Western power. Once this
had happened, as in the ancient myth, the gods could mete out punishment but could not take back the fire.

After World War I, Vietnamese recruits were gradually repatriated,
and formed a pool of skilled manpower and foremen for French colonial industry.[42] However, they had learned more than technical and
industrial skills in France. Through contact with French workers and
labor organizations, they had also learned about union organizing
and the socialist workers' movement. It is no coincidence that French
sources date the first serious labor disputes in Vietnam to 1920.[43]

Several Vietnamese revolutionary leaders were first introduced to
Communism as workers in France, among them Ton Duc Thang, the
second President of the DRV. Just as the biography of Ho Chi Minh,
the first President of the DRV, illustrates the route to Communism
taken by patriotic Vietnamese intellectuals, so the biography of his
successor illustrates an alternative route taken by many leaders of
the Vietnamese Communist movement: from proletarian to labor organizer.

Ton Duc Thang was born in 1888 to poor peasants in Long Xuyen,
Cochinchina. As a boy he left his family for the city, where he worked
as a servant and got his first schooling—a part-time class from which
he was expelled for leading a protest against the teacher's favoritism
for students who offered presents. In 1910, while working as a mechanic in Saigon, he set up a friendship society for workers and a
mutual-aid association; these were the first workers' organizations in
southern Vietnam. In 1912, while working at the ship repair yard of
the Saigon technical school, he organized a strike of the apprentices,
which spread to the repair shop proper. Both strikes were successful.

That same year Thang took a job as a mechanic on a French ship
and made his way to France, where he enlisted in the navy in 1914.

In 1918, when his ship was in the Black Sea under orders to intervene against the Soviet government, he joined with other sailors in protesting the action and was chosen to hoist the red flag on the French flagship. Back in France, he worked at the Renault automobile factory and was active in the Confédération Générale du Travail.[44]

In 1920 Thang returned to Saigon and formed a secret labor union dedicated to mutual aid, protection of workers' interests, and struggle against French domination. Its members paid dues according to their earnings, usually the equivalent of one day's salary a month. There was no fixed headquarters; the union met once a month at the home of one member or another on the pretext of observing the anniversary of a parent's death. By 1925 the union had some 300 members in private firms and public services in the Saigon-Cholon area.

In 1925 Thang joined the Thanh Nien and was elected to its executive committee. In August of that year he organized Vietnam's first political strike. The strikers' aims were ostensibly economic: a 20 percent wage increase, a full complement of workers in each workshop, and resumption of the former practice of closing 15 minutes early on pay day. But the purpose behind the strike was political: to support Chinese workers against the attempt of the great powers to "restore order" in China after the outbreak of a wave of strikes there, and in particular to prevent the *Michelet*—one of three warships promised by France for the Western show of force in China—from leaving Saigon. A strike was called for August 4 at the military shipyard where the *Michelet* was being repaired; the strikers were aided by collections in Saigon's factories and supported by the Chinese workers' union in Cholon.

By August 11 the Governor of Cochinchina was ready to negotiate, and the negotiations ended shortly afterward in a total victory for the workers, who even received their wages for the days they had been on strike. Nor did they hurry to repair the *Michelet*, which was unable to leave Saigon until November 28. As a strike that differed markedly from earlier ones, which had had purely economic aims and had been for the most part spontaneous, this strike represented a turning point in the history of the Vietnamese workers' movement.[45]

Ton Duc Thang was arrested and deported to Poulo Condore prison in 1929, where he was to spend the next 16 years. He was not freed until August 1945, when he became an energetic leader of the Nam Bo (Cochinchina) Vietminh resistance.[46] He is by no means a unique example. Other leading Communists with worker or labor union backgrounds include Hoang Quoc Viet, of the Lao Dong Party Central Committee, and Politburo members Van Tien Dung and Le Thanh Nghi.[47]

The workers of Vietnam never constituted a large percentage of the population at any given time. In 1929, just before the depression, the number of workers reached a high of about 221,000, of whom some 140,000 were industrial workers (53,000 in mines and 86,000 in factories) and some 81,000 were agricultural workers, primarily on rubber plantations.[48] This compares with a total population of some 20,000,000 at about this time. Yet the figures for any one year are misleading because of the rapid turnover among Vietnamese workers, and because they include only workers in French enterprises. As a French official in the International Labor Office wrote in the 1930's, "The Annamite working class undoubtedly exists, and its numerical importance can be assessed by multiplying the figures given in the statistics by 4 or 5."[49] Joseph Buttinger puts the figure still higher:

> It is safe to say that between 1910 and 1940, millions of peasants for shorter or longer periods enjoyed the dubious blessings of proletarian life under the colonial regime. Only a small fraction became permanent members of the working class, but the impact that the development of capitalism in Vietnam had upon the outlook of large segments of the population was nevertheless great. . . .
>
> The working class remained small, but the nature of colonial capitalism spread the negative effects of modern labor exploitation over a vast number of people. It thus prepared not only the people in factories, mines, and towns, but also those in the villages, for the days when revolutionary leaders would seek the support of the masses.[50]

The depression had a severe impact on the Vietnamese industrial labor force, reducing it from some 221,000 workers in 1929 to a low of 150,000 after the depression hit.[51] Declining employment and Thanh Nien agitation soon sparked a widespread movement of strikes, demonstrations, and protests in most of Vietnam's urban centers, and above all in two cities of Nghe An province, Vinh and its port, Ben Thuy. Some 8,000 workers were concentrated in this area, employed in an electric plant, several mechanized sawmills, a large match factory, and a locomotive repair shop in Vinh, and as dockworkers in Ben Thuy. Drawn from the surrounding countryside, most of these workers retained their rural family and economic ties. Because Nghe An was an overpopulated area with a large labor supply, industrial wages in Vinh and Ben Thuy were among the lowest in Vietnam.

On May 1, 1930 (a date chosen by Indochinese Communist Party organizers), some 1,200 workers, followed by peasants from the surrounding countryside, paraded in the streets of Ben Thuy. On the same day, some 3,000 peasants marched to the concession of a Vietnamese collaborator and demanded the return of land "stolen from the people." For the next few months there were nearly continual strikes in Vinh and Ben Thuy, and peasant unrest spread from Nghe An to the adjacent province of Ha Tinh. Many strikers went to the countryside to participate in the peasant movement, and peasant demonstrations were launched in support of workers' strikes. By the end of 1930 the "worker-peasant alliance" was a reality.[52]

In sum, the proletariat made a major contribution to the development of the Vietnamese revolution. The labor movement produced a number of leading Communists; the familiarity of many peasants with proletarian working conditions helped bridge the gap between the traditional and modernized sectors of Vietnamese society; and workers played an important role in starting the first Communist-led mass movement in Vietnam, the Nghe-Tinh soviets of 1930. However, the proletariat was far too small to provide the mass base of the Vietnamese revolution. That role was played by the peasantry.

## The Peasants

The first French troops in Cochinchina in 1861 were amazed at the extent of peasant resistance. As one chronicler wrote: "The resistance center was everywhere, subdivided *ad infinitum*, nearly as many times as there were living Annamese. It would be more exact to regard each peasant fastening a sheaf of rice as a center of resistance."[53]

Although, as we have seen, most of the initial peasant resistance to the French was led by scholars, their most tenacious antagonist was a man of peasant background, De Tham, a Robin Hood figure who took from the rich to give to the poor, and whose followers were peasants whose land had been taken during the period of conquest. De Tham and his peasant forces waged an off-and-on battle with the French until his death in 1913, 16 years after the defeat of the Scholars' Resistance.[54] Thus from the first, anti-French resistance that combined social with nationalist causes proved more powerful than patriotism alone.

Fear of peasant rebellion had provided some check on the rapaciousness of Vietnamese rulers under the previous feudal system, but after the completion of "pacification" in 1897, the French, confident of their overwhelming military superiority, were under no such constraint. By means of regressive taxation measures including a head tax, the gabelle, and a government liquor monopoly, the Vietnamese peasantry was made to foot the bill for the high salaries of French administrators (the largest colonial civil service per capita in any Asian colony) and to pay for capital development with both money and corvée labor. Whereas traditionally village landlord notables had played a certain role as defenders of local interests against the state, the French made them an extension of a strongly centralized system, obliging them, on pain of personal punishment, to enforce French colonial laws, to collect peasant taxes, and to force the peasants to buy French monopoly liquor.

Not only did the French grant peasant land to Frenchmen and outstanding Vietnamese collaborators as concessions; their taxation policies also made it possible for landlords to expand their holdings greatly. Besides repeatedly raising head and land taxes, the French required payment in cash. Most peasants had to borrow the needed tax money, and many lost their land as a result, for at usurious rates of interest each year's tax loan threw them further into debt. Others were forced to meet their tax and loan payments by selling their crops immediately at harvest time, when prices were lowest; they therefore had to buy food for their family later, when prices were higher. Some of the rice they sold ended up in the hands of exporters, who sold an average of nearly 10 percent of the annual Tonkin rice production in the high international market of the pre-depression years.[55] As a result, even after a good harvest peasants had to live in a state of semi-famine for part of the year.

As the French and their local collaborators tightened this vise on the Vietnamese peasantry during the first decades of French rule, the peasants were victims of forces they did not understand and were powerless to oppose in any but futile, uncoordinated local struggles. Their traditional leaders, Confucian scholars, either were completely demoralized in the face of French power or had become allies of the French. Although modernizing scholars sympathized with the peasants' plight, they did not provide leadership for peasant struggles. Although the major causes of the peasant demonstrations of 1908 in central Vietnam were taxes and the corvée, the peasants, as the French suspected, had been inspired to some extent by the modernizing scholars. Some of their writings, couched in easily memorized verse, had circulated among the peasantry, and Phan Chu Trinh's associates had made village lecture tours. However, as David Marr has pointed out in his excellent study of this period, "those scholar-gentry who had set the stage intellectually and emotionally for the tax protests apparently had stayed home and refused to lead the immediate confrontations."[56]

By the late 1920's, however, a new generation of revolutionary intellectuals with a doctrine of mass organization was waiting in the wings. The depression that hit Vietnam in 1930 created a revolutionary situation in which they could act.

Like the 1908 tax protests, the peasant upsurge of 1930 was essentially sparked by economic conditions. Because of the fall in the price of rice, concessionaries left hundreds of thousands of acres of riceland untilled. Evicted tenant farmers and unemployed farm workers could not find jobs in the cities, where a large percentage of the urban work force had been laid off. With stocks in the hands of merchants worthless because of the collapse of the market, some French factories burned rice for fuel. The colonial regime, far from alleviating the situation, made it worse by raising peasant taxes in an effort to compensate for depression losses. These conditions, combined with bad harvests, produced famine in some areas, particularly Nghe An. Beginning in early 1930 there were widespread strikes and peasant demonstrations throughout Vietnam, and in Nghe An and Ha Tinh these developed into a full-scale uprising.

On September 12, 1930, French airplanes bombed an unarmed peasant demonstration in a district of Nghe An, killing 217 peasants and wounding over 100. When the peasants returned to bury their dead, the planes struck a second time. Anger in the whole province over the savagery of this attack escalated the struggle into a new phase, that of peasant "soviets." In what is known as the Nghe-Tinh soviets movement, French administrators and their Vietnamese collaborators were driven out of whole districts of Nghe An and the adjacent province of Ha Tinh for several months, and village administrations consisting of poor peasants were formed. Land that had been usurped by Vietnamese landlords was distributed, rents reduced, debt payment suspended, schools and adult literacy classes opened, and self-defense militia organized. The most popular part of the Communist Party program, however, was the confiscation of rice from the rich to give to famine victims.[57]

A revolutionary intellectual from Nghe An, Nguyen Duy Trinh (now Foreign Minister of the DRV), has written an account of that period in his native village. Trinh had been a student of Tran Phu (first Secretary-General of the Indochinese Communist Party) in the high school at Vinh. After a brief period of imprisonment, Trinh was released in early 1930—the French apparently thought that their threats, plus family influence, would be sufficient to deter him from further revolutionary activities. Trinh, however, was excited at the prospect of putting his years of study of revolutionary theory into practice, and immediately returned to his native village. There revolutionary intellectuals like himself were able to apply their lessons in mass organizing and teach the peasants the new ideology. Peasants would pour into the street, form parades, shout political slogans. Then,

> arriving at a large field, the demonstrators, in good order, listened to the speakers, members of the Party, who popularized the doctrine, roused the minds of the masses, stirred up hatred and called for action. In each struggle [session] there were about a dozen speeches delivered by speakers until their voices became husky, while tens of thousands of people listened in complete silence and rapt attention. Sometimes the struggle lasted all night; at times it was so exciting that it went from one day to the other without the demonstrators showing signs of tiredness.[58]

But while peasants throughout the Nghe-Tinh soviets were attending day and night demonstrations and lectures, no one was tilling the fields, and soon this created a major problem, aggravating the already severe famine situation. The French were able to take advantage of this development by handing out rice to those who would surrender to the colonial side. Furthermore, the Communist leadership's encouragement of the peasants' hatred of rich Vietnamese led to disastrous consequences: the French were able to recruit wealthy villagers to help suppress the revolutionary movement; with their knowledge of the local situation, they were even more effective than the indiscriminate slaughter practiced by Foreign Legionnaires.[59]

Though the Nghe-Tinh soviets were defeated by this combination of violent military suppression and counterrevolutionary measures, the Communist leadership learned from its mistakes. When, in 1945, famine once again contributed to creating a revolutionary situation, the Vietminh's attacks were focused on Japanese and French rice depots, not the granaries of rich Vietnamese. One of the first acts of the DRV government in 1945 was to launch a campaign for increased agricultural production; an appeal was also made to well-off Vietnamese to contribute some of their rice to the famine-stricken. Through such measures, the Vietminh united rich and poor Vietnamese against the French.

For Vietnamese Communist leaders, the Nghe-Tinh soviets movement was "the dress rehearsal for the August Revolution [1945]."[60] In it they had learned many important lessons, including the danger of stressing class conflict and social revolution in a colonial context. In the early 1940's they worked out a compromise agrarian program which, while improving the poor peasants' lot, took account of the interests of rich peasants and patriotic landlords as well.[61] Thus adjusting Marxist theory to the reality of the Vietnamese colonial situation, they were able to lead a national united front of anticolonial Vietnamese to victory.

As this brief account makes clear, the Vietnamese revolution was far from being simply a "peasant revolution." Though the peasantry provided the bulk of the supporters and soldiers of the revolution, its leaders were those who were familiar with modern organization, technology, and ideas, namely revolutionary intellectuals and workers. During the anti-French Resistance (1946–54), the militarily superior French were able to reoccupy the cities of Vietnam in a matter of months. The revolutionaries of the urban areas withdrew into the countryside and continued to fight alongside a peasantry they had already led in revolutionary movements as early as 1930. The force that ultimately overthrew the French colonialists was that of the mobilized Vietnamese peasantry, but without the nonpeasant mobilizers, with their modern skills, Marxist ideology, and knowledge of the national and international situation, this force might have been squandered and defeated, like that of a strong but unarmed man trying to defend himself against an opponent with a knife. In revolution, as in judo, skill is more important than strength, for brute force alone usually favors the counterrevolutionary side.[62]

## PART TWO

*Organization-Building and Leadership Strategies*

# Traditional Modes and Communist Movements: Change and Protest in Indonesia

REX MORTIMER

A leading Southeast Asian historian, Harry J. Benda, has made two comments on Asian Communism that are highly pertinent to the evaluation of the role of Indonesian Communism in the 1950's and 1960's. "Ideology apart," he notes, "it is not inconceivable that in Asia (as elsewhere) Communist movements as such provide a substitute for decayed or vanishing social institutions. For it is exactly these institutions—the family, the clan, the tribe, or the village community—that have suffered most heavily under the eroding onslaught of the economic and political systems carried to Asia by the West in the course of the past century or so."[1] But ideology too must be taken into account, and Benda has something relevant to say on this aspect of the interaction between Asian Communists and their followers: "For whatever urban-oriented 'modern' leadership might have decreed, at the local level Communists quite soon learned to speak—or slipped into speaking—the language of peasant expectations of apocalyptic change leading to immediate justice on earth. [Peasant audiences] may themselves have taken an active, dynamic part in distilling from the new gospel laid before them what they needed and could assimilate, weaving old and new together into a kind of 'folk Marxism'—just as they had for millennia done with the gospels of other sophisticated creeds."[2]

Although there is insufficient evidence to test these hypotheses in depth, I will attempt in this paper to demonstrate the validity of both propositions as applied to the Indonesian case. Communist organi-

In delineating PKI policies in this article, I have drawn on material contained in my book *Indonesian Communism Under Sukarno: Ideology and Politics, 1959–1965* (Ithaca, N.Y.: Cornell University Press, 1974).

zation, it will be argued, did indeed prove to be a substitute for decayed or vanishing institutions; and not only did the peasant follower of Communism adapt Communist doctrine to his needs, but the doctrine itself, in the circumstances confronting the Communists, had to be diluted to be consistent with perceptions to which the peasant was attuned.

In some instances, the combination of Communist organizing skills and an ideology assimilable to peasant needs has proved to have a devastating revolutionary dynamic. So it seemed to many observers that this would be true also of the Indonesian Communist movement in the early 1960's. But in the event, this expectation was unfulfilled. Although the movement came to represent a huge tide of protest and impatient aspiration, the very terms of the PKI's accommodation to its environment rendered it incapable of directing that tide toward the destruction of the obstacles in its path. To explore the reasons for the failure of Indonesian Communism to convert grass-roots support into revolutionary force, it is necessary to range widely among the traditional and contemporary phenomena of Indonesian society.

### The Javanese Peasantry

In most respects, the conditions conducive to agrarian unrest that Donald Zagoria identifies earlier in this volume as characteristic generally of Monsoon Asia are to be found in Java.* The area is marked by acute land hunger, a high incidence of landlessness, and an increasing trend toward "pauperization" of the peasantry. But one important factor that is applicable to much of the region Zagoria surveys is missing: in Java, there is nothing approaching the incidence of "parasitic landlordism" found in India, the Philippines, South Vietnam, and other countries of Monsoon Asia. Indeed, Java differs notably from these countries in the smallness of the landowner class as a social grouping, the smallness of landowner holdings, and the low order of economic differentiation among the peasantry. Inequalities abound, to be sure, but they are inequalities set within an overall pattern of subsistence or below-subsistence farming.[3]

In addition, Java exhibits strongly one of the characteristics Zagoria has elsewhere identified as inhibiting revolutionary potential.

* I have confined my discussion to Java since information on Communist organization elsewhere in Indonesia is too scanty to warrant analytical study. The fact that both general political developments and Communist operations centered on Java during the period I cover somewhat compensates for this deficiency.

"A landless class that is divided by caste, language, tribe, or religion will inevitably have great difficulties in achieving unity," he notes.[4] In the Javanese case, the peasantry is sharply divided into two hostile religio-cultural groups: the *abangan*, the majority of ethnic Javanese, who wish to preserve the basically animist but part Hindu-Buddhist, part Islamic lifeways derived from the customs followed by their ancestors from time immemorial; and the *santri*, or activist Moslems, whose most important cultural referent is their religion.*

These two "exceptional" features of Javanese society together posed a formidable obstacle to the revolutionizing efforts of the PKI and played a significant part in forcing it to accommodate to its social and political environment. The more closely we examine traditional society and its cultural content, the more forcefully are we impressed by the need to view Communist tactics and dilemmas in mobilizing protest in this historical context.

Traditional Javanese society was notoriously loose in its organizational structure. As Sartono Kartodirdjo points out:

> The strongest institutional link in traditional Javanese society was *suwita*, a system of client relations extending through society from top to bottom. The essence of this institution was an asymmetrical exchange of services, with the client providing products of labour in return for physical protection, chances for advancement, and enhanced status. . . . Thus the hierarchy of the state, and the bureaucracy in particular, was integrated not by formal institutional or organisational means, but by the myriad dyadic linkages of the client system. Since the traditional state had no functionally specialised political and economic organisations separate from these particularised pyramids of patrons and retainers, political relations were always preponderantly particularist, ascriptive, and diffuse in character.[5]

The relatively formless nature of the authority structure was replicated at the village level. The traditional Javanese village appears to have been only loosely integrated by work exchanges, the political authority of the village head, and various cultural mechanisms for promoting harmony and a sense of community. By comparison with the Chinese or Vietnamese village, say, it lacked marked gradations

---

* Abangan and santri represent the two major cultural-cum-ideological streams (*aliran*) in Javanese society. A third stream, that of the *prijaji*, or Javanese nobility, constituting the great tradition of old Java in its modern antecedents, also has to be incorporated into the cultural patterning. For an extended discussion of the aliran and their modern political expressions, see Clifford Geertz, *The Religion of Java* (Glencoe, Ill.: Free Press, 1960).

of wealth and landholding, and it was deficient in articulated solidary bonds over and beyond the base unit of the nuclear family.

Traditional protest and rebellion likewise demonstrated an absence of enduring, tightly knit, and more or less continuous vehicles for the expression of discontent comparable to the clans, guilds, or secret societies of China and Vietnam. Rebellion in Indonesia has customarily taken the form of sudden, passionate outpourings of violence and agitation or equally idiosyncratic acts of withdrawal, rather than carefully laid and constructed designs of subversion. Although specific social conditions and structures certainly influenced the locale and timing of dissident movements, the coherence of such movements seems to have been created through the medium of common cultural experience.

Magical-mystical movements of a messianic kind, in a word, have formed the leitmotif of traditional rebellion. In precolonial society, the spirit of political estrangement was epitomized in the sage-like figure of the *adjar*, together with his pupils, "whose typical role is to diagnose decay within the kingdom and warn of the impending downfall of the dynasty."[6] Although "the classical *adjar* vanished from the scene with the penetration of Islam and the later superimposition of bureaucratic colonial authority . . . his social and political role [was taken over by] the rural Islamic *kjai* [religious teachers] of the late pre-colonial and colonial periods."[7] The colonial order acted to spur revolt by undermining the traditional economic, political, and cultural system and creating "a chronic state of crisis in society."[8] By inducting the traditional ruling groups into their apparatus, but repelling and persecuting the kjai, the Dutch ensured that, in times of stress and breakdown, the masses would turn to these counterelites for the inspiration and organization of resistance. Meanwhile, the Moslem zealots, impelled by the activist cast of their religion to be more assertive in their opposition than the adjar, responded by emerging at times of disorder and distress at the head of their faithful santri (pupils) "to play brief but at times decisive roles in the collapse of an old order and the emergence of a new, before retiring again to their former isolation."[9] As Benedict Anderson emphasizes, the very distance of the kjai from constituted authority enhanced their popular standing: perceived as being free of self-interest, they radiated a pure flame of dissident power that attracted adherents.[10] Both the colonial and postcolonial orders abound with examples of revolt sparked and led by Islamic teachers and holy men.[11]

## Some Consequences of the Colonial Era

The overall effect of Dutch rule was to sap whatever vitality there was in Javanese village society and undermine its fragile organizational structure. Traditional elites, from the nobility down to the village headmen, were drawn into the colonial administrative apparatus and rendered less capable than before of acting as mediators for peasant interests. At the same time, Dutch economic penetration had the effect of stifling the emergence of differentiated strata in the countryside, so that no equivalent of a gentry class developed to provide local leaders for revolt, resistance, or renovation. The prevailing system of commercial agriculture practiced in Java intensified tendencies toward involution and "shared poverty," while simultaneously weakening the social mechanisms that might have enabled the village to cope in some measure with the increasing poverty and distress. Viewing the resultant social fragmentation from the vantage point of the early post-independence years, Clifford Geertz characterized the evolution of Javanese small town and village society as "an unbroken advance towards vagueness."[12] The village in particular, with virtually no informal but clearly bounded social groups such as cliques and gangs,[13] was notable for "the general formlessness of the life [and] the looseness of ties between individuals."[14] A number of anthropologists and sociologists have noted that the nuclear family represents the only stable village corporate group in Java.[15] Town life has not been very different in this respect, at least at the provincial level. Relations among upper-class urban dwellers are governed primarily by elaborate and intimate rituals of status, ceremonial, and influence that seldom coagulate into more than informal cliques of a generally limited kind;[16] and relations among the poorer kampong dwellers have tended to replicate the village pattern.[17]

As for the estate laborers and other marginal economic groups created by Dutch intervention, various factors appear to have inhibited their conspiratorial organization. In addition to the lack of a cultural tradition conducive to such a development, to say nothing of close Dutch supervision, most agricultural laborers were merely seasonal workers whose strongest ties continued to be with their nuclear families and home villages.

We find further confirmation of social and cultural impediments to lasting organization in the fact that even among industrial and semi-industrial workers in the modern era, trade unions and similar associations have been susceptible to pronounced membership "drift" and multiple allegiance, solidarity consciousness apparently finding little focus within such organizations *qua* organizations.[18] Even the PKI, with its undoubted organizational skills and drive, was never able to overcome this problem completely in its heyday.

In the colonial era, as we have seen, in the absence of any social organization capable of promoting protest and rebellion the vacuum was filled by the kjai, a figure standing outside the formal structures of Indonesian society and drawing elements from within these structures toward him only at times and under conditions of local unrest. Even after the formation of nationalist movements and trade unions, the religio-cultural broker of dissidence retained a good deal of power and influence on events. Anderson argues persuasively that the struggle for independence itself was ignited on a mass scale by forces working within the tradition of the adjar and the kjai. In this case, however, a new twist was given to the traditional formula under the influence of the Japanese style of rule on Java. As George Kahin observes, "The central thrust of revolutionary power in the critical generative stage of the struggle for independence . . . lay primarily, and to a decisive degree, with Indonesian youth," and these youth were products of an experience akin to that of the traditional religious training schools.[19] According to Anderson:

> The institutions created for youth by the Japanese authorities bore certain common features that, by an irony of history, replicated some of the essential characteristics of the traditional *pesantren*. Accordingly, the experience of being part of these institutions reinforced the cultural power of that tradition no less than it instilled new conceptions and cemented new relationships.
>
> *       *       *
>
> The impact of the Japanese style was powerfully enhanced by the familiar traditional resonances it evoked. . . . Victory in the war and independence for Indonesia depended on the *semangat* [spiritual power] and discipline of the Indonesian people themselves. The similarity between these ideas and Javanese conceptions of power as cosmic energy, to be concentrated and accumulated by ascetic purity and spiritual discipline, was quite apparent.[20]

Alongside the activities of the *pemuda* (youth), and sometimes converging with them, especially in the rural areas, there appeared once again on the historical stage the more truly traditional figure of the kjai, biding his time in isolated oblivion until the portents of dynastic collapse became evident.[21] Together, but only in a very limited sense coordinated, these forces supplied the diffuse militant energy of the national revolution and its impulses toward social radicalism, but, lacking effective leadership and a uniting ideology, the radical wave gradually spent itself and left control of the national revolution in the hands of moderate and upper-class leaders of the older nationalist movements.[22]

In the latter stages of the revolution, and especially in the early years following independence, political parties and their networks of voluntary associations came to fill the empty shell of the village with organizational activity. It is testimony to the dearth of solidary bonds in small town and village society that the parties made such decisive inroads in these communities, providing the major focus of group loyalties and activities. The principal mode of entry of the parties was via patron-client relationships streamed along the lines of long-standing cultural cleavages. This was a pattern to which, as we shall see, the PKI adhered in at least some essentials.

A number of factors account for the rapid and extensive upsurge of the Communist movement in Indonesia after independence. The expectations aroused by the Indonesian national revolution, in part fueled by a long millenarian tradition, were not matched by any program or vision of social change that gave promise of satisfying those expectations. The independence settlement itself heavily compromised the achievement of independence by making extensive concessions to Dutch economic and political influence. Moreover, the parties mainly responsible for effecting that settlement established a distance and remoteness from the populace that left the latter in a representational void. Over a longer span of time, there was little in the way of development in Indonesia that held out any hope of alleviating the acute problems of land hunger, underemployment, and material distress, which were most pronounced on Java.

The thrust of the Communist movement, from the time of its revitalization in 1951 after a disastrous and bloody setback in 1948, was toward the creation of political conditions that would make far-reaching social change possible. Its message was initially directed toward those very groups that felt most acutely disadvantaged and disenchanted by the post-independence settlement—urban workers and lowly state functionaries, estate laborers, squatters on estate lands, and the young people in the more detraditionalized villages. But even if the PKI had fully mobilized and organized these groups, they would not have constituted a sufficient base of support for a challenge to the established order. The PKI felt obliged to seek a wider clientele among the peasants, and for that purpose to appease a section of the elite that could afford it political protection while it pursued its grass-roots mobilization. Both prongs of this extended strategy obliged the Communists to bend toward an accommodation with traditional forces and ideas; both embroiled them too in the religio-cultural divisions that bit deep in Indonesia and cross-cut their efforts to agitate along class lines. By the imperative of survival, the PKI thus gave sustenance to the very forces it needed to overcome in order to reach its objective. The tension between the pressures toward adaptation and the desire for transformation hence lies at the center of the ideological dynamics of the Communist movement between 1951 and 1965.

The character of the PKI has to be gauged from two overlapping viewpoints: that of the leadership as expressed in its goals and strategies, and that of the cultural perceptions of the huge peasant mass it rallied behind it in the 1950's and 1960's. Although from the first angle one can detect a continual, if circuitous, striving to use the Party to promote change, from the second, the movement seemed to be concerned rather with defending the material and sociocultural interests of the abangan Javanese against the inroads of both activist Islam and urban-sponsored "modernization." The pressures of change, slow as their pace was in Indonesia, affected the PKI leaders and the peasants alike. The former were impelled to dilute their doctrine to make it palatable to the peasant; the peasant, for his part, was induced by his need for a social and cultural champion to accept new ways of organization and thinking promoted by the Communists so long as they could be harmonized with his basic urge to conserve a past that represented his frail peg of security. Certain features of the leadership and cadre force of the PKI placed the Party in a uniquely favorable position to appeal to the dispositions of the abangan. But, by the same token, the special character of abangan society and culture sharply limited the PKI's ability to transform this large social grouping into a disciplined political resource.

### The Social Choices in the Early Years of the PKI

In the first phase of its existence, the PKI worked some direct accommodation with the Islamic tradition of revolt, which played a significant part in the Communist uprisings against the Dutch in 1926–27.[23] The failure of the revolts, and the consequent punitive measures visited upon the PKI by the Dutch, effectively put the Com-

munists out of action for almost two decades. Although a weak underground Party nucleus was reestablished in 1935 and gathered adherents during the Japanese occupation, it was not able to organize a
successful anti-Japanese movement. In this, the Communists, like
other political factions, were deterred in part by the effectiveness of
Japanese counterintelligence work and in part by the cultural inexperience in conspiratorial techniques already referred to. But the
main thing that worked against the development of a popular resistance movement was the Japanese policy of catering to nationalist
sentiment in Indonesia. By sponsoring a myriad of organizations that
were designed to rally the population to their side but at the same
time held out the ultimate promise of independence, the Japanese
managed to co-opt most of the actual or potential nationalist leadership.[24]

In the early stages of the independence struggle, the PKI, reestablished openly in October 1945, pulsed in tune with the pemuda
rhythm, and tried to reach the youth with a militant social program
formulating goals for their struggles. This bid for pemuda support
was launched by a maverick Communist, a lawyer with pronounced
mystical leanings named Mohammed Jusuf, who had no close connections with the prewar PKI apparatus and whose political style was
quite out of character with that of conventional Communist leaderships.[25] It is more than doubtful that Jusuf's attempt to unite the radicals could have succeeded, but in any case in March 1946 he was
thrust aside by older generation PKI leaders returned from long years
of exile and detention in Dutch prisons and camps.[26] These men were
disinclined to follow in Jusuf's footsteps. Long out of touch with the
situation in their country, bound by long-standing ties to the elite
nationalist leaders, and inured (by many years of Comintern experience or influence) to the politics of maneuver and compromise, they
elected to follow the then current international Communist line of
accommodation to the purely nationalist objectives of the Republican leaders, and endorsed their policy of compromising with the
Dutch and other Western governments. But a large number of
younger PKI or future PKI members, including those who were to
become the top leaders and key cadres of the movement in the 1950's
and 1960's, were caught up in the pemuda wave, some of them as
prominent activists and leaders. These young men retained and later
revived the sense of radical mission and nationalist purpose that animated them in the hectic years of 1945 and 1946.

By this time it had become more difficult for Communism to effect the kind of conjunction with Islamic militancy that had occurred in the 1920's. Communist attacks on orthodox Moslem leaders of Sarekat Islam in that period, the hardened division between Islamic and secularist nationalists that developed during the 1930's and early 1940's, and the formal expression of this division in the Japanese-sponsored organizations during the occupation had all combined to rouse the ire of Moslem religious leaders against the "atheistic" Communists. After the outbreak of the national revolution, Islamic groups were sufficiently well-organized and militant to cater adequately to their own communities, and they erected formidable barriers of sentiment against Communist infiltration. The Communists found it easiest to gain adherents among the abangan Javanese of central and east Java. The road to the abangan was relatively open, since many of their accustomed leaders, the prijaji, had lost all standing because of their collaboration with the Japanese in depredations against the peasants. The abangan, alarmed by the zeal and organizational advantages of the Moslems, were susceptible to the appeals of any radical non-Islamic group that showed a concern for their material and cultural needs.

How much the santri-abangan schism intensified during the revolution was demonstrated in 1948, by which time the pemuda drive was long spent and the political stage dominated by relatively regularized Party and military structures. The PKI, affected by the increased intransigence of Moscow in the opening rounds of the Cold War, took a more militant stance in opposition to the Republican leadership, culminating in a confrontation between Republican and pro-Communist armed groups at Madiun in September.[27] The PKI was then set upon by the loyalists, and in the ensuing fighting and disorders Communist supporters and Moslems slaughtered each other with wild abandon in the hinterlands of east and central Java, with the latter having by far the better of the contest.[28] The PKI was decimated for the second time; of more lasting significance, it was from this time forward identified for better or for worse with the abangan outlook, and was to find devotion to Islam a major limiting factor on the growth of its mass membership and influence.

### The Party After Independence

After languishing for some years, the PKI was taken in hand in January 1951 by a new leadership that was to remain intact for 14 years, that was to bestow on the movement its greatest political gains and inflict on it its most devastating setback, and that was to devise a most subtle and intricate relationship between modern and traditional influences. The young leaders and cadres who came to the fore in 1951 and the years immediately following belonged to the pemuda generation and, in many cases, had been pemuda stalwarts.* They were imbued with the radical nationalist spirit characteristic of their age group, and animated by the pemuda ideal of creating a strong, independent, and "progressive" Indonesia.

By virtue of their own and their followers' experiences in the revolution and their relatively low-status origins, the new PKI leaders were quick to respond to the deep dissatisfaction with the fruits of independence already in evidence by 1951.

They hit out strongly against the style and policies of the government, labeling the settlement with the Dutch a betrayal of the revolution and the status of Indonesia following independence that of a "semicolonial, semifeudal" state. Their programmatic utterances called for the repudiation of the Round Table Conference Agreement ending the war with the Dutch, the nationalization of foreign enterprises, and the reconstruction of Indonesian society along prescribed Communist lines—industrialization, the modernization of the country, the inauguration of a technological and social revolution in the countryside, and the elimination of superstition and backwardness.[29] These policies struck strong chords among the disaffected lower strata; insofar as they emphasized Indonesia's dependent status, they also echoed the feelings of those elite groups that aspired to establish and lead a strong, independent, and assertive nation. These groups were most heavily represented within the "radical" wing of the PNI (Partai Nasionalis Indonesia), which captured the leadership of that party, repudiated coalition with the more Westernized parties, and took over the government early in 1953.

At this stage, the ideology and style of the PKI gave it the unambiguous stamp of a modernizing force. Its program, as we have noted, strongly reflected the modernizing thrust of international Communist doctrine. In addition, alone among the political parties the PKI sought to appeal to the populace across ethnic, religious, regional, and cultural boundaries, and to rally them to the Communist banner along the lines of actual or incipient class solidarities. It

* The top leaders of the PKI in this period—D. N. Aidit, M. H. Lukman, Njoto, Sudisman—had all been prominent activists. All were 30 years old or under in 1951.

strove to implant trade union and socialist consciousness among the workers, and to educate the peasants to an awareness of their common needs and aspirations as a class.[30] Organizationally, the Party sought to transcend patron-client and *aliran* modes by promoting participant consciousness, applying universal standards of recruitment, promoting able members on merit and irrespective of status, developing specialized roles in the organization, and establishing a disciplined system of authority based on normative rules of conduct. Part of the PKI's success as a mobilizing force, it seems reasonable to assume, sprang from its ability and willingness to provide scope for the talents of thousands of cadres who in more tradition-bound parties and organizations would have been denied upward mobility.

It would be highly misleading to overlook or minimize in any way these modernistic features of the PKI, which all commentators have recognized. But since we are here concerned with the PKI's impact on and interaction with its huge peasant base, there is every reason to look carefully at those factors that pulled the Party in the direction of the traditional ideas and practices which prevailed among the peasants. The Communist leaders, overwhelmingly persons of lower-status and urban background who had experienced their greatest inspiration and sense of mission in the early years of the revolution, felt no explicit allegiance toward a traditional order that had become seriously attenuated in the last half century or so of Dutch rule, and that moreover had shown itself utterly incapable of coping with the challenges and stresses of the occupation and national resistance. Nor were they, like so many of their higher-status, better-educated nationalist competitors, drawn in an ambivalent fashion to worship the order, rank, and routine of the Dutch colonial system. At the same time, they were strongly anti-Western, and heavily influenced by the mystique of the revolution and national awakening associated with the pemuda efflorescence, which as we have seen contained strongly traditionalist undertones. Part of this ideological inheritance included a reverence toward the Indonesian or, more specifically, the Javanese precolonial past, which was seen to have represented a period of national greatness, "primitive communist" customs, and cultural values superior to foreign ways. These precious traditions of the past were believed to live on among the common people, overlaid by oppressive and colonial layers, and to bear the seeds of national revival and adaptation to "national democratic" change.[31] In this respect, then, the PKI leaders and cadres were attuned to traditions consonant with the outlooks of both the Javanese elite and the Javanese peasantry. They were open to induction into a neotraditionalist political and social framework under certain conditions; and these conditions were in many respects created by their relative weakness in relation to their adversaries.

The Communists might have hoped to elevate class to a primary place in the political stakes, but prevailing social and political circumstances weighed heavily against them. The urban workers were relatively few in number, and predominantly employed in small and scattered semicraft enterprises where patron-client relationships between owners and workers remained strong.[32] A great part of the urban work force was casual, itinerant, and underemployed. But one step away from the peasantry, or in many cases still partly dependent on farming for their livelihood, these workers (a high proportion of them village women augmenting their family incomes) were far from ideal material for the promotion of class-based politics.[33] Additionally, they were acutely vulnerable to governmental and military repression, as the clampdown in August 1951 following a wave of PKI-led strikes had confirmed.[34] Industrialization failed to make headway between 1951 and 1965, and the PKI was unable to put muscle into its proletarian nucleus; it felt compelled to adopt moderate tactics in the unions under its control while seeking to implant stronger class and political consciousness among the workers through education and propaganda alone.*

Among the peasantry, there was considerable discontent in some areas, but the PKI was in a poor position to exploit it for revolutionary purposes. Like all the other parties, the PKI was urban-based and lacked cadres in the countryside; where these did exist, the Party was in no position to direct and discipline them until it had gained greater political experience. A local target for use in mobilizing the peasantry was also difficult to identify. In contrast to many other Asian societies, the "shared poverty" system common in Java had kept social differentiation in the villages down to a minimum and prevented the growth of a substantial landed class; in comparison

---

* It is notable that PKI programmatic declarations and conference reports provided virtually no directions for labor agitation after 1953, even though the Party led the largest trade union federation, SOBSI. Apart from a short period of industrial militancy in 1960, when the PKI was testing its ability to influence the government by radical pressures, the Communists' efforts on behalf of the industrial workers were almost completely reserved for political ends in broad conformity with government policy. Nevertheless, the PKI was considered the most active intervener on behalf of workers' interests. See Lance Castles, *Religion, Politics, and Economic Behavior in Java* (New Haven, Conn.: Southeast Asia Studies, Yale University, 1967), pp. 81–84.

with patron-client ties organized along the santri-abangan axis, class lines of identification were weak and submerged. Local village officials could serve, and did serve, as objects of competition and conflict, but these too tended to take on religio-cultural coloring and in any case to offer only minimal opportunities for radical mobilization in a system where preponderant power lay in the hands of urban officials outside the villagers' reach. Although the PKI sought to implant class consciousness among its worker and peasant followers, and succeeded to some extent in doing so, social and political circumstances combined to delay and dilute the impact of this effort, while the PKI masses, at most partly detraditionalized, tended to interpret even those PKI policies that were directed toward tangible political goals from the standpoint of their traditional belief system. For its own reasons, the PKI leadership itself found it necessary over time to lend power to this traditionalist image of itself.

The directly political constraints on a radical, class-based strategy were no less compelling. The Indonesian Communists, unlike their counterparts in China, Vietnam, Burma, Malaya, and the Philippines, had failed during the World War to marshal nationalist sentiment and traditional sources of revolt under the umbrella of a resistance movement against the Japanese invaders, and, largely as a result of this failure, they were not equipped with nationalist credentials or resources built up in armed struggle when the nationalist revolution broke out in 1945. With these handicaps, they not only failed to gain hegemony of the national revolution, but in the aftermath of the Madiun affair emerged from that revolution to face the challenges of independence weak, divided, and with their nationalist claims sullied. Ranged against them was an ongoing political system dominated by a coalition of high-status nationalists and Islamic elites backed by a substantial army, which, if resistant to civilian control, was at the same time strongly anti-Communist. For the Aidit leadership, both armed agrarian revolution and militant political opposition based on radical elements in the towns and countryside were ruled out by the stark fact of Communist weakness in relation to the government forces.* This conclusion was fortified by the August 1951 episode,

---

* Aidit specifically rejected the path of armed guerrilla struggle in his report to the Fifth Congress of the PKI in 1954. See D. N. Aidit, *Problems of the Indonesian Revolution* (Bandung: Demos, 1963), p. 254. The PKI leadership seems never to have contemplated it seriously thereafter. A policy of urban opposition was implicitly ruled out by the character of the PKI's united national front strategy.

when the union militancy that led to heavy punitive measures against the PKI was not matched by an equal willingness on the part of the PKI's followers to rally to its aid at a time of travail. Ever present, too, in the minds of the PKI leaders was the memory that violence had cost them dearly in the past, whereas the Republic, whatever its deficiencies, was in part the product of their struggles and sacrifices; the PKI could not lightly put itself in the same position as the Moslem insurgents of the Darul Islam or of secessionist groups by openly seeking its overthrow.

By 1952 the PKI leaders had come to the conclusion that they must pursue a gradualist, moderate, and flexible strategy, hinged upon an alliance with one of the major parties and the extraction from this alliance of maximum freedom to pursue the amassing of grass-roots support in the expectation of ultimately opening wider political options for themselves.[35] The strategy was cast in the form of a united national front program, following Soviet-disseminated precedents, but it very soon came to have a distinctive Indonesian flavor imparted by sociocultural and political conditions. In 1952, the governmental alliance between the two largest parties, the PNI and the Masjumi, began to break down, and the opportunity the PKI had been waiting for appeared. The PNI began to adopt a more radical nationalist stance congenial to the PKI, which eagerly offered the PNI its parliamentary support in return for an understanding that its legality would be respected so long as it did not engage in anti-government agitation or the promotion of class conflict.[36] The effect of this informal agreement was to bind the PKI as a junior partner to a party that was strongly Javanist, based on the prijaji class and its partly Westernized offshoots, and basically conservative in social policy and outlook. Thus the Communists were driven by social and political circumstances toward an adaptation to traditionalist forces.

As the PKI's support began to grow within the framework of the alliance strategy, the accommodationist pressures on it intensified. The Party's appeal spread out rapidly into the villages of central and east Java, whereupon the influence upon it of vertical alignments and other traditional ties became more salient and inhibiting. In locales with a record of radicalism not already preempted by Islamic groups, the PKI effected its penetration via detraditionalized elements, particularly village youth partially uprooted by the disorders of the occupation and revolutionary war.[37] Through their agency, the Communists agitated against traditional barriers to change and reform, such as authoritarian *lurah* (headmen) and their subordinates. Once again, however, the pace of these "vanguard" villages had to be adapted to the requirements of overall strategy and the lower order of militancy displayed by the mass of villagers influenced by the PKI, so that the promotion of agitational politics was increasingly replaced by an accent on welfare programs and the nationalist consensus that united the Communists and the PNI-led governments from 1953 onward.

In other villages in which the PKI established its influence in the 1950's and early 1960's and in which there was no easy line of access via existing radical tendencies, the Party relied mainly on traditional patron-client and authority relationships to establish its organization. Some Communist patrons were recruited through kinship links with urban leaders attached to the Communist cause, others through their desire to advance their interests against competitors in the village domain with the support of a well-knit and active Party machine, and still others through their opposition to Islamic groups in the village power structure.* Later, as the PKI's moderate and patriotic stance and the respectability it gained by association with the government and Sukarno became more pronounced, important village patrons were attracted by the Party's image and its promise of providing them with opportunities for personal advancement.

The PKI was aided in its effort on the village front by the failure of the PNI to use its base among the prijaji and *pamong pradja* (state bureaucracy) to bid for active peasant allegiance; as an urban elite used to taking rural acquiescence for granted, the PNI leadership failed to appreciate the extent to which disruptive change and alarm at Islamic resurgence had induced the abangan Javanese to look for a social and cultural champion with greater dynamism and concern for their interests. The PKI, with its activist organization and under-dog's drive, began to fill the village vacuum to an ever-increasing extent at the expense of the PNI, as the 1955 general elections and

---

* Generally speaking, Communist patrons seem to have come from among well-to-do and frequently "modern" (in terms of occupation and urban orientation) villagers. See Selosoemardjan, *Social Changes in Jogjakarta* (Ithaca, N.Y.: Cornell University Press, 1960), p. 176; Robert Jay, *Javanese Villagers* (New Haven, Conn.: Yale University Press, 1969), pp. 422–28; and Jay, *Religion and Politics in Rural Central Java* (New Haven, Conn.: Southeast Asia Studies, Yale University, 1963), pp. 98–99. With all hypotheses concerning Communist bases among the peasantry, however, it is well to bear in mind Sartono's caution that "Studies of Indonesian political developments since Independence contain scarcely any sustained analysis of the rural population." "Agrarian Radicalism in Java," in Claire Holt, ed., *Culture and Politics in Indonesia* (Ithaca, N.Y.: Cornell University Press, 1972), p. 71.

the 1957 regional elections amply illustrated.[38] In the process, the PKI took on more and more the role of a broker for abangan cultural values.

Whatever the Party's view of its aims and tactics, the humble peasant could be excused for interpreting its actions on his behalf through traditional spectacles. The PKI vigorously promoted the radical nationalist issues that fed the restlessness and disorientation of large numbers of small-town dwellers and villagers, and by so doing stirred in them that sense of oneness of the *rakjat* (common people), which was deeply rooted in Javanese culture.[39] It reminded the villagers of the glories of Indonesia's (non-Islamic) heritage, and insisted both on the relevance of this heritage to the transformation of society and on the superiority of Indonesian ways to all foreign ways.[40] It defended communal customs and rights, interpreted in the broadest possible sense, against "feudal" demands and capitalist inroads alike.[41] It administered indefatigably to the elementary needs of the peasants, just as the righteous kings and officials of popular legend had done in the past. It propounded the promise of a better future for the common people, after the style of jealously preserved treasures of folklore and prophecy. With respect to the prijaji, the PKI adopted an attitude in accord with the ambivalence of the abangan toward their superiors, giving critical support to "progressive" officials and organizing concerted opposition to "reactionary" ones.[42]

This combination of appeals by the PKI, outstandingly successful as it was in the parliamentary period in building up the Party's numbers and mass influence and in maintaining the government's general benevolence toward it, did not bring the Communists appreciably closer to their goal of national power; their relationship with the PNI was predicated on that party's right to determine the central political issues. PNI plans did not include extending to the PKI a share in government office or introducing any significant part of its social program. The government's main attention was given to international affairs, and to the promotion of the interests of the political-bureaucratic-entrepreneurial cliques with which it was closely connected. Yet the PKI could not press the claims of its clientele beyond moderate limits without endangering the alliance that had brought it its gains, especially since the anti-Communist parliamentary opposition was sufficiently strong to represent a continual threat to its security. The Communist appeal perforce had to be cast increasingly in terms of the nationalist temper which it shared with the government, and which exercised a strong hold over the minds of the political public.

By 1957 the Communists' electoral advances had raised a distinct possibility that they might capture an absolute parliamentary majority in the general elections scheduled for 1960. But they can hardly have counted strongly on being given the opportunity of coming to power in this manner, especially in view of mounting dissatisfaction with the way in which the parliamentary system was functioning and the army's determination to take a hand in the country's political future. At the same time, given the political constraints on the PKI and the diffuseness of its bases of support, the Communists had little alternative but to play a waiting game. The longer the Party waited, however, the more strongly its ideology and policies came to reflect the weakening of its class stand and its accommodation to neotraditionalist modes. The PKI's material by this time was beginning to reflect the actuality, rather than the doctrinal symbolism, of its political position. It stressed what was common among the interests and outlooks of the parties forming the government alliance, thus reinforcing the disposition of both the elite and the political public to see the contours of politics in aliran terms, and prompting its own followers to view its role as one associated with rather than sharply distinct from that of the other parties in the alliance.* Similarly, by seeking to accumulate the largest possible membership and following from all strata of society as a means of pressing its claims to a share in office while at the same time deterring repression, the PKI was impelled to broaden the ambit of its appeal along nationalist lines and to downgrade specifically class demands.[43]

## The PKI and Sukarno

With the PKI denied political initiative, and discontent and rebellion mounting in the country, Sukarno and the army moved in to oust the parliamentary regime and inaugurate the system of Guided Democracy. Once again, fundamental social change was deferred by the device of institutional rearrangement and a still stronger resort to neotraditional and nationalist appeals. At the same time, Sukarno undercut the drawing power of the PKI's radical program by introducing measures to cushion strategic sectors of the society against economic distress. The PKI, caught between the Scylla of the Sukar-

---

* This point should not be overstressed, however. Part of the PKI's appeal lay in the fact that it was simultaneously identified with popular government policies and dissociated from unpopular government actions and behavior.

no-army partnership and the Charybdis of the anti-Communist regional rebels, could see no option other than to follow and adapt its coalition strategy to the new dispensation, with Sukarno as the key figure in its moves to gain security for itself. Inescapably, this decision dictated a further and more extensive accommodation to traditional forces.

Sukarno cast his magnetic appeal in images that evoked widespread devotion from Indonesians of all kinds, but more especially from the Javanese abangan heartland. The themes he stressed—completion of the national revolution, national unity, Indonesian identity, anti-imperialism, democracy with guidance—were all traced in an imagery striking deep chords among this aliran. National pride was fostered by an idealized picture of the Javanese past drawn from historical legends and the *wajang* plays, in which the traditional emphasis on harmony, the mediation of conflict by consensus practices, mutual assistance, and a sense of order fused with his modernist ideas into a dynamic conception of a future harmony based on the values of the Javanese personality and culture. His populism was modern in its promise of some participant role to all citizens, but it was also cast in an authoritarian mold justifying the leadership of the common people by their traditionally sanctified leaders. His formula for national unity through Nasakom,* while notionally according equality to all *suku* (nationalities), in practice promoted unity on Javanese terms by repressing regional ambitions and strengthening the role of the political center; it accorded first place in politics to expressive leaders and native sons with traditional merit or its pretense behind them; it strengthened the bureaucracy, a Javanese instrument, as against local and regional autonomy.

Sukarno's analysis and prescription were pertinent enough to account for their appeal. Their implicit authoritarianism was if anything welcomed by a great part of the political public, for whom the novel practices of Western-style democracy had proved deeply disenchanting, and who were ready to follow a leader with charisma and a panacea. As such, Sukarno's most pronounced appeal was to the alienated public and the abangan, who read into his ideas (with his aid) a sign of the return of a strong and just ruler who would restore the stability and prosperity of the realm and make of the *kraton*, or palace, a center of power and attraction. His ideology embraced mil-

---

* An acronym signifying the unity of nationalist, religious, and Communist groups in society.

lions in the psychological rewards of integration into the national crusade and the struggle to achieve utopia.[44]

The almost contrived blend of past- and future-oriented elements in Sukarno's ideology was duplicated in the structures of his political system. Many of the formal institutions of the regime were outwardly modern and "progressive" in character, although all were imbued with the mystique of national oneness and elite guidance that derived from powerful precolonial traditions. Of greater significance, however, was the fact that other structures, and particularly the informal modes of decision-making that were more crucial than the institutional panoply, were more obviously traditionalist in inspiration and style. The powerful court circle, the modern prijaji at the head of bureaucratic units converted to appanages, the imposition of loyalty tests as the main criteria of worth—these, along with the formal restoration of the *pamong pradja* to something approaching its former glory and power, resounded with echoes from the Javanese imperial past.[45]

By underwriting Sukarno's ideology and political structure, glorifying his national role, and agreeing to conform with his guidelines for the country, the Communists were drawn toward a more explicit accommodation to tradition. There were sound pragmatic grounds for their alliance with the President, who represented their strongest protection against the army and their best hope of obtaining a strategic position in the power apparatus without a fight they could not expect to win. At the same time, there were more than pragmatic reasons that made their coming together possible and mutually agreeable. As we have noted, both Sukarno and the PKI struck their strongest chords among the same clientele—the lower urban strata caught between the influences of tradition and modernity and seeking a strong *pegangan* (mooring post) to attach themselves to and give them their bearings; and, more extensively, among the abangan of central and east Java, who longed for security and the promise of a better life. It is not stretching things too far, then, to suggest that both Sukarno and the PKI, in not very different ways, were seeking to define and articulate the needs and interests of these strata, providing the urban public with a utopian message to counter its psycho-cultural disorientation and the abangan with an assurance that their material interests would be met and their cultural values defended against the challenge of orthodox Islam.

The subtle but significant shifts that took place in PKI ideology in this period indicate the degree to which the Communists were adapting to the new dispensation at the expense of doctrinal fidelity. In 1960 class was explicitly downgraded in favor of national alliance against external foes and their domestic allies.[46] The undifferentiated rakjat became the repository of all national virtues and aspirations, which ran in a continuous line from the precolonial past to the socialist future.[47] The aliran, rather than class groupings, became the central pivot of the united national front program.[48] Instead of class forces, the spectrum of Indonesian society was conceived in the political, and sociologically neutral, categories of "right, left, and middle forces."[49] The struggle for the overthrow of imperialism in Southeast Asia and the entire world, rather than the fight for the internal reconstitution of Indonesian society, became the central preoccupation of PKI policy and action.*

In the absence of direct evidence, we must draw on the general principles of cultural analysis to hypothesize how the peasantry of Java interpreted the joint Sukarno-PKI ideological mélange. If traditional agrarian radicalism can be said to have contained four characteristic symbolic features—"millenarianism, messianism, nativism and belief in the Holy War"[50]—then the ideational link is certainly highly suggestive. In catering to traditional millenarian urges, Sukarno promised a "just and prosperous future" whose contours resembled a modern version of the blessed kingdom of legend. The PKI, likewise, if it refrained from spelling out the ultimate nature of its constantly reiterated goal of a Communist future, nevertheless made two things about it clear: it would build on (non-Islamic) village traditions of mutual help, cooperativeness, and consideration; and it would bring the common people the abundance of food and clothing, freedom from crushing tax burdens, and equal distribution of cultivated land foretold in millenarian prophecy.[51] The messianic element was provided by Sukarno's charisma alone, at least at the national level; though Aidit's picture was to be found in quantity in every Javanese village penetrated by the PKI, and the personalization of his role was promoted assiduously by the Party propaganda machine, he never achieved anything approaching a mystical aura even among those strongly influenced by the Communists. Nativism was fully supplied by the radical anti-imperialist, antiforeign themes

* This orientation was justified in doctrinal terms by the claim that Indonesia remained a "semicolonial" country even after the nationalization of most foreign capital in 1958.

that loomed so large in both Sukarno's ideological armory and that of the Communists. Finally, with campaigns to liberate West Irian and confront Malaysia, the Javanese received their secularist, non-Islamic variants of the Holy War, and its potency as a source of support for the regime and the Communists is attested to both by the enthusiasm engendered by the crusades and by the alarm shown by anti-Communists at the strides made by the PKI under their umbrella. Whatever the intentions of the PKI leadership (and this can only be conjectured as ambivalent or, more likely, acquiescent), it would appear that the Communists were providing the radical proclivities of the peasants with ample fuel in terms consonant with their traditional aspirations and outlook.

Yet despite the convergence of the ideologies and, to a large degree, the interests of Sukarno and the PKI, there was an implicit conflict between their respective aims. Whereas Sukarno, as the incumbent source of power and embodiment of prijaji values, was seeking to integrate the Javanese and Indonesian masses into a socially conservative order managed and directed by their superiors, the Communists, as power aspirants and articulators of lower-status abangan values, were trying to mobilize the masses for the supercession of that order. In practice, however, the conflict was vitiated to a considerable degree by certain facets of Sukarno's temperament. Although he jealously safeguarded his own prerogatives and probably considered that not much in Java ought to be different, his romantic Jacobin leanings led him to value the appearance, if not the reality, of change and "revolution." The PKI appealed to him intrinsically for its dynamism, as well as for its usefulness as a counterweight to army power, and he was content to let officeholders be harried and humiliated if a case could be made out for their halfhearted commitment to the causes he held dear. This gave the Communists opportunities for resisting the consolidation of the new "bureaucratic capitalist" power structure by constant campaigns and agitations against "reactionaries" and "hypocrites" in high places.* With all their political guerrilla tactics, however, they were unable to arrest the tide of socioeconomic processes, and found power coalescing in a civil-military bureaucracy strongly antithetical to their ambitions.

At length the PKI felt constrained to make a partial break with

---

* These "retooling" campaigns reached a crescendo during the PKI's "revolution on all fronts" in the first nine months of 1965.

consensus politics and the neotraditional pattern in order to prevent the doors to power being firmly closed against them on Sukarno's death or incapacitation. Fortunately for them, in September 1963 Sukarno's anti-imperialist crusade precipitated a head-on clash with the Malaysian Federation, backed by British armed forces, and Indonesia succumbed for a time to a heady radicalism, which the President embraced more fervently than any other. The PKI decided on a "revolutionary offensive" to isolate and crush the anti-Communist forces and throw off the chains keeping them from a share in governmental office.[52] The hub of the PKI effort was directed toward the peasantry, and the chosen issue was land reform. Seizing on the government's failure to implement vigorously its own 1959 and 1960 laws on the subject, the PKI in the early months of 1964 launched a campaign of "unilateral actions" by the peasants, seeking to carry the laws into effect through organized strength and in some respects to go further toward applying the PKI's more radical demands in this respect. The Communists succeeded in promoting widespread actions of this kind, particularly in central and east Java, with the object of impressing their allies and deterring their enemies by demonstrating their control of the countryside. They aimed in the course of the campaign to radicalize and discipline their own followers so as to create a class-type force of poor peasants and landless laborers committed to their cause.[53]

## The Destruction of the Communist Party in Indonesia

Ultimately, however, the campaign was a failure. Ranged against the Communists, despite Sukarno's benevolence, were the local military and civilian officials, the PNI branches and their supporters, and, most violently, the Moslem religious leaders and their santri following. For all the radicalism that could be called on by the PKI in areas of the key provinces, it was no match for this array of opposition. In the end, the abangan peasants, reared on a moderate political diet, led in many cases by men of wealth and substance in the villages, fearful of Moslem intransigence, and confirmed too often by the PKI itself in their traditional cultural disposition toward harmony and deference to authority, recoiled from the furor their activities stirred up and obliged the PKI to beat a careful and screened retreat.[54]

Here was substantial evidence that the PKI had failed to bridge vertical lines of social division, to implant a tough class consciousness in the rural poor, or to transcend the basis on which its phenomenal mass support was based—its ability to protect its clientele from official and Moslem wrath and bring them benefits without undue cost.

From that time onward until its obliteration in the aftermath of the 1965 coup attempt, the PKI confined its efforts to shift the balance of power to maneuver within the metropolitan superculture of Djakarta, replacing its fire-eating village mass campaign of 1964 with ineffectual efforts to establish People's Science Institutes to combat superstition and fatalism.[55]

The coup attempt itself has been persuasively interpreted as primarily a nativist reaction on the part of mystically tinged abangan military officers from central and east Java against the unpatriotic, self-interested, and corrupt behavior of their high command—offenses both to the interests of the line men and to traditional concepts of the purity and devotion of the *kesatria*, or warrior.[56] Whatever the final verdict on this episode, if there ever is one, there is no doubt whatsoever that the ensuing massacre of Communists and Communist sympathizers turned into one more round in the repeated conflict between the santri and the abangan, with the santri, backed again by the forces of government and army, having a still more signal victory than they had had in 1948.[57]

The response of the Communists to their sudden precipitation into the void, if more fully explored, would likewise sound traditional resonances, judging by what little we do know about it. The seeming belief of the PKI leaders that their proximity to the ruler, in this case Sukarno, would save them, is fully consonant with Javanese notions of power. What the Communists forgot, however, is that a decayed power center is already a powerless one. The extraordinary passivity displayed by most PKI activists and organizations in the face of their persecution, amounting in some cases to voluntary surrender to the authorities, betrays a like dependence on a disintegrated center, as well as a more deeply rooted peasant recognition that when the tides of the cosmic order run against you, it is useless to resist.

The decimation of the PKI left the neotraditional structures built up in Indonesia from the time of independence, and particularly after 1957, fundamentally intact and now reassertive. Though the Party touched hundred of thousands of Indonesians with a new spirit of dynamism and political modernity, its imprint was light overall and poorly distinguished from the official state ideology as a result of the compromises it had been forced into. The abangan peasants of Java

are still seeking a social and cultural champion. With the demise of
the PKI, they have been unable to find a more satisfactory alternative
than to vote Golkar* in 1971 as the only permitted protection against
Moslem pretensions,[58] and to seek sanctuary in Javanese mystical and
Hindu revival movements.[59] With the ever-increasing economic and
political pressures bearing down on them, these resources are liable
to prove all too ineffective to meet their needs, but the present regime
has anticipated any attempt to reorganize them politically by designating them a "floating mass," to be denied any direct political representation or participation.†

Unless and until Indonesian society crystallizes in more conven-
tionally modern forms of social structure and consciousness, the central paradox that afflicted the PKI must mark any potential successor
to it. The crux of this paradox was that the closer the Communists
remained within Javanese cultural lifeways, the greater the strength
and influence they were able to amass, but the weaker their power to
convert these resources into a revolutionary force. On the contrary,
the further the PKI moved away from these cultural underpinnings
by tapping radical and proto-revolutionary elements in the society,
the more it demonstrated the radicalism latent in Javanese society but
at the same time the greater became its vulnerability and isolation.
Never being in a position to put all its stakes on the revolutionary
road, the Party eventually fell victim to the cultural plurality and
vertical allegiances that are the mainsprings of elite dominance. The
conclusion seems inescapable that "*aliran* identification, while it provides a base of support relatively impervious to persecution by the
authorities, creates an enormous problem for any political movement
trying to mobilize for social revolutionary purposes, for it is extremely
likely that efforts at open class struggle will dissolve into communal
conflict."[60]

* Golongan Karya, the army-sponsored equivalent of a state party, which routed
the Nationalist and Moslem parties in the 1971 general elections.

† The "floating mass" doctrine, enunciated by government spokesmen following
the 1971 elections, prohibits all political party organization (including Golkar) below
the *kabupaten*, or regency, level. Thus it effectively debars direct political participation by the residents of small towns and villages.

# The Ethnic and Urban Bases of Communist Revolt in Malaya

MICHAEL STENSON

The Malayan Communist Party (MCP) was founded and flourished in the mainly Chinese populated towns of British Malaya during the 1930's and 1940's.[1] Although its political influence among Chinese may well have reached a peak during the Japanese occupation, when it led the Malayan People's Anti-Japanese Army (MPAJA) from the fringes of the interior jungles, its long-term political strength continued to lie in urban areas, where the civilian branch of the MPAJA, the Malayan People's Anti-Japanese Union (MPAJU), appears to have exerted a considerable authority during the occupation.* It is significant that instead of continuing to fight an anticolonial independence campaign from the relative security of the interior in late 1945, the Party returned as quickly as possible to the familiar milieu of the towns and the organizational tactics and forms that were associated with them.[2] Moreover, when the Party again resorted to armed operations from rural bases in mid-1948, it did so less of its own volition than as a response to its inexorable exclusion from significant influence in urban areas by the colonial government. The subsequent failure of the MCP's armed revolt underlined the Party's exceptional dependence on urban bases for successful political action.

---

* It was the MPAJU that maintained contact with the bulk of the Chinese population, whether squatting in rural areas or remaining in the towns. Its cadres collected subscriptions, which were close to taxes, gathered supplies and intelligence, recruited members, and exterminated traitors. G. Z. Hanrahan states that the MPAJU political campaign resulted in the fourfold growth of the MPAJA and the creation of a "sympathetic mass base numbering hundreds of thousands." He also alleges that the extermination of traitors was pursued with considerably more vigor than the anti-Japanese campaign. *The Communist Struggle in Malaya* (New York: Institute of Pacific Relations, 1954), pp. 36–37, 40, 44.

In the Malayan context, however, it was the identification of the towns with the Chinese that was crucial both to the origins and to the outcome of the revolt. For although elements of class conflict were essential to the MCP's genesis, the full magnitude of the Party's support derived more from its ethnic than its class base. The ghetto character of Malayan towns and the ethnic nature of Party membership were sufficient in themselves to preclude successful revolution. Whereas both the Chinese Communist Party and the Vietminh were to benefit from enforced resorts to the countryside, where they consolidated peasant support in areas relatively safe from enemy attack, the MCP was driven into a countryside that most of its members had always feared and where it was isolated from its bases of urbanized Chinese support by hostile Malay peasants. There could be no possibility, in Malaya, of the successful application of the strategy of mobilizing the peasantry to surround and isolate the towns. These were already surrounded by hostile, if as yet not very highly politicized, Malay peasants. The political assault on the towns was not to begin until the late 1960's and was to take the shape of an ethnic attack on the bastions of Chinese radicalism.

The pluralistic nature of Malayan society was indeed to be a major impediment to the development of any interracial and national political movement. A "glorified commercial undertaking rather than a 'State,' " British Malaya was established on the constitutional fiction of Malay sovereignty and the reality of the efficient organization of immigrant peoples for predominantly commercial ends. The term British Malaya itself was merely one of administrative convenience, bearing no connotation of a national state and covering over the continued existence of nine protected Malay States and three colonies. Rule was essentially limited and largely indirect. The social styles, commercial roles, and resident locations of the three main racial groups, Malays, Chinese, and Indians, were clearly and for the most part exclusively defined. Such distinctions not only inhibited the development of proto-national mass-based political movements, but indeed contributed to the polarization of politics along racial lines. Thus when the MCP espoused the objective of an independent, multiracial Malayan Republic in 1935, it adopted a political cause that altogether lacked the sanction of tradition on the one hand, and that was socially and politically at least twenty years ahead of its time on the other.

The appeals of Communism were to be limited, in the main, to one racial group, the Chinese, who maintained throughout the period of British rule a high degree of sociopolitical autonomy. Such autonomy derived initially from the existence of the tightly knit secret societies. Originally anti-Manchu in motivation and always of political significance, the secret societies were essential for the rapid expansion of Chinese tin-mining in the hostile environment of the nineteenth-century Malay States. Following the decline of the previously all-embracing societies at the end of the nineteenth century, a decline that related to rapid social and economic change as well as to British controls, Chinese autonomy was largely a matter of economic specialization and cultural exclusivity, on the one hand, and of British unwillingness or inability to promote social or political integration by the granting, for example, of common citizenship on the other. Autonomy was to be, in this respect, both an asset and a major disadvantage in the development of revolutionary politics. The important asset of the veil of secrecy was to be more than counterbalanced in the long term by the inability to appeal to a potentially national constituency.

However, relative sociopolitical autonomy should not be equated with sociopolitical cohesion, for the Chinese in Malaya never constituted a truly cohesive political or social community. British intervention in the administrative affairs of the Western Malay States was intimately related to the internecine warfare of competitive secret societies. Even after the decline of the secret societies, Chinese in Malaya remained divided by the primordial loyalties of dialect group and clan, and then in the course of the twentieth century by additional class and other social divisions. The political significance of the spread of a common language, *Kuo yu*, after 1917 was to be severely limited by the fluidity of what remains a society of recent migrant origin, a society primarily oriented to the acquisition of wealth and status. If the plural society as a whole was a medley, so too was Chinese society itself.

In the light of considerations such as these, the inherent difficulties of extending Communism within Malayan Chinese society in particular will be readily appreciated. For all that, Communism developed as a significant force among the Chinese in the 1920's, throve in the late 1930's, and reached a peak in the mid-1940's, when it appealed at times not only to many Chinese, but also to some Malays and Indians. Moreover, political and military defeat in the 1950's was never absolute.

*Early Sources of Communism in Malaya*

The early sources of Communism in Malaya are regrettably obscure. Although there are hints of Communist ideological influence prior to 1920, specifically Communist agitation seems to have made no headway until after the Chinese Communist Party (CCP) and the Kuomintang (KMT) agreed to join forces in 1923. Thereafter the Malayan Revolutionary Committee of the Kuomintang, assisted from 1925 by agents sent by the Far Eastern Bureau of the Comintern, set about serious organizational activity. Their efforts seem to have been concentrated on two groups that were most susceptible to the influence of radical, utopian political ideas and were often most directly affected by rapid social change—students in Chinese schools and laborers in the larger industries, especially those in urban areas. Both groups were to be the mainstays of Communist support in subsequent years. Young schoolteachers, who were commonly recruited direct from China, were also effective in the propagation of Communist concepts.

In this respect two features require emphasis. The first of these was the continuing influence of the tradition of secret-society-type autonomous and antigovernmental activity. Such traditions were to be essential for the survival of Communism in the face of efficient police and security service supervision. In a broader sense it is probable that the ritualistic and secretive aspects of Communism contributed to a coalescence of modernity and tradition, providing a continuity that gave Communism considerable appeal during periods of often bewildering and unsettling change.[3] The second important feature to be borne in mind was the coalescence of modernist political influences emanating from China with rapid internal social change in Malaya. The enthusiasm of the Malayan Chinese response to the cultural and political awakening of China was undoubtedly related to specifically Malayan factors, such as the decline of the previously all-embracing, exclusive secret societies, the rapid opening up of the west coast hinterland by mining and plantation enterprise, the growth of large industrial-type establishments in the towns, greatly improved communications, greater mobility of labor, and, above all, the rise of towns that served not only as commercial centers but also as centers for the dissemination of modern ideas. It was through the Chinese schools, which were first erected by Chinese clan, guild, and district associations in the major towns, as well as the Chinese newspapers, reading rooms, dramatic associations, old boys associations, commercial guilds and associations, and labor unions, all of them urban-centered, that modernist Chinese concepts were most effectively propagated in the 1920's, 1930's, and 1940's.

The intensity of the impact of such concepts related also to the fact that urbanization in Malaya was unusually extensive and essentially Chinese. By the late 1920's the west coast was covered with a host of lesser commercial and distribution centers, sufficient in size to maintain most of the organizations mentioned above and thus playing a vital role in the dissemination of modern concepts into otherwise isolated rural areas.*

As Malayan Chinese society became more permanently established in the 1920's and 1930's, as the sex ratio improved, and as the nuclear family became increasingly widespread, the role of the local town became even more important.[4] It was to the nearby town that the children of the migrants went for their schooling; it was to the town that they increasingly went for entertainment; it was in the town that the young congregated on holidays; and it was to the dynamic new associations there that the socially and politically active were attracted.

This is not to suggest that the dissemination of what one may loosely term modernist concepts and forms was steady and unfettered. It was not. The world trade depression, with its associated mass unemployment and the resulting repatriation of thousands of laborers, halted the rising tide of change in the 1920's and obliged most who remained in Malaya to concentrate on survival. The impact in Malaya of the KMT-CCP split in 1927 eventually contributed to the formation of the MCP in 1930 but in the meantime probably retarded the process of political mobilization as a whole. Even more disruptive were the controls of a colonial government increasingly worried by the effects of Chinese politicization in theoretically sovereign Malay states. An efficient security service closely controlled KMT activities in the

---

* In 1931 in the Straits Settlements, the Federated Malay States, and Jahore (comprising two small islands and a strip of land less than 400 miles in length, and, with the exception of isolated Pahang, rarely more than 30 to 40 miles in width) there were two towns of between 25,000 and 50,000 inhabitants; eight of between 10,000 and 25,000; nine of between 5,000 and 10,000; and 80 of between 1,000 and 5,000. The percentage of the Chinese population classified as urbanized was also at the high levels of 73.8 for the Straits Settlements, 38.5 in the Federated Malay States, and 21.9 in Johore. C. A. Vlieland, *British Malaya: A Report on the 1931 Census* (London: Crown Agents for the Colonies, 1932), pp. 44, 48. In the towns of the main commercial areas of the west coast, the Chinese comprised 66.5 per cent of the total urban population in 1947. In Singapore they comprised 78.7 per cent.

1920's, and captured and banished the top leaders of the newly formed MCP from mid-1930 to mid-1931.[5]

## The Creation of a Mass Base, 1937–1942

Revival began only with the easing of the depression in 1933–34, and truly widespread politicization only with the full-scale Japanese invasion of China in July 1937. Virtually all politically active Chinese then united behind the British-sanctioned China Relief Funds Movement, which set up China National Salvation Associations in almost every town with extraordinary speed.*

As in China, it was via the anti-Japanese campaign that the Communists were to achieve their greatest successes. And yet one must ask why this was so in a society not subject to KMT misgovernment or as yet directly affected by Japanese attacks and occupation, a society that was, moreover, geared above all to the rapid acquisition of wealth, that was supposedly socially mobile and upward moving. Most writers have suggested that the answer lies in the strength of overseas Chinese patriotism. And some support is given to this thesis by the otherwise inexplicable conversion of the commercial magnate Tan Kah Kee to at least verbal praise of the Communist cause after visiting China in 1939.[6]

However, one should not discount the intensity of social and class conflict among the Chinese of Malaya as an essential precondition for the extraordinarily rapid extension of Communist organization and influence in the years 1937–42. The immigrant society was by no means one of open opportunity for the great majority of the Chinese population. Rags to riches stories were much publicized but were increasingly the rare exception rather than the rule. Such groups as the Hailams from Hainan, for example, remained bound to menial employment as servants and coffee-shop employees by virtue of Hainanese custom and non-Hainanese prejudice. They were to be consistent supporters of a Party that promised to end their social and economic subordination. Chinese society tended, indeed, to become increasingly stratified along socioeconomic lines. In the early part of the twentieth century there emerged increasingly clear distinctions between Straits-born Chinese (many of whom were English educated)

---

* The British sanctioned the movement because of their concern at continuing Japanese aggression. The decision was to be of the utmost importance for the MCP, which gained a brief respite from police harassment.

and those born on the mainland, and also between Chinese *towkays*, or businessmen, and Chinese laborers. Such distinctions were by no means parallel or absolutely defined, and continued to be cut across by traditional loyalties to clan, guild, or language group. Class divisions did not emerge as exclusive or dominant categories. Nevertheless, popular awareness of the existence of distinctive interests was clearly indicated by the widespread trend toward the decline of the inclusive guilds and the formation of separate employers' and employees' associations in the 1930's.

It is interesting, in this respect, that though Communist ideology seems to provide a peculiarly convincing explanation of the situation of the Chinese in British Malaya, the Party's purely ideological appeal does not appear to have been especially strong. Would-be members tended to be attracted to the MCP because of its patriotic efforts in the anti-Japanese campaign or because of its attempts to improve the lot of Malayan workers. Study of Communist ideology was a consequence rather than a cause of Party membership.

Far more significant was the appeal of a generalized anticolonial, anti-British, utopian patriotism to Chinese-educated youth.[7] Lacking opportunities for employment in the colonial administration or large European companies, young Chinese were especially frustrated during times of depression and unemployment. Alienated from the "respectable" Chinese leadership by virtue of their poverty and their inability to speak English, they turned readily to radical political causes as an outlet for their energies and a means of improving their lot. Leadership of the Party itself was characterized by its youth, the Secretary-General being only thirty-three years of age and the members of the Central Executive Committee averaging only twenty-six years of age in 1940.[8] Youth was both a consequence of the appeals noted above and a guarantee that appeals would continue to be made to the same group. Extreme youth was in fact to characterize Party leadership into the 1940's because of the added factor of a very high attrition rate as the result of large-scale arrests by both British and Japanese.

The success of the MCP in the years 1937–42 seems to have related, in short, to its effective association of appeals to Chinese patriotism with measures to ameliorate concrete social and economic grievances. Under the respectable aegis of the China National Salvation Associations, whose public leadership was dominated by conservative KMT supporters, the MCP set about organizing the Chinese workers and the students in the Chinese schools. The result was a host of associations, ranging from reading rooms and dramatic clubs to rickshaw pullers' associations, which were directed in their activities by the secret, Communist-controlled Anti-Enemy Backing-Up Societies (AEBUS) and disciplined by its Traitor Elimination Corps. A common technique was coupling the collection of China relief funds with didactic plays and lessons or with demands for higher wages, better conditions, and shorter hours. Between 1937 and 1940 the AEBUS took up the cause of most groups of Chinese urban workers with considerable success, particularly in the years 1939–40. Chinese patriotism and the material improvement of workers' wages and conditions were thus deliberately and inextricably interwoven.*

Moreover, by means of the Special Affairs Committee of the AEBUS an increasingly effective control was exercised over the whole of Chinese urban society. Operating very much in the fashion of the secret societies and employing various forms of intimidation, such as tarring, ear clipping, and destruction of property, the enforcement sections of the Special Affairs Committee collected subscriptions, gained concessions for workers, and ruthlessly supervised the boycott of Japanese goods.[9]

The extent of the MCP's organizational influence in rural areas and the smaller towns should not be overestimated during the period prior to 1942. There is, for example, little evidence of truly widespread and consistent organization of the Chinese who worked the tin mines and rubber plantations. However, in the main towns, and particularly in Singapore, the Party was plainly a force to be reckoned with. Far more revealing than its own claim to the leadership of over 70 unions in the Singapore General Labor Union was the fact that in the face of an imminent Japanese invasion of Singapore, the British turned to the illegal and detested MCP for assistance in providing labor for essential services and volunteers for guerrilla squads and local defense corps.†

* The Pan-Malayan General Labor Union, one of the MCP's most important fronts, was relegated to the background in favor of relief funds committees that acted as trade unions among Chinese workers. Membership of the AEBUS was officially estimated at 30,000.

† The British would never have turned to the MCP had they not believed it was the only group that could guarantee the cooperation of Chinese labor. Within the Chinese Mobilization Council set up in December 1941, and comprising KMT, China Relief Funds, and MCP leaders, the crucial labor and propaganda sections were

## The Japanese Occupation—a National Liberation Campaign Foregone

Having served to demonstrate the depth of existing Communist influence, the Japanese occupation thereafter created an environment in which the MCP rose to preeminence as the most effective antagonist of the hated Japanese and the protector of specifically Chinese communal interests.

The second aspect was undoubtedly to be of major advantage to the MCP, particularly in the brief interregnum period immediately following the Japanese surrender on August 15, 1945. But at the same time it highlighted the basic distinction between the Communist struggle in China and that in Malaya. Whereas the one was potentially national, the appeal of the other was at best limited to not much more than 44 per cent of the population of the country in which it was based.[10] It was this factor as much as any exclusively geographical factor, such as the relative lack of isolated refuge, that severely circumscribed the military and political effectiveness of the MCP-controlled MPAJA and MPAJU.[11] Although the MCP had extensive influence among the Chinese population, its identification with Chineseness was to prohibit any possibility of widespread support from Malays.* The creation of liberated zones and the leadership of a credible national independence movement were precluded by the fact that Chinese rural dwellers were invariably interspersed with and often numerically dominated by antagonistic Malays or culturally alien Indians. Malaya lacked what has been termed revolutionary space in social as well as purely geographic terms.

One wonders whether such considerations influenced the MCP's decision not to oppose the British return with a national liberation campaign in August 1945. Whether they did or not, there can be little doubt that the decision was an act of political realism.[12] On the one hand, it may have seemed an opportune moment to stage such a campaign. Politicization and anticolonialism were at a higher level than ever before. Moreover, effective armed resistance to a forcible reoc-

---

headed by MCP representatives. By Hanrahan's estimate, the Party had no more than 5,000 members at that time, but sympathizers and members of front groups numbered many thousands. *Communist Struggle*, pp. 25–26. Although the MCP's influence in rural areas was probably small, it should be noted that the Party cooperated with the British in forming a guerrilla force of about 300 in remote Kelantan.

* Malays commonly referred to the MPAJA and the MCP as "the Chinese Party" in 1945.

cupation might have united the main racial groups in common antagonism to a reoccupying force that could hardly have avoided hurting the interests of all groups at one stage or another. Rehabilitation of the economy and administration and the promised amelioration of the people's immediate suffering may well have been greatly delayed and popular resentment turned against an unimaginative, authoritarian, colonial British Military Administration. But on the other hand were certain immediate realities: the possibility of an advantageous British-MPAJA agreement to cooperate against the Japanese and then in restoring order, a well-armed British invasion force based in nearby India and capable of landing men at any part of a long narrow peninsula, and the existence of unprecedented racial antagonism, which had manifested itself in violent Sino-Malay clashes even before the MPAJA took over control of many towns in the interregnum after the Japanese surrender. MPAJA trials of alleged Malay collaborators, predictions that the country would be liberated by the Chinese army, and assertions that the Chinese intended to run the country thereafter, brought racial feeling to a peak of intensity. Indeed, violent racial clashes in which many lives were lost continued until mid-1946. A communal bloodbath was a far more likely eventuality than a united anticolonial struggle.

## The Peaceful United Front Policy

In lieu of an immediate, armed national liberation movement, the MCP reverted, not without some dissension, to its prewar policy of mobilizing popular support by means of a variety of front groups, this time far more openly and on a far larger scale. The main assumptions on which the policy was based were a degree of cooperation from, or at least toleration by, the British administration, the existence of popular political awareness based on a substantial working class capable of leading a powerful radical movement, and British willingness to introduce electoral politics and to grant independence in the not too distant future. The basic strategy was that of the peaceful united front, in which the MCP itself was to form and directly control most of the constituent organizations.*

* These assumptions were never set out in Party documents but may be deduced from public statements during the period. Both the tactic of the united front from above and that of the united front from below were employed, depending on the group. In the case of the Malayan Democratic Union, for example, the MCP deliberately encouraged the development of what it hoped would be a broad-based nationalist party appealing to the traditional leaderships of all races and only indirectly

The united front was developed and extended with extraordinary speed and effectiveness. Between August and October 1945 the Party set up People's Associations in most towns and many villages. Between October and December 1945, Women's Association, New Democratic Youth League, and MPAJA Ex-Comrades Association branches were set up throughout the country. In the same period General Labor Unions were established to serve almost every section of the work force. The Party also openly sponsored the formation of the democratic nationalist party, the Malayan Democratic Union, in December 1945 and January 1946 and was to play a leading and probably decisive role in the formation of the All-Malayan Council of Joint Action (AMCJA) in December 1946 for the purpose of arousing popular support behind demands for a more democratic constitution. By such means the Party exploited and generated an unprecedented politicization among non-Malays. With the important exception of Malay opposition to the new Malayan Union constitution, the MCP directly controlled or was closely associated with every major political movement in the immediate postwar period. It undoubtedly constituted by far the best organized political party in the country.

## *Flaws in the United Front Strategy*

However, from the first there were signs of serious weaknesses in MCP strategy.

First, the British never granted the MCP the political latitude it had hoped for. Thus, the People's Committees that were elected by the People's Associations between August and October 1945 and that initially exercised considerable administrative authority were denied recognition and were soon severely discouraged by the British. By February 1946 plans for an all-Malayan conference of People's Committees had been dropped, and most committees had been quietly discontinued. The MPAJA was disarmed and disbanded in December 1945, the MCP's request that it be included in a Malayan self-defense force being ignored. The General Labor Unions were denied official recognition, and every attempt was made to minimize their influence on the work force. Allegedly subversive newspapers were banned, and a number of MPAJA leaders were tried and jailed for handing out

---

influenced by the MCP. In the case of the Malayan Indian Congress, by contrast, the Party, though accepting the existence of a racially based party and cooperating with it in the campaign over the constitution, adamantly refused to share leadership of Indian labor with it.

summary justice to alleged collaborators. An attempt to stage a countrywide stop-work demonstration on February 15, 1946, in protest of such repressive measures, in support of the MCP's new "United Racial Emancipation War Front of all races in Malaya," and in celebration of the British humiliation over the fall of Singapore was effectively checked.

Moreover, in May 1946 the British gave way to concerted Malay pressure against the Malayan Union constitution. Secret discussions with representatives of the Malay Rulers and the United Malays National Organization resulted in the recommendation in December 1946 of an even more restrictive constitution than the already restrictive Malayan Union.[13] Far fewer Chinese and Indians were to be eligible for citizenship; elections were explicitly ruled out for the near future; the prospect of independence was quietly relegated to the background. Despite widespread protests organized by the AMCJA, the Pusat Tenaga Ra'ayat (PUTERA), and the Chinese Chambers of Commerce in 1947, the Anglo-Malay proposals were adopted with minor modifications and the new Federation of Malaya inaugurated in February 1948.

At the same time, the British set about the systematic reimposition of their administrative authority. The reorganization of the police in 1946 steadily reduced the capacity of the MCP and its front groups to exert their own coercive authority. Above all, the British decided in midyear to insist on the registration and supervision of all trade unions, a policy that was deliberately and effectively enforced from late 1946 to early 1948 in order to break centralized Communist control of the trade union movement. The significance of this policy, the full implications of which did not become apparent to the MCP until late 1947 or early 1948, cannot be underestimated.[14] For the Pan-Malayan Federation of Trade Unions (PMFTU), as the Pan-Malayan General Labor Union had been renamed in late 1946, was by far the most popular, powerful, and wealthy of the MCP's front groups. Without the centralized authority of the PMFTU there could be no hope of successfully pursuing a peaceful united front policy.

Second, so keen were the MCP leaders to return to the towns in 1945 that they neglected the solid core of Chinese squatter support which had been so important to them during the Japanese occupation and which was to be of decisive importance again in 1948. Even the MPAJA Ex-Comrades Association was not as vital as it should have been, failing to maintain a cadre of disciplined volunteers ready for coordinated action at any time.[15] The MCP thus placed almost total reliance on the open urban struggle, making little attempt to maintain a capacity for simultaneous armed operations in rural areas. When the Party began seriously considering armed revolt in late 1947, it experienced unanticipated difficulties in arousing former MPAJA members to their old militant enthusiasm.

Third, the MCP overestimated the size, political awareness, and potential power of the "working class." Its assessment of the "working class" as comprising 30 per cent of the total population was both an exaggeration and an oversimplification in a society where nearly 50 per cent of the population relied on traditional agriculture, where employment patterns were extremely variegated, and where many workers, such as tin miners and rubber plantation workers, were located in relatively isolated rural areas.[16] As the General Labor Unions demonstrated in 1945–46, tin miners, plantation workers, and even hawkers, dance hostesses, and bar girls could be aroused to militancy and persuaded or obliged to join unions in exceptionally favorable circumstances. However, it was quite another matter to maintain membership and enthusiasm when conditions were much improved (partly as a result of the General Labor Unions' agitation), when employers were much more determined to resist union demands, when the labor shortage was less acute, and when the government was ever more closely supervising union activities. Even in the relatively favorable environment of the Batu Arang coal mine, where the workers had far longer experience of unionization than most, the consolidation of a militant General Labor Union could not be accomplished in the less favorable circumstances of middle and late 1947.

Moreover, the mid-1940's witnessed the beginning of a trend that was to be of major long-term significance, the entry of increasing numbers of Malay peasants into the industrial labor force.[17] After 1948 there was never again to be widespread employer concern about labor shortages. The effect was twofold: first, to reduce the bargaining power of the existing labor force, and second, to delay indefinitely the formation of a truly united, self-conscious working class. The significance of this trend was to become apparent in April-June 1948, when a number of strikes aimed at disrupting the economy and laying the groundwork for more militant action were broken by the introduction of Malay workers.[18]

Fourth, despite some signs of top-level recognition of the need for Malay support, the grass-roots cadres of the MCP and its front groups remained actively hostile to, or contemptuous of, Malays.[19] The directness of the challenge to Malay lives, authority, and ethnic survival that MPAJA and MCP activities posed in the interregnum period of 1945 was the primary cause of the exceptional Malay politicization in opposition to the Malayan Union proposals under which most Chinese would become citizens. In effect the MPAJA succeeded in doing precisely what broader MCP strategy dictated that it should not do. It had helped polarize politics along ethnic rather than class lines. Thereafter, MCP attempts to create a "United Racial Emancipation War Front of all races" in February 1946, to create Malay trade unions, and to draw Malays into radical peasants associations were doomed to failure. A few Malays of the Malay Nationalist Party and its associated organizations were prepared to cooperate—albeit uneasily, after much bargaining, and as a separate group (PUTERA)—in the 1947 campaign for a more liberal constitution. But for the most part the ethnic lines were rigidly drawn prior to the 1950's. Indeed, the MCP, appealing as it did to grass-roots Chinese cultural and political loyalties and standing for Chinese as much as class struggle, was peculiarly ill-fitted to develop strong intercommunal ties. Very few Malays were enrolled in its ranks, and those who were tended to be as despised by Chinese cadres as they were by their own communities.* And the formation of a broad, multiracial left-wing alliance was to founder in the 1940's, as it did again in the 1960's, on the rock of Malay refusal to accept Chinese-educated leadership.†

Fifth, prolonged pursuit of the united front strategy during a period when economic conditions were improving and governmental authority was being reestablished contributed to two other disadvantageous trends. On the one hand, it permitted the reemergence of rival leader-

---

* A predominantly Malay Tenth Regiment was formed as part of the MCP-controlled Malayan Races Liberation Army in February 1949. Its support, however, was based on the distinctive features and discontents of the Malays of one state, Pahang. When subjected to strong counterinsurgency pressure later in the year, it quickly disintegrated. In recent years Malay support for the MCP has revived and grown in Pahang, Trengganu, and Kelantan, and a Malay has been appointed chairman of the Party's central executive committee.

† In 1965 the radical Socialist Front alliance of the Labour Party (then led by Communist-influenced, Chinese-educated activists) and the Party Ra'ayat broke up after six years of uneasy cooperation. Deep-seated Malay cultural antagonism toward the Chinese-educated and intense Malay fears of Chinese political domination seem to have been the crucial factors. Conservative alliances between English-educated and less culturally distinctive leaders on the basis of Malay political supremacy have proved far easier to form and sustain in the short term.

ship within Chinese society. Chinese commercial groups, initially discredited because of their abdication of leadership or active collaboration during the occupation, and forced to accept and pay for MPAJA or MCP "protection," quickly exploited the reassertion of British authority to revive their own political organizations. Thus, the KMT was revitalized in 1946, as was the disciplined, paramilitary San Min Chu I Youth Corps. In July 1946 there was a concerted attack by KMT elements on MCP front groups in the Sitiawan district of Perak.[20] In the course of 1947 many Chinese businessmen used the San Min Chu I or secret society gangs to protect themselves from labor union demands. By 1948 rival conservative Chinese leadership was so well established that a major objective of the militant MCP policy adopted in May was the elimination of the bourgeoisie and of KMT elements. Soon after, there were violent clashes between KMT and MCP groups in a number of places during KMT celebrations of Chiang Kai-shek's inauguration as first constitutional president of China.

The existence of rival leadership within Chinese society was to be of fundamental importance in a situation where the MCP proved incapable of appealing to many Malays, or over 40 per cent of the population. It was, for example, to contribute to the failure of the campaign for a more liberal constitution, for whereas Malay opposition to the Malayan Union had been universal, Chinese opposition to the Federation of Malaya proposals was deeply divided. Conservative, old-established Chinese leaders refused to join the Malayan Democratic Union because of its Communist associations, and the Chinese Chambers of Commerce probably refused to join the AMCJA for the same reason.[21] Although the Chambers did join in the protest to the extent of cooperating in a major protest *hartal* in October 1947, they were prepared to come to terms when the British proved adamant and to accept seats on the new Federal Legislative Council.

On the other hand, many MCP cadres either became totally involved in open front activities or became disillusioned at the lack of progress toward explicitly revolutionary goals. In the case of some PMFTU leaders, for example, British officials believed they had so identified with the organization they had created with such success, and had become so impatient of MCP demands on it, that they were prepared to turn to violent revolutionary activity in 1948 only under extreme duress.[22] In fact, the MCP had encouraged them to pursue the constitutional struggle for two and a half years by that time and had openly discouraged militant strikes between mid-1947 and April 1948.[23] It is hardly surprising, then, that some took MCP policy at its face value and proved unwilling to revert to the discomforts of guerrilla warfare. At the same time, there is evidence of continuing dissension on the part of militant cadres who had always opposed the policy of a peaceful united front.[24] Some of them persisted to win the day in March and May 1948, but it is probable that others became disillusioned and defected.

Sixth, such trends related to the MCP's fundamental tactical problem. Having adopted the broad strategy of the peaceful united front, how was it to maintain and extend popular support when economic circumstances were improving and in face of an increasingly unsympathetic and restrictive British administration? Above all, how and when was it to use its popular support for the transition to more openly revolutionary politics?

## The Problem of Transition to Revolutionary Politics

The first attempt to resolve these tactical problems was made in February 1946, within a few days of the formal ratification of the peaceful united front policy at the Plenary Executive Committee meeting of January 22–27, 1946. The "Letter to the Brethren of All Races in Malaya from the Central Executive Committee of the Malayan Communist Party on the Realization of the Compendium of Democracy" explained that because of the "fascist" and "reactionary" policies of the British the Party was obliged to enunciate a new program. It had concluded that it was both necessary and propitious to begin an anticolonial independence movement in which the MCP itself would provide the leadership for the "United Racial Emancipation War Front of all races in Malaya." The appeal was directed to all groups and parties, which were promised the right to criticize and maintain their organizational independence. The "Letter" insisted that the "All Peoples Anti-Fascist Strike is not to put into practice Communism in Malaya but rather to effect first of all the total emancipation and independence of the races."[25] However, when the British served warning that any attempt to use the strike weapon to coerce the administration would be suppressed with the full power of the government, the MCP backed down. The one-day work stoppage that was to be held on February 15 as a protest demonstration was called off. The United Racial Emancipation War Front began with a tactical retreat in the face of superior strength.[26]

Having eschewed open revolt for the time being, the Party responded to British firmness by retreating further into the background in an attempt to make itself less exposed to British police actions, while at the same time granting its front groups an air of greater independence. MCP offices, which had commonly been shared with, or had stood alongside, those of the New Democratic Youth League, the Women's Associations, and the General Labor Unions, were closed down in all except the major towns. Subsequently, every attempt was made to conceal MCP leadership or influence on the various groups. Leadership of the united front was to be disguised.

The open united front groups continued to expand rapidly. The General Labor Unions, or Federations of Trade Unions as they were later called, utilized enhanced popular awareness in a time of exceptional economic hardship and social confusion, calling and enforcing more strikes than at any other time in Malayan history, winning major concessions for most groups of workers, and enrolling a claimed membership in the Malayan Union of 263,598 in April 1947, or slightly over 50 per cent of the total work force. The AMCJA-PUTERA also succeeded in staging a series of rallies culminating with the hartal on October 20. Never before had the MCP possessed such widespread support, whether direct or indirect.

But many within the Party were discontented at the lack of revolutionary fervor, and some may well have appreciated the superficial and exposed nature of much of the new support the Party had apparently gained. A few may have begun to consider the fundamental problem of the transition to revolutionary politics, a transition that appeared all the more difficult in the light of the Party's retreat from open leadership of the united front and of increasingly effective British controls. Doubts such as these may well have contributed to growing concern about the loyalty of the Party's Secretary-General, Lai Teck, and to his defection prior to the Executive Committee meeting of March 1947.[27]

In any event, none of the MCP leaders appear to have had a convincing answer to the Party's dilemma. Lai Teck's successor, the youthful Chin Peng, served as acting head of the Party until March 1948, when his position was confirmed; he is believed to have spent much of his time seeking the advice and possible support of foreign

Communist parties.[28] Party leadership, which had always been characterized by inexperience and lack of incisive analytical and tactical skills, was more inexperienced and indecisive than ever. Meanwhile, from the end of March 1947 the Party deliberately subordinated all other activities to the waging of the struggle for a more liberal constitution. Trade union militancy was discouraged, partly in order to concentrate on the political struggle and partly in order to persuade government authorities that the Federations of Trade Unions were moderate, responsible, and deserving of official registration and recognition. Both campaigns were misguided, demonstrating the lack of decisive strategic direction by the MCP during a crucial period of about one year. Success in either case would merely have gained the MCP a more secure position within the existing constitutional order while providing it with little more opportunity for radical political action, thus magnifying the problem of making the transition from legal to revolutionary politics.

In the event, neither campaign achieved its object. By November 1947 the failure of both should have been apparent to any moderately acute observer. By February 1948, when the Federation of Malaya was inaugurated and when the payment of subscriptions to unregistered Federations of Trade Unions was banned, the writing was on the wall for all to see. The twin foundations of the peaceful united front policy had been completely undermined. Instead of operating in a political environment where the relatively free play of political forces was permitted and where progress toward responsible electoral politics was rapid, the MCP and its front groups found themselves on a steadily constricting political stage with no prospect of rapid expansion in the future. The formation of the AMCJA-PUTERA had represented a last-ditch attempt to reverse the tide of political change. Its failure to embody a sufficiently united front, and thereby to induce significant changes in official constitutional policy, meant the removal of an essential precondition for the effective pursuit of a peaceful united front policy. At the same time the centralized authority of the MCP's main mass movement was being inexorably undermined. If the Party's intelligence organization had been even moderately efficient, it would have known that the British were already preparing for the final destruction of the PMFTU. The MCP could no longer avoid facing up to the contradictions in its own policy.

Two broad alternatives then remained open to the Party. It could accept the elimination or destruction of its main front groups, and thus the loss of most of the tremendous gains in mass support achieved over the previous two and a half years, and retreat further into the background, salvaging what it could. Or it could resort to armed revolutionary action in which it could exploit the mass support it had so carefully nurtured and much of which yet remained under its influence. In the long term, the former tactic may have been well advised, permitting the MCP to harbor its existing leadership resources, to retain most of its existing links with popular organizations, and to wait for more favorable circumstances before reverting to open mass action.[29] In the short term, however, it was totally unacceptable to youthful Party activists who were imbued with revolutionary enthusiasm and could not have accepted what would have appeared as yet another ignominious retreat in the face of imperialist aggression.

At this stage, internal and external pressures coincided: on the one hand, the onset of the Cold War was associated with an atmosphere of crisis in which revolutionary Communism confronted resurgent capitalism, and on the other, the successes of the CCP seemed to demonstrate that the democratic revolutionary forces were the wave of the future. In light of the continuing debate regarding alleged Soviet "instructions" to revolt, remitted via the Calcutta conferences of February–March 1948, it is necessary to emphasize this coincidence of internal and external trends. Whether actual "instructions" were sent or not (and I am of the opinion that it is unlikely they were), the essential point is that the new Soviet interpretation of international trends made sense in the light of Malayan events.[30] The thesis that reactionary capitalist forces were ruthlessly intent on crushing all democratic revolutionary groups and regimes in an attempt to achieve absolute international dominance, and its corollary—that militant revolutionary struggle was essential if resurgent capitalism was to be defeated—fitted in perfectly with Malayan experience.

The Party therefore finally formulated clearly militant strategies at its March and May plenums in 1948. But here again it is necessary to note some qualifications. Many accounts of the period, including my own, have referred to an MCP decision to revolt.[31] In fact, the fullest available summaries of the resolutions passed at the two plenums indicate that though eventual civil war or armed revolution was anticipated, no specifically revolutionary program was prepared. C. B. McLane's summaries of the three resolutions of the Fourth Plenum of March and the 12-point "plan of struggle" of the Fifth Plenum of May are the most detailed and are substantially the same as those of

J. H. Brimmell.[32] McLane summarizes the three resolutions of the March conference as follows:

> The first was a political analysis of the situation in Malaya which concluded that inasmuch as the Labour Government in Britain had shown itself no different from its predecessors in protecting Britain's imperialist interests, the struggle for independence must *ultimately* take the form of a "people's revolutionary war"; the MCP stood ready to provide leadership in this glorious task. The second resolution, regarding political strategies, set two tasks before the party; reversal of the former "ostrich policy" of "surrenderism" (manifested in the dissolution of the MPAJA, the acceptance of self rule instead of full independence, and the party's retirement behind front organizations); and *preparation* of the masses for an uncompromising struggle for independence, without regard to considerations of legality. The third stressed the need to restore party discipline, after the laxness of the Loi Teck era.[33]

Both McLane and Brimmell suggest that a "plan of struggle" or "directive" was adopted at the Fifth Plenum in order to counter government reaction to the Party's more militant activities of April–May, in particular its encouragement of a wave of strikes.[34] As McLane summarizes the plan, it

> emphasized the primacy henceforth of illegal work; urged that trade unions be used as vehicles of anti-British propaganda; called for strikes specifically aimed at the disruption of the Malayan economy; demanded a more vigorous assault on the democratic parties and on the national bourgeoisie (including Chinese elements sympathetic to the Kuomintang); [and] proposed measures to attract intellectuals and peasants to the Communist cause.[35]

Brimmell and McLane seem agreed that the Fourth and Fifth plenums moved the MCP "closer to open rebellion" but did not in fact prepare an explicitly revolutionary program.[36]

In retrospect it seems clear that the MCP anticipated a fairly prolonged period of increasingly militant activity in which both legal and illegal tactics would be employed.[37] It is probable that it had not prepared a specifically revolutionary program at the time of these meetings, and that it did not prepare one until some months later.[38] And it is undeniable that many leading MCP members were forced to flee to the jungle in fear and uncertainty after the British outlawed the Federations of Trade Unions on June 13 and then declared a state of emergency throughout the Federation of Malaya on the eighteenth.

The MCP hastily resorted to open revolutionary warfare as a necessary response to unexpectedly severe British repression.*

The fact that the MCP was taken by surprise attests not only to the inadequacy of the Party's response to changes in governmental policy and practice, but also to the essential dangers of overreliance on exposed, urban-centered front groups as the basis for revolutionary action.[39] When it came to the pinch, the Party's most powerful front group, the PMFTU, could be banned, its offices raided, its administration completely disrupted, and a number of its leaders arrested. So effective were such government measures, so inadequate, if any, were PMFTU plans to go underground, so superficial was worker solidarity, that the wave of strikes that had preceded the ban collapsed within a mere 12 days. It was to be some months before the MCP could attempt to revive its links with the work force after the debacle of June. Meanwhile, government and employer controls had been so effectively enforced that the MCP was never again to emerge as a practical champion of worker interests in the Federation of Malaya.[40] Indeed, after June 1948 the MCP tended to prey on workers, who were forced to supply money and food or to carry goods, and to endure slashed rubber trees, sabotaged mines, and confiscated identity cards as a consequence of the Party's attempts to disrupt the economy and nullify governmental controls.

In the panic scramble for the safety of the jungle all the other open front groups were left to their own fate without leadership or guidance. The Malayan Democratic Union dissolved itself in protest at government repression, which made it impossible, the Party claimed, to carry on meaningful political activity within the law. The AMCJA-

---

* Three points stand out with regard to MCP planning. First, it was naïve in the extreme to expect intensified militancy to be tolerated by a colonial regime that had shown every sign of increasing repression. Second, it was unwise not to work out a more precise revolutionary strategy, including a draft timetable and responses to likely government action (a three-stage program culminating in the declaration of liberated zones in August 1948 was mentioned by Malcolm MacDonald, the Special Commissioner for Southeast Asia, but is not confirmed in subsequent official accounts and seems to have no firm foundation in fact). Third, it was absolute folly to assume that the revolutionary struggle was potentially national in aim and character. In this respect above all, the parochialism of the MCP or perhaps its essential ethnocentricity blinded it to the realities of Malayan life. The militant policy of March and May 1948 was adopted, it appears, in a mood of revolutionary fervor that paid little heed to previously acknowledged weaknesses in the Party's influence among non-Chinese. One suspects that the name Malayan Peoples' Anti-British Army, which was altered to Malayan Races Liberation Army only in late 1949, most clearly illustrates the driving animus but restricted scope of Party motivation and policy.

PUTERA, having agreed under strong MCP influence to donate $4,000 from its "fighting fund" to provide relief for striking workers in April 1948, simply faded away. The New Democratic Youth League and the Women's Associations also ceased activity.* No doubt the associations developed by means of such groups were to be useful for subsequent MCP recruitment, the distribution of propaganda, the collection of funds, and similar activities; the MPAJA Ex-Comrades Association was undeniably so. But it is noteworthy, first, that even in the case of the MPAJA, many members had to be coerced into going underground and, second, that such groups as the New Democratic Youth League, the Women's Associations, and the Ex-Comrades Association had never been at the center of united open front policy. Their membership had been relatively small, their appeals restricted almost solely to the Chinese, and their activities therefore of less public appeal and of a more secretive character.

After June 1948 the Party was obliged to revert to the techniques of the Japanese occupation period when urban support was relatively less important and more difficult to maintain. The control and support of Chinese rural squatters once again became a paramount concern.

The enforced reversion was in itself an adequate guarantee of the Party's failure. It was forced away from its areas of proven and preferred influence within urban Chinese society into rural areas where Chinese comprised small minorities in the midst of hostile Malay peasants. When the Chinese squatters were successfully relocated and isolated in a new village, as they were during the course of 1950–52, the Party's position became even more tenuous.[41] When the government succeeded, almost despite itself, in stimulating the formation of a stable, conservative, multiracial political alliance, committed to electoral politics and the attainment of independence, the Party's fate was virtually sealed.[42] That the Party recognized this is indicated by its attempt to negotiate a settlement in 1955 whereby it would be permitted to return to constitutional politics and its urban bases on favorable terms. The failure of those negotiations committed the remnants of the MCP to protracted guerrilla warfare fought spasmodically from the security of the jungles on the Thai-Malaysian border.

Having surveyed the origins of the Communist revolt in a largely chronological fashion, we may now examine the background to the revolt in the light of Chalmers Johnson's analytical framework.[43]

* The Malayan New Democratic Youth League, the MPAJA Ex-Comrades Association, and the MCP itself were banned on July 23, 1948.

First, between the end of the nineteenth century and the gaining of independence in 1957, British Malaya lacked a prevailing myth of social order. The official view that British Malaya was comprised mainly of sovereign Malay states, in which Malay custom and religion were to be scrupulously observed, became increasingly anachronistic with the influx of Chinese and Indian laborers and the development of the modern economy alongside of, but separate from, traditional Malay society. By 1931, when Chinese and Indians outnumbered Malays and other Malaysians in British Malaya as a whole, the myth had become all too patently meaningless. The consequence of Malay agitation for the decentralization of much more real power to the Malay state administrations, however, was the continued exclusion of Chinese and Indians from adequate participation in the colonial polity. Although large numbers of Chinese and Indians had settled permanently in the Malay states, they were still classified as aliens.

The presentation of the Malayan Union scheme in 1945, whereby most Chinese and Indians could become citizens, indicated official recognition of the need to involve all *de facto* permanent residents in a single polity. However, rejection of the scheme, consequent upon intense Malay opposition, and its replacement by the Federation of Malaya constitution, under which most Chinese and Indians initially remained aliens, illustrates the immense difficulties of integrating a plural society that lacked a convincing tradition of previous political unity. The Malayan Union aroused little support from Chinese because the prevailing myth of social order remained the acceptance of the regulation and altruistic guidance of the colonial power. Most politically aware Chinese rejected colonial rule, demanding representative, responsible self-government leading rapidly to independence. Malays were, by contrast, intensely fearful of any attempt to integrate the competitive Chinese into a common polity. And, in the event, the reaction generated by the fear of ethnic extinction proved to be infinitely more intense than Chinese demands for elections and self-government. Partly for this reason, partly because Malays expressed a strong desire to retain the buffer of colonial rule, and partly because the colonial administrators had already been antagonized and challenged by intense Chinese Communist agitation, the British gave way in mid-1946 and negotiated a secret settlement with the Malays.

As a result, the overwhelming majority of Chinese, though more firmly committed to Malaya than ever before, remained aliens in a society where Malay political supremacy within the context of the colonial regime was more firmly established than ever. The intense

Communist-led agitation of the postwar years culminating in the open revolt of 1948 was partially consequent upon the failure to provide most Chinese with constitutional avenues of political expression. Indeed, in many respects the revolt represented a radical ethnic, rather than a class, bid for power in a polity that recognized neither the culture nor the political aspirations of the Chinese.

One must note, however, the inherent difficulties in attempting to integrate such a society, difficulties that the MCP was itself to face in the attempt to create an alternative polity. That the British made no attempt to begin round table discussions involving all races in 1946 is undeniable. That such discussions would have succeeded is extremely doubtful, for the disparity of Malay and Chinese political attitudes and aspirations was greater than at any other time in Malayan history. On the one hand, Malays retreated to the security of traditional institutions and leaderships, stood united on the retention of the Sultans' sovereignty, accepted limited Chinese citizenship with reluctance, and adamantly refused to contemplate the prospect of open political competition by means of elections. On the other hand, active leadership of the Chinese was in the hands of young, Chinese-educated, chauvinistic, Communist-inclined radicals. Communication across the chasm between utterly divergent political aspirations and social styles would have been almost inconceivable.

In the light of existing racial tension, of exceptional politicization, of a nearby Indonesian independence movement, and of concurrent difficulties in India and Burma, one may understand why the British declined to risk the inevitable competitive political rallying, walkouts, provocative statements, and demonstrations that would have accompanied round table discussions. The choice, in all its stark reality, was the appeasement of the Malays, who had traditionally provided a secure base for imperial authority, or the risk of intensifying Malay politicization, the probability of a pan-Indonesian independence struggle, and the certainty of extreme ethnic tension. But the corollary of Malay appeasement was Chinese alienation and the possibility of militant Chinese anti-government agitation. In short, revolutionary activity of one form or another was probably inherent in the nature of postwar Malayan society.

Moreover, Chinese society itself, though retaining a high degree of autonomy, lacked social or political coherence, becoming increasingly differentiated in the course of the twentieth century. Despite the many inadequacies of the secret societies, their decline at the end of the nineteenth century left a political gap that was to be filled in the twentieth century by competitive political groupings—the KMT and the MCP—based on increasingly distinctive socioeconomic classes. The politicization of the Chinese-educated youth from the poorer sections of Chinese society was to be accelerated by a series of major social, economic, and political changes in the 1920's, 1930's, and 1940's—notably the nationalist awakening in China, the great trade depression, the Japanese invasion of China in 1937, the Japanese occupation of Malaya from 1941 to 1945, and the exceptionally fluid postwar situation. Yet in the colonial plural society they remained alienated with no possible avenue for the effective, constitutional expression of political aspirations, and often few enough avenues for the fulfillment of personal social and economic aspirations. Young Chinese students and workers therefore responded to the only party that took substantial and concrete measures to involve them in political activity and to ameliorate or resolve the major crises through which they lived—a party that held out, moreover, the prospect of a new utopian social order.

Finally, the Japanese occupation and the postwar period provided the MCP with an opportunity to build up a mass base that even included some Indian worker support. The exceptional social upheavals of the period, the disruption of established authority, the existence of extreme economic hardship, the creation of a new youthful leadership during the occupation, and the discrediting of the old, all provided the MCP with unusually favorable circumstances, particularly when the British failed to fulfill popular Chinese and Indian aspirations for a new postwar political order.

Such were the general preconditions for revolutionary political action. But revolt was not precipitated by the intensification of such factors. Dysfunctions within the political system as a whole were being markedly reduced by 1948. The major movements of population to and from the towns during and after the occupation had come to an end. Economic circumstances were markedly better than in 1946. Established Chinese and Indian leaderships were being restored. Youthful hopes of a new postwar political order had waned. The constitutional issue had been decided and had, moreover, been accepted by the more conservative Chinese and Indian leaders.

The resort to armed revolt came therefore not at the peak of popular frustration and political mobilization, but as the result of the specific frustrations of a radical minority. Popular politicization had

reached a peak in early 1947, when widespread strikes and agitation
against the proposed constitution coincided. Having failed to exploit
the opportunity, the MCP found itself being inexorably excluded
from substantial political influence by an increasingly restrictive colonial power.

It was in such circumstances that international events, notably the
atmosphere of militant Cold War confrontation and the successes of
the CCP, convinced an inexperienced, provincial leadership that what
was in reality an act of desperation was both necessary and timely.
Above all, international trends, as interpreted by the conference of
revolutionary youth and the Indian Communist Party in Calcutta,
seem to have contributed to an atmosphere of exaggerated revolutionary enthusiasm in which the Party was able to convince itself,
contrary to all experience, that decisive action would induce the
British to retreat from their restrictive policies. In the event, the
strikes of April and May 1948 precipitated further government restrictions and a hasty Communist retreat to the jungle. Unfortunately for the MCP, international events could exert no influence
whatsoever on the objective Malayan situation. Begun in disarray
and isolation from the Party's bases of mass Chinese urban support,
the revolt exposed the MCP as the leader of a minority group of
radical Chinese within a plural society where politically awakened
Malays regarded Communism as a specifically Chinese disease. The
MCP was doomed to stage a festering revolt which, in the absence
of fundamental social and political transformations, could never develop into a true revolution.

# Burmese Communist Schisms

JOHN BADGLEY

Placing the Burmese Communist movement in the context of the Asian Communist experience sharpens our insight into what is uniquely Burmese and what is generic to Asia. A second context, the Burmese historical experience under the monarchy and the British colonists, further explains the behavior of many contemporary leaders, including several key Party members, who were as captive of their culture and physical environment as were noncommunists. Here we deal not with speculation about motives, but rather with observed behavior patterns that persist, probably because Burma's agrarian milieu sanctions a kind of political protest comparable to, but not the same as, ideologically inspired insurgency.

To begin, let us mark the watershed dividing Asian parties linked to the Comintern in the 1920's from parties springing out of depression-motivated anticolonialism in the 1930's. The major countries, India, Japan, China, and Indonesia, all had significant movements by 1920. So also did Mongolia, and there was a growing movement among dissident Koreans in the Soviet Union. Intellectuals in the first Asian parties grappled in their publications with the theoretical struggles among European Marxists, thereby developing an important body of indigenous literature.[1] Nationalists-cum-revolutionaries could identify with their domestic Communist Party a decade later (or two decades in the Indonesian and Indian cases) during the final phases of anticolonial struggle. Some of this first-generation literature formed two fountains of influence, from China and India, which second-generation Communists in nearby colonies used to

Support for translations in this paper was received from the Translations Committee, Southeast Asia Regional Council, Association of Asian Studies, through a grant from the Ford Foundation.

legitimate their own views—for the issue of the legitimacy of one's revolutionary organization had become a significant problem in mainland Southeast Asia by the end of World War II.

The Indochinese, Thai, and Burmese had twice-born Communists, those who were first inspired by the European revolutionaries and the turned to the younger Chinese or Indian movement for their models.[2] The orthodox within the Comintern had established an authority pattern that paralleled the intellectual influence of the European colonialists. Continental Communist theorists shaped the thinking of their progeny in the colonies. That relationship prevailed among the mainland Southeast Asian revolutionaries until the mid-1930's. To that point, French writers and Europeans translated into French had served as primary sources for the Viets, Khmer, and Lao, and for the Thai as well. But after Mao's Long March, many of the Communists in the neighboring countries moved from the theoretical European to the more practical peasant revolution in China. Ho Chi Minh's service in Mao's Red Army is illustrative, predating by some 15 years the trickle of Burmese Communists along the same course.

While comparable, the Burmese case is distinguishable from the Indochinese case on two counts. Instead of French, the Burmese revolutionary leaders of the 1930's turned to English sources for their literature, and found in the British experience a weaker Communist Party and a more successful Socialist movement than in the European countries. Furthermore, they found in the Irish revolutionaries a practical model for their movement.[3] Marxism in Burma tended to take on a Fabian tinge, even among the mainstream revolutionaries in the Dohbama Asiayone, who led the protests in the 1930's and spawned the youthful leaders of the anti-Fascist People's Freedom League (AFPFL).[4]

Because Burma's educational system, like its government, was administered through the India Office until Dyarchy (separate rule) was introduced in 1937, the young revolutionaries at the University of Rangoon had close ties with the Indian student radicals at Rangoon's parent institution in Calcutta. Their "Asian Front" stretched across the subcontinent rather than into Southeast Asia or China. It was the members of the Bengali Communist Party of India (CPI), in fact, who initiated Comintern sanction for the fledgling Communist Party of Burma (CPB) in 1939, though they had to act through a Vietnamese Comintern agent stationed in Singapore.[5]

Although the CPB collapsed within the year, after the British imprisoned their leaders, the organization was resurgent a few years later as the center of Burman anti-Japanese activities. With British assistance the first contact was made in 1943 between the Burmese and Chinese Communists. Thein Pe Myint, a CPB liaison agent who had been arrested on arrival in Calcutta, was released after eight months' imprisonment and traveled to Chungking to meet with Chinese leaders, hoping to coordinate the anti-Japanese activities in the two countries. Chiang Kai-shek gave him short shrift; and Chou En-lai, though he listened with interest and expressed enthusiasm for the revolution, did not offer any support to the Burmese movement.[6] Almost a decade was to pass before the Chinese would take a serious interest in the Burmese Party. Meanwhile, the Burmese Communists survived their first major schism and, in 1948, set an insurgent course to which they still adhere.

## The Emergence of Postwar Factions

Factions are conventional within political parties, especially among Communists concerned with orthodoxy. However, in Burma the first division was ethnic, not ideological: when discussion cells first began to be organized in January 1939, two racially constituted groups were formed, one Burman and the other Bengali. Although they were merged at the First Congress, on August 15 of that year, the element of racial (cultural) distrust flourished later, when Burmese who had been trained in China returned to lead the purge of those who had ties with the Indian movement.

During the Japanese occupation and the struggle for independence the tension between these two groups was glossed over. Rather a fissure appeared that was more typical of other Asian Communist parties. The Party Chairman, Thakin Soe, who led the CPB (or Red Flag Party) during the dangerous years of Japanese occupation, believed firmly that imperialism must be fought militarily, and accused Aung San, the President of the AFPFL, of forsaking fundamental Leninist principles to negotiate with the British for independence. Rather than be a part of any coalition, Thakin Soe took the Red Flags underground, leaving Thakin Than Tun with the majority of Party cadres. Than Tun inherited Thakin Soe's status as leader of the mainstream faction and institutionalized his position by forming a second Communist Party, the White Flag Burma Communist Party (BCP). The Cominform was to sanction Thakin Soe's tactic in January 1948 at the Calcutta Conference,[7] but in 1946 his departure for the jungle was labeled "leftist adventurism" by Than Tun.

Thakin Than Tun had played a cautious political game since his student days. Although sympathetic to the formation of the CPB in 1939, he had not joined a cell; instead he had taken the post of Secretary in the Dohbama Asiayone, hoping thereby to have wider influence.[8] During the occupation, he served as Agricultural Minister in the collaborationist Ba Maw government, and only approached Thakin Soe about joining the Party and appointment to the Central Committee in late 1944. Never a theorist, Than Tun always worked as an organizer and depended on others to articulate his ideological views. His decision to forgo further compromise in the spring of 1948 was apparently compelled by the Socialists' refusal to grant him a portfolio in the government.

Than Tun had been a comrade-in-arms of Aung San and the others who formed the People's Revolutionary Party (PRP) as an alternative to Thakin Soe's CPB in 1944; his wife and Aung San's wife were sisters; and his friends of ten years' standing took over the government from the British. It must therefore have been a difficult personal decision to follow his mentor, Thakin Soe, into the jungle in May 1948. Indeed, had Aung San not been assassinated in 1947, Than Tun and the majority of the BCP probably would have been cajoled, as the PRP was, into joining the coalition cabinet.[9]

The AFPFL's policy of unity collapsed into empty slogans immediately after independence when the Socialists excluded representatives of the ethnic minorities (save for a British-trained Indian) from their Executive Council. First the Karens, then dissident Mons, Kayah, and Shans, and finally the Kachins turned against the Burman Socialists who controlled the AFPFL. The BCP followed suit, but used ideological rather than ethnic reasons for its protest. Through the remainder of 1948 and most of 1949, the government struggled to maintain control over the major cities and relinquished all of rural Burma to one or another insurgent group. Only the failure of the disparate insurgent forces to unite saved the government. The dissident groups on the Right were mistrustful of the Left, which included not only the two Communist parties, but also the 20,000-man People's Volunteer Organization (PVO), a body Aung San had created out of the Burma Independence Army in 1946 against the possibility the British would not fulfill their promise of independence.

After Aung San's assassination the leftist groups had little faith in his Socialist-sponsored heir, U Nu, who was of no greater stature than Than Tun at the time. The British commercial firms continued their operations, and the government was perceived by the Left as dominated by officials spawned in the Indian and Burmese civil services, satraps of colonial rule. Though the PVO too eventually split, the larger faction went underground and controlled most of central Burma for nearly two years. U Nu's appointment of General Ne Win as Defense Minister (and for a short period Prime Minister) in 1950 forestalled a large-scale conflict with the PVO, and it was then courted by some BCP leaders advocating a united front. But the mainstream of the White Flag Central Committee supported Thakin Ba Tin (Goshal), who contended in a widely circulated memorandum that the Party should strike for power with no further compromise.

The emergence of Goshal as the BCP's principal theorist accounts for the second major ideological schism within the Burmese movement. Once again, as with the earlier Thakin Soe split, the issue was strategy: should power be gained by compromise and political maneuver, or should the purity of the struggle be maintained so that the Party could legitimately claim to represent the revolutionary forces of Burma? Thein Pe Myint advocated compromise and circulated a memorandum to Central Committee members to that effect, but in the critical months of April and May, 1948, the Goshal thesis was accepted, and Thein Pe Myint found himself purged a second time (he had been purged from the Dohbama Asiayone in 1939).[10] Goshal wrote the justification for the purge, and as one of the original CPB founders (in the Bengali cell in 1939), stepped into the key role of Party theorist for Than Tun. He held that position until April 1968, when Peking returnees persuaded Than Tun to purge him at the height of the Burmese version of the Cultural Revolution.

Having taken the decision to pursue a rural peasant revolution, the Burmese finally turned away from their initial colonial link with Indian Communists and established a formal tie with the Chinese Party. The first contact was made in 1950, when two BCP representatives, Yebaw Aung Gyi and Bo Than Shwe, made their way overland to Peking. A full Party delegation followed in May 1953, when

> a group of Party leaders led by Thakin Ba Thein Tin, then Vice-Chairman of the Central Committee, left Burma for China via Myitkyina. There were 40 people in [this second group]. Their guide and contact was Chi Teng-chi. He was trained for clandestine activities in Burma by the Chinese Party and was an undercover agent in the Overseas Chinese Association in Burma.[11]

Ba Thein Tin was a district police officer from lower Burma who had joined Thakin Soe's CPB in 1944, then remained with the White Flags after the 1946 split. He rose to Politburo membership in 1948 and supervised Party communications within Burma and later with the Chinese, using equipment provided by them. He rose to even higher position when elements of the BCP went into exile in China, becoming Chairman of the Central Committee-in-exile. From his headquarters in Peking he supervised about 80 cadres, the bulk of whom were scattered around China for training in military, political, and management techniques. According to one of the Central Committee members:

> The exiled C.C. in China established contacts with Communist parties in 49 countries on six continents, and exchanged views with representatives from other parties. [It] also met and discussed problems with representatives of 27 brother Communist parties in bourgeois nations. [Further, it] took part in congresses of other parties when it had the opportunity to do so. It participated in 11 such congresses.

In an address to one such gathering, another member of the committee stated that some Chinese Communists saw the BCP as the cornerstone of the movement among Southeast Asian nations because, as one CCP leader had put it, the Burma Party "has been under the direct guidance and supervision of the Great Mao's thought." Though it was true that the Vietnamese were fighting against the Americans, the CCP man had remarked, they were not waging a class struggle. "They are merely fighting a defensive war for their nation. Moreover, revisionism has been increasing day by day in the Vietnamese and Lao Dong parties. It even overwhelms the highest leaders. That is the main difference between other parties and the Burma Communist Party."[12]

## BCP Approaches to Rangoon and Peking

There seems to have been consensus within the Central Committee about the decision to work with the CCP; certainly Goshal is on record as favoring the dispatch of Ba Thein Tin in 1953.[13] And there is no evidence of conflict during the 1950's in the biographies or memoranda published thus far about the CCP role as senior adviser in theory and strategy, as well as occasional supplier of light military equipment, communications materials, and funds (the last, via the Rangoon Chinese associations). Of particular significance is the Burmese acceptance of two major proposals for peace negotiations with the government, one in 1955, the other in 1963. It was the discussions following on the second proposal that led to the blood-letting among senior White Flag leaders in 1968 and the reconstitution of the Party in a new locale along the Yunnan border, distant from its previous base of operations.

Consider the first of these developments. Though the White Flag Central Committee rarely assembled because of increasingly effective surveillance by the Burmese army and police and the difficulty of communications between committee members scattered from the Shan hills to Arakan, a meeting was arranged in June 1955. This extraordinary effort was occasioned by the need to develop a response to U Nu's offer for negotiations and amnesty for most insurgents, a mark of his success in recent elections and of his confidence in his ability to out-negotiate the White Flags. Than Tun had received a wire from Peking outlining a counterproposal, which was to be approved by the Central Committee, but was not to be revealed as a policy formulated jointly by the Chinese and Russian parties. The committee duly approved it as the "Ending the Civil War and Obtaining Internal Peace Program."[14] An open letter to U Nu under Than Tun's signature, a response to the peace overture to be disclosed at a press conference, also reportedly originated in Peking.

Yebaw Mya, a ranking division chairman and editor of *The Last Days of Than Tun*, from which this information is drawn, notes that at this time BCP headquarters was fleeing from the government's military offensive, and that Than Tun simply typed the letter out as it came by wire, signed it, and sent it to U Nu by messenger. According to him:

> All communications and contacts between the BCP and the CCP were highly classified and not known even among Central Committee members. At the Burmese end, Thakin Than Tun alone controlled and managed the communications, which he submitted to the Politburo only when necessary. On the Chinese end, a Central Committee member in charge of Burmese affairs, chosen by the Chinese Party for that purpose, and Thakin Ba Thein Tin handled the arrangements. No other Burmese comrades were permitted to know of this. Therefore all other members of the exile BCP, in the earlier phase, were ignorant of the real relationship between the BCP in Burma and the CCP.[15]

The Internal Peace Program called for such great compromises by the government that the negotiations were certain to fail; indeed they never progressed to the stage where Than Tun could leave the jungle.

The second round of negotiations came in 1963, following Ne Win's second ascension to power in 1962 and his consolidation of a Revolutionary Council bent on nationalizing all industrial production and foreign trade. *The Burmese Way to Socialism* had been released as his ideology,[16] and a number of Marxist ex-insurgents were brought in as advisers to his colonels and brigadiers. The time was propitious for a direct confrontation, Peking determined, apparently believing that Ne Win would collapse under the combined weight of a unified insurgent front.[17]

The news of the Revolutionary Council's offer reached Peking on June 11, 1963. Allegedly only one senior member was at the BCP headquarters there; most of the other Party members were "participating in all kinds of socialist construction in various parts of China." Cell meetings were held immediately throughout China by the Burmese, and their views were submitted to Peking and digested by July 7, at which time Thakin Ba Thein Tin and Thakin Pu sent for Yebaw Tin Shein and explained the committee's plans.

> Taking advantage of the Burma military government's offer for negotiation, Yebaw Aung Gyi and Yebaw Tin Shein will be sent back to Burma's Party headquarters. In reality they are going back not for peace negotiation. They will be establishing contact with the Burma Communist Party. However, it must appear to outsiders that their mission is to negotiate peace. Most important of all is to recognize that the military government's offer for peace negotiations is, in fact, an attempt "to sell dog's meat for goat meat, fitting a deceiving goat's head to a dog's body."
>
> Thakin Ba Thien Tin and Thakin Pu discussed [the issue] with members of the group, instructing them to return with this line and gave detailed instructions. Moreover, owing to a change in circumstances, the number of people to be sent back home was increased [to 32]. On July 10, 1963, Chinese Communist leaders . . . gave briefings regarding ideological guidance and practical activities. . . .
>
> After briefings and necessary detailed instructions, a State dinner was given in honor of the group of exile BCP members who were chosen to return to Burma. At the dinner, top Chinese leaders toasted, drinking mai tai liquor: "Let's meet at liberated Rangoon soon." They prayed and toasted the same theme repeatedly.[18]

The BCP representatives returned in three groups. The first seven arrived in Rangoon on July 8 and immediately contacted the Chinese Embassy, where they were reportedly briefed about current developments in economic, political, and military affairs, and told how to pick up their daily instructions. They brought with them a political statement issued by Ba Thein Tin as a basis for discussion with leaders of other leftist parties. "In case the Government assassinated all seven members of the group, they intended to expose the assassination to the people by publishing the prepared statement, . . . charging the government with spoiling the peace, cherished by all monks and laymen alike. . . . The incident was to be made public throughout Burma and to the world simultaneously . . . to be determined at a time cued over Peking radio."[19]

A second group of returnees was flown to Rangoon on July 23 with instructions to travel immediately to BCP headquarters. Although the Burma army provided them security and transportation on August 11, the Chinese Embassy instructed the delegation to divide into two groups because of the danger of traveling together. One flew by helicopter, the other by an army Dakota plane to Prome, and then, again in two groups, they went on by helicopter to a village in the Pegu Yoma Mountains, 12 miles south of the headquarters.

> The first group of Peking returnees arrived at headquarters on August 13. Thakin Than Tun welcomed each returnee with an embrace, receiving all of them with tremendous emotion. Tears fell from his eyes. Prior to their arrival the headquarters camp was almost empty, with only 15 persons in residence. It was quiet, with little activity. The people living there spoke quietly and moved slowly, but when the returnees entered, the headquarters filled with different kinds of noises. It echoed with Thakin Than Tun's laughter, which broke out frequently.
>
> He welcomed the returnees as follows: "Your arrival at this moment saves the whole revolution, and all of us as well. We were like people with broken necks, so cursed that we could not even raise our heads. . . . I have tried to keep matters in the Party under control so as to prevent it from splitting into factions. If I had not prevailed it would have collapsed like the Alanni Party [Red Flag] long ago. Now your arrival represents a tremendous shot in the arm.[20]

In the next five days the Politburo prepared and adopted several resolutions on the negotiations, including proposals forwarded by the Peking returnees. Members of the preliminary delegation were chosen, and in this action the shift in power from Goshal and the Burma-based Politburo toward the Peking returnees was clearly marked. Yebaw Mya, a member of Goshal's faction, was slated to represent him on the delegation, but Than Tun and Aung Gyi, who were forming the group, rejected him, contending that the "people of Burma held the Peking returnees in high esteem. Even the militarist government and its army respected and valued the returnees."[21]

The delegation left for Rangoon on August 26 and during the first week of September met with every delegation that was to enter into the negotiations in the hope of arranging a united front. The third group of returnees, Ba Thein Tin and several aides, arrived on September 3 to take over the political and administrative responsibilities, and met throughout the month with every communal and ideological group. The returnees made Madanyata, an umbrella organization for a number of communal and underground parties, their prime target, reasoning that if the negotiations were conducted through that organization rather than by the BCP as a separate group, the status of the Communists would be enhanced even if the negotiations failed. These efforts were successful, and the first meeting with the government, held October 8, 1963, was conducted with Madanyata as the lone delegation.

Since the BCP headquarters had been cut off from some of its branches for as much as three years, the clandestine meetings between headquarters representatives and the other cadres were of enormous benefit. The discussions lasted a month and permitted various insurgent groups to meet with the press and move about freely (though undoubtedly under military surveillance) in Rangoon. One of the most poignant gestures was a press conference given by Thakin Soe, flanked by his latest wife and a large photograph of Lenin. However, there was nothing sentimental about the BCP program, which was planned in detail to recoup the erosion of the Party's authority over the past decade of isolation in the jungle.

## Schism Again

The consensus that had prevailed during the first decade of close collaboration with the Chinese was shattered by the events leading to the amnesty discussions of 1963 and the dominating role of the Peking returnees during the negotiations. The last negotiating meeting was held November 14, and ten days later, at a new BCP headquarters, the Politburo met to discuss why the peace talks had failed. Present at the meeting were Politburo members Than Tun, Goshal, Thakin Chit, and Yebaw Htay (a returnee); and Central Committee members Aung Gyi, Thakin Pu, and Bo Zeya (all three returnees).[22]

Than Tun argued that the government had effectively demanded their surrender and therefore was responsible for the failure. But

Goshal submitted that the BCP was responsible because Party dele-gates had gone to Rangoon "to expand underground organizations," and because the timing of a mass rally was such that it had seemed like blackmail to the government. Furthermore, he charged that Than Tun and the returnee Aung Gyi were directly responsible for these errors, and that Thakin Chit, who was sent to Rangoon to take charge of un-derground activities, "had an extreme leftist attitude and must bear no small part of the responsibility."[23]

The meeting ended in an impasse, as might be expected, and the contentions of the two sides were sent to Peking for resolution. Three months later the Chinese replied with "Our Opinion Regarding Peace Negotiations," a document marked secret and directed to the Central Committee only. As a cover, the document was purported to be "The Chairman's Original Proposal Regarding the Peace Negotiations." In essence, it stated that the Politburo was bankrupt politically fol-lowing the negotiations, and that a concrete political program would be formulated in Peking.

> Commencing with the fourth week of April 1964, the Burma Party received from Peking political, organizational, and military programs. As soon as they were received at Politburo headquarters the Party arranged for a Central Committee meeting. In June the Politburo met to prepare for the Central Committee meeting, but though it was termed a Politburo meeting, non-Politburo members—mere Central Committee members and Peking returnees—were admitted. Other Central Committee members from various regions of Burma were not permitted to participate. They accordingly discussed problems arising from the program dispatched from Peking well in advance.[24]

Relations between the two factions deteriorated steadily, to the point where Than Tun was meeting alone with the returnees, and Goshal was scrambling to hold his Central Committee loyalists to-gether in similar ad hoc meetings.

The conflict was one that Goshal could not win, and by the end of 1964 Than Tun had created a set of teams to tour Burma and launch the new Party program. Soon after, on March 25, 1965, he established a "college" for cadres under the guidance of Aung Gyi and Myo Tint. Taught exclusively by returnees and based on the training they had received in China, the Central Marxist-Leninist School offered classes in such subjects as ideology, economics, and party- and army-building.

A further step toward the dissolution of the Party leadership that had been in control since 1948 was taken at a Politburo meeting in

June 1965. "It was actually a scene of collision between two opposing
political programs advocated by two hostile camps. Thakin Than
Tun and Yebaw Aung Gyi led the camp that stood for amendment of
the 1964 program, and Yebaw [as he now called himself] Ba Tin
(Goshal) led the opposing camp."[25] Than Tun eventually obtained
passage of a completely new Party program by using teachers and
trainees of the Central Marxist-Leninist School to override the forces
Goshal could marshal. The niceties of the debate can be omitted here;
in essence it centered on Goshal's contention that Than Tun had vio-
lated procedure by creating a new program.

In 1966 Myo Tint, one of the two men in charge of the BCP school,
presented a major lecture on ideology, contending that previous Party
concepts of the type of states "accepted" by Marxist-Leninists were
incorrect: "There are only two types of states, Capitalist Dictatorship
and Proletarian Dictatorship. This concept is the real essence of
Marxism, Leninism, Stalinism, and Maoism. Thus, the goal of the
present people's democratic revolution must be none other than the
Proletarian Dictatorship [of Burma]."[26] This lecture caused great
ferment within the Party, since it was sanctioned by Than Tun's
forces. The thesis directly contradicted the 1955 Central Committee
resolution that the goal of "the national democratic revolutionary
forces in Burma shall be a joint dictatorship of four classes, with the
proletariat as the vanguard. The four classes are Workers, Peasants,
Petty Bourgeoisie, and National Bourgeoisie."[27] The notion that an
instructor in an ideology course who was not even a member of the
Central Committee could challenge a fundamental principle unani-
mously adopted by the Party leaders was appalling to those who had
constituted the mainstream of the BCP.

At a series of discussion meetings held under the aegis of Than Tun
and Aung Gyi, returnees argued against the 1955 policies, quoting
appropriate passages from the literature they had studied in China.
By the spring of 1968 Than Tun had marshaled sufficient votes within
the Politburo to purge Goshal and his followers. Goshal was executed
in April 1968.

In the following days a number of White Flags defected to the government, including Yebaw Mya and Thakin Ba Khet, who were to
edit the voluminous papers seized at Party headquarters when it was
overrun in late September. Than Tun was assassinated by an em-
bittered young Chin guard whose friend had been purged and executed after Goshal's death. The Party headquarters was reestablished

in the northern Shan States with Thakin Zin, a mild elder, as Chairman, and the Politburo reconstituted with Peking returnees in control. But the bloody purges did not cease. Throughout 1969, defectors reported ritual horrors in connection with the executions, such as women hacking at still-living opponents of their husbands and persons bathing their feet in the blood of the executed. Rituals of this type were never reported prior to 1968 and suggest either a marked deterioration in morale, even the sort of insanity associated with the last dynasty, or an extension of the worst excesses of the Cultural Revolution, or both.

## A Search for an Explanation

One can still do no more than speculate about the several causes of the repeated schisms in the Burmese Communist movement. The first, the division between Thakin Soe and Than Tun, seems to have arisen in Thakin Soe's compulsion to develop his own theory of revolution without consideration of what his own Central Committee and Communists elsewhere believed. Than Tun was a modest thinker, quite prepared to place himself in a subservient intellectual position to a theorist who could rationalize Party action in a grand fashion. Goshal performed that role prior to the linkup with the CCP; thereafter both men seem to have genuinely appreciated the contribution made by the Chinese to their cause.

For a decade the BCP fought a holding action, constantly on the move around central Burma to evade the army and never seriously challenging the authority of the government. Without the substantial forces of the PVO, which had surrendered by the mid-1950's, the BCP could never hope to seize even a district town for its capital. By 1963 the Party was no more than a pathetic band of insurgents hiding in the monsoon jungle, isolated and remote from the scene of any revolution. One can well understand why Than Tun was so overwhelmed at Peking's clear interest in the conduct of the negotiations with the government.

If Than Tun's quoted remarks represent his actual sentiments at the time, and the context supports that interpretation, then it reasonably follows that he would be willing to accept Chinese initiatives on almost every Party activity. Bear in mind that the Revolutionary Council's policies were a fundamental challenge to the Communists, for the rhetoric was Marxist. Moreover it was harder and harder to recruit new cadres from the university because the BCP's revolutionary activities had diminished through the years. Although many Burmese intellectuals were in despair over the excesses of the Ne Win dictatorship, few saw the White Flag as a credible alternative. The revolution had passed the Party by unless a new image could be created. The returnees offered that potential, even though this meant abandoning the organizational procedures so painfully developed during the first two decades of Party history. The irony in all this was that Than Tun found himself accused of the same heresy Thakin Soe had committed in arbitrarily taking the Red Flags to the jungle.

The Chinese motive for this intensive involvement in Burmese Party affairs is more difficult to explain. There is no record of any parallel in Indonesia. Aidit and the other leaders of the PKI had an independent base and a successful movement, and they went to Peking more or less as comrades and equals of the Chinese. The Vietnamese Party likewise operated independently, consulting the Chinese but usually maintaining a neutral stance between the Soviets and the Chinese, even during the years of amity between the Communist superpowers. The Khmer and Thai Party links with the Chinese are probably more like those the Burmese maintained, but to date there is no published documentation to support that supposition.

Two things may have conditioned the character of the Sino-Burmese relationship. First, the Burmese seem to have been viewed by the CCP as merely another minority within China. This is reflected in an organizational structure that made Ba Thein Tin responsible to Li Wei-han, a member of the CCP Central Committee, and Li in turn accountable to the Chinese Politburo for minority affairs within China. (It was Li, we might note, who handled the negotiations with the Tibetans in the 1950's.) Moreover, the separation of the Burmese exiles from one another and the severe Party discipline imposed on them were in line with the kind of treatment meted out to other minorities. To be sure, Ba Thein Tin himself was treated like a visiting dignitary—for example, he occasionally appeared at public functions in the company of Liu Shao-ch'i or Chou En-lai—but his committee-in-exile was rarely given the opportunity to meet, let alone direct Party affairs. The 1963 negotiations were an exception, but even then the procedure followed in formulating a response clearly reveals the subservience of the Burmese.

Second, the Chinese leaders' concern with developments in Burma, particularly their vital interest in the negotiations in 1963, may be related to their perception of a threatening encirclement of their country. The American buildup in Vietnam was under way, the Russians had been less than amicable during the Sino-Indian war in 1962, and India had become an implacable foe. The investment in Burma's revolution was a low-risk, low-cost affair, and was certainly encouraged by the BCP.

The subsequent behavior of the Chinese youth in Rangoon and of the BCP itself during the Cultural Revolution is less easily explained. It is possible that the occupation of the Foreign Ministry in Peking by Red Guards for several weeks in 1967 affected the operations of the Chinese embassy in Rangoon. Certainly the embassy had played an important role during the peace negotiations, and a number of its staff members may have had close ties with leftist and Chinese groups in Rangoon. And the playing out of a Burmese Cultural Revolution within the BCP in the following months could have reflected the fervor of younger returnees who saw themselves as the vanguard of a movement sweeping up their comrades in China. Unquestionably, they had considerable influence owing to their training, and they had been carefully treated as an elite by Than Tun ever since their return.

The persistence of behavior patterns associated with traditional Burmese rule may also be an explanation. However, since seeking explanation in historic parallels is a dangerous business, I turn now to a discussion that is decidedly speculative, but that is also suggestive of the beliefs that many Burmese hold concerning their own politicians.

## Historical Perspectives on Rebellions in Burma

Burmese history, both monarchical and colonial, has been marked by repeated rebellions, a fact that Aung San noted in the "Blue Print for Burma" he prepared for several Japanese friends in 1941. "In the olden days," he wrote, "the stability of the administration was frequently disturbed because of the rivalry of claims to the kingship, either in the life-time of the king or on his death. In the conception of the Burmese people, everything goes well if the head leads correctly but everything goes wrong if the head misleads or is unable to lead. . . . The Burmese temperament . . . demands always a strong, capable leadership."[28]

According to *The Glass Palace Chronicles*, Burma's earliest history saw frequent attempts at regicide or attacks on the monarch's forces in the countryside by disaffected relatives. The Konbaung Dynasty, the last monarchical line, suffered more than its share of such violence.

Although no king in the line was assassinated, over the years several dissident princes fled to protective villages or abroad to avoid the executioners. Others led protests against the court, and one fought for years against Mindon, the last strong monarch. By custom, monarchs executed their competitors, occasionally having them tied in a velvet bag and trampled to death by elephants. In the eyes of the Burmese, this practice ensured a graceful end for the victim (who as a Buddhist revered the elephant) while allowing his rival to avoid a loss of merit as a result of killing another person. The British, however, felt otherwise; indeed, the revival of this practice by the last reigning monarch, Thibaw, accounts for much of the popular support in England for the third Anglo-Burmese War, which saw the whole of Burma finally incorporated into the British Empire.

The British governors were successful in pacifying the country, but at considerable cost, for insurgents struggled on for a decade after the 1886 conquest of Mandalay. The battles were mostly fought in the region between the Irrawaddy River and the Pegu Yoma Mountains, the same territory that was to provide sanctuary for the BCP some 75 years later. Rebellions recurred time and again in the next half century, the most savage coming near the end of British rule—the Saya San revolt of the early 1930's. Thousands were killed before the protest ran its course, and in repressing the rural followers of the ex-monk, the British fed the nationalist impulse that created the Dohbama Asiayone, which was founded within a year of Saya San's execution.

Buddhist scripture teaches that the quality of the rule of a regime can be no better than the ethics of the ruler. Alongside this is the folk belief in the necessity of a firm hand at the tiller. At the outset, I noted that several key CPB and BCP leaders were captive of their culture, just as one would expect the more middle-of-the-road government leaders to be. Thakin Soe fought his insurgency in a style very like that of the classic protestors. His was not a pitched war of attrition, but an aloof struggle for moral ascendancy within the revolutionary movement. Moreover, he did not lead the life of a puritanical or dedicated Communist; he was more like the Burmese princes of the past, with a host of consorts and several wives. That fact alone cost him substantial support after the Japanese occupation when he emerged as a courageous leader but one who was also wholly undisciplined in his personal life.

Than Tun's life-style was more typical of an insurgent leader in the

Leninist mold; he lived simply, with little in the way of material goods, and seems to have had an exemplary married life. In the end, however, his movement developed into a mere cult of the jungle. For two decades he and his followers perceived the world from obscure villages, dependent on smuggled magazines and the Chinese radio for their reality. World events, even Burmese politics, passed them by, and the romance of "The Revolution" wore thin. All but a handful of those who joined the movement before 1948 had defected or been killed by 1963, and by 1969 the Party leadership of 1962 was entirely altered except for the Peking returnees and Thakin Zin. Indeed, by being in exile for a decade, the returnees gave the BCP more continuity and stability than the leaders who remained on the scene. The most significant fact about the Burmese movement, which must have plagued the key Politburo figures and contributed to their bloody end, was its ineffectiveness. It is hard for an outsider to understand what such a failure of leadership means to a Burmese. For those steeped in the tradition of the need for leadership to be strong and commanding, the BCP experience in the final years must have been excruciating. Passions long repressed, particularly among wives who had suffered through the years with none of the security of a settled family life, must have influenced those who indulged in the savage ritual. All the same, the ritual itself in no way derived from the Burmese heritage, but is more properly attributed to the model of the Maoist Cultural Revolution.

Next to the mass warfare that accompanied the Korean, Vietnamese, Lao, and Khmer Communist movements in the past two decades, or the wholesale slaughter by reactionary groups in Indonesia after the Gestapu affair, the schisms and even the bloodshed that marked the Burmese movement seem almost trivial. Fortunately for Burma, it has kept itself out of the politics of the Cold War. Yet one cannot study the Communist movement and feel secure about the future. China has demonstrated a long and unusual interest in Burma, and manipulated the major Communist Party there to a greater degree than in any other country. Because Burmese politics do not inspire confidence in the ability of any Rangoon regime to control dissident groups, the potential for substantial warfare persists. Although the Cold War has become less intense, it has been replaced by a Sino-Soviet hostility that inspires another type of intervention, as in Bangladesh.

The fractures in the Burmese Communist movement have all developed in response to changes in the political environment. Although personalities have influenced the situation, they have not shaped it, for the movement has consistently lacked the power to direct even its own affairs. This condition has invited outside involvement in the past, especially when it was a low risk for the actors, and we should anticipate more of the same in the future. The BCP is already enjoying a resurgence in central Burma, apparently under the leadership of Burmans disaffected from the White Flag group situated near the China border. Because economic conditions in Burma are improving only slowly and because communal divisions continue to be wounds on the body politic, the issues that inspired protest insurgency over the past three decades remain unresolved. Barring a thorough purge in the movement, we can anticipate that the China-trained cadres and leaders will greatly influence the future course of Burmese Communism. This younger generation of returnees may well be capable of considerable self-criticism because of their training. But they clearly must depart from their own Party heritage if they are to avoid the schisms that to this point have been the most prominent characteristic of the Burmese Communist movement.

# Toward an Exchange Theory of Revolution

JEFFREY RACE

Today's student of revolution faces the same riddle posed by Tolstoy a century ago in *War and Peace*. "Napoleon commanded an army to be raised," wrote Tolstoy, "and to march out to war." The riddle thus is, "why six hundred thousand men go out to fight when Napoleon utters certain words." Why, when revolutionary leaders utter certain words, do men march off to their death? In Vietnam, conversely, when President Diem ordered his army to go off to fight, why did it not do so? Or, to pose the same riddle in more contemporary terms, what must the aspiring political leader do to "make power"?

Each of these situations is an instance of the same empirical and conceptual difficulty: how one can gain "something for nothing," i.e., create influence relationships where none existed before, and with no material resources. The solution proposed here seizes upon a salient structural similarity between the empirical development of a revolutionary movement and the sociological concept of an "emergent structure."[1] This concept, coined to warn against the fallacy of psychological reductionism in the study of group behavior, denotes new patterns of behavior that appear when individuals interact. For us it is pregnant with implications for the emergence of revolutionary movements.

What follows is an attempt to go beyond the conceptualization of revolution set forth in my book *War Comes to Long An*.[2] The analysis there was limited in two important respects. First, it was a static theory rather than one incorporating explicitly dynamic variables. Second, it was inadequate to cope with what I call the genetic problem: the actual process by which individuals in an environment of favorable disposing conditions become "one" in a coherent organization.

Social exchange theory and the concept of "emergent structure" have much to tell us about the fine structure of group processes that lead to the development of revolutionary movements. A knowledge of this fine structure will help us to avoid some errors and oversimplifications in dealing with gross phenomena and to see relationships that may not be evident from an examination of macrostructures alone. In particular the use of social exchange theory can offer us important insights into the processes occurring between various components within a revolutionary movement, and between the movement and its ecological and human environments. Furthermore, we will be better able to avoid the ambiguities of such terms as mobilization, participation, support, and nationalism. The conceptualization proposed here will also, I believe, move us beyond such explanations of revolution as "grievances," "fanaticism," and "roboticism" (i.e., organizational theories). The perspective of revolution that comes into view is instead one of revolutionary participation as an adaptive response to changing circumstances.

In what follows the reader may be struck by the similarities between the predictions of exchange theory and the dictates of common sense. This much should be reassuring. However, the reader may also be tempted to ask what exchange theory *adds* to common sense. I think several observations can be made. First, this analytic structure formalizes many intuitive but vague notions, so that they may be operationalized. Second, it provides a series of bridging propositions to link static theories of individual and group behavior with dynamic theories of political and economic change. Third, it provides a means of integrating the role of group values with the role of incentives in organizational development. There is finally the awkward fact that, for all its similarities to common sense, nothing like exchange theory was used by official American analysts and policy makers in their analyses of and attempts to put down social revolution in Vietnam. Thus we may say that, to the extent exchange theory resembles common sense, it did not seem very compelling to those for whom Vietnam was an affair of state and not just an intellectual exercise.

The emphasis here is principally theoretical. In the first part the theory will be elaborated using examples and empirical data from Vietnam. The penultimate section will shift our attention to northern

Thailand, which, just because it is so different, well illustrates some important similarities. Finally, some unresolved problems and some fruitful topics for further research are suggested.

## An Exchange Analysis of Revolution

In *War Comes to Long An* I attributed the strength of the revolutionary movement in Long An province to proper "policies," but this is inadequate as an explanation of revolutionary emergence. "Policies" imply the existence of a functioning "organization" that can "promulgate" them and (in the earlier formulation) motivate cooperation. Motivating cooperation is still germane, but the use of exchange theory permits us to move back a step to explore the conditions of emergence.

A brief review of the concept of emergence in the context of organization theory will serve as the introduction to our problem. For our purposes a revolutionary movement may most fruitfully be viewed as a cooperative system. At the same time, as a formal organization, it includes an authority structure, i.e., a structure in which participants execute orders because they feel it is right to do so, despite individual preferences to the contrary. Both components—voluntary cooperation and authoritative coordination—are present, and our specific question is how such a cooperative-authoritative structure comes into being where none existed before.

We will recapitulate here the theoretical account of this process given in a standard work in the field of organization theory, *Formal Organizations*, by Peter M. Blau and W. Richard Scott.[3] Blau and Scott describe authority relations as beginning in dyadic relations of compliance. Authority may develop out of the expansion of dyads into one structure headed by the same individual:

> To establish authority over his subordinates, the supervisor must be able and willing to furnish services that command their respect and allegiance. For the collective loyalty of subordinates is what legitimates his exercise of control over them and transforms it into authority. When respect for the supervisor and feelings of obligation to him prevail in a group, they give rise to a consensus that, since it is in the common interest to maintain his good will, his directives and requests must be followed. Once these group norms enforce compliance with the supervisor's directives, his influence becomes independent of the use of coercive sanctions, or of persuasion, or even of the need to oblige particular subordinates in exchange for every request made of them.[4]

Several features stand out here for our purposes. First, an "authority structure" emerges from the formation of a group where previously no group relations existed (i.e., where there were no common norms). Second, one basis for the initial dyadic compliant (cooperative) behavior was the furnishing of services by the supervisor, which we will pursue below as "exchange." Third, both voluntary (dyadic) compliance and subordination to authority exist in the group structure. Here we introduce an important postulate, namely, that the collective compliance will be greater the greater the extent of the exchange. Though such compliance might in fact continue in the absence of exchange because of the *individual* expectation of group members that all others would participate contrary to individual preferences, we postulate that this type of compliance will be less stable than compliance accompanied by continued exchange.

Our examination of the logic of this postulate will be facilitated by an extract from a later work by Blau, in which exchange as a "starting mechanism" is explicitly combined with the concept of emergence.

> The social norms and values of subordinates that legitimate the power of influence of a superior transform it into authority. Simultaneously, indirect processes of social exchange become substituted for the direct exchange transactions between the superior and individual subordinates. Before legitimating norms have developed, subordinates offer compliance with the superior's directive in exchange for services he furnishes. . . . The emergent social norms that legitimate authority give rise to two exchange processes that take the place of this one. Individual subordinates submit to the authority of the superior because group norms require them to do so and failure to conform evokes social disapproval. The individual exchanges compliance with the directives of the superior for social approval from his peers. The collectivity of subordinates exchanges prevailing compliance with the superior's orders, which it has to offer as the result of its social norms that enforce compliance, and which legitimates the superior's authority, for the contribution to the common welfare his leadership furnishes.[5]

From this account we may extract the diagrams in Fig. 1, clarifying both the role of exchange and the emergent structure.

In this conceptualization an emergent authority structure arises from, and is perpetuated by, exchange processes. The first formal statement of exchange theory in sociology was by George Homans.

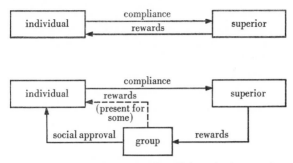

Fig. 1. *Above:* Initial dyadic relationship. *Below:* Authority relationship
(emergent structure)

However, Chester Barnard's classic study of business organization
employed exchange analysis implicitly, and as Alvin Gouldner has
pointed out, assumptions about the primacy of exchange processes
have an extremely long tradition. The most extensive and rigorous
use of exchange analysis is now in economics, but some writers have
begun to develop frameworks for its application to sociology. Exchange theory has thus far found very limited use in political science and, to my knowledge, none in the study of revolution.[6]

With exchange theory we can explain the development of one kind
of social bond between individuals and, as we have seen above, the
subsequent emergence of new group structures. Such social bonds
develop since each party exchanges something less valued (by him)
for something more valued. However, we can go beyond the framework of exchange theory developed thus far, in which two parties
exchange values they already possess. The development of a revolutionary movement is more complex than this, precisely because the
participants have "nothing" to start with except their own two hands
and the extremely limited resources of those at the bottom of the
social order. Whence the rewards that motivate cooperation? We
should first clarify that what is *exchanged* is certain behaviors (or
promises, i.e., agreements, to perform them). Two kinds of rewards
then follow (though a third type will be discussed later). First, there
are existing material resources, which may be redistributed through
the "power" of the resulting authority structure.* Second, the emer-

---

* At a more sophisticated level, however, we should note that "ownership," for
example of real estate, is not an intrinsic property but just another form of generalized agreement. This is clear from the legal definition of ownership as an ensemble
of state-protected rights, which may be disaggregated in practice as well as in theory.

gence of a *new* structure of coordinated action creates new values. This deserves a bit of elaboration. For one thing, such a new structure, having a hierarchy of status, will *ipso facto* provide new status roles, at least with reference to the organization's members. For another, individuals in a cooperative relationship with one another have a different impact on surrounding structures than would the same individuals not in cooperation. Thus cooperation, which each individual promises to the others, leads to an "emergent structure," new influence relations, and thereby new "power" and new "power roles." Putting this into diagram form so as to distinguish it from the Blau concept presented in Fig. 1, we have the configurations shown in Fig. 2.

Thus the "promises made" are motivated by rewards, some redistributive of existing values and some resulting from the new values created by these promises. To review a bit, once an organization exists, person *A* receives value from person *B* for compliance with *B*'s wish. This much is clear and not at issue (though, as an analysis of the functioning of organizations, it was poorly understood by the Saigon government). The genetic problem is rather how, with both

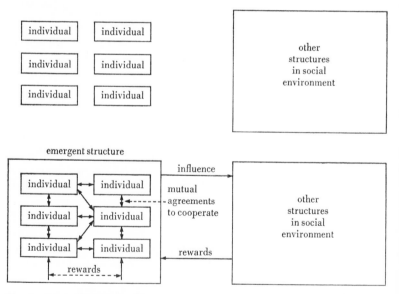

Fig. 2. *Above:* Structure prior to exchange relations. *Below:* Emergent structure secures rewards from environment.

*A* and *B* possessing practically "nothing," they can get "something." The answer can be clarified with some mathematical notation. If in the absence of cooperation *A* has accrued values totaling $X_{a1}$ and *B* has accrued $X_{b1}$, and if they can have $X_{a2}$ and $X_{b2}$, respectively, with coordinated action, where $X_{a2} > X_{a1}$ and $X_{b2} > X_{b1}$, then there is an incentive to both to achieve cooperation. This in a nutshell is the answer to the dilemma of the revolutionary seeking to create forces and of the political leader seeking to "make power." Through such an exchange process all are better off, or, in economic language, all move to a higher indifference curve.

From this conceptualization the following observation can be made about the "power" a cooperative system will "have": we identify this "power" with the amount of effort participants are willing to expend to maintain the exchange relationship. In our notation, it is the effort equivalent of the difference in value position before and after cooperation, i.e., $X_{a2} - X_{a1}$, $X_{b2} - X_{b1}$, summed over all the participants. This identification should create no conceptual problems as long as we understand power not as a generic term, but simply as the aggregate of all the specific behaviors participants are motivated to perform. This interpretation of power is different from Blau's, which identifies power with the relationship between individuals that holds when there is an imbalance of resources.[7] The difficulty with this interpretation is that, as we have shown, it is possible for an organization to "have power" though it begins with practically no resources at all.

A major conclusion from this analysis, and an analogy with economics, is that if various conditions discussed below are present, there can be an enormous expansion of cooperative activity and thus of "power" in the system. That is, new structures of influence may emerge, just as new wealth may be created in the economy.[8] Conversely, like the economy, the system may stagnate at low levels of power if participants are not willing to make the exchanges that permit an enlarged cooperative system to emerge.

Expanding on this insight a bit, cooperative systems do not evolve at random. They are shaped by what we may call constraining factors, that is, those factors that determine which out of all possible states is actually realized. Exchange analysis focuses our attention on the following:

1. *The objective situation.* By this is meant components both of

the physical world and of the existing social structure that make exchange attractive (e.g., population density; productivity; terrain configuration; a perceived threat; distribution of status, wealth, and income; and so forth).

2. *Values.* By this is meant those prerational beliefs about what is right that establish limits on permissible maximizing behavior. (Thus many actions that would enhance the value position of an individual in fact are not performed; we need not peer very far into human behavior to take this as given.) Particularly in regard to politics, this category subsumes "ideology," or the goal- and means-defining part of the belief structure. Values (in this sense) delimit the scope within which the exchanges specified by 3 and 4 may take place.

3. *Policies.* These are the rational, maximizing component. For the organizational context, policies define the terms of trade of an exchange; that is, they represent a statement of the kind of exchange the "organization" is willing to make. They are thus in some sense an "offer" to trade. (We should note that the actual exchange, when fully decomposed, might consist of numerous policies. Thus, within an administrative bureaucracy, the government's terms of trade are composed of policies of salary, promotion, and fringe benefits, and policies regarding degree of effort expected. Owing to the composite nature of the exchange, the structure of the situation may not be apparent.)

4. *Preferences.* This refers to a component of the psychology of the individual potential cooperators that defines (a) the ordering of the various values they desire; and (b) the intensity of that desire, i.e., the amount of effort the individual is willing to expend to obtain the value.

Looking back now over these four factors, we see that each one specifies an indefinite number of possible structures of cooperation. As each additional constraining factor is overlaid on those previously considered, the number of possible cooperative structures diminishes. In the relatively short run, which we will consider here (secular changes are treated further on), factors 1, 2, and 4 are constants, with factor 3 being the proximate determinant of which cooperative structure—*if any*—emerges in a particular instance. It is important to note that unless the potential structures permitted by each of the four factors are isomorphic for at least one structure, *none may emerge.* The empirical interpretation of this phenomenon is exemplified by the performance of numerous "paper" organizations in southern Vietnam during the Diem period.

## Values and Preferences

At this point we will expand our discussion of factors 2 and 4 above. The use of exchange theory presupposes some kind of maximizing behavior by individuals, i.e., the social equivalent of "economic man": search behavior that will move the individual to a higher indifference curve. Yet men do not do this indiscriminately: they do not pursue some exchanges that would move them to a higher indifference curve. We may accordingly introduce a variable that determines the probability of an exchange on a given issue. This variable thus is an index for the facilitation or blockage of an exchange. Here we go a bit beyond Blau, who views values as integrative mechanisms for large numbers of individuals who do not know each other personally.[9] Instead we view values as the releasing *or inhibiting* factor.

There are many vague political terms in the literature regarding this phenomenon, for example, legitimacy and alienation. We propose to subsume these under the value variable and define it operationally as follows: holding incentives constant, the value coefficient is measured by the quantity of exchange (empirically this might be measured as the number of man-hours of a given level of effort motivated, or some similar quantity).

We must distinguish a second variable that comes into play: individual preferences. Values are here meant to denote the effect determined by *group* structure. Preferences are meant to denote the effect determined by individual personality structure. Though the two operate jointly to determine the extent of exchange on a given issue, they are distinct both empirically and conceptually.[10]

With this conceptualization we can now identify one component (the means component) of political ideology as the set of coefficients attached to each possible type of exchange. This will be useful below in explaining a major anomaly of the Saigon government's response to revolution: that it did not offer certain exchanges which would clearly have been in its own interest. One consequence of the relative consistency of social values is that they permit stability in complex systems of indirect exchange. Yet here, as we will see, a perverse consequence also occurred: the prerational limitation of flexibility in government response.

## Policies

As noted above, I feel that a revolutionary movement may most fruitfully be conceptualized as a successful cooperative system, which neatly solves the genetic problem. Viewing revolution in this way also permits us to incorporate many diverse lines of inquiry, as we will attempt to do further on. Nevertheless, the theoretical exposition is not enough; there remains the question of what the actual exchanges might be.

Plainly, the first question is, who are the parties to the exchange? At one level it is clearly a question of "leaders" versus "followers" within an organization. Numerous observers have noted that revolutions are not made by peasants alone, for various excellent reasons such as limited cognitive competence and a non-futuristic orientation. Thus there is, at this level, an exchange (in the organizational division of labor) of leadership, insight, and "vision" on the part of superiors for compliance on the part of subordinates. Even if there were complete *formal* equality in the founding of a revolutionary organization (e.g., in a village), stratification would still occur because of differences in individual capacities and contributions.[11]

A second way to view exchange is to aggregate individuals into groups and see the exchange as taking place between one clearly corporate entity, e.g., a government (or, alternatively, a revolutionary movement), and various social groups whose members behave similarly, e.g., different classes of peasants, intellectuals, or small merchants.

What then, empirically, were the actual exchanges that took place in Vietnam and aided the success of the revolutionary movement; or, alternatively, what were the exchanges that failed to take place and weakened the government? As noted earlier, we tend to think of the terms of trade of an exchange as being set by "policies." But though we may unambiguously use the term policy to denote a course of action pursued by an existing organization, this usage is meaningless for an organization that does not yet exist: the exact problem of an emergent structure. For this special instance, then, I use the term policy to denote a *promised* course of action, which is actualized as the incipient cooperative structure emerges. Thus the exchange, as described earlier, is mutual agreement to perform specified activities, as a consequence of which the parties jointly will enjoy the future rewards.

We can identify several important policy differences (in this sense) between the revolutionary movement in Vietnam and the Saigon government. Furthermore, since the factors of objective situation, social values, and individual preference-orderings were relatively constant, whereas these policy differences were subject to human discretion, we may identify these policy differences as the final determinant of the differing organizational performances in Vietnam.

One set of policies were those pertaining to wealth and income. As I have pointed out in *War Comes to Long An*, the revolutionary land policy not only was able to achieve a far broader distribution of land than did the government program, but also was coupled with policies aimed at redistributing income between social groups: progressive (versus regressive) taxation, rent and interest reduction, and reduction in amounts charged for use of agricultural animals and implements.

The redistribution of wealth and income assumes a fixed amount of both. By the process described above, an emergent structure of cooperative activity might direct to its members some larger proportion of each. This could be done in Vietnam without harmful consequences for production since landlords had ceased playing a significant role in the production process.[12] No *addition* to either wealth or income was necessary—through some "development policy," for instance—for the revolutionary movement to succeed in inspiring voluntary cooperation in its effort. This constant volume of values did not hold regarding a second category of policies, those concerned with the distribution of power and status.

To a limited extent the revolutionary movement's policies of redistribution of power could be said to be identical in structure to those regarding wealth and income: simply dividing a fixed quantity differently, or in this case installing different persons in positions similar to those previously occupied by government personnel. However, this simple redistribution of power roles to different social groups, interesting as it is, was not the actual structure of revolutionary success. The movement did more than redistribute roles: it permitted *new structures of cooperation* to emerge, through the process I described earlier. It is here that the use of policies in the sense of agreements is most clearly distinguished. Here, also, the sense is clear of an exchange between the government (or the revolutionary movement) and social groups.

What did the Party do that permitted these new structures to emerge? Several contributing factors can be identified. First, the Party "placed more authority" at lower levels in its organization than the government did. It is important not to reify authority; it is not something "given." Rather, the Communist leadership adopted different policies from those of the government concerning which levels would be permitted to make certain types of decisions. Thus, organizational roles at the lowest levels in the revolutionary structure specifically called for the making of more important decisions than could be made by the corresponding government echelon. At the same time, the policy of decentralizing some decision-making was matched by the "policy" of demanding more risk-taking and effort. Government leaders were not willing to agree to such decision-making authority at these levels, and so were not able to receive the risk-taking and expenditure of effort in exchange.

A second contributing factor was the contrasting promotional structures of the revolutionary movement and the Saigon government, as shown in Fig. 3. Within the revolutionary movement there was a continuous promotion system from the village Party chapter to the Central Committee, the recruiting at the bottom being done principally from among groups of low rank in the stratification order. In contrast, the government continued the system established at the turn of the century, recruiting rural elites only into the village-canton structure, and relying on a completely different career system for positions in the central administrative structure. There was no mobility path from the one to the other.

We may analyze this structural difference from an individual view-

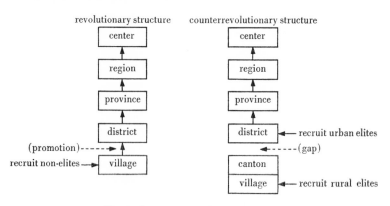

Fig. 3. Contrasting mobility structures

point and see that no matter how hard a government village chief worked, he could never hope to be more than a canton chief, whereas within the Party a poor peasant could aspire to a position at the village level, the district level, or even higher. Thus the Party policy of a continuous promotion system (in effect a social mobility mechanism) was actually one-half of an exchange, the other half being the comparatively greater risk-taking and effort demanded, and produced, within the revolutionary system. This promotion system had an independent structural effect, although it was combined in practice with a class-sorting mechanism (at least until 1945, when the social origin of those recruited into government local organs began to shift). The independent structural effect becomes clear after 1954, from which time the Saigon government was increasingly forced to recruit persons of more humble origin into its local organs. The motivation of these recruits was still weak compared with that of their revolutionary counterparts, however, due to this important structural asymmetry.*

We should note that this same structural difference may be seen from a group viewpoint as well. That is, the leadership of the revolutionary movement, a national structure, was willing to make exchanges with local structures—villages. The Saigon government, however, was unwilling to make this national-local exchange. Consequently, compared with the government, the revolutionary movement gained in its ability to influence local activity and in its degree of national-local integration, while yielding something in autonomy. (This trade-off between influence and autonomy will be discussed in more detail below.)

Here we must hypothesize that the exchanges offered by the Party fit better with popular preferences than those offered by the government. As a result, structures emerged that were not permitted by the exchanges the government leaders were willing to make. These structures were not just duplicates of government structures, staffed by different people; they were *expanded* structures compared with those of the government.

What is the contribution of status to this phenomenon? Status here

---

* Party policy similarly dictated increased upward mobility to power positions in the military forces for non-elite groups. The government officer corps was recruited from elite groups because of the educational requirement of the *baccalauréat*; enlisted personnel had little hope of achieving officer rank. In Party military forces, by contrast, officer-level positions were filled directly by promotion of the most qualified men in the ranks.

is much more amorphous than power, the dimensions of which are plain from a structural analysis of Party institutions. We should be clear that status is a separate type of reward from power, though it may co-vary: it is deference and approval from a collectivity for contributions to group goals; it is characterized by both ranking and distance.

Regarding the first element, ranking, the revolutionary movement's "power" vis-à-vis individuals permitted it simply to abolish old forms of deference behavior, e.g., gestures of salutation and terms of address. Beyond this, however, the greatly expanded structures of cooperative activity just discussed undertook redistributive measures that favored large numbers of people within rural villages. These enlarged structures permitted many more individuals to be *associated* with the group-benefiting redistributive effort, even though only in a contributory and not in a decision-making role. Thus, many more individuals could gain group approval through the revolutionary movement than through the government, and this was of course carefully orchestrated by the movement through contests, competitions, award ceremonies, and the like. Combined with this policy was the principle of explicit preference for persons of humble origin as objects of praise. Within the government system the honor ranking was traditionally *si nong cong thuong* (scholar-official, farmer, worker, merchant); within the revolutionary movement the second and third were transposed with the first.

In respect to social distance, too, it is clear that there was a lesser degree of status differentiation within the revolutionary movement than within the government. Party leaders emphasized identification between members of the movement and the general population in terms of dress, custom, speech, and other forms of status differentiation. Since it is well established experimentally that status differentiation impedes communication, we infer that there was a preference for cooperation with the revolutionary movement over the government because of the greater probability of positive reinforcement through community approval. Furthermore, the reduced status differentiation between the movement's operatives and the population had an independent effect in increasing the frequency of interaction.[18]

A third important type of exchange carried out by the revolutionary movement in Vietnam was not "social" at all, but pertains instead to the special circumstances of revolutionary war. I refer here to policies of protecting certain people in return for their cooperation. As I noted in *War Comes to Long An*, several groups of people were prominent in this exchange issue. The first chronologically were those former Vietminh adherents who were persecuted, either on an official basis or on a personal basis, by agents of the Diem regime. A second significant group were youths who wished to avoid the national draft after its promulgation in 1957. A smaller group consisted of those fleeing government jurisdiction for common crimes.[14]

## Starting Mechanisms and a Periodization

One plain implication of this analysis is that non-elites could always improve their position by cooperating to undo their "betters." Since this in fact happens with surprising rarity, we would like to know with more precision when it might occur. Some secular factors will be considered below. Here, however, we can identify some short-run variables that facilitate emergence of revolutionary organizations; conversely, their absence may hinder emergence despite otherwise favorable disposing conditions. At the same time a useful four-stage periodization comes into view: first, a situation of favorable disposing conditions (unequally distributed values); second, the appearance of direct (dyadic) exchanges; third, the phase of emergence, in which indirect exchanges and an authority structure appear; and finally, the phase of goal succession.[15]

The problem is that a successful organization (revolutionary or otherwise) can function only through a complex series of indirect exchanges in which rewards for many participants are mediated by the group and dispersed as social approval. Yet this authority structure is individually coercive only when the group structure actually emerges, i.e., when there is a simultaneous expectation of coordinated group action to realize group rewards. Otherwise, no one may act, despite an objectively favorable situation, since there is no expectation that others will do likewise.

Thus the question is how this simultaneity of expectations may be induced, leading to indirect exchanges. The answer lies in the existence of certain kinds of "starting mechanisms," or more specifically, direct exchanges in which the rewards to the individual are contingent only on his own behavior and not on the simultaneous action of the collectivity. Such direct exchanges are illustrated by the dyad in Fig. 1. Multiple dyads, headed by the same individual, may then (in favorable circumstances) evolve into an authority structure.

The key word here is contingency: whether the reward is so divisible that its receipt depends on individual behavior. This phenomenon of contingency, its function as a starting mechanism, and the special character of revolutionary organizations in the direct exchange (dyadic) phase can be illustrated by events in Vietnam. We might first refer back to the period between 1955 and 1957: the revolutionary organization, in attempting to preserve and rebuild itself,[16] relied to a considerable extent on those seeking *protection* (ex-Vietminh, draft evaders). Slightly later, in expanding into new villages, the movement relied on another contingent exchange: land. This is illustrated by the hamlet of Ai Ngai in Phu Ngai Tri village in Long An.[17] Sometime in 1958 a Party member from outside the village approached Nguyen Van Cu, a poor farmer, offering him land if he cooperated to drive out the Saigon government presence. Cu agreed to cooperate, and thus a direct exchange relationship was initiated in which both parties would be better off if cooperation succeeded. Together they interested several people from other hamlets in the same offer, and thus a number of direct exchange relationships, but not yet an authority structure, developed.

The conclusions we draw are several. First, the mechanism at work here was the divisibility of the reward, which permitted multiple direct-exchange dyads to develop, preparing the way for a solution to the "inertial" problem of lack of simultaneous expectations. Second, if the development of the movement were halted in this phase (by eliminating the reward issues or the leaders of the exchange dyads), it would be more serious than later, since the group structure would not yet have emerged. The third conclusion is that a revolutionary organization is more likely to develop the more there are contingent exchanges, i.e., the more important is protection as an issue and the more divisible are the social values to be redistributed. Conversely, the less there are contingent exchanges, the less likely is a revolutionary organization to emerge (or the more slowly will it do so), despite otherwise favorable disposing conditions. Here we see the peculiar role of land as a starting mechanism: there are many types of distributive inequalities, but land is amenable to individual redistribution in ways that other values are not (e.g., a progressive taxation system or a school building, which are collective goods).[18]

The third phase is that of emergence proper, in which the simultaneity of expectations appears (through the prior working of multiple direct-exchange dyads). In this phase there is an authority structure, with many individuals cooperating not for material rewards but for the social approval mediated by the group. Once at this point, the movement is much more resistant to assault, not because so many more persons cooperate (though this is true), but principally because the idea of cooperation (i.e., the simultaneity of expectations) exists independently of any individual in the organization. The organization could conceivably be reconstituted from memory; and in fact this is exactly what happened in Vietnam in the late 1950's.

The phase of emergence may be illustrated by pursuing the example of Ai Ngai. During 1960 the government was driven out of the hamlet—by the men noted above, motivated by the powerful direct exchanges previously discussed. The types of exchanges the movement was willing to make were so manifestly beneficial to the community that cooperation led to social approval. Many villagers thus cooperated without receiving the direct exchange benefits that had served to initiate the process. Within two years the number of active participants rose to about 70—far more than the government had ever motivated.

The fourth phase we can identify with this analysis is that of goal succession. Emergence occurred through an expansion from direct exchange, but on a limited number of issues (in which rewards were divisible). The goal succession phase sees the exchanges moving to indivisible rewards, beginning first with such things as a progressive taxation system and the reduction of interest rates, and coming ultimately to innovations with more remote collective payoffs, such as labor exchange and socialization into new work and expenditure habits. Once in the goal succession phase, the revolutionary organization is much more firmly consolidated, since its motivational structure is spread across so many more exchange issues. Furthermore, as the organization expands its activities into new spheres the process of "interlocking" noted by Talcott Parsons occurs, leading to greater stability.[19]

This periodization assumes the "worst case" for heuristic purposes, i.e., a completely atomized collection of individuals having no experience of current cooperation or memory of past cooperation. Even in such a case, new cooperative structures may emerge. However, there is an important alternative route to revolutionary organization: turning existing patterns of cooperation to new purposes. Thus, existing organizations could move directly to the fourth stage of goal succession, reducing or eliminating the need for divisible incentives to catalyze action. Accordingly, in attempting to predict the likelihood of revolutionary organization in a society, we should also look at the degree of organizational density, the amount of coordinated group activity independent of (or in opposition to) authority, or even the strength of historical memory of such activity. That is, to the extent that there already exist solidary bonds among a population—of clan, religious, political, or other types—we expect emergence to be facilitated.

## Exchange, Parties, and Bureaucracies

The discussion thus far has focused on competing military and bureaucratic structures. When we think of political conflict we ordinarily think of a struggle between national political parties. The absence of such conflict (leading instead to the type of conflict we have been discussing here) is one of the major anomalies of the struggle in Vietnam. Consequently, we should shift our attention for a moment to investigate why political party competition simply was not a serious element in Vietnam. Here we encounter an example of how cooperative systems are shaped by group values of political leaders. This is best illustrated by the problem of political parties in Vietnam. The examination of this problem is useful not just as an illustration here, but also because it helps to clarify a more general problem in the theoretical literature. On the one hand there are those (often government officials) who argue for civil bureaucracies or military bureaucracies, or both, as effective mechanisms of rule in transitional societies;[20] on the other hand there are those, such as Samuel Huntington, who advocate parties, arguing the rigidity and inevitable breakdown of administrative regimes. It is the purpose of this section to point out the error of the first position and to elaborate the theoretical basis of the second position in a way that its advocates themselves have not done.

There appear to be three major "exchange systems" in which individuals can achieve mobility. First among these is economic activity in general, both in the sense that historically it may precede the other two, and in the sense that in modern noncommunist systems most individuals operate principally in this exchange system. The second major system is the government bureaucracy, to include both the civil administration and the military establishment. The third broad possible system is that of political participation.

In one frequent formulation these exchange systems are called "co-optation mechanisms," since in certain circumstances potential revolutionary participants may be so attracted by rewards available elsewhere as not to engage in revolutionary activity (itself one form of political activity). Thus these exchange systems are in some way alternatives to one another, depending on both the terms of trade in each and the volume of exchange available. In our discussion here we will hold the economic system constant and deal with the remaining two systems, which may be expanded much more rapidly and with greater precision than the economic system. We should bear in mind, however, that an alternative to revolutionary participation may have been participation in favorable exchanges in the economic system. Several observers have emphasized how the Diem regime placed obstacles in the way of the expansion of economic activity just as it did in the way of political activity. However, this point will not be pursued here.

Both bureaucracies and political party systems are structures of cooperation in which cooperation improves the value position of the participant. What are the important differences between the two for our purposes? A political party is a cooperative system established for the purpose of giving expression to constituent sentiment. At a higher level, a political party *system* aggregates interests and resolves conflicts. An administrative organization, by contrast, is a cooperative system established for the purpose of command and accountability.

In both cases, however, we are concerned not with the formal goal of the organization, but with the organization's functioning as an exchange system. In particular, how does this functioning relate to search behavior for maximally beneficial exchange relations? The superiority of parties as exchange systems is apparent. First, let us acknowledge that both parties and administrative systems can offer rewards to participants. If the number of individuals seeking improved terms of trade is limited, a bureaucracy may suffice to co-opt them. It is when the number grows larger than the absorptive capacity of the bureaucracy that the weakness of bureaucratic organization as a vehicle of exchange becomes apparent. Here we come to the superiority of party systems as cooptation mechanisms.

In what does this superiority consist? In a bureaucracy both the maximum volume of exchange and the terms of trade are relatively fixed. Thus entrance standards are (ideally) fixed; tables of organization are fixed in size; and the rewards for compliance (security, salary, promotion, pension) are relatively static. Parties in comparison are easily expandable structures of cooperation; that is, there is no *a priori* limit either on volume of exchange or on terms of trade: "entrance standards," if any, are easily adaptable; there is no fixed size; and the rewards may be very great, even for a given size, e.g., "capture" of political power, corruption, or redistribution of property.

We should move now from analysis of one party to analysis of a competitive party system. If such a system is permitted to emerge, any one party may lose rewards for participants, but the system *as a whole* amounts to an implicit exchange between the government and political participants: the government permits the emergence of systems of cooperative activity (parties, legislatures) that influence government policy; in exchange the participants "agree" to refrain from anti-system activity. On the other hand, if the government places prior restraints on political activity (i.e., is not willing to make such an exchange), the rewards available through "legal" cooperation may fall below the level sufficient to bring about the emergence of a competitive system. Potential participants sit by; their efforts are not even motivated against "anti-system" actions by others. In short, the emergent structure of legal activity does not emerge. Better yet, from the point of view of the revolutionaries, an alternative anti-system structure may emerge.

We thus see that when the demand for access to values exceeds the absorptive capacity of a bureaucracy, a bureaucracy will suffer in competition with an expanding structure of cooperation like the revolutionary movement in Vietnam. The "rational choice" in such a situation, as Harold Hotelling and Arthur Smithies have suggested, is for the "sufferer" to move closer to the competitor (in physical terms), or to offer more competitive terms of trade (in exchange terms).[21] In other words, he should spur the development of co-optation mechanisms, in our case expandable structures of cooperation represented by parties and, at a higher level, a party system.

Though this discussion has been framed in terms of coopting individuals, the analysis might equally be applied to the cooptation of competing organizations. One of the most intriguing questions in the comparative study of Communist movements is why some choose a revolutionary path whereas others remain "domesticated." Our analysis here suggests that "domesticated" behavior is a rational response either to the perceived viability of the existing institutional order (since enough other actors have been bought off to make the revolutionary path unsuccessful) or to the co-optation of the Communist leadership itself. Rex Mortimer's paper in this volume provides an excellent case study of the latter phenomenon.

Why did the Diem regime not pursue such a rational policy of co-optation? Two possibilities suggest themselves. One is that there may have been an *a priori* abhorrence of political party conflict, a consequence of the strong Confucian influence on Diem's political thinking. In terms of our earlier fourfold classification of constraining factors, the values of the principal actors in the Diem regime did not permit this type of exchange relationship to develop even though it would have been beneficial to do so. John McAlister's statement of the consequence is accurate and succinct: "Instead of political mobilization [Diem] saw his major task as political control of such effectiveness that it prevented anyone else from mobilizing power."[22] This is apparent in the regime's behavior toward both the party system and the legislative system. Robert Scigliano, writing in 1963, well summarized the party situation:

> There is from a legal standpoint no opposition party in Vietnam. The approval of the Secretary of State for Interior is required for any political party to function, and his disapproval need not be explained and cannot be appealed.... The only parties which have thus far received this approval have been the pro-government groups. All opposition activity in Vietnam is either suppressed, and its participants arrested, as in the case of the communists and a number of too energetic nationalists, or watchfully tolerated, so long as its scope is restricted to small group discussions and the issuance of mild criticisms against the government.[23]

By constitutional provision, statute, or interpretation, numerous restrictions were similarly placed on the legislative system. The National Assembly did not install the Cabinet, nor could it overturn it; it could not alter the budget, nor did it have any post-appropriation control over expenditure; many policy areas did not even come before the legislature but were handled by administrative action. And, in any event, legislative elections were carefully manipulated by the government to produce safe deputies.[24]

This analysis permits us to specify more exactly than is currently the case in the literature just what political leaders must do to bring about a functioning party system as an alternative to anti-system violence. In the most succinct statement of the problem in the literature, Huntington asserts:

Whether a society evolves through a more or less revolutionary path thus depends upon the choices made by its leaders and their urban opponents after the city asserts its role in the political system. At this point either the leaders of the system mobilize the peasantry into politics as a stabilizing force to contain urban disorder, or the opposition mobilizes them into politics as a revolutionary force to join in the violent destruction of the existing political and social order.[25]

What makes the decisions of the political leaders right is more ambiguous. Huntington correctly asserts that it is not holding elections. But "creating organizations" that will "organize participation" and "structure it into legitimate channels,"[26] though excellent as a goal, is not yet a specification of the means. Our analysis shows that the "right decisions" are those that expand the volume of exchanges and improve the terms of trade, leading to the evolution of complex exchange systems between government and party system, between party and party, and between party and party member. A greater volume of exchange leads to stronger integrative bonds, while "organizations" without exchanges remain, as Diem's did, hollow shells.

Because we are dealing with a complex system of exchanges in which some units are actually systems themselves, we may apply this analysis as well to the so-called nationalist parties in the South. These were commonly criticized for failing to present a united front to the Communists, for bickering, for restricting themselves to "tearoom politics," and for failing to go out to "mobilize mass support." Yet it is clear from the values of "nationalist" political leaders that they were not prepared to make the exchanges, as were the Communists, that would motivate the cooperation of poor or landless peasants. As John D. Powell points out,[27] the problem for such groups is subsistence; their margin of safety is small. Political activity is an alternative to subsistence and so will have little appeal unless it provides rewards that are immediate, direct, and guaranteed. Such rewards were available through the types of exchanges the Party was willing to make, but not through the types of cooperation offered by "nationalist" leaders, which centered on symbolic, impersonal, corporate, and universalistic appeals and rewards.

An alternative possibility explaining the failure of the Diem regime to pursue the "rational choice" is a more instrumental one: that the regime sought autonomy for itself and had a genuine fear of autonomy for any other organization. This quest for autonomy, however, was based on a fatal misunderstanding of the relationship between autonomy and influence, which our exchange analysis will permit us to clarify.

The Diem regime's obsessive quest for autonomy is apparent in its political behavior: abolition of village autonomy, effective elimination of the role of the region and regional delegate, destruction of the power of the sects and the Binh Xuyen, removal of French influence, and abolition of the monarchy.[28] In short, the regime handled the autonomy problem by limiting cooperation, i.e., by throwing legal and extralegal obstacles in the way of all forms of cooperation except those whose rewards were strictly regulated by the regime. Yet as we have seen, organizational power derives from exchange, and exchange implies that *each party has power over the other.*[29] Diem was obsessed with autonomy and therefore became so completely divorced from social forces (i.e., bereft of exchange relations) that his government lost all ability to operate in its social environment. By denying others influence over himself, he denied himself influence over others as well.

This analysis also suggests an important qualification to one frequent view of autonomy in the literature: that it is desirable as an index of "institutionalization." Huntington's presentation exemplifies this view:

> Where the political system lacks autonomy, [new social groups] gain entry into politics without becoming identified with the established political procedures.
>
> . . .
>
> As political participation increases, the complexity, autonomy, adaptability and coherence of the society's political institutions must also increase if political stability is to be maintained.
>
> . . .
>
> If a society is to maintain a high level of community, the expansion of political participation must be accompanied by the development of stronger, more complex, and more autonomous political institutions.[30]

I believe such formulations should be qualified to make it clear that they refer to *autonomy from any one group*, and not to autonomy in general (as one might infer from the passages quoted). Autonomy from any one group derives from successful exchanges with a multiplicity of others. Autonomy in general, Diem's obsession, leads instead to the kind of isolation and collapse suffered by his political system.

*Exchange and Secular Development Processes*

We have just examined a static theory of exchange that makes revolution comprehensible as a rational act for thinking participants, rather than as the frenzied response of ideological fanatics. What we would like to know, however, in order to amplify the theory, is: why did a revolution occur at this particular moment? It is a puzzling question, for the static analysis just elaborated suggests that the less well off could always improve their situation by collaborating to undo elites.

We should begin with the structure of traditional stability in the South. Three elements stand out here. First, the number of candidates for effective anti-system leadership was limited by the narrowness of educational opportunity. Second, in the political sphere, an effective co-optation system existed, via the mandarin examinations, to absorb into the ruling elite those who might otherwise have gone into anti-system activity. This system provided mobility from villages into the national bureaucratic structure, and it ensured a place even for those who tried and failed the examinations.[31] At the same time, those retiring from the system returned to reside in villages and play an important leadership role there. A third important component of traditional stability was economic redistribution, both by automatic social processes and by conscious policy of the Emperor. The former is the well understood consequence of measures to prevent threats to social solidarity in relatively closed village societies, through various pressures toward economic leveling of the wealthy, e.g., obligatory rituals, feasts, and contributions. Over time the result was considerable mobility—up and down—in village society; at any one time, the result was to mitigate intra-village differentials of wealth.[32] Furthermore, at various times the Emperor broke up for redistribution large landholdings that were accumulated despite local leveling pressures.[33] Thus, the number of those with the mental preparation for leadership was limited; they were effectively co-opted; and one of the programs on which an anti-system movement might have based its appeal—land redistribution—was executed from time to time by the regime itself.

A number of significant changes disturbed this traditional system of stability mechanisms and facilitated a mass movement against the central authority. One was the erosion of the position of the local elites, who were a crucial linkage between the mass of the population and the central authority. The traditional system provided exchanges with very favorable terms of trade for village elites. Under the existing system of village autonomy, local elites had almost plenary authority, with only a post-decisional accountability to the central government. The latter had only limited functions, in the religious and military spheres. Furthermore, individuals dealt with the central authority only through the medium of their local leadership. The local elites thus were favored in the types of exchanges the central power was willing to make: plenary local authority in return for some limited forms of compliance with the central power (furnishing taxes, corvée laborers, conscripts, and so forth).

The new exchanges between central and local authorities under the French were much less favorable at the local end. Under so-called modern ideas of rationalization of administrative structures, many more responsibilities were placed upon local elites, e.g., for individual tax payment records (with personal responsibility by officials) and for individual census rosters (something never required under the traditional system). This so-called rationalization also called for the separation at the local level of administrative and religious offices, though appointment to religious office was an important part of the incentive for performing administrative duties. In addition, many of the earlier powers of the local elites were no longer endorsed, e.g., certain types of adjudication and punishment. Finally, in response to changing administrative fashions in Saigon, local authorities in Cochinchina were at various periods to be elected, which seriously detracted from the prestige rewards of local administrative roles.[34]

The result of these changes was to diminish the formerly favorable terms of trade the local elites had enjoyed in this national-local exchange. Increased effort was demanded while rewards decreased. At the same time, as Paul Mus and others have pointed out, Frenchmen occupied many of the higher positions in the national administrative system, clogging elite positions and damaging the co-optation mechanism.

The effect, we may deduce, was to erode a long-emergent structure of authority, namely, the village council, as the leadership organ of the corporate village and linkage with the national system. This disintegration weakened the village council both as a potentially repressive weapon again the village population and as a means to co-opt elite candidates into the system. Thus the stage was set for the process described above: potential cooperators might sit by, their energies not motivated on behalf of the system; or alternatively, with old structures disintegrating, the appeal of forming new structures was proportionately greater, and the risk less.*

Another process occurring here is described by Karl Deutsch as "social mobilization," one consequence of which is the "proliferation of new social forces" elaborated by Huntington.[35] Deutsch defines social mobilization as "the process in which major clusters of old social, economic and psychological commitments are eroded or broken and people become available for new patterns of socialization and behavior." It is thus a type-concept composed, in Deutsch's formulation, of a number of indices, such as literacy, exposure to mass media, and urbanization. Three components of this process can be neatly integrated with exchange theory.

First, social mobilization places traditional people in new situations where they have new needs. Compliance with the elites was based on their fulfillment of certain needs, but in the changed situation of urbanization and new means of livelihood, the old exchanges may not —probably will not—be relevant, and the earlier forms of compliance will no longer "fit." Traditional stability implies a complementarity of expectations between each actor and all others regarding their respective behavior, a complementarity that is reinforced by the persistence of the objective situation. When this situation is altered, the stability of mutual expectations declines, leading to the type of chaotic, patternless political behavior that Huntington has aptly called "praetorianism."[36]

A second meeting-point between the mobilization hypothesis and exchange theory concerns the consequence of expanding literacy. At the upper end of the scale, expanding literacy may create new elite candidates who cannot be absorbed by existing structures. Thus, there is a growing lack of fit between the structurally permitted volume of exchanges and terms of trade, on the one hand, and the volume and terms expected, on the other. There appears a group intellectually capable of leading an anti-system movement, and with the incentive to do so as well. Lower down on the scale, a similar principle operates among potential followers. In the traditional system the mass of people will be participants in highly unequal exchanges. As literacy spreads, leading to greater equality between elites and masses on this continuum, dissatisfaction appears with the persistence of greater

---

* It is interesting to observe that the formal rationalization of administrative structures had such a substantively irrational consequence.

inequality on other continua. Along with the dissatisfaction appears the intellectual capability for coordinated group action to do something about the situation. Some empirical studies suggest the individual psychological process at work here: the tendency to behave so as to bring different value dimensions into congruence.[37] Donald Zagoria's paper in this volume also discusses recent empirical evidence on the behavioral consequences for politics of expanding literacy.

A third important interface between social mobilization and exchange theory centers on the role of communication: without communication there could be no exchange. Three components of Deutsch's formulation of social mobilization have implications for communication: per capita income, which is an index of improving physical communication; circulation of mass media; and literacy. As physical communications improve, as mass media develop, and as literacy spreads, it becomes *possible* for new, expanded, complex systems of exchange to develop. Two consequences are plain in the context of Vietnam. First, the simple volume of exchange expands, increasing the amount of power of the system and, *pari passu*, proportionately diminishing the power of existing structures that do not expand (e.g., a centralized bureaucracy, which is limited in its exchange potential for reasons specified above).* Second, from a distributive point of view, entirely new groups of people are now *enabled* to participate in new and far more comprehensive exchange systems. The actual shape of the new systems, however, depends on the kinds of variables mentioned in previous pages.

Another aspect of the social mobilization process worth noting here concerns the shifting nature of the linkages between rural and urban areas, and why in particular the linkages failed as they did in Vietnam. As communications and literacy expand, we expect new groups —particularly middle peasants and small businessmen—to move into local leadership positions, replacing traditional elites. Such individuals have the cognitive competence, the resources, and the extra-village connections necessary to sustain a linkage role. As Powell points out,[38] they are connected to both worlds, and they experience a tension between individual mobility and village solidarity. Which way they turn depends on the type of linkage permitted by the larger structure.

---

\* The same process explains the decreasing role of individuals and the correlative "institutionalization" of modern life.

Why did such individuals not lead a vigorous "pro-system" effort in Long An, as we might expect them to do? The answer appears to be that under the arrangements perpetuated by the Saigon government in its areas, such individuals could go on making profits under the market system *without exerting leadership in the political sphere* (and ultimately the military sphere). In fact they were not even encouraged to do so by the government; its bureaucratic structure had little absorptive capacity to incorporate new social groups ready for expanded participation. Within the existing structures, furthermore, the burden of risks and expenditure of effort were not rewarded by comparable incentives; consequently, the terms of trade in the exchange did not encourage middle peasants to seek these roles for their intrinsic rewards.

Another set of processes occurring in Long An converge in what has come to be known as the "exploitative landlord" phenomenon. The first general theoretical treatment of this question was Alvin Gouldner's important article "The Norm of Reciprocity." It was posed in its present form by Barrington Moore, Jr.; and valuable empirical work has been done by Robert Sansom and Sydel Silverman.[39] The processes center on changes in the land-labor ratio and in the inputs of the various actors, including both local elites and the central government. The crucial point of convergence of all these processes can be neatly described in exchange theory as the shifting terms of trade between elites and non-elites. Earlier we discussed the secular shift in terms of trade between national and local elites; now we will focus on local elites and those under them.

As noted above, traditional local elites formed an important linkage between the national structure and local villagers. From the viewpoint of the villagers, the local elites performed an important protective function in preserving the autonomy of the village and the anonymity of its members vis-à-vis the outside. The local elites also performed important ritual functions and provided significant inputs to the production process. For these, of course, they were generously rewarded in terms of wealth and status. Even so, there were periodic land redistributions and considerable mobility up and down.

This traditional stable relationship at the local level was upset by a number of changes that took place in the decades following the French invasion. For one, the French policy approach to developing the Mekong Delta, requiring enormous capital investment, dictated that it would be opened up in the form of large estates. In the early decades of clearing and cultivation this system was both successful and stable, since the elites provided important resources of management, capital, and know-how. A concurrent process, however, was that of population growth (accelerated by French-sponsored improvements in health), leading around 1930 to the exhaustion of new land.

Other important processes were going forward simultaneously. The expansion of the market and general improvement in communications facilitated the growth of extra-village ties; beyond this, local elites came to depend on the power of the central authority for their protection as the government, under the influence of the French "modernizing" reforms, came to depend on village elites for its extractive functions. The result was to attenuate intra-village leveling pressures. At the same time the French-supported monarchy no longer followed earlier leveling practices from the top. Finally, a number of other activities previously performed by local elites began to diminish with the growing differentiation of Vietnamese society: political functions came under the purview of an evolving corps of administrators; military affairs fell to a distinct military force; credit came from an expanding merchant class, and so forth.

The confluence of all these changes was on the terms of trade between local elites and non-elites. In brief, the elites provided fewer inputs to the exchange while non-elites at the same time provided more (as signified by increasing tenancy and rising rental rates). Focusing for a moment solely on the economic sphere, Sansom's evidence indicates clearly that Vietnamese cultivators are economic maximizers, and so they should be sensitive to a changing economic role for the landlord. This is entirely consistent with the evidence in *War Comes to Long An* that economic redistribution was one motivational component in the success of the revolutionary movement.

The changing terms of trade between social groups had two significant consequences. One was the changing subjective characterization of the relationship. Silverman's evidence from Italy indicates a shift from a subjective perception of "collaboration" to one of "exploitation," that is, a decline in the "legitimacy" of the elites; we may infer that a parallel change took place in Vietnam. The other consequence, taken to its extreme in Vietnam, was decreasing cooperation with elites and, finally, armed revolt.[40]

The final dynamic process to be considered here is that explored by Joel Migdal in an as yet unpublished work; the process may be characterized as a growing "crisis of unbalanced accounts" occurring in a situation of "structural incompleteness."[41] These new elements make attractive certain new exchange relationships.

Migdal's analysis begins with the structure of village stability in subsistence peasant society. Two elements stand out: first, the prevention of outside multiple alliances or even linkages, both by the overlord and by the villagers themselves; second, economic leveling mechanisms of the type I described earlier. In a relatively closed community, social controls against deviance are strong; and the closed character of the village is perpetuated by well-founded fears of uncertainty and exploitation lying outside.

Certain changes destroy the viability of this inward-looking subsistence economy, bringing about what Migdal calls the "crisis of unbalanced accounts": a continuing cash deficit. He here identifies three particularly important changes: population growth; demands for cash to satisfy the state's taxes or the requirements of new production methods; and a decline in cash receipts from handicrafts owing to foreign or domestic competition. Migration and clearing new land are only stopgap measures for the village; ultimately villagers are forced from subsistence production into market production, as well as into labor for cash outside the village. The increasing competition for village resources increases intra-village conflict, and at the same time the developing extra-village linkages lead to a decline in the efficacy of social control mechanisms—both those that support the poor and those that temper the selfishness of the rich. The result is increasing stratification in a situation of "structural incompleteness" (one in which elements are absent that would facilitate the use of market opportunities). This combination favors the emergence of a revolutionary response. In Migdal's words:

> As the crisis of unbalanced accounts results in a greater degree of external relations, peasants interact increasingly with an active network of economic institutions outside the village. What is particularly relevant for the peasants—and especially the less powerful ones—is that this network . . . is fraught with shortcomings: it is marked by corruption and monopolistic practices and is structurally incomplete.
>
>                                      · · ·
>
> The hypothesis put forth here is that peasant participation in institutionalized revolutionary movements is an attempt on their part, at least initially, to solve [these shortcomings].[42]

Thus, in Migdal's interpretation, a revolutionary movement is a mechanism for effecting a new integration at a higher level, in keeping with the now shrunken world, to replace the traditional mechanisms of social exchange and social control that had existed in the subsistence village.

Whatever the validity of the secular processes just described, each is a gradual one producing "disposing conditions." Is there any more specific point in time, or any more specific condition, with which the emergence of a revolutionary movement might be identified? Here I think we should refer back to our earlier discussion of starting mechanisms and the importance of self-protection as an exchange issue. Such self-protection often becomes salient in the context of a war against a colonial power and this, it seems to me, has led to considerable confusion in discussions of the role of "nationalism."

In one common presentation nationalism is considered a "general law" of the form "whoever is nationalist gains popular support." It then serves as the major premise of a syllogism explaining the success of some nationalist revolutionary movement. This form is primitive but ubiquitous. Thus, for example: "That side will win peasant support which can demonstrate that it represents the cause of Vietnamese nationalism and the vague aspirations of a new life which form part of its appeal."[43] Or, as another writer puts it: "The French were definitely the 'aliens' and the Communist-led Viet-Minh forces could count on the instinctive support of the native population."[44]

Viewing the phenomenon of "nationalism" in exchange terms shifts our attention from the kind of prerational xenophobia implicit in the preceding quotations back to the realm of rational calculation. This is not to deny an emotive, symbolic aspect to revolutionary behavior; it is only to deny that a disciplined long-term movement can be constructed on this basis alone. Opposition to foreigners may provide value integration that facilitates cooperation, but it does not explain the *amount of effort* expended, that is, why the revolutionary forces fought so much more effectively than the counterrevolutionary forces in Vietnam.[45]

Another important distinction will help to clarify the role of nationalism: that between the ultimate value the group seeks to further and the value of group approval participants gain for furthering that ultimate value. Social approval is what motivates the effort, even though it is approval for contributing to the group goal of, say, nationalism. It is easy to see how an observer might mistakenly believe that the group goal itself is what motivates cooperation, but the distinction between the two values must be maintained, for it is otherwise impossible to explain how the group continues to function despite shifting means and goals.

My own interview evidence in Vietnam suggesting that "nationalism" was not a motivating factor seems confirmed by Chalmers Johnson's evidence concerning the differences in the Chinese response to the Japanese presence where Japanese policies differed. In the North, the Japanese pursued policies of compulsory labor, indiscriminate violence, and "kill all, burn all, destroy all." In Central and South China the Japanese effort was much more restrained and achieved greater success, leading the Party to observe that "in areas in which the peasants were offered reasonable security by Nanking and the Japanese, propaganda alone was not sufficient to induce them to join the guerrillas."[46]

These points suggest that "nationalism," understood as opposition to invading foreigners, is neither necessary nor sufficient to motivate a revolutionary movement. The mechanism at work in bringing about the emergence of the revolutionary *organization* is instead *self-protection*; it may be one group against another, where both are of the same national origin (the case of Long An); it may be the special "nationalist" case of native defenders versus foreign invaders; or it may be some peculiar variant, such as an ethnic minority versus a dominant majority, all within one national territory—in fact we shall discuss just such a case in the next section.

What is of interest to us is that the urgent need for self-protection is the type of individual contingent incentive peculiarly suited to be a starting mechanism. Once the organization emerges, due to this special circumstance—i.e., once the special pattern of mutual expectations is developed—then the organization, by a process of "goal succession," may shift its activities and its motivational structure into other areas. Thus through this mechanism an organization may rapidly emerge where, despite favorable disposing conditions, it might otherwise have developed only slowly, or possibly not at all. A clumsy invader may restructure the situation such that self-protection becomes important, but a clumsy compatriot may do this just as well.

## An Unlikely Case: Northern Thailand

There is hardly a less likely setting imaginable for a Communist-led revolutionary movement than in the jungles and teak forests along Thailand's northern border. Communications are poor; there is little literacy; the residents are so close to primitive cultivation that stratification by wealth has not proceeded very far. Yet just for this reason events there powerfully illustrate some of the propositions advanced in earlier pages: about the phenomenon of emergence; about the exchange functions performed by a revolutionary leadership; and about the role of agreements that political leaders are (or are not) willing to make. Space limitations dictate a highly condensed presentation of the empirical data; documentation is less than ideally complete also, due both to the sensitivity of the subject in Thailand and to sheer physical problems of research. Considerably greater detail is presented in my article "The War in Northern Thailand."[47]

The northern region of Thailand comprises roughly one-fifth of the territory of the kingdom. It consists of a series of mountain ranges stretching south from Laos and Burma and then bending westward to merge with the long mountain range extending the entire length of the Thai-Burmese border. A series of migrations over the last ten centuries, continuing to today, has populated this region with from 200,000 to 300,000 people belonging to several major ethnolinguistic groups. The diversity among the hill tribes makes generalization difficult. However, it can reasonably be said that distaste toward the upland peoples is the commonest attitude on the part of the valley-dwelling Thai, who consider the upland peoples primitive "savages" of low cultural level and unappealing hygienic practices. This distaste is aggravated by tribal swidden agricultural practices.

There are a number of distributive issues over which the tribal peoples and the Thai are in conflict. First, of course, is the land itself. According to Thai law, the upland areas are royal preserves, and the hill tribes are, technically, illegal squatters. Tribal swidden techniques destroy the forest, another infraction of the law; and the opium grown by some of the tribes is yet a third. A second major source of conflict is that the citizenship status of the tribal peoples is ambiguous at best, and thus they are unable to serve in, much less achieve any kind of mobility through, such government organs as the military, the police, or the civil administration. This total exclusion of tribal leaders from influence in the government has left the tribal peoples defenseless against petty victimization by low-level government officials. There has similarly been no alternative mobility channel through education, since until 1955 there was no system of education for the tribal peoples.* The full potential for difficulty in

---

* In 1955 the Border Patrol Police began a school program, but the well-intended BPP effort has been greatly hampered by interagency conflicts in Bangkok. In 1970 I interviewed the then best-educated Meo in Thailand—who had completed five years of schooling.

this situation has not been realized because of the limited contact between the Thai and the upland peoples, the limited education of the latter, the government's restraint in enforcing the letter of the law, and, most important, the lack of "power" within the upland system itself.

We should devote a moment to this point. It is clear that the Thai government, through its unwillingness to enter into exchange relationships with tribal peoples in the spheres of political, military, police, or bureaucratic participation, forfeited an opportunity to develop influence among them. Yet the tribal peoples themselves did not possess "power" as we have described it, at least beyond the village level. The Meo, for example, the most important tribe involved in the current violence, were once a powerful kingdom in southern China. But though the memory of a Meo king has survived through the twelve centuries since the destruction of their kingdom, until recently the Meo have not had the supra-village organization that would have permitted their coordinated action in great numbers.

It was in such a low-power system that the Communist Party of Thailand (CPT) began recruitment efforts around 1962. Significantly, it began with offers, by Thai and Sino-Thai assigned to the upland areas, for educational opportunity abroad (in Laos, Vietnam, and China) of a type simply not available through cooperation with the Thai government. Coupled with this was the offer of a public service career in the revolutionary movement. By 1967 the movement was still in the dyadic phase, with between 100 and 200 activists, according to government sources, spread in small numbers principally in the border provinces. At this point, in response to two incidents, a massive and violent government reaction took place, and this will illustrate for us the phenomenon of emergence.

The first incident was the so-called Opium War in July 1967, in which the KMT groups resident in the north since fleeing China in 1949 engaged in a rare public brawl over 16 tons of opium. To preserve the fiction that Thailand was being "invaded," the government sent a number of army units up into the hills. For reasons too complicated to go into here, the tribal peoples engaged these units in some small brushes, and the army retaliated by napalming and burning villages, firing indiscriminately with mortars, and forcibly resettling the hill tribes.

The second incident was actually a series of small engagements growing out of an assassination, a small attack on a government militia outpost, and an extortion attempt by police officials. The result was similar, but in new areas: a violent and indiscriminate reaction that restructured the situation so as to make self-protection an urgent matter. Some idea of the extent of the violence can be gained from the size of the refugee population created: some 6,000 in June 1968, 9,000 in January 1969, 10,000 in mid-1970, and 15,000 in 1972.

Correlating with this massive government assault was the emergence of a true authority structure, in fact an incipient "government," at least in the Meo areas. The number of people taking an active part in the movement, according to government sources, jumped from 200 or fewer in 1967 to more than 2,000 in 1972. At the same time, large areas became "liberated zones" from which the Thai government was (and is) completely excluded. This "void" left in the hills by the Thai government was filled by the first integrated supra-village political and military structure the Meo have had in more than a thousand years. Given the conditions described above, it is unlikely that such a structure would have emerged for a very long time, if at all, without the "starting mechanism" lent by the Thai authorities. The irony of course is that the movement, in cooperation with ethnic Thai CPT cadres, began in turn to put pressure on the Thai communities in the foothills. Indeed, one of the remarkable features of the movement is just this degree of Thai-tribal collaboration. It attests to the power of favorable exchanges to overcome lack of value integration, given the proper catalyst.

This brief example thus illustrates several points. First among these is the phenomenon of emergence, resulting from the peculiarly potent starting mechanism of self-protection. It illustrates again the rationalistic common core of what in the Chinese case was called nationalism: that the mechanism is not emotional opposition to foreigners; the tribal people cooperate well with the "foreign" CPT leaders. A second point well illustrated is the importance for emergence of the kinds of agreements the existing authorities are willing to make. The establishment's discriminatory practices, legal and customary, against the tribal peoples deprived the central government of exchange relations with the tribesmen, and thereby of authority as well, thus recapitulating Diem's quest for autonomy and the resulting self-isolation of his regime. In both cases an emergent anti-system structure was the result. A third point concerns the phase of goal succession. The preliminary findings of studies now being completed reveal that the movement is being consolidated by goal succession into broad literacy training, introduction of sanitation and public health measures, formation of cooperatives, institution of new agricultural methods, and the like.

My purpose here has been to introduce at least the beginnings of a framework for analysis of revolution that describes both the subjectively rational aspect and the (at least in principle) objectively calculable variables. One important task for elaborating the framework is operationalization of the dimensions and, through further empirical work on various revolutions, a more precise specification of the functional relations involved and of the "prices" of the exchanged values. Silverman's work is a suggestive beginning to the pricing problem. Another important task, as I see it, is the integration of the emotive and inner-psychological aspects of revolutionary participation into this rational-calculating framework. Both individual and group components are relevant here, e.g., early socialization of revolutionary leaders and crowd behavior.

I think one virtue of this framework is that it directs our attention to certain measurable aspects of the real world. Thus "legitimacy" is seen as a function of the terms of trade in exchange relationships, though an important empirical issue here is the extent of the lags involved. We will thus want to look at the structure of exchange networks, and particularly at the absence of exchange bonds between significant actors. An important correlative variable here is the amount of power in the various parts of the system under examination.

Dynamically, we will want to know how the networks are shifting in structure, and how the terms of trade between groups vary. In particular, as new groups appear, what kinds of exchange linkages will they be able to develop? And how do shifts in other variables, such as education, communications, physical mobility, marketing patterns, and technology, affect existing structures and the potential for new ones?

Finally, I would add, this framework emphasizes the volitional aspect of revolutionary emergence: we see revolution as an adaptive response to a particular kind of situation, and whether such a situation exists depends on the willingness of various participants to enter into certain agreements. This is by no means to say that this choice is not influenced by other factors as well. But an awareness of choice itself is important in determining the decisions of participants. Here it seems to me exchange analysis hints that a more just and less violent world is not just a matter of structural determinism.

## PART THREE

*Revolution: Town and Countryside*

# Utopian Socialist Themes in Maoism

MAURICE MEISNER

Modern history, Karl Marx once wrote, "is the urbanisation of the countryside, not, as among the ancients, the ruralisation of the city."[1] Mao Tse-tung, seemingly, has been intent on reversing the direction of the modern historic process. In Maoist theory and practice, modern revolutionary history is made by peasants in the countryside, who culminate their revolutionary efforts by overwhelming the presumably conservative inhabitants of the cities. And in the post-revolutionary era, Mao's "ruralism" is reflected in an emphasis on socioeconomic development of the agrarian sector, a perception that the true sources for socialist reconstruction reside in the countryside, and the notion that urban dwellers can acquire "proletarian" revolutionary virtues by going to the rural areas and living and working with peasants.

Yet before concluding that Mao has stood Marx completely on his head, it should be noted that though Marx celebrated the modern dominance of the city over the countryside as a historically progressive development, he was more concerned with the phenomenon of the separation between town and countryside as an expression of man's alienated "pre-history" under the social division of labor. For Marx, moreover, the resolution of the problem was not the urbanization of the countryside in the present, but the abolition of the distinction between town and country in the socialist and communist future.

Maoists fully share this Marxist utopian goal; indeed, there is no feature of the original Marxist vision of future communist society that occupies so prominent a place in Chinese Marxist theoretical writings. And the theoretical concern not only expresses a utopian hope, but reflects a preoccupation with pressing practical problems of development. In China, as in other predominantly agrarian countries, no social question is more critical than the gap between the modern cities and the backward countryside. It is a gap that is political and cultural as well as economic, and the manner in which the problem is perceived has crucial implications for virtually every aspect of public policy. For those seeking egalitarian social ends, the Marxist historical analysis of the separation between town and country is a matter of special theoretical and practical relevance, and the Marxist goal of abolishing that separation is especially attractive.

Although Maoists share the utopian goal Marx proclaimed, they differ significantly in their historical understanding of the problem, and the means by which they strive to resolve it are profoundly different from anything Marx or Lenin might have conceived. In examining this matter in the history of Maoist thought and action, one is struck by a more general phenomenon—the appearance in Maoism of conceptions and notions similar to those characteristic of a variety of nineteenth-century Western non-Marxist socialist theories, especially those pejoratively labeled "utopian" by Marx and Lenin.

It should hardly be surprising—and especially not to Marxists—that where Marxist theory has taken root in underdeveloped lands it should take on certain characteristics of earlier "pre-Marxian" socialist ideologies. Whereas Marxism presupposed the existence and development of modern industrial capitalism, utopian socialist theories had their intellectual origins in an earlier era of modern economic development; like Marxism, they were protests against the injustices of early industrialism, but, unlike Marxism, they did not accept or take into account the historical and social consequences of modern capitalism. If there is a causal relationship between sociohistorical environments and modes of thought, as is here assumed to be the general historical case, then it seems not illogical that ideas appropriate to a preindustrial or early industrial culture should appear (however implicitly and unconsciously) in the revolutionary Marxist ideologies that today flourish in the economically backward areas of the world.

This essay will attempt first to identify certain of the "utopian socialist" strains in Maoist thought, particularly as they are revealed in the Maoist conception of the relationship between town and countryside in modern history and in the making of modern revolutions, and then to assess their theoretical implications and their sociohistorical function. This will necessitate not only a comparison between aspects of original Marxism and the contemporary Maoist variant of the theory, but also, to begin with, an inquiry into some of the theoretical and historical differences between Marxism and other nineteenth-century Western socialist ideologies.

## Marxism

All history, according to Marxist theory, is marked by a "constant war" between town and countryside. On this view, one of the distinguishing features of "civilization" (as opposed to primitive communalism) is the "fixation of the contrast between town and country as the basis of the entire division of social labour."[2] The perennial antagonism between urban and rural areas is a phenomenon of central importance in Marxist historical theory. As Marx formulated the matter in *Capital*: "The foundation of every division of labor that is well developed, and brought about by the exchange of commodities, is the separation between town and country. It may be said that the whole economical history of society is summed up in the movement of this antithesis."[3]

Although a universal historical phenomenon, the distinction between town and countryside became a dynamic "antithesis" only in the Western line of historical evolution leading from classical antiquity to modern capitalism. As Marx described the process, town and countryside have existed in a continuous and antagonistic relationship, alternately providing the basis of successive historical stages. For the purposes of the present discussion, the salient feature of the Marxist analysis is that historical progress is identified with the supremacy of the city, whereas the dominance of rural areas is associated with periods of historical stagnation or regression. For example, Marx summarized the decline of Greek and Roman antiquity and the rise of feudalism as follows:

> If antiquity started out from the town and its territory, the Middle Ages started out from the country. This different starting point was determined by the sparseness of the population at that time. . . . In contrast to Greece and Rome, feudal development therefore extends over a much wider field. . . . The last centuries of the declining Roman Empire and its conquest by the barbarians destroyed a number of productive forces; agriculture had declined, industry had decayed for want of a market, trade had died out or been violently suspended, the rural and urban population had decreased. From these conditions and the mode of organisation of the conquest determined by them, feudal property developed under the influence of the Germanic military constitution.[4]

It is noteworthy that Marx attributed the emergence of the new rural-dominated feudal sociohistorical formation not to any underlying process of economic development, but rather primarily to a fortuitous political factor, i.e., the barbarian conquests and their retrogressive effects on population and production. Nowhere is it suggested that feudalism was the inevitable or historically logical result of the "ancient" mode of production; nor is there any implication that feudalism was a stage in a process of progressive historical evolution. To the contrary, the rural-based feudal system is described as a retrogressive development resulting from a decline in productive forces and population.

The major Marxist concern, however, is not with the origins of feudalism, but with the question of the transition from feudalism to capitalism. Here the gradual emergence of commercial towns on the fringes of feudal society—with the consequent conflict between the burgher towns and the feudal countryside—becomes crucial in the Marxist explanation of the genesis of modern capitalism. With the growth of large-scale trade in the late medieval era, the accumulation of commercial capital, the specialization of urban craft industries, and the influx of a surplus rural population, the towns became increasingly separated from the countryside—a division that reflected the separation between capital and landed property and intensified the "constant war of the country against the town." It was a war that the towns were bound to win, though now the changing relationship between town and countryside is attributed to economic factors—in contrast to the political-military origins of feudalism and the earlier dominance of the countryside. The rapid extension of the division of labor in the towns (especially the development of modern manufactures) led to the disintegration of feudalism and the triumph of the modern bourgeoisie, a class that tended to absorb all earlier possessing classes while turning the majority of the population of the emergent towns into a new oppressed class, the modern urban proletariat. For Marx, the rise of capitalism was not only inseparable from the dominance of town over countryside; it also foreshadowed the dominance of urbanized industrial nations over rural peasant countries—for the permanence of the productive forces of capitalism could be assured only if capitalism achieved worldwide dominion.[5] Marx had little doubt that this universal triumph was immanent in the modern historic process. As the "Manifesto" proclaimed:

The bourgeoisie has subjected the country to the rule of the towns. It has created enormous cities, has greatly increased the urban population as compared with the rural, and has thus rescued a considerable part of the population from the idiocy of rural life. Just as it has made the country dependent on the towns, so it has made barbarian and semi-barbarian countries dependent on the civilized ones, nations of peasants on nations of bourgeois, the East on the West.[6]

Despite this celebration of the supremacy of the modern capitalist city over the internal and external "countryside" as a historically progressive and indeed revolutionary development, Marx morally condemned the separation between cities and rural areas: "The antagonism of town and country can only exist as a result of private property. It is the most crass expression of the subjection of the individual under the division of labour, under a definite activity forced upon him—a subjection which makes one man into a restricted town-animal, the other into a restricted country-animal, and daily creates anew the conflict between their interests."[7] Thus the abolition of the distinction between town and countryside was a precondition for achieving the "truly human life" the socialist revolution promised. It is interesting to observe that despite his well-known distaste for "the idiocy of rural life," Marx (in one of his rare glimpses into the future communist utopia) pictured the ideal society in almost rurally idyllic, pastoral tones: "In communist society, where nobody has one exclusive sphere of activity but each can become accomplished in any branch he wishes, society regulates the general production and thus makes possible for me to do one thing to-day and another to-morrow, to hunt in the morning, fish in the afternoon, rear cattle in the evening, criticize after dinner, just as I have a mind, without ever becoming hunter, fisherman, shepherd or critic."[8] Moreover, it is noteworthy that among the measures Marx proposed for the transition to a communist society once the proletariat achieved political supremacy was the "combination of agriculture with manufacturing industry" accompanied by the "gradual abolition of the distinction between town and country, by a more equable distribution of the population over the country."[9]

Yet the Marxist conception of the revolutionary process that would lead to the realization of this goal was firmly centered on the modern industrialized city. Capitalist forces of production had led to the definitive economic and political dominance of town over countryside and at the same time had established the essential (and urban-based) material and social conditions for the future socialist transformation of society—large-scale industry and the modern proletariat. For Marx, the modern historical stage was the city, and its principal actors the two urban classes into which capitalist forces of production inevitably were dividing society as a whole: the bourgeoisie and the industrial proletariat. In this conception of modern history, the countryside and its inhabitants had a minimal role to play at best, and possibly a retrogressive one. It was assumed that a substantial portion of the peasantry would be thrown into the ranks of the urban proletariat, and the remainder would be transformed into "rural proletarians," working as wage-laborers in large agricultural enterprises organized on a capitalist basis of production. As Engels typically put the Marxist position on the matter: "Our small peasant, like every other survival of a past mode of production, is hopelessly doomed. He is a future proletarian."[10]

Thus it was assumed that the peasantry *qua* peasantry would largely disappear from the historical scene. And insofar as it did not, Marx viewed the persisting peasant population either as politically irrelevant in the making of modern history or, more sinisterly, as a potentially reactionary force that could serve as the social basis for historically retrogressive Caesarist-type dictatorships and Bonapartist cults—a possible development that raised the specter of the resurgence of the reactionary social forces of the countryside over the progressive social forces of the modern city.[11]

It is significant to note that neither in the Marxist analysis of the transition from feudalism to capitalism nor in the Marxist conception of the forthcoming socialist revolution does one find any place for the peasantry as an independent or creative force in modern history. Although peasants are the main victims of exploitation in feudal society, it is the urban bourgeoisie that plays the historically progressive role in overthrowing feudal socioeconomic and political relationships. The peasants are largely passive victims of the transformation. To be sure, Marx and Engels did not wholly preclude the possibility that the peasants might make some positive contribution to the final class struggle between urban workers and capitalists. But they would be able to do so only as "auxiliaries" of the proletariat and only insofar as they accepted the ideological and political leadership of the working class of the cities. As Marx succinctly put the matter in his analysis of the Paris Commune of 1871 (a document enshrined as the Marxian model of proletarian revolution and the dictatorship of the proletariat despite the abortiveness of the historical event itself), the Communal Constitution of the Parisian proletariat "brought the rural producers under the intellectual lead of the central towns of their districts, and there secured to them, in the workingmen, the natural trustees of their interests."[12] In original Marxism, in short, the sources of historical progress and the creative forces of revolution resided in the cities; and modern history, insofar as it was to be modern and progressive, was indeed no less than the "urbanization of the countryside."

Furthermore, Marx placed a positive value on the forms of political and economic centralization that industrialism entailed. The large-scale organization of both industry and agriculture and the increasing specialization of the division of labor based on an ever more complex technology were seen as creating the necessary conditions of economic abundance on which the future socialist society must rest. Not only did Marx and Engels champion the superiority of centrally directed, large-scale economic enterprises, they also saw as historically progressive (and a prophetic pointer to the socialist revolution) the modern, centralized bourgeois state. In describing the revolutionary accomplishments of capitalism as the prelude for socialism, Marx observed: "The bourgeoisie keeps more and more doing away with the scattered state of the population, of the means of production, and has concentrated property in a few hands. The necessary consequence of this was political centralization."[13] Although the centralized bourgeois state apparatus was to be "smashed" (and not merely taken over) in the socialist revolution, the ensuing "transition period" would temporarily intensify centralized political and economic control. "The proletariat," Marx predicted, "will use its political supremacy to wrest, by degrees, all capital from the bourgeoisie, to centralize all instruments of production in the hands of the State."[14] Moreover, among the specific measures proposed following the success of proletarian revolution were "centralization of credit" and "centralization of the means of communication and transport in the hands of the State."[15]

Needless to say, the processes of political and economic centralization that Marx saw as historically progressive in both capitalism and the early phase of socialism presupposed urbanization; they were processes that fortified the dominance of town over countryside, as modern historical progress demanded. Marx was not unaware of the social costs of centralization and urbanization. He wrote with

great sympathy about the tragic human price involved in the uproot-
ing of peasants from the land and from their old social world of sanctified custom and tradition, as well as the dehumanization of the
growing proletariat in large factories and overcrowded cities. But, in
the Marxist view, this was the price of historical progress, and the
price had to be paid. It was, after all, precisely a "dehumanized"
proletariat that was to be the agent of a universal process of human
liberation, and it was a large-scale industrialization that was creating
the economic prerequisites for the birth of the new society. Just as
the abolition of the state had to be preceded by its centralization, so
the eventual abolition of the distinction between town and country
had to be preceded by the dominance of the cities over the rural areas.

Moreover, there could be no retreat from the course that history
dictated, and there was no hope of "bypassing" the social consequences of urbanization and industrialization. To those who hoped
to do so, Marx replied that "the country that is more developed industrially only shows, to the less developed, the image of its own future."[16] Indeed, a "premature" social revolution—one that took place
before capitalist productive forces were fully developed—would be
futile at best and possibly historically retrogressive:

> If the proletariat destroys the political rule of the bourgeoisie [Marx
> argued], that will only be a temporary victory, only an element in the
> service of the bourgeois revolution itself, as in 1794, so long as in the
> course of history, in its "movement," the material conditions are not
> yet created which make necessary the abolition of the bourgeois mode
> of production. . . . Men do not build themselves a new world out of the
> fruits of the earth, as vulgar superstition believes, but out of the his-
> torical accomplishments of their declining civilization. They must, in
> the course of their development, begin by themselves producing the
> material conditions of a new society, and no effort of mind or will can
> free them from this destiny.[17]

More ominous was the potential for regression in any attempt to force
the pace of history. Marx and Engels raised this possibility in responding to Russian Populist proposals to "skip over" the capitalist stage
and thus avoid the evils of industrialization and urbanization. Engels
summed up the general Marxist position on the matter in 1875:

> Only at a certain level of development of the productive forces of so-
> ciety, an even very high level for our modern conditions, does it become
> possible to raise production to such an extent that the abolition of class

distinctions can be a real progress, *can be lasting without bringing about stagnation or even decline* [my emphasis] in the mode of social production. But the productive forces have reached this level of development only in the hands of the bourgeoisie. The bourgeoisie, therefore, in this respect is just as necessary a precondition of the socialist revolution as the proletariat itself. Hence a man who will say that this revolution can be more easily carried out in a country, because, *although* it has no proletariat, it has no bourgeoisie *either*, only proves that he has still to learn the ABC of Socialism.[18]

Marx's characterization of modern history as "the urbanization of the countryside" was thus no mere rhetorical turn of phrase; the proposition is central to his analysis of the modern historical process and its socialist outcome. For Marx the city was the symbol of historical progress, for it was in the cities that the prerequisites for socialism resided. The social evils of urbanization and industrialization—the degradation and dehumanization of man in modern factories and in large cities, his increasing enslavement to an ever more complex and specialized technology and division of labor, his further alienation under the unbearable weight of gigantic forms of economic and political organization—were the historical costs that mankind had to pay for its eventual liberation. The new society could only be built on the material accomplishments of this past and would bear the burdens of the past. Socialism could only be the product of capitalism, and thus "in every respect" socialist society would be "still stamped with the birthmarks of the old society from whose womb it emerges."[19] For Marx the historical process had to be carried to its modern breaking point before mankind could break away from his alienated "pre-history." Just as man's total alienation in modern capitalist society was the precondition for his total liberation, so the total dominance of town over countryside was the necessary price and prelude for achieving the abolition of the separation between town and countryside.

## Marxism and Utopian Socialism

Utopian visions of a future egalitarian social order are as old as the history of social thought, recurring throughout the ages in the histories of all major civilizations. But socialism, though in this tradition, is a distinctively modern intellectual response to early industrial capitalism in Western Europe. More precisely, the emergence of socialist theories should be seen as the specific responses of workers and intellectuals to the twin upheavals of the French Revolution and the industrial revolution, not simply (and simplistically) as an ageless quest for freedom and social justice.

Marxism is but one socialist response to the traumatic social and political transformations wrought by Western European industrial capitalism. It is neither an eternal truth, as some of its adherents present it, nor a modern expression of the ancient Judeo-Christian prophetic tradition, as some critics would have us believe.* What distinguishes Marxism from its nineteenth-century rivals, those social-ist doctrines that Marx and Engels pejoratively characterized as uto-pian, are, broadly put, three major issues: first, the acceptance of modern industrial capitalism as a necessary and progressive state in sociohistorical development; second, the belief that the urban indus-trial proletariat is the truly creative revolutionary class historically destined to transcend the bourgeois order and usher in the new class-less society; and, third, a belief in an objective historical process amenable to a scientific analysis that reveals the potentials men can seize on to realize what is immanent in history itself—as opposed to any reliance on moral examples or the innate goodness of human nature.

These are perspectives not present in the various utopian social-isms of Fourier, Saint-Simon, Owen, and others—however much else Marx shared with them and derived from them. Nor were they present in similar "utopian" views found in the anarchist and populist social-ist ideologies (of which Rousseau and Proudhon were the intellectual forerunners) that flourished in the less economically advanced Euro-pean countries. Although the utopian socialists were no less vigorous than the Marxists in condemning the social evils of capitalist indus-trialism, their critiques tended to be based more on moral judgments of the injustices of the new economic order than on any historical analysis of the nature and function of the system. As Engels noted: "The socialism of earlier days certainly criticized the existing capital-istic mode of production and its consequences. But it could not ex-plain them, and, therefore, could not get mastery of them. It could

---

* Perhaps the most vulgar expression of this widely held, but highly misleading, notion is to be found in Toynbee: "Marx has taken the goddess 'Historical Necessity' in place of Yahweh for his deity, and the internal proletariat of the Western World in place of Jewry for his chosen people, and the Messianic Kingdom is conceived of as a Dictatorship of the Proletariat; but the salient features of the Jewish Apocalypse protrude through his threadbare disguise." *A Study of History* (New York: Oxford University Press, 1947), p. 400.

only simply reject them as bad."[20] Moreover, as George Lichtheim observes, the utopian socialists were inclined "to identify the critique of capitalism as a system of production with the rejection of industrialism as such."[21]

Quite naturally accompanying this ambiguous attitude toward modern industrialism were ambiguous and uncertain solutions for the social problems it produced. In utopian socialist writings, the proletariat appears as the object of exploitation but not as the subject in any future process of emancipation. Rather the solution is to be wrought by means of education and the force of moral example, through the working out of ideal social models by those who have grasped reason and understand social truth. As Marx acutely put the matter: "In the formation of their plans they [the utopian socialists] are conscious of caring chiefly for the interests of the working class, as being the most suffering class. Only from the point of view of being the most suffering class does the proletariat exist for them." While recognizing the existence of social class divisions, they nonetheless "consider themselves far superior to all class antagonisms," Marx further observed. "They want to improve the condition of every member of society. . . . Hence, they habitually appeal to society at large. . . . For how can people, when once they understand their system, fail to see in it the best possible plan of the best possible state of society?"[22]

What is striking about utopian socialist (and populist) ideas in this respect are their highly elitist political implications. Although utopian socialist theorists rose in protest against the social injustices of capitalist industrialization, they did not assign to the proletariat—the principal victims of capitalism—the main role in correcting those injustices and transforming society. Rather, they appealed to man in general, premised on the fundamental goodness of an essentially unchanging human nature; and the populists looked to the peasant masses in particular as a class with instinctive socialist strivings. But despite this faith in the powers of reason and the moral goodness of man, the ultimate bearers of the new and perfect social order remain the Social Planners themselves; in the end the historical initiative rests with those supra-class men of genius who alone possess truth and reason.

Utopian socialist theories emerged out of a relatively early stage of modern capitalist development, at a time when the social and historical consequences of capitalist industrialism and urbanism could not have been fully recognized. The resulting tendency was to view capitalism as an "unnatural" phenomenon as well as a morally evil one, to view the industrial workers as its passive and unfortunate victims, and to emphasize human consciousness and moral appeals as the forces that would bring about a socialist utopia consonant with the needs of a universal and constant human nature.

Utopian socialism and populism can thus be seen as essentially "precapitalist" rejections of capitalism, as a general mode of thought that had its greatest appeal to social groups threatened by the early phases of modern capitalist development (artisans and peasants, along with their self-appointed intellectual spokesmen), and as ideologies that as a result tended to find their roots in the less economically advanced countries of Europe in the nineteenth century. Marxism, on the other hand, was an intellectual product of a more mature phase of capitalist development and found its "natural home" among the intellectuals and urban workers of the economically advanced countries, for it was a theory that accepted modern capitalism and all its social consequences. It is in the light of these general historical and theoretical differences that one must understand the very different conceptions of the relationship between town and countryside characteristic of non-Marxian socialist ideologies.

For the purposes of the present inquiry no attempt will be made to distinguish between the many different socialist predecessors and contemporaries Marx and Engels condemned as "utopian." Nor will we be particularly interested in the differences between the utopian socialist theories that arose in the Western European countries in the first half of the nineteenth century and the Populist theories that flourished in Russia during the second half of the century. The concern here will be to characterize in broad outline a general mode of thought that underlies a wide variety of non-Marxian responses to the social consequences of early capitalist industrialism. Indeed, in large measure, it is only in contrast to the Marxist analysis of capitalism that "utopian socialism" becomes a historically definable intellectual-political tradition.

One general and fundamental feature of utopian socialist thought is the perception of history as basically a struggle between "natural" and "unnatural" forces of development. Like Rousseau, the nineteenth-century utopian socialists attributed social evils to unnatural institutions that had imposed themselves on society and tended to pervert a basically good human nature. Thus the solution of social problems was seen in terms of removing unnatural institutions (or preventing their further development); an ideal social order would then emerge as a result of the release of natural human desires. The achievement of the task was based on a profound faith in the powers of human consciousness, a faith that the moral suasion and social examples of "enlightened" men would naturally appeal to the instincts of all men to do away with false institutions.

From this rationalist, unhistorical perspective, capitalism and its social forms and consequences were seen as unnatural phenomena, and the modern city—the symbol and center of capitalist industrialism—as the principal source of social corruption and dehumanization. The condemnation of the bourgeois city, accompanied by a strongly agrarian orientation, appears in the Babouvist doctrine[23] that grew out of the French Revolution, a doctrine that marks the earliest expression of modern socialist and communist ideas. Philippe Michel Buonarroti, the major ideologist of Babouvism, advocated that the urban masses should go "back to the land" to achieve an egalitarian order: "Agriculture and the arts of first necessity, being the true nutritive supports of society, it is to the scene of these occupations that men are called by nature to live, whether it be to till the soil or furnish the agriculturalists with commodities and recreations."[24] Buonarroti, as J. L. Talmon observes, "saw in the great cities and capitals 'symptoms of public malady, an infallible forerunner of civil convulsions.' The evils of the old regime were to him indissolubly interwoven with the huge cities, which have condemned one portion of the people to overwhelming toil, and the other to demoralizing inaction. The countryside has been crushed, the cities overcrowded. The latter became seats of 'voluptuous pleasure' of the rich, the source and manifestation of most glaring inequality, greed, envy, and unrest. Agriculture should be restored to its ancient primacy and glory." Thus to realize the ideal society, the large cities had to be broken up, "by scattering their inhabitants over the country to live in healthy smiling villages."[25]

The anti-urban biases expressed in the first crude stirrings of modern communist egalitarianism became one of the major themes of utopian socialist thought in general and received its most powerful expression in Russian Populism. The assumption was that the modern division between town and countryside was not (as in Marxism) a logical historical development, but rather an unnatural phenomenon that separated men from each other and dehumanized them. Just as capitalism in general was unnatural, so the modern bourgeois city was an external intrusion that forced men to live in a manner alien to their "true" human needs. This assumption is reflected in the utopian socialist solution to the social evils wrought by capitalism and industrialism: the creation of a network of small, rural-based socialistic communities, which by moral appeal and social example would spread to undermine the urban-based capitalist system.*

What is particularly striking is the strongly agrarian character of the ideal communities the utopian socialists envisioned and attempted to establish. Their self-sufficient socialistic communes were to be set up in relatively remote areas of the countryside as much out of preference as necessity—not simply because they had to grow and function independently of capitalist socioeconomic relationships and political control (in order to serve as alternative models of social development), but also because of what were perceived to be the social virtues of rural life in general. Fourier's famed phalansteres, for example, were to be voluntary associations of 1,600 persons cultivating some 5,000 acres of land. Generally hostile to modern large-scale industry and technology, the Fourierists believed that agriculture was the natural occupation of men and celebrated the virtues of agrarian simplicity.[26]

Even those utopians who recognized the potential social benefits of modern industry and technology, and thus wished to bring them under the collective social control of the producers, envisioned ideal communities in which the cultivation of the soil occupied a prominent and honored place. Etienne Cabet, perhaps more properly characterized as a "utopian communist" than as a "utopian socialist," was an ardent advocate of industrialization. Yet, deeply tied to the eighteenth-century tradition of Natural Law ethics, he believed, as Lichtheim notes, "that there are certain universally true propositions about

* There is an interesting similarity between the utopian socialist conception of how socialism would come into being and the generally accepted view of the process of the transition from feudalism to capitalism. In the latter case, bourgeois towns developed outside the feudal system and eventually undermined and overwhelmed it. The utopian socialist communes, which were to be established beyond the confines of capitalist society, presumably were to function in a similar manner. In the Marxist view, of course, the transition to socialism presupposed a qualitatively different historical process: socialism could emerge only on the basis of the material and social foundations of capitalism and only through the working out of the contradictions within the capitalist mode of production itself. In addition to producing the necessary economic conditions for socialism, capitalism also produced the modern proletariat, the agent of socialist historical redemption. In short, as Marx put it in the "Manifesto," the bourgeoisie necessarily creates "its own gravediggers."

human nature which, once understood, can lead only to one conclusion: that by going back to 'nature' (i.e., to the precapitalist order of things) men will go back to their own 'true' nature."[27] In Cabet's visionary description of the competely egalitarian Icaria, one finds the majority of the inhabitants engaging in agriculture, albeit with the assistance of modern technology.[28] Even Robert Owen, himself a wealthy industrialist with a profound faith in the powers of science and industry to yield unlimited economic abundance, eventually proposed that the restructuring of society should be brought about by the establishment of model agrarian-based socialist communities— the more or less self-sufficient "Villages of Cooperation."[29]

Although the utopian socialists' attitudes toward modern industry and technology were highly diverse, ranging from hostility to celebrations of the social benefits their proper use would yield, they stood on common ground (for the most part) in rejecting the modern industrial city as the starting point for socialist transformation. Rather, they saw the model socialistic communities, operating outside the capitalist system in the more remote areas of the countryside yet untouched by modern capitalism, as the agency of transformation. And these models, as a general rule, pictured the ideal society as one where agriculture and industry were combined (in varying fashions and degrees) in a new rural setting. This ideal, which implicitly rejects the modern industrialized city, became a cornerstone of utopian socialism. More explicitly advocated later by Proudhon and especially by the Russian Populists, it remains the cornerstone of the contemporary utopian socialist tradition. "The union of agriculture, industry and handicraft in a modern village community," according to Martin Buber (the most eloquent twentieth-century spokesman for utopian socialism), is the ideal social arrangement and the means by which the socialist society is to be achieved.[30]

The generally anti-urban thrust of utopian socialist thought is reflected in a variety of characteristic beliefs that negate the features associated with the modern city. One of the most prominent themes in early socialist literature is a profound distrust of all forms of large-scale organization. The hostility to centralization—represented in the political realm by the modern, bureaucratic state and in the economic realm by capitalist forms of industrial organization—that is implicit in the ideal of a society reorganized on the basis of self-sufficient communes appears most explicitly and forcefully in the writings of Proudhon: "The prime cause of all the disorders that visit society, of the oppression of the citizens and the decay of nations," he wrote, "lies in the single and hierarchical centralization of authority. . . . We need to make an end of this monstrous parasitism as soon as possible."[31] His remedy for the problem (and it was in accord with the general utopian socialist solution) was a free federation of autonomous communal units unfettered by centralized, bureaucratic entanglements. "The dispersion of the masses and their redistribution is beginning," he proclaimed, and thus the center of social life was moving from the overpopulated cities to "the new agricultural and industrial groupings."[32]

Closely associated with this hostility to modern large-scale and centralized organization was a distaste for occupational specialization. The inhabitants of Fourier's ideal phalansteres, for example, were to engage in various occupations and activities and switch from one to another every two hours. The ideal was the well-rounded individual, a person who would combine many different kinds of physical labor with a wide variety of cultural and intellectual pursuits, thus satisfying a natural human desire for diversity and self-fulfillment. This bias against specialization was also a source of anti-intellectualism. In this ideal society, there was no need for formal institutions of education, for the young would educate themselves spontaneously in a natural social setting based on the unity of living and working;[33] and there would be no place for university-educated intellectuals, whose specialized training necessarily created a sharp separation between mental and manual labor incongruous with the new order. This notion was later to be emphasized by Kropotkin in his anarchist-populist variant of the utopian socialist tradition; Kropotkin advocated the wholesale abolition of institutions of higher education in favor of "school-work-shops" that would integrate study with work, thus eliminating the distinction between mental and manual labor.[34] Among the earlier utopians, anti-intellectualism—in the form of a Rousseauist distrust of intellectuals in general—is particularly marked in the writings of Proudhon and Wilhelm Weitling, the most noted German exponent of French utopian socialist ideas.[35]

Other prominent (though not universal) themes in utopian socialist thought are asceticism and complete egalitarianism. As opposed to the opulence and extravagance that marked urban bourgeois life, the utopians advocated the virtues of a simple and spartan life-style. And in reaction to the gross inequalities and rigid social stratification of the modern industrial city, there arose demands for wholesale and immediate social leveling. For Marx, by contrast, asceticism in general reflected total human self-alienation, and egalitarian social leveling a crudely premature (and, for its time, reactionary) ideological demand that flowed from a still underdeveloped industrial capitalism and a still immature proletariat.*

As we have seen, the centralization and specialization the utopian socialists so strongly condemned were identified with the modern city. It was in the city that large-scale industry developed and where its horrendous social consequences were most evident; it was in the city that the human personality was fragmented by an increasingly complex and specialized division of labor; it was in the city that the bureaucratic state power resided; it was in the city that university-trained specialists and intellectual elites were produced. And it was to be by going *outside* of the city that the utopian socialists hoped to negate all of the evils and inequities associated with urban capitalism, including the unnatural division between town and countryside.

The utopian socialist views that arose in the Western European countries, especially France, in the early nineteenth century, received fuller and more systematic expression in the latter half of the century in Russian Populism. Although classical Russian Populism (circa 1850–80) was well within the mainstream of utopian socialist thought in general—and, indeed, was a direct intellectual descendant in large measure—it emerged under particular historical conditions (and in a historical time) that made it a distinct variant of the general ideological pattern. Like their Western predecessors, Russian Populist theorists were responding to the social disruptions of early capitalism and industrialism, but their response was conditioned by a consciousness of "backwardness," by a recognition that they were dealing with the specific problems of a largely agrarian country, where modern capitalism was in its infancy, in confrontation with the economically advanced capitalist countries of Western Europe. As Walicki points out, "Russian Populism was not only a reaction to the

---

* Marx generally viewed utopian socialism as an ideological expression of the first futile strivings of the emergent proletariat, strivings that "necessarily failed, owing to the then underdeveloped state of the proletariat, as well as to the absence of the economic conditions for its emancipation, conditions that had yet to be produced, and could be produced by the impending bourgeois epoch alone. The revolutionary literature that accompanied these first movements of the proletariat had necessarily a reactionary character. *It inculcated universal asceticism and social leveling in its crudest form*" (my emphasis). "Manifesto," in Marx and Engels, *Selected Works* (Moscow: Foreign Languages Publishing House, 1949), 1: 58.

development of capitalism *inside* Russia—it was also a reaction to capitalism *outside* Russia."[36] Moreover, whereas utopian socialism in the West preceded Marxism, Populism appeared when Marxism was already a well-formulated theory; thus not only were the Populists influenced significantly by Marxist ideas, but they developed their own ideas as an explicit alternative to the Marxist analysis of capitalism and its historical outcome.[37] One further general distinction might be noted: the utopian socialists (in their rejection of capitalism) spoke for what they perceived to be the interests of society in general, with a particular sympathy for the urban workers as the most exploited segment of society, whereas the Populists presented themselves as the spokesmen for "the people," defined essentially as the vast peasant masses, who were held to be the main victims of capitalist encroachment. These features—the consciousness of "backwardness," the awareness of Marxism, and the special concern with the fate of the peasantry—gave Populist theory an ideological dimension not present in earlier utopian socialist ideologies and give it a particular contemporary relevance.

Nonetheless, the Populists shared with the utopian socialists certain fundamental assumptions, beliefs, and ideals; indeed, Plekhanov and Lenin characterized Russian Populism as a form of utopian socialism, and their lengthy polemical critiques of it were similar to the critiques Marx and Engels had leveled against the early-nineteenth-century formulators of the socialist ideal.[38] Like the earlier utopians, the Populists perceived history not as a process, but as an eternal struggle between natural and unnatural tendencies of development. What was most unnatural was the developed capitalist system of Western Europe and the possible intrusion of this alien force on Russian society. Paradoxically, it was Marx's *Capital* that was partly responsible for the Populist image of Western capitalism as an unnatural and dehumanizing development;* from Marx's analysis, the Populists derived a picture of the horrifying social evils following

---

* The first translation of *Capital* appeared in Russia, a fact that Marx viewed as "an irony of fate"; translation work was undertaken by Populists in 1868, only a year after the original German publication, and the Russian-language version was published in 1872, 15 years before the first English translation. Russian Populists, many of whom were in semi-exile in Western Europe in the 1850's and 1860's, were of course generally familiar with Marx's analysis of capitalism (and Marxist theory in general) well before the publication of *Capital*. For a perceptive analysis of the influence of *Capital* and other Marxist works on Russian Populist theorists, see A. Walicki, *The Controversy Over Capitalism* (Oxford: Clarendon Press, 1969), pp. 132–53.

on capitalism, not one of its promise for a socialist society. To the unnatural character of Western social and economic development they counterposed the natural forms of collectivistic social life embodied in the traditional Russian village *mir* and placed their hopes in the inherent socialist aspirations of the "precapitalist" peasantry. They accordingly condemned all forms of modernity identified with capitalism and urbanization: large-scale industry and economic organization, centralization and bureaucracy in all its manifestations, and the state were unnatural institutions that had imposed themselves on society and prevented true human solidarity. A further source of social inequality was formal higher education, which produced specialists who were separated from the masses; the general Populist hostility to occupational specialization was expressed in a celebration of the inherent goodness of simple men and a belief that the basis for a true human life resided in the spartan, ascetic, simple, and egalitarian virtues of the uncorrupted countryside.

These characteristic features of Populist thought emanated from a central concern with the immediate social costs and ultimate historical consequences of modern capitalism. The degradation and dehumanization wrought by nineteenth-century industrialism were nowhere more vividly portrayed than in the writings of Marx and Engels, and this aspect of the Marxian critique became deeply etched on the Populist mentality. But whereas Marx assumed that the transformation of the masses into a dehumanized and alienated proletariat was the social price mankind must pay to achieve liberation, the Populists were neither willing to pay the price nor convinced that doing so would lead to the socialist outcome Marx predicted. It was not capitalism but rather precapitalist agrarian society that held socialist potentialities. That being the case, it was the duty of "enlightened men" to release the socialist instincts of the peasantry and build the new society on the basis of the collectivistic traditions of the mir— and to do so before these instincts and traditions were destroyed by capitalist forces of production.

The Populists' determination to "bypass" capitalism thus reflected more than just a desire to avoid the social evils of urban industrialism; it reflected their profound belief that capitalism led not to, but away from, socialism. Whereas the Western European countries had become so exhausted and corrupted by their economic "over-maturity" that they no longer had the energy and morality to realize their own socialist ideal, backward Russia, precisely because she was yet relatively unburdened by capitalism—and thus her "precapitalist" (and allegedly socialist) traditions were yet relatively uncorrupted— would be able to leap to the forefront of world civilization.[39] It was this consciousness of "backwardness"—a consciousness molded by agrarian Russia's coexistence with advanced industrialized nations and sharpened by the Marxist description of the tragic aspects of modern historical development—that shaped the specific Populist response to modern capitalism. It was a consciousness, moreover, that gave rise to two notions of particular contemporary relevance: the purported advantages of backwardness and the idea of national uniqueness in historical development.

The Populist conception of the road to socialism was similar to that advocated earlier by the utopian socialists of Western Europe. The road led outside the cities, the source of all political and economic evils, to the countryside, where the village mir would be the basis for socialist reconstruction. The new order of justice and equality was to rest on a free federation of largely self-sufficient communal units incorporating modern industry and technology in an agrarian framework and based on the unity of "living and working," a conception very much in line with the schemes of Fourier and Proudhon. In this setting there would emerge the new all-round man, who would develop all of his latent capacities, engage in a variety of productive pursuits, and be free to develop his true human personality.

In the realization of this socialist utopia, the Populists, like the utopian socialists, placed an extraordinary faith in both the powers of the human consciousness to determine social reality and the force of moral example. Whether an innate socialist consciousness resided in the people and needed only to be naturally released by a catalytic agent (as the early Populists who were determined to "go to the people" believed) or whether (as in later variants of Populist ideology) that consciousness had to be imposed on the masses by an "enlightened" intellectual elite, the Populists shared with their utopian socialist predecessors the belief that the ideas, the will, and the morality of men were the decisive factors in determining the course of social development. They rejected the Marxist notion that there were objective laws of historical development to which the activities of men must conform. Insofar as there were impersonal historical forces, such forces were moving in the wrong direction—toward an "unnatural" capitalist future and not to a socialist one. Thus the Populists insisted that the task of socialist reconstruction could and must be undertaken in the here and now by men endowed with the proper consciousness and moral values. Time was of the essence, for the rapid development of capitalism and the Marxian analysis of that development gave rise to a fear that time was not on their side. For the Populists as well as the utopian socialists neither "objective" historical reality nor conditions of economic scarcity were seen as barriers to the achievement of socialism. Indeed, in the case of the Populists, the factor of economic backwardness was converted into a prime revolutionary virtue.

In the Populists' conception of socialist revolution, the abolition of the distinction between town and countryside was not a distant goal conditional on the achievement of a high level of economic development, but rather an immediate task to be accomplished in the very process of the revolutionary transformation they believed to be imminent—or believed could and must be made imminent by a natural alliance between peasants and laymen intellectuals. A backward country could achieve a more or less immediate transition to socialism by benefiting from the experience of the advanced Western states (and thus avoiding the attendant social evils), by appropriating the technological and scientific achievements of the West and integrating them with agricultural production in the countryside, and, above all, by relying on the latent socialist aspirations of the peasants and their traditional collectivistic institutions, which were still independent of the capitalist market and relatively uncorrupted by the bourgeois city. The Populist notion of bypassing the capitalist stage presupposed bypassing the industrialization of the cities and its undesirable social consequences as well. And the Populist goal of a decentralized society composed of a federation of egalitarian village communities combining industry with agriculture left no role for the city in the revolutionary process and no place for the city in the new socialist society that presumably would emerge from that process. The general decentralization of political and economic life, upon which the Populists as well as the utopian socialists placed so high a value, demanded an immediate end to the distinction between town and countryside.

The realization of this goal was made all the more urgent by the Populist image of the city as an unnatural creation, whose alien political and economic tentacles were constantly reaching out to corrupt the countryside, always threatening to undermine and destroy rural collectivistic life and institutions. One of the most pervasive themes in Populist literature is the contrast between the artificial, immoral, oppressive, and dehumanized character of urban life and the essential goodness and purity of the countryside, where, as Alexander Herzen typically and romantically described it, the peasant "has no other morality than that which flows quite instinctively and naturally from his communal life."[40] The city was the site and source of all the principal evils that afflicted society—modern capitalism, the modern centralized state bureaucracy, and modern industrialism in its bourgeois form. The very forces that Marxists saw as progressive and as moving inexorably toward a socialist resolution were seen by the Populists as alien and retrogressive phenomena that threatened to overwhelm and dominate the countryside. Thus, the abolition of the distinction between town and countryside was seen, not as the long-range goal and product of an eventual socialist future, but as an immediate and pressing task in order to preserve the essential agrarian sources of socialist renewal. Neither the utopian socialists of Western Europe nor the Populists of Russia were disposed to wait for the full development of capitalist productive forces to bring about a socialist society, a process that would only further the unnatural separation of town and countryside and the separation of men in general. The socialist regeneration of society, on the basis of communal units operating autonomously of the urban capitalist system, had to be undertaken in the here and now.

### Leninism, Stalinism, and the Soviet Experience

The history of Marxism in Russia is, in one sense, the history of the triumph of the town over the countryside. The ascendancy of Marxist over Populist ideas at the end of the nineteenth century, which coincided with a period of rapid industrial growth, marked the ideological dominance of town over countryside in the history of the Russian revolutionary intelligentsia. The Bolshevik victory of 1917 proved to be the political triumph of the city over the countryside. And Stalinist industrialization culminated the process with the economic dominance of the city based on the exploitation of the rural areas.

If Russian Populist ideology was conditioned by the Marxist analysis of Western capitalism, and thus contributed to the Populist idealization of traditional agrarian life, Marxism arose in Russia out of the Populist intellectual milieu as a specific rejection of the Populist faith in a noncapitalist road to socialism. In denying the possibility of bypassing the capitalist phase of development and reaffirming (and universalizing) the original Marxist analysis of the dominance of town over countryside, Plekhanov and Lenin proved more "orthodox" Marxists than Marx—and on this point, Lenin was no less orthodox than his Marxist mentor Plekhanov. In his lengthy anti-Populist polemics, Lenin argued that modern capitalist forces of production had already achieved dominance in Russia, that the collectivist features of traditional agrarian institutions had been undermined by modern economic forces and class divisions, and that the inevitable development of urban industrialization and the consequent emergence of a modern urban proletariat had transferred the revolutionary arena from the countryside to the cities.[41] Rejecting the Populist view, Lenin believed, with Plekhanov, that "no historical peculiarities of our country will free it from the action of universal social laws."[42] Those laws dictated a capitalist future with all of its social consequences, including the complete domination of town over countryside. "The separation of town from country," Lenin insisted, "their oppositeness, and the exploitation of the countryside by the town" are the "universal concomitants of developing capitalism. . . . Therefore, the predominance of the town over the countryside (economically, politically, intellectually, and in all other respects) is a universal and inevitable thing in all countries where there is commodity production and capitalism, including Russia: only sentimental romanticists can bewail this. Scientific theory, on the contrary, points to the progressive aspect given to this contradiction by large-scale industrial capital."[43]

The Populists, in refusing to recognize the progressive character and potential of modern capitalism and instead basing their hopes for a socialist future on an atavistic idealization of the "primitive" forms of traditional agrarian life, were condemned to historical oblivion by the same universal and immutable forces of modern socioeconomic development that had already destroyed the precapitalist social relationships they romanticized. Although the Populists had been progressive in their time by first posing the problem of capitalism, they now had become "utopian reactionaries" still "dreaming about 'different paths for the fatherland,' "[44] the carriers of a reactionary petty-bourgeois ideology that represented the interests of the doomed small producer and promoted "stagnation and Asiatic backwardness."[45]

When Lenin turned to the peasantry as a potential revolutionary ally after 1900, he did so essentially for immediate tactical political reasons, not because of any newfound faith in the socialist potentialities of the countryside. The peasantry found a place in Leninist revolutionary strategy only because the Russian bourgeoisie had compromised with Tsarist autocracy and thus failed to play its appointed political role in the bourgeois-democratic revolution. Without entering into all the complexities of Lenin's views on the revolutionary role of the peasantry, the essence of the matter is that the peasantry was to serve as the surrogate for the bourgeoisie in the "democratic" phase of the revolution. The peasantry remained petty bourgeois, in Lenin's eyes, but the hitherto reactionary petty bourgeoisie of the countryside could be politically useful because the liberal bourgeoisie of the cities had proved politically useless.

Whatever the implications of this revised strategy for original Marxist theory, Lenin retained his basic Marxist faith that the genuinely progressive economic, social, and intellectual forces in modern history resided in the cities. Nor did this strategy dispel his basic distrust of the peasantry and the backward countryside or in any way mitigate his hostility to Populist ideology, which he continued to regard as a basically reactionary expression of the interests of a still petty-bourgeois peasantry. The alliance of the proletariat and peasantry was simply an alliance of political expediency confined to the bourgeois-democratic phase of the revolution, a means by which to hasten history on its proper course in the absence of a revolutionary bourgeoisie; when the revolution reached its socialist phase it was assumed that the alliance would prove untenable. Moreover, even in performing the necessary bourgeois-democratic tasks, the peasantry was the junior partner in this unorthodox alliance; the proletariat was not merely to ally itself with the peasantry, but was to "lead" it. Further, Lenin took it for granted that the proletariat and the peasantry would be represented by two different political parties, one "socialist" (i.e., the Bolsheviks), and the other "democratic." The Bolsheviks remained an urban-based party and acquired no roots in the countryside; the latter was left to the Socialist Revolutionaries, whom the Bolsheviks took to be the political representatives of the "democratic" peasantry.

The political formula for this unorthodox version of a bourgeois-democratic revolution was to be a "democratic dictatorship of the proletariat and peasantry." There is no need to discuss here the ambiguities involved in this curious notion or its ambiguous history in Leninist theory and practice except to note that it became irrelevant to political realities with the Bolshevik triumph. State power rested in the hands of an urban-based party that claimed to embody "pro-letarian consciousness." The suppression of the Socialist Revolution-aries in 1918 destroyed even the pretense of peasant political partici-pation. Further, the traditional peasant distrust of the towns and of the state was intensified by the extension of Bolshevik political power to the countryside and the dispatch of urban Communists to the rural areas to requisition grain from an increasingly hostile peasantry.

With the failure of the anticipated socialist revolutions in the ad-vanced industrialized countries, the Bolsheviks were confronted with the problem of what to do with a successful anticapitalist revolution in an economically backward and isolated country—a country that not only existed in a hostile international arena but also contained within it a vast and largely hostile peasantry. Their response to this problem, a problem anticipated in neither Marxist nor Leninist the-ory, was largely determined by orthodox Marxist perspectives, and most notably on the question of the relationship between town and countryside. However unorthodox Lenin may have been in other areas and however unorthodox the revolution he led, he and his fol-lowers were wedded to the Marxist assumption that the cities held the progressive forces of modern history and the countryside the forces of stagnation and potential regression.

To be sure, Lenin had the gravest doubts about attempting to build a socialist society in an economically and culturally backward land. Indeed, in his last years, he was plagued by a profound sense of guilt about the moral and historical validity of the Bolshevik Revolution. The brutalities and irrationalities of Stalinism were in no sense in-herent in Leninism. But insofar as Lenin confronted the problem that Stalin later formulated as "socialism in one country," the general thrust of his views and policies foreshadowed the "revolution from above" over which Stalin was to preside. Lenin concluded that the Bolshevik Revolution, if it remained confined to backward Russia, could be no more than a bourgeois revolution, whose first and most pressing priority was to carry out the unfulfilled tasks of capitalist economic development, albeit under socialist political auspices. This meant, above all, urban industrialization, which required a strong state apparatus that could impose its political control over the coun-tryside and extract from agricultural production the capital necessary for the industrial development of the cities. Lenin's preoccupation with the need for rapid economic development (which he stressed increasingly after mid-1918) was reinforced by his own strongly held views—notably his "technocratic bias" (epitomized by his striking formula that "electrification plus Soviets" equals socialism, his slogan "learn from the capitalists," his fascination with the economic efficiency of "Taylorism," and his emphasis on heavy industry); his unqualified acceptance of the virtues of centralization in general; his persisting anti-rural sentiments; and his distrust of all forms of "spontaneity." Such were the Leninist ideological points of departure for the Stalinist strategy of urban industrialization based on forced rural collectivization, the nature and social consequences of which are too well known to require discussion here. It is sufficient to observe that although Stalinism, in its particular fashion, has perhaps confirmed Marx's original characterization of modern history as the "urbanization of the countryside," it has contributed nothing to the realization of Marx's goal of abolishing the distinction between town and countryside. Indeed, if anything, the Soviet model of industrialization— and the urban elites it has spawned—has widened the gap between town and countryside.

## Maoism

It is one of the great ironies of modern history that Marxism, a theory addressed to the urban working class of advanced industrialized nations, should have become the dominant ideology of anticapitalist revolutionary movements in the "backward" peasant countries. And it is one of the ironies of the history of Marxism that many contemporary versions of that theory incorporate socialist ideas and conceptions that both Marx and Lenin condemned as "utopian" and "reactionary." It is not the case that contemporary Communists in economically backward lands have consciously adopted, or have been intellectually influenced by, utopian socialist or populist theories. Utopian socialism and populism are not easily definable ideological systems and are not self-conscious and shared intellectual-political traditions; unlike Marxism-Leninism, the tradition with which Communists identify, utopian socialism and populism are primarily analytic categories designating general modes of thought that have appeared in various forms in different historical environments. If some of the same ideas and assumptions have emerged in contemporary variants of Marxism-Leninism, they are not perceived as "populist" or "utopian socialist" by their modern-day Communist carriers. The similarities are nonetheless quite striking.

The crucial factor in the emergence of "utopian"-type conceptions within contemporary Marxist-Leninist ideologies is the manner in which modern capitalism is perceived. As we have noted, utopian socialism, both in its early-nineteenth-century Western European varieties and in its later Russian Populist form, assumed that capitalism was an unnatural and alien phenomenon—and thus was unnecessary to the achievement of a new socialist order. Marxist theory, by contrast, holds that the full development of capitalist forces of production (with all of their consequences) is historically necessary to create the social and material prerequisites for socialism. Lenin, despite all his unorthodoxies in the realm of revolutionary strategy, never abandoned the fundamental Marxist premise that socialism presupposes capitalism.

The modern Chinese historical situation was hardly conducive to the acceptance of this Marxist faith in the progressive nature of capitalism. Modern capitalist industrialism was not an indigenous development, but one that came to China by way of foreign imperialism. Insofar as industrial capitalism developed in twentieth-century China, it not only created all the social evils associated with early industrialism in the West (and in more extreme form), but also developed in areas under foreign influence, primarily the treaty ports. If a perception of capitalism as alien and evil is a general response to the effects of early industrialization, it was a perception that the modern Chinese historical experience served to intensify. Although some of the more Western-oriented Chinese Marxists attempted to adhere to the orthodox Marxist-Leninist view, the Chinese situation did not encourage holding to a faith in the socialist potential of a capitalism so alien in origin and so distorted in form. The general tendency, as it emerged in Maoism, was to identify capitalism with imperialism, to see both as external impingements, and to look elsewhere for the socialist regeneration of Chinese society.

On the intellectual level, Chinese Marxist rejections of the Marxist historical analysis of capitalism were facilitated by the absence of competing socialist ideologies—in clear contrast to both original Marxist theory, which arose in opposition to various socialist theories that failed to appreciate the sociohistorical significance of the new capitalist forces of production, and Marxism in Russia, which developed in direct opposition to the Populist view that capitalism could and must be bypassed. Chinese Marxists, never seriously confronted with the ideological-political opposition of non-Marxian socialist theories, had less need to defend or affirm (as did Lenin) the Marxist view that socialism presupposed capitalism, a proposition that many viewed as incongruous both with Chinese historical reality and with their own socialist hopes. Moreover, Chinese converts to Communism were politically committed to the Marxist-Leninist program of revolution long before they became intellectually committed to Marxist theory; in a country that lacked a social-democratic tradition, Chinese Marxists were much less firmly tied to Marxist theoretical concepts than their Western and Russian counterparts. Thus, many Chinese Marxists (and most notably, Mao Tse-tung) found it relatively easy to ignore or reinterpret the Marxist view that capitalism was a historically progressive phenomenon, much less an essential condition for socialism.

There are many ambiguities in the treatment of capitalism in Maoist theory, and much that is obscured, whether by the ideological need to appear to conform to Marxist-Leninist orthodoxy or by tactical political considerations. Leaving aside such ideological and tactical considerations, two major themes dominate this realm of Maoist thought. First, capitalism in China is seen as insolubly bound up with foreign imperialism. Second, the Chinese revolution (both in its bourgeois-democratic phase, as that term is radically redefined in Maoist theory, and in its socialist stage) is perceived as part of the world-wide struggle of the forces of socialism against those of capitalist imperialism, with China appearing (at least implicitly) as a vanguard nation in a global revolutionary process. Both propositions serve the larger Maoist need to deny that China's socialist future hinges on the social and material results of modern capitalist forces of production—or that the relative absence of such forces constitutes any barrier to the pursuit and achievement of revolutionary socialist goals.

The identification of capitalism with imperialism—one of the most prominent themes in Maoist theoretical literature—is intimately related to the manner in which the relationship between town and countryside is perceived in both the Maoist strategy of revolution and the Maoist strategy of post-revolutionary development. The theme appears in Mao's earliest writings as a Marxist[46] and is later theoretically formulated in the notion that the "principal contradiction" in Chinese society (and thus the principal impetus for revolution) is between "imperialism and the Chinese nation."[47] Excluded from membership in the nation are classes and groups "in league with imperialism" (as Mao put it in 1926[48] and as he has maintained ever since)—warlords, landlords, and the comprador big bourgeoisie and their intellectual representatives. These, in effect, are internal foreigners—groups dependent on an alien capitalism imposed on the Chinese nation from without, and socially, economically, and above all (for Mao) ideologically tied to the external capitalist-imperialist order. Potentially excludable from the nation and potentially alien is the remainder of the bourgeoisie, politically wavering groups that stand on a precarious middle ground. Mao's distrust of the bourgeoisie in general is expressed in its most pristine form in the original version of his 1926 "Analysis of the Classes in Chinese Society," a seminal document in which he undertook to define the attitudes of social groups toward a revolution whose aim was "to overthrow world capitalist imperialism":

> As to the vacillating middle bourgeoisie, its right wing must be considered our enemy; even if it is not already, it will soon become so. Its left wing may become our friend, but it is not a true friend. . . . How many are our true friends? There are 395 million of them. How many are our true enemies? There are a million of them. How many are there of these people in the middle, who may be either our frinds or our enemies? There are four million of them. Even if we consider these four million as enemies, this only adds up to a bloc of barely five million, and a sneeze from 395 million would certainly suffice to blow them down.

The passage concludes with the injunction: "Three-hundred-and-ninety-five millions, unite!"[49] Here we have a populist organic conception of "the people," not a Marxist class analysis.

Despite the celebrated distinction between a reactionary comprador bourgeoisie and a presumably progressive national bourgeoisie, the latter does not loom large in the Maoist revolutionary scheme of things. Indeed, Chinese capitalism in general is viewed as potentially reactionary and alien. "National capitalism," Mao wrote in 1939, "has developed to a certain extent and played a considerable part in China's political and cultural life, but it has not become the principal socio-economic form in China; quite feeble in strength, it is mostly tied in varying degrees to both foreign imperialism and domestic feudalism."[50] Moreover, the perceived alien character of even national capitalism is reinforced by the general Maoist analysis of Chinese history. In applying (perhaps halfheartedly) the standard Marxist periodization of Western historical development to China, Mao observes that although China has "a rich revolutionary tradition and a splendid historical heritage," she nonetheless "remained sluggish in her economic, political and cultural development after her transition from slave system into feudal society."[51] Chinese feudalism lasted some 3,000 years, Mao notes, and "it was not until the middle of the nineteenth century that great internal changes took place in China as a result of the penetration of foreign capitalism." It was this foreign intrusion that undermined the traditional feudal economy and "created certain objective conditions and possibilities for the development of China's capitalist production," possibilities that were partially realized in the emergence of a "national capitalism . . . in a rudimentary form."[52]

Thus, like the comprador capitalism of the big bourgeoisie, the national capitalism of the national bourgeoisie owes its origins to foreign imperialism and so has an alien character. Although national capitalism has certain interests opposed to imperialism, nevertheless, as Mao constantly emphasizes, it remains strongly tied to the external force that gave birth to it.

One cannot escape the impression that capitalism and a bourgeoisie in whatever form are perceived as somehow alien to China. Formal Maoist theory takes as universally valid Marx's periodization of Western history;* Mao thus feels compelled to argue that "China's feudal society . . . carried within itself the embryo of capitalism," and that "China would of herself have developed slowly into a capitalist society even if there had been no influence of foreign capitalism."[53] Yet Mao's strangely non-Marxian analysis of this embryonic Chinese capitalism raises doubts about whether even an indigenous bourgeois development is seen as desirable. In Marx's analysis of the transition from feudalism to capitalism in the West, the dynamic historical force is the development of a bourgeois mode of production in cities, operating at first *outside* the confines of feudal society, and the major class struggle is between the newly arisen bourgeoisie and the old feudal aristocracy; the peasants, though major victims, are not actors in the process. In Maoist theory, by contrast, we are told that in Chinese feudal society the "main contradiction" was between peasants and landlords (not between a bourgeoisie and the feudal classes). This is accompanied by the wholly non-Marxist proposition that the class struggles of the peasantry "alone formed the real motive force of historical development in China's feudal society."[54] The implication that capitalism is appropriate for the West but not necessarily

* The whole notion of a universal, unilinear scheme of historical evolution is a distinctively Stalinist invention, foreign to Leninism as well as to original Marxism.

for China is also suggested in the historical examples Mao offers to distinguish between "perceptual" and "rational" knowledge in his essay "On Practice." In the West, he observes, the proletariat arrived at a true knowledge of the world from its experiences with modern capitalism and, through the scientific summation of those experiences in Marxist theory, "came to understand the essence of capitalist society." In China, however, "the Chinese people arrived at rational knowledge when they saw the internal and external contradictions of imperialism, as well as the essence of the oppression and exploitation of China's broad masses by imperialism in alliance with China's compradors and feudal class; such knowledge began only about the time of the May 4 Movement of 1919."[55] Thus, although "capitalism" and the "proletariat" are the appropriate categories for socialist development in the West, the appropriate categories for the Chinese road to socialism are "imperialism" and the "Chinese people."

However one wishes to interpret Mao's view of the "sprouts" (*meng-ya*) of an indigenous capitalism in traditional China that proved abortive, he quite clearly sees the modern capitalism introduced by imperialism, if not as an unnatural phenomenon, then certainly as an alien one—and in no sense the historical prerequisite for socialism. From the beginning Maoism looked not to the Marxist-defined socialist potentials of capitalist forces of production, but rather to the "Chinese people" for the sources of a socialist future. And "the people," of course, are basically the vast peasant masses, the overwhelming majority of that organic entity of 395 million identified in 1926 as the true friends of revolution. It is significant that in his "Analysis of the Classes in Chinese Society," Mao employed an almost wholly numerical criterion in assessing the revolutionary potential of classes.[56] If the four million members of the potentially reactionary "middle bourgeoisie" are expendable, so also, implicitly, are the members of the urban proletariat, who when all is said and done constitute only a tiny percentage of the 395 million. Even more noteworthy is the famous "Hunan Report" of early 1927, where Mao is drawn exclusively to the spontaneity of peasant revolt, that creative and elemental tornado-like force "so extraordinarily swift and violent that no power, however great, will be able to suppress it."[57] In this lengthy document, which expresses the Maoist vision of revolution in its most pristine form, neither capitalism nor the modern social classes it produced are even mentioned in passing.

Logically flowing from the Maoist rejection of the Marxist proposition that socialism presupposes capitalism is a relative lack of concern with the bourgeoisie and the proletariat, the two Marxian-defined revolutionary classes in modern history. Just as the national bourgeoisie is unnecessary in the national or bourgeois-democratic phase of the revolution, so the proletariat is unnecessary in its proletarian-socialist phase. There is no need to dwell here on the well-known abandonment of the urban proletariat in Maoist practice even if not in formal theory. The "leadership of the proletariat," of course, means no more than the leadership of the Communist Party, or more precisely, those members of the revolutionary intelligentsia who are deemed to possess the appropriate proletarian socialist consciousness; whatever institutional form this "consciousness" might take, there is no need for any organic or organizational tie with the actual proletariat. And though Maoist theory makes a formal distinction between the bourgeois-democratic and socialist stages of the revolution, the distinction all but vanishes in the redefinition of bourgeois-democratic revolution. Without entering into the tortuous argument that converts "a bourgeois-democratic revolution of the general, old type" into "a democratic revolution of a special, new type," let us note simply that the aim of this "new-democratic revolution" is to "steer away from a capitalist future and head towards the realization of socialism," and that the leadership of the revolutionary process in general "rests on the shoulders of the party of the Chinese proletariat, the Chinese Communist Party, for without its leadership no revolution can succeed."[58]

The utopian socialist character of Maoism is nowhere more apparent than in the rejection of the fundamental Marxist premise that socialism presupposes capitalism and the historical activity of the classes directly involved in modern capitalist relations of production. The Maoist tendency is to find the sources of socialism in those areas of society that are least influenced by capitalism—in a peasantry relatively uninvolved with capitalist socioeconomic relationships and with intellectuals ideologically uncorrupted by bourgeois ideas. As in utopian socialist and populist theories, capitalism and its modern social and material products and accomplishments are not perceived to be the preconditions for the socialist reorganization of society. Whereas Marxism is concerned with the bourgeoisie and the proletariat as the dynamic classes in modern history, Maoism is concerned with the relationship between peasants and intellectuals.

There are other affinities with utopian socialist theories in Maoism, which logically accompany these departures from Marxism. In Maoism, as in utopian socialism, economic backwardness is not seen as an obstacle to the achievement of socialist goals. To the contrary, backwardness is converted into a revolutionary advantage and a socialist virtue. Just as the Russian Populists proclaimed Russia to be closer to socialism than the countries of the West precisely because of her economic underdevelopment, so Mao proclaims the special Chinese revolutionary virtues of being "poor and blank" and sees preindustrial China pioneering the way to a universal socialist and communist future. To celebrate the "advantages of backwardness" is to abandon the Marxist faith in the objective determining forces of history, to deny, in a word, that socialism is immanent in the progressive movement of history itself. Rather the historical outcome turns on "subjective factors"—the consciousness, the moral values, and the actions of dedicated men. Maoism shares with the utopian socialist tradition the view that socialism rests, not on the development of material productive forces, but rather on the moral virtues of "new men" who can and must impose their socialist consciousness on historical reality. Here, essentially, we find the populist belief that what is decisive in the remaking of society, "as it should be," is the emergence, in Herzen's words, of "men who combine faith, will, conviction and energy."[59] And there is nothing non-Maoist (although much that is non-Marxist) in Buber's utopian socialist formulation that the realization of socialism "depends not on the technological state of things" but rather "on people and their spirit."[60]

One also finds in Maoism a hostility to the organizational and institutional forms identified with modern economic development, not unlike that expressed by the nineteenth-century utopian socialists. The bias against occupational specialization, the antipathy to large-scale and centralized forms of political and economic organization, the deep aversion to all manifestations of bureaucracy, and the distrust of formal higher education are aspects of the Maoist mentality too well known to require elaboration here. Like the utopian socialists and populists, Mao is unwilling to accept the consequences of "modernity" as the necessary price of historical progress. And not merely because the price is regarded as too high; if there is no objective historical process culminating in socialism, there is no assurance that paying the price will lead to the predicted socialist end.

In the special value Maoism places on an ascetic life-style and in its strongly egalitarian orientation, we find still other prominent themes in utopian socialist and populist literature. Asceticism in general, it might be noted, was regarded by Marx as one of the principal expressions of human self-alienation; and egalitarianism, in the Chinese historical situation, would have been condemned by Marx as a primitive and crude form of social leveling—primitive and crude because the conditions of economic abundance for genuine equality are not present.

In sum, on the basis of the three broad questions that generally distinguish Marxism from utopian socialism, Maoism is clearly more akin to the latter than the former. First, Maoism rejects the Marxist premise that modern industrial capitalism is a necessary and progressive stage in historical development and a prerequisite for socialism. Second, Maoism denies (implicitly in theory and most explicitly in practice) the Marxist belief that the industrial proletariat is the bearer of the socialist future. Third, Maoism replaces the Marxist belief in objective laws of history with a voluntaristic faith in the consciousness and the moral potentialities of men as the decisive factor in sociohistorical development. These departures from Marxism bear directly on the Maoist conception of the relationship between town and countryside in modern history.

Just as the Maoist attitude toward capitalism was fundamentally conditioned by the imperialist origins and implications of that development in China, so the Maoist attitude toward the relationship between town and countryside was molded by the association of foreign political and economic domination with the development of the modern cities of China. For Mao the city was not the modern revolutionary stage posited by Marxism, but a foreign-dominated stage. It was a situation that bred powerful anti-urban biases and, correspondingly, a strong agrarian orientation; the city came to be identified with alien influences, the "countryside" with the "country." Such a perception gave rise to a more general suspicion of the city as the site and source of foreign bourgeois ideological, moral, and social corruption, a suspicion that lingered on long after the foreigners were removed from the cities. And this suspicion tended to foster a rejection of the Western (and Marxist) assumption that industrialization implies urbanization in favor of an alternative non-urban (and thus non-alien) path to modern economic development. The Marxist ideal of eliminating the distinction between town and countryside is particularly appealing because it is seen as not only a desirable social revolutionary goal but a desirable national one as well.

There may well be traditional Chinese precedents for this anti-urban impulse. As Rhoads Murphey has observed, the traditional Chinese admiration for nature expressed itself in a Confucian tendency to find wisdom and truth in the virtues of rural life, whereas "in the cities, where man disregarded nature, truth was clouded [and] virtue weakened."[61] We shall not pause here to speculate on whether traditional anti-urban views survived to influence modern Chinese attitudes. Whatever the influence of the Confucian gentry's preference for the rural virtues (or the possible influence of old peasant resentments against the essentially parasitic administrative-based town in traditional China),[62] certainly the most important factor in conditioning present-day perceptions was the modern imperialist impingement, which did in fact make foreign enclaves of the cities and the city the symbol of foreign domination. An early modern precedent might be noted in passing. During the Opium War, as Frederic Wakeman points out, the British intrusion stimulated anti-urban as well as anti-foreign sentiments among the gentry and peasantry of Kwangtung province; the rural inhabitants saw the city of Canton as being filled with "traitors" (*han-chien*), urban merchants, and corrupt Imperial officials who were collaborating with the enemy intruders.[63]

This "prenationalist" perception of the city as infested with internal foreigners becomes a much more prominent theme in twentieth-century Chinese nationalism. As modern Chinese cities developed in a Western mold, thus widening the cultural as well as the socioeconomic gap between town and countryside, one nationalist response was to look to the rural areas (relatively uncorrupted by foreign influences) for the true sources of national regeneration. It is by no means a coincidence that the most nationalistic of the early Chinese Communists (such as Li Ta-chao and Mao) were the first and most ardent advocates of a peasant-based revolution and were willing, and indeed eager, to abandon the cities that they viewed as alien bastions of conservatism and moral corruption—as opposed to Chinese Communists who accepted Marxist-Leninist theory in its more or less orthodox Western form as an international revolutionary message and who placed their socialist hopes in the development of urban industry and in the revolutionary potential of an urban proletariat formed in a Western image. Populist impulses and nationalism are closely related phenomena in modern world history, and this is nowhere more dramatically demonstrated than in modern China, where a revolution based on a populist modification of Marxism-Leninism necessarily assumed the character of a war of the Chinese countryside against the foreign-infected cities.

Mao's anti-urban bias is not simply the product of what became a rural-based revolution. It is apparent in his early writings and most strikingly in the "Hunan Report." Quite apart from his well-known statement relegating the city to a minor role in the revolutionary process, we find here (among other remarkable things, for a Marxist) the view that the knowledge and culture of the urban intelligentsia, which is equated with foreign knowledge and culture, is not only unsuited to the needs of the peasantry, but inferior to that which the peasants were acquiring on their own. As he put it:

> In my student days, I used to stand up for the "foreign-style schools" when, upon returning to my native place, I found the peasants objecting to them. I was myself identified with the "foreign-style students" and "foreign-style teachers," and always felt that the peasants were somehow wrong. It was during my six months in the countryside in 1925, when I was already a Communist and adopted the Marxist viewpoint, that I realized I was mistaken and that the peasants' views were right. The teaching materials used in the rural primary schools all dealt with city matters and were in no way adapted to the needs of the rural areas. . . . Now the peasants are energetically organizing evening classes, calling them peasant schools. . . . As a result of the growth of the peasant movement, the cultural level of the peasants has risen rapidly. Before long there will be tens of thousands of schools sprouting in the rural areas throughout the whole province, and that will be something quite different from the futile clamour of the intelligentsia and so-called "educators" for "popular education."[64]

In the same document, moreover, he suggests that revolutionaries who remain in the cities are likely to become ideologically corrupted and politically conservative. When news of "the revolt of the peasants in the countryside" reached Changsha, "there was not a single person who did not summarize the whole thing in one phrase: 'An awful mess!' Even quite revolutionary people, carried away by the opinion of the 'awful mess' school which prevailed like a storm over the whole city, became down-hearted at the very thought of the conditions in the countryside, and could not deny the word 'mess.' "[65] The remedy, of course, was for potentially "revolutionary people" to leave the corrupting life of the cities for the countryside, where revolutionary creativity resides. In vastly different political and historical circumstances, it remains the Maoist remedy to this day.

Mao's early hostility to the city persisted to govern the Maoist conception of the relationship between town and countryside in both the revolutionary and post-revolutionary eras. Implicit in Maoist theory (and quite apparent in Maoist practice) is the identification of the city with what is foreign and reactionary and the countryside with what is truly national and revolutionary. Consider, for example, one of Mao's "antagonistic contradictions," that between town and countryside. We are told that whereas in Western capitalist society "the town under bourgeois rule ruthlessly exploits the countryside," in modern Chinese society it is *"the town under the rule of foreign imperialism* and the native big comprador bourgeoisie [that] most savagely exploits the countryside," thus creating an antagonism between the two of a particularly extreme character.[66]

No doubt the Maoist suspicion of the city and the general Maoist view of the relationship between town and countryside in modern revolutionary history were greatly fortified by the whole Chinese Communist revolutionary experience, in which the rural forces of peasant revolution did in fact "surround and overwhelm" the cities. But the unique revolutionary strategy that led to that outcome was itself determined in part by a pre-existing faith in the revolutionary potential of the countryside and a negative conception of the city. Long before that strategy was formulated, much less proved in practice, Mao viewed the cities as bastions of conservatism; the cities were dominated by the forces of foreign imperialism and infected by alien social and ideological influences, were the strongholds of the bourgeois, who were seen as the agents (or potential allies) of imperialism, were the centers of domestic political reaction and the breeding places for social and ideological corruption in general. To be sure, the cities also held the urban proletariat, but however much one might sympathize with its plight, it was not, for Mao, a class that held much revolutionary potential. Numerically speaking—and Mao often spoke in numerical terms—it was but a tiny percentage of "the revolutionary people."

These views on the place of city and countryside in the revolutionary process flowed from a larger (and strikingly non-Marxian) conception of revolution characterized by a belief that a socialist-oriented revolution need not be dependent on modern industrial capitalism or its product, the urban proletariat, and need not proceed according to any Marxist-defined laws of objective historical development. Rather, revolutionary success depended on the vast peasant masses and "de-urbanized" intellectuals who were willing and able to "unite" with the peasants and guide them along the correct path.

Both early ideological impulses and the concrete experience of the Chinese revolution contributed to the dichotomy between the revolutionary countryside and the conservative cities. It is a notion that is deeply ingrained in the Maoist mentality, and one that was to have profound implications for the pattern of post-revolutionary Chinese history, as well as one eventually to be projected into a global vision of a worldwide revolutionary process in which the "revolutionary countryside" of the economically backward lands would triumph over the "cities" of Europe and North America. Where Marx believed that modern history made the countryside dependent on the towns and "nations of peasants on nations of bourgeois," Mao believes that modern revolutionary history is the victory of the countryside over the town and the victory of peasant nations over bourgeois nations. The Maoist belief has nothing in common with Marxism or Leninism, but it is similar to the Russian Populist claim, as Walicki has put it, that "Russia, and the backward countries in general, were more ripe for the great social upheaval than the economically developed bourgeois Western countries."[67]

Although the Chinese Communist Revolution was rural-based (and the Communists, or at least the Maoists, rural-oriented as well), the "ultimate target" of the revolution, as John Lewis has pointed out, "was always the cities."[68] As early as 1939 Mao called for more attention to "work in the cities," for though the revolution would necessarily take the form of "a peasant guerrilla war" and would "triumph first in the rural districts," "the capture of the cities now serving as the enemy's main bases is the final objective of the revolution."[69] And in March of 1949, when the Communists were capturing the cities in the last phase of the civil war, Mao announced that "the center of gravity of the Party's work has shifted from the village to the city."[70]

Yet the Communist capture of the cities in 1949 was the rather anticlimactic consummation of a revolution in which the decisive battles had been fought by rural people in the countryside. Communist control of the cities did not involve revolutionary political action but rather assumed the form of a military occupation of the urban centers by a largely peasant army. The Maoist suspicion of the cities and their inhabitants (who had contributed so little to the revolutionary victory) remained—and it was later to reemerge in a confrontation with new problems in vastly different historical circumstances. Indeed, in the same report in which Mao announced the inauguration of the period of "the city leading the village," he warned that revolutionaries might be susceptible to urban bourgeois corruptions—to "sugar-coated bullets"—and that the rural style of "plain living and hard struggle" might give way to the "love of pleasure and distaste for continued hard living" that city life encouraged.[71]

Nonetheless, it was Mao himself who was as responsible as anyone for establishing the early post-revolutionary policies that gave rise to the social consequences against which he later was to rebel and condemn others for creating. Shortly before the formal establishment of the People's Republic, in the essay "On the People's Democratic Dictatorship," Mao postponed Marxist utopian goals to some indefinite time in the future in favor of the "immediate tasks" of building a strong state power and promoting rapid economic development.[72] With the city now established as the new "center of gravity," it was only logical that the "immediate tasks" should be pursued in accordance with the Soviet model of development: a priority on building urban heavy industry and establishing centralized (and urban-based) political and economic bureaucracies. The social and political results of the First Five-Year Plan are well known: the growth of bureaucratic structures and practices; the emergence of new patterns of social inequality, manifested especially in the appearance of political-administrative and technological-intellectual elites in the cities; urban economic development to the detriment of the agricultural sector; processes of what Maoists perceived as ideological decay (most notably, the tendency for Marxian socialist goals to become ritualized, and the abandonment, in practice if not in rhetoric, of the rural revolutionary values of an egalitarian style of "plain living" and hard work); and a growing political, economic, and cultural gulf between the modernizing cities and the backward countryside.

In the Maoist response to this familiar pattern of "post-revolutionary institutionalization," the Marxist goal of eliminating the distinction between town and countryside assumed a special prominence. And Maoist affinities with utopian socialist and populist ideas emerged with particular clarity, especially in the rural communization movement of the Great Leap Forward and the accompanying theoretical literature on "the transition from socialism to communism." The Maoist remedy for the social consequences of urban industrialization was to industrialize the countryside, to move the political as well as the socioeconomic center of gravity from the cities to the new peasant communes. These were to serve not only as the main agencies for economic development but also as the basic social units for China's "leap" to a communist utopia. Although it is by no means the most utopian document of the times, the chiliastic expectations of the era are conveyed in the official Party resolution of December 10, 1958, which defined the nature and sociohistorical function of the communes.

> In 1958, a new social organization appeared fresh as the morning sun above the broad horizon of East Asia. This was the large-scale people's commune in the rural areas of our country which combines industry, agriculture, trade, education and military affairs and in which government administration and commune management are integrated. . . . The development of the system of rural people's communes . . . has shown the people of our country the way to the gradual transition from collective ownership to ownership by the whole people in agriculture, the way to the gradual transition from the socialist principle of "each according to his work" to the Communist principle of "to each according to his needs," the way to the gradual diminution and final elimination of the differences between rural and urban areas, between worker and peasant and between mental and manual labor, and the way to the gradual diminution and final elimination of the domestic functions of the state. . . . It can also be foreseen that in the future Communist society, the people's commune will remain the basic unit of social structure.[73]

These are some of the themes elaborated on *in extenso* in the voluminous Great Leap literature on the communes and their assigned role in "the transition from socialism to communism." For obvious reasons of space, I cannot here discuss the massive body of literature, much less the realities, of the communization movement. But two aspects of this Maoist vision of the Chinese road to socialism are worth noting: first, the decidedly anti-urban implications of the communes, as they were originally envisioned, and second, the extraordinary emphasis placed on the role of human consciousness and moral qualities in achieving ultimate Marxist goals.

The whole Great Leap Forward vision of decentralizing social, economic, and political life in relatively autonomous and self-sufficient rural communes marked not only a drastic reversal of the pre-1957 policy of post-revolutionary development, but also the emergence of policies and strategies that were intended to undermine the power and prestige of the new urban elites. The emphasis on the "industrialization of the countryside" and the much-heralded scheme of combining industrial with agricultural production meant a radical deemphasis on the role of the cities and their inhabitants in achieving economic growth and revolutionary social change. Similarly, the new educational policies demanding the combination of education with productive labor (through "Red and Expert Universities" and various "half-work, half-study" programs) devaluated urban-centered and urban-oriented institutions of higher education. The new universities would produce "new peasants" who combined a socialist consciousness with scientific expertise; the masses themselves were to become the masters of science and technology. Moreover, the communes were to be not only the primary socioeconomic units, but also the primary organs of revolutionary political power. Assigning the administrative role of the *hsiang* to the commune was interpreted at the time as giving it the task of "performing the functions of state power."[74] Indeed, it was argued that "the integration of the *hsiang* with the commune will make the commune not very different from the Paris Commune, integrating economic organization with the organization of state power."[75] The Paris Commune (or, more precisely, Marx's interpretation of it) is of course the classic Marxist model of the "dictatorship of the proletariat"; thus the people's commune implicitly became the model Maoist instrument for carrying out the socially revolutionary measures of the transitional "proletarian dictatorship," including the all-important one of abolishing the distinction between town and countryside.*

The radical policies pursued during the abortive Great Leap Forward campaign reflected long-standing Maoist hostilities to those features generally associated with urban industrialism: occupational specialization, bureaucratic rationality, large-scale centralized organization, and formal higher education. And they posed a grave threat not only to the new urban elites, but to state and Party bureaucracies in general. Had the communes developed in accordance with the original Maoist vision, economic decentralization logically would have been accompanied by the dismantling of centralized bureaucratic political power.

The anti-urban thrust of the communization movement was accentuated by a general celebration of the virtues of rural life and an assault on "decadent" urban life-styles. Cadres were called on to practice and glorify the rural revolutionary social tradition of "the fine work style of leading a hard and plain life" and to condemn those

* It might be noted that an ideological prelude to the Great Leap policies was the abandonment (in 1956) of the notion of a "people's dictatorship" as the political formula for the Chinese road to socialism and communism in favor of the notion of "the dictatorship of the proletariat." The key document here is Mao's treatise *On the Historical Experience of the Dictatorship of the Proletariat* (Peking: Foreign Languages Press, 1956).

corrupted by city life, bringing them to indulge in extravagance and waste and to adopt the "bureaucratic airs" of lethargy, conceit, and effeminacy. The way to correct these vices was for city dwellers to live and work with the peasants in the countryside and there acquire true proletarian revolutionary virtues. It is noteworthy that the official Party resolution on the communes (of December 1958), while calling for the transformation "of the old cities" into "new socialist cities," observed that the communization of the cities would be more difficult and lengthy than the communization of the countryside, not only because of the greater complexity of urban life, but also because of the persistence of bourgeois ideology in the cities.[76]

Another striking feature of the Great Leap Forward era was the enormous emphasis placed on human consciousness and spiritual transformation. The utopian social goals of the movement could be realized in the here and now; one had only to rely on the "enthusiasm and creativity of the masses," believe that the people would respond as enthusiastically to moral and ideological appeals as to purely monetary incentives, recognize that "man is the decisive factor," and trust in the emergence of "new men" of "all-round ability," whose consciousness and actions would bring about the new society.[77] This celebration of "the people's creativity" took on a strongly rural orientation, for revolutionary creativity and the potential to achieve the appropriate morality and consciousness were attributed essentially to "the pioneering peasants."[78] Those who argued that China lacked the objective economic basis for communization and the transition to communism were accused of holding to the heretical "productive force theory" and of refusing to recognize "the great role and revolutionary enthusiasm of more than five hundred million peasants." They were reminded of Chairman Mao's words, "Poverty inclines one to change, action and revolution," which meant that "under all circumstances attention should be given to the full display of the subjective activity of the masses."[79]

Although the utopian elements in Maoism received their fullest expression in the Great Leap Forward era, they remained on the ideological scene after the forced retreat from the radical communization program and the reassertion of the power of urban-centered economic and political bureaucracies in the early 1960's. And they reemerged on the political scene with apocalyptic fury in the Cultural Revolution. However one wishes to interpret this extraordinary phenomenon, it was certainly (among other things) a direct attack on urban elites and an attempt to reverse the growing political and economic dominance of the industrializing cities over the countryside. It is perhaps overstating the case to describe the Cultural Revolution as "a movement of the countryside against the cities, and of the peasants against the workers," as Stuart Schram suggests,[80] if only because peasants were not principal actors in the political drama. Nonetheless, the Cultural Revolution marked the resurgence of an ideology that speaks on the peasants' behalf and the reestablishment of policies that tend to benefit the countryside rather than the cities and their "urban overlords." It resolved, at least for the time being, one of the central policy issues involved in Chinese Communist political struggles over the past decade and a half. The view, generally identified with Liu Shao-ch'i, that urban industrialization must precede the full socialist reorganization of the countryside gave way to the Maoist policy of committing a greater share of energy and resources to industrializing the countryside and increasing its access to education and health services. If it is not a policy that has achieved, or is likely to achieve, the ultimate goal of abolishing the distinction between town and countryside, it is nevertheless a policy that promises to narrow the economic, social, and cultural gap between urban and rural areas, and thus at least leaves open the possibility for future generations to pursue the more utopian ends so ardently proclaimed in the Great Leap Forward era.

Perhaps the most significant implication of the utopian socialist strains in Maoism is the inversion of the Marxist-Leninist view of the relationship between town and countryside. Nothing could be more repugnant to the Maoist mentality than Marx's characterization of modern history as "the urbanization of the countryside," the assumption that industrialization demands urbanization, and the proposition that the complete dominance of town over countryside is a historical prerequisite for the achievement of communism. Just as Mao's revolutionary strategy was based on a faith in the radical potential of the peasantry, so his post-revolutionary strategy focuses on the countryside as the point of departure for radical socioeconomic change. It is a strategy designed to avoid what Marx regarded as the inevitable social consequences of industrialization and to eliminate the social inequalities and ideological impurities that the city is seen to foster even in a presumably socialist society. The Maoist aim is neither to "ruralize" the city nor to "urbanize" the countryside. It is, rather, to modernize the countryside. The cities are gradually to be absorbed into a modernized and communized rural milieu as society moves to the ultimate goal of abolishing the distinction between town and countryside.

Maoists, to be sure, have adopted many of the measures Marx proposed as means to this end in the "transition" period following the socialist revolution: the "combination of agriculture with manufacturing industries," "a more equable distribution of the population over the country," and the "combination of education with industrial production."[81] But they flatly reject his assumption that such measures can be pursued successfully only in advanced industrialized countries under the leadership of the cities and the urban proletariat. Maoists insist that they must be undertaken in the here and now in a situation of economic scarcity, with the impetus coming from the countryside and a peasantry armed with the appropriate consciousness, morality, and leaders. It is not the utopian goal that distinguishes Mao from Marx (and Lenin) and that gives Maoism its "utopian" character, but in what manner and under what conditions that goal is pursued.

The inversion of the Marxist view of the relationship between town and countryside in modern revolutionary theory is by no means a distinctively Chinese Marxist phenomenon. Along with similar intellectual affinities with utopian socialist thought, it is found in contemporary Marxist ideologies in other areas of the world—most notably in the Castroist version of Marxism-Leninism, in the neo-Marxist writings of Frantz Fanon, and in the "African socialism" of Julius Nyerere. For Castro, for example, "the city is a cemetery of revolutionaries";* and for Fanon, the peasantry is the only revolutionary class, since the foreign-built towns are populated by a privileged and conservative proletariat as well as a parasitic bourgeoisie.†

---

* Quoted in Regis Debray, *Revolution in the Revolution?* (New York: Grove Press, 1967), p. 69. In Castroism, the city is not only physically dangerous for the revolutionary but also spiritually corrupting. As Debray puts it (pp. 70–77), revolutionaries who remain in the city will "lose sight of moral and political principle"; thus they are to "abandon the city and go to the mountains" because "the mountain proletarianizes the bourgeois and peasant elements," whereas "the city can bourgeoisify the proletarians." Similar anti-urban sentiments appear prominently in the writings of Che Guevara.

† The argument is developed in detail in Frantz Fanon, *The Wretched of the Earth* (New York: Grove Press, 1966), esp. pp. 29–163. For Fanon, the city, along with its sociopolitical life, is "the world that the foreigner had built" (p. 110); thus revolutionaries, who are to incarnate the elemental will of the peasantry, must live in the countryside both before and after the political victory and "ought to avoid the capital as if it had the plague" (p. 148).

The appearance in contemporary Marxist (or neo-Marxist) ideologies of ideas and conceptions similar to those characteristic of nineteenth-century European utopian socialist theories can be seen as a
function of economic backwardness—as modern variants of a universal intellectual response (in new historical circumstances and ideological frameworks) to the effects of early industrialization or to the
anticipation of them. Since these effects are most evident in the city,
they have historically tended to foster strong anti-urban biases. In
non-Western countries the hostility to the modern city has been particularly intense because the city not only manifests all the undesirable
social consequences of early industrialism, but is also the symbol of
foreign political, economic, and cultural dominance. The response,
accordingly, is both a nationalist and a social one. It is this powerful
combination of nationalist and socialist aspirations that has led many
contemporary non-Western Marxists to endorse Marx's goal of abolishing the distinction between town and countryside while rejecting
his analysis of the historical function of this division and his assumptions on the means by which it would be eliminated.

Such "utopian" departures from orthodox Marxism-Leninism have
influenced profoundly both the revolutionary and post-revolutionary
strategies of contemporary Marxists. In the making of revolution,
perhaps the most important implication is the rejection of the urban
bourgeoisie and proletariat as revolutionary classes in favor of the
peasantry. And in the making of new social orders, what is involved
is a special concern with the social price of modern economic progress,
an explicit rejection of Western and Soviet models of development,
an attempt to achieve industrialization without urbanization, and a
search for means of economic growth that seem consistent with the
ultimate achievement of socialist and communist goals. A good case
can be made (although I will not attempt to make it here) that non-
Marxian "utopian heresies" have served the needs of revolution well
where revolutions have been needed, and are better suited than standard Marxist and Leninist assumptions to the socioeconomic realities
of economically backward lands. Certainly there is nothing in the
modern Western historical experience to confirm Marx's prediction
that socialism is the logical and necessary result of modern capitalism,
and there is little in the Soviet historical experience to offer much hope
that this particular "socialist" pattern of urban industrialization is
likely to lead to any genuinely socialist future. It would be one of the
supreme ironies of modern history (and of the history of Marxism

in the modern world) if it should turn out that the peasant countries become the pioneers in the quest for Marxist socialist ends.

Yet before celebrating the "new roads" to socialism, one might do well to keep in mind some of the dangers that Marx long ago warned against: the possibility of historical regression inherent in any attempt to create a socialist society in the absence of highly developed productive forces; the particular forms of political elitism that tend to grow from historical situations characterized by a general weakness of social classes; and the tendency of countries with large peasant populations to foster Bonapartist personality cults—a phenomenon apparent in the appearance of charismatic leaders like Mao, Castro, and Nyerere who emerge on the historical scene with special "spiritual bonds" to the masses.

Perhaps we are simply witnessing in Maoist China and elsewhere a rather more mundane and familiar process, in which socialist ideologies and ostensibly socialist societies—as in the Soviet case but in new and strange forms—are performing the historical work of capitalist economic development with ultimately more or less similar social results. Will it turn out, as Marx believed, that "the country that is more developed industrially only shows, to the less developed, the image of its own future?" Or is it rather the paradoxical case that old utopian ideas in new ideological gestalts and operating in unforeseen historical circumstances are projecting the image of a new future?

# Urban and Rural Strategies in the Chinese Communist Revolution

YING-MAO KAU

Studies of the causes and processes of Communist insurgencies tend to fall into two broad categories. One emphasizes the socioeconomic roots of the revolutionary movement by analyzing conditions of economic poverty, social injustice, and political repressions. Such conditions generate "systemic frustration" in society, which ultimately leads to social aggression and political revolt.[1] The other category tends to stress the roles of leadership and strategy. The ability of the insurgents to formulate new ideologies, creative leadership techniques, and effective strategies of mobilization is treated as the determinant of revolution.[2] The first kind of study focuses on objective and quantifiable sociological variables that constitute the environment of politics, the second on the more elusive elements of political choice and formulas that activate and organize potential resources for the attainment of normatively defined goals.[3]

Analytically, such conceptual differentiation is useful and necessary. However, the close relationship of interaction between environment and strategy should not be overlooked. Evidence shows that unlike the primitive types of amorphous violence, Communist movements have never occurred due to the "systemic frustrations" of poverty and deprivation alone (without a well-organized and determined Communist leadership). Similarly, no revolutionary insurgency has ever become viable with a strategy that fails to appreciate and make full use of the environmental forces. Moreover, no single

This study was supported in part by grants awarded by the Social Science Research Council and the Howard Foundation. I am grateful for the valuable suggestions and comments given by Frederic J. Fleron, Philip E. Ginsburg, John W. Lewis, Suzanne P. Ogden, Pierre M. Perrolle, Lucian W. Pye, Charles Tilly, and Donald Zagoria.

society today is completely free from tensions and conflicts generated by the scarcity or unjust distribution (or both) of desired values, such as wealth, status, and power. The key problem facing all Communist leaderships, accordingly, is to devise a modus operandi that can maintain an optimum relationship between environment and strategy, guiding the movement to overcome obstacles and make the best use of supportive forces.

This paper aims at examining the stages and sequence of the Communist movement in China between 1919 and 1949, with special emphasis on the relationship between changes in the operational environment and corresponding adjustments in strategy. Particular attention is given to the crucial shifts between the urban and rural orientations of strategy and the role the cities played in the process of revolution. Most analyses of the Chinese Communist movement tend to characterize the Maoist strategy as one marked by its exclusive emphasis on the rural-based agrarian movement, mass mobilization, and guerrilla warfare. The long period of its isolation in the countryside, it is argued, turned the CCP into a "peasant Party."[4]

Although such a characterization has some validity, it grossly neglects the significance of the stages and sequence of the revolutionary process, alternating between the cities and the countryside, and discounts the importance of the cities and towns in the Chinese Communist movement. As will be shown, the urban centers played a crucial role to begin with in the creation of the Communist movement as a viable organizational and ideological force. Even during the rural seclusion and guerrilla activities, the cities and towns remained the indispensable source of manpower for the top and middle levels of leadership. Moreover, the Maoist rural-oriented strategy was designed to respond to the changing environments of operation, with the aim of moving into the cities from the countryside in the final stage of the movement. In the final analysis, the success of Mao's revolution rested on its ability to adjust its strategy to the changing context of insurgency, rather than on what is often believed to have been a strong adherence to a rural-oriented strategy.

## The Urban-Centered Stage, 1919–1927

The Communist movement in China can be divided into three periods in terms of the environmental settings: a period of organization among intellectuals and workers centered in the cities between 1919 and 1927; a period of peasant mobilization and guerrilla warfare based in the countryside between 1928 and 1945; and a period of large-scale political and military operations to encircle the cities from the countryside between 1946 and 1949.

The first stage began, for all practical purposes, with the 1917 October Revolution in Russia, which gave a tremendous boost to the appeal of Marxism-Leninism as a viable political alternative for China among radical urban intellectuals.[5] Indeed, a small number of professors and students immediately decided to study and practice the example of the Bolsheviks. Led by such prominent professors at Peking University as Ch'en Tu-hsiu and Li Ta-chao, a Marxist study society was organized in Shanghai in 1918. With the moral and material support of agents dispatched by the Comintern, similar societies quickly sprang up in other cities. Moving beyond disseminating Marxist-Leninist principles and operating Russian-language institutes to prepare Chinese youth for study in Moscow, these societies soon began engaging in agitation and organization among workers in urban centers.[6]

Activity in this embryonic period was centered primarily in the cities and remained so after the study groups gave way to the CCP, formed in Shanghai in July 1921. The Party was active in these early years mainly with students, intellectuals, and workers. The rapid expansion of Communist-led trade unions from 1922 to 1927 (see Table 1), in comparison with the neglected agrarian movement, testifies to the urban-centeredness of the strategy. Almost the first act of the newly formed Party was to organize a Secretariat of the Chinese Trade Unions to coordinate labor organizations. Virtually all the youthful leaders of the Party were involved in the labor movement. By the time the Second All-China Labor Congress met in May 1925, the "red unions" had succeeded in capturing the leadership of

TABLE 1

*Expansion of the Communist-led Trade Union Movement*

| Date | All-China Labor Congress | No. of Communist-led unions | Membership |
|------|--------------------------|-----------------------------|------------|
| May 1922 | 1st | 100 | 270,000 |
| May 1925 | 2d | 165 | 540,000 |
| May 1926 | 3d | 699 | 1,241,000 |
| June 1927 | 4th | — | 2,900,000 |

SOURCES: Teng Chung-hsia, *Chung-kuo chih-kung yün-tung shih* (A history of the Chinese labor movement) (Peking: Jen-min ch'u-pan she, 1953), pp. 69, 153; Suzue Gen'ichi, *Chugoku kaihō tōsō shi* (A history of the Chinese liberation struggle) (Tokyo: Ishizaki shoten, 1953), pp. 361–401; Nym Wales, *The Chinese Labor Movement* (New York: John Day, 1945), p. 54.

the workers; they now set out to organize the All-China Labor Federation (ACLF). When the ACLF convened the Fourth All-China Labor Congress at Wuhan in 1927, Liu Shao-ch'i reported that the Party had organized nearly 3,000,000 workers.[7]

The Party's stress on the labor movement was also reflected in the steady increase in urban labor unrest in the same period. Unofficial statistics show that the number of labor strikes grew from 25 in 1918 to 535 in 1926, an average increase of about 64 strikes per year.[8] Meanwhile, the Party itself grew just as impressively. Between 1921 and 1927 its membership jumped from 57 to 57,967. In this period, the recruits were predominantly students and urban workers.[9]

But the rapid growth of the Communist forces in the cities under the shield of the United Front with the KMT after 1923 began to worry the Nationalist leadership, and after some preliminary moves in 1926, Chiang Kai-shek launched the first all-out purge of Communists in Shanghai on April 12, 1927. Soon after, he extended the repression to other cities. The purges, effectively executed by the police and military forces of the KMT and associated warlords, quickly wiped out most of the Communists' gains in the urban areas. In the year 1927 alone the CCP membership dropped from a peak of nearly 58,000 to about 10,000. The frantic attempts to reestablish the Party's urban bases made by Ch'ü Ch'iu-pai in 1927 and by Li Li-san in 1930 failed disastrously. With the consolidation of his power after 1928, Chiang was able to use his superior military forces to destroy Communist-led organizations in the cities systematically in the so-called White Terror.[10]

*The Promises and Obstacles of the Urban-Based Movement*

The first stage of the Communist movement in China highlights some features of theoretical significance. The Communist leaders were able to score impressive successes by concentrating their energies in the cities and skillfully manipulating a number of urban forces. However, the urban setting also presented serious obstacles and limitations to the movement. Several generalizations and hypotheses can be made.

First, the Chinese experience in 1919–27 suggests that Communism as a viable ideological and revolutionary movement is likely to start in the cities rather than in the countryside. The position of the city as the center of intellectual and political activities and the link with other societies seems to be of decisive importance in the initiation of a movement. The modern urban center is clearly the place in which new ideas and information are generated, transmitted, and disseminated. This is particularly true if their sources are extra-societal. It is inconceivable, for example, that an alien ideology like Marxism-Leninism could have entered China without passing through the gateway of the treaty ports.

Second, the urban intellectuals (teachers and students) and workers of China proved to be the social groups most susceptible to Communist mobilization in the 1920's. Though both groups were politicized and involved, they played different roles. The intellectuals provided the nucleus of the ideological and organizational leadership, and the workers the popular base of the movement. Yet, functionally they were mutually complementary and supportive. In terms of the psychological theory of "frustration-aggression," both groups were "frustrated," and thus politically "aggressive,"[11] though with their distinctly different socioeconomic environments and life goals, their frustrations were presumably of a different order. It is likely that, in most cases, value and ideological conflicts play a dominant role in making intellectuals Communists, whereas socioeconomic deprivation and the hope of a better life persuade workers to support Communism.

Third, external stimulation and support clearly played a critical role in the launching of the Communist movement in China. Despite the serious mistakes that Moscow made in China, the help given to the CCP in its first years played a far more important role than is generally appreciated. It was men like Gregory Voitinsky and Michael Borodin who helped lay down the organizational and ideological foundations of the CCP, recruit and train the core of the leadership, and arrange the coalition with the KMT. It may be generalized that even a relatively small amount of external assistance can play a vital role in the initiation of a Communist movement in a society where experience and organization are lacking. The importance of such external aid will probably decline over time, once the movement begins to generate its own internal supports.

Fourth, the Chinese experience also suggests that once a reasonably successful movement arises in the urban centers, inertia tends to develop to keep it there. As Max Weber argues, all organizations, when routinized, tend to preserve their existing relations with the environment, and become reluctant to change.[12] The CCP was no exception. The bulk of the Party leaders in the early years were men of urban background, who undoubtedly felt most comfortable operating in the familiar setting of the cities. The convenience of modern technology, communications, and other facilities worked as both incentive and justification for keeping the movement in the cities. The pressure from the Comintern to apply the Bolshevik model of revolution in China and form a coalition with the urban-based KMT further confined the operation of the CCP to the cities. It should be noted that when the Communists moved out of the cities in 1927, they did not do so voluntarily. They were in fact forced into it for their own immediate security and survival.[13]

The preceding analysis shows that a number of sociological forces characteristic of the urban scene can be effectively used by a Communist movement. However, these same forces and others in the cities may also be hazardous. For example, by taking advantage of the concentration of intellectuals and workers and the availability of modern mass media and transportation facilities, the Communists succeeded in creating a Party structure and a labor movement in a relatively short time. But as the tragic events of 1927 show, all these urban elements could also be used by the government against the Communists. In a few short months Chiang Kai-shek in alliance with conservative forces in the cities (secret societies, traditional labor bosses, and so forth) was able to carry out a thorough suppression. Clearly, the government's means and capability of repression were at their most effective in the cities.

Second, certain structural characteristics of the city also hinder the development of a Communist movement. In comparison to villages, which are geographically dispersed and structurally diffuse, cities are marked by a greater concentration of population (under integrated administrative control) and a greater structural and functional differentiation of socioeconomic life. Industrialization and urbanization generate a relatively more complex pattern of social grouping and occupational organization; trade associations, industrial enterprises, and professional organizations emerge with a high degree of structural independence, functional autonomy, and organizational regimentation. For the Communists this means that the infiltration and expansion of Communist forces will require a large number of professionally competent cadres to penetrate and work in different specialized sectors and organizations.

As the sociologist Marion J. Levy, Jr., has argued, the process of modernization tends to strengthen organizational integration and administrative centralization in society.[14] A good example of this process is seen in the expansion of the functions and powers of modern urban governments. Broadly speaking, the increased centralization of governmental power and the increased interdependence of subsectors in the urban setting make it impossible for the Communists to achieve "partial control" or "partial liberation" of a city. In the urban setting the Communists have to fight an all-or-nothing "positional warfare"; there is no real alternative save small-scale, clandestine infiltration with minimal organized activities.

Finally, the statistics on the labor movement cited earlier show impressive growth in the Chinese Communist movement in its first years. But the quick collapse of the movement after the 1927 purge raises important questions. The effectiveness of the White Terror and the shaky organization of the early Red Unions may have played a significant part in that collapse, but the central cause seems to be related to the psychological basis on which the workers were mobilized. If it is true that workers join a revolution because of their socioeconomic deprivation, then the millions of workers who responded to Communist agitation in the early 1920's would have harbored strong expectations for the improvement of their lowly status and poor living conditions. The CCP thus had to secure concrete benefits to satisfy some of these expectations or see the political enthusiasm of the workers wane. But under the circumstances in the 1920's, the range of actions open to the Communists was severely limited; short of the seizure of power and administrative control over an entire city, there was no way they could have carried out reform to bring demonstrable results to the workers. What this proves is that using ideological mobilization to induce desired political responses and commitments has limits. At a certain point, ideology without evidence of achievement or of a credible potential for success will lose its attractions and become empty propaganda.

## The Rural-Based Peasant and Guerrilla Movement, 1928–1945

After 1927, the environment and strategy of the Communist revolution underwent a fundamental change. To paraphrase Mao, the "center of gravity of Party operation" shifted from the urban centers to the vast countryside of China.[15] With the KMT forces in relentless pursuit, Mao and his followers retreated in 1928 into the remote mountainous areas bordering Kiangsi, Hunan, and Fukien provinces. In the relative security provided by geographical isolation, Mao was able to organize revolutionary bases and a Red Army. At the same time, he began to reinterpret Marxist-Leninist theory within the context of an agrarian China and to elaborate his strategy of peasant movement and guerrilla warfare. In five years he succeeded in organizing five peasant Soviets and 15 revolutionary bases scattered over 74 hsien. The Communists' strategic shift to the countryside became almost complete in 1932, when the skeleton Central Committee of the Party had to leave its underground bases in Shanghai and move to Mao's Kiangsi Soviet for protection.

The series of encirclement campaigns launched by Chiang Kai-shek in 1930, however, forced the Communists to liquidate the Kiangsi bases in 1934 and to begin the legendary Long March to the isolated northwestern hinterland. Despite the enormous losses the Communists suffered in the course of that retreat, they managed to reestablish rural bases in the remote areas of Yenan after 1936. The full-scale Japanese invasion of China in 1937, followed in 1940 by the creation of the Wang Ching-wei "puppet regime" to govern the occupied areas, apparently further convinced Mao that "the countryside, and the countryside alone, can provide the broad areas in which the revolutionaries can maneuver freely. The countryside, and the countryside alone, can provide revolutionary bases from which the revolution can go forward to final victory."[16]

Throughout the 1930's and 1940's, Mao repeatedly directed the Communist forces to avoid the cities and main transportation lines, and warned against the "military adventurism" of fighting reckless and premature positional war in the cities, where the enemy was strong. Ideal places for building bases, carrying out reforms, and fighting guerrilla warfare, he argued, were the mountainous and border areas, where poor communications and transportation, along with the typically ambiguous division of provincial administrative responsibilities, made military and police control largely ineffective.[17] It was not until 1947, when the Red Army had been brought up to strength and final victory was obvious, that Mao ordered a strategic shift in the center of operation from the countryside to the cities, and from guerrilla warfare to positional war aimed at seizing and occupying those cities.

*The Benefits and Costs of Shifting to the Rural Strategy*

The development of the rural-based movement was by no means smooth and easy. There were, for example, the difficult years of organizing the Kiangsi Soviet and the painful costs of the Long March. But by the end of the Sino-Japanese War in August 1945 the Yenan-based Communist forces were able to claim control of about one-fourth of the nation's territory (primarily in the rural areas) and about one-third of its population.[18] This success attests to the correctness of Mao's strategy, which called for the concentration of effort in the countryside through mobilization of the peasantry, agrarian reform, and protracted guerrilla warfare.

The Communists benefited in several important ways in their shift to the rural sector. First of all, thanks to the relative inaccessibility and primitive rural conditions of the border areas, they were able to solve their most pressing problem, the need for military and political security. The rugged terrain, poor transportation, and weak administrative control in these isolated areas made effective repression by the government impossible. By taking refuge in the countryside, the Communists traded the convenience of urban life for the physical security essential to the survival and growth of the Party.

Second, the rural strategy enabled the movement to develop autonomous territorial bases out of the easy reach of government forces, where basic economic and administrative structures could be created. Here, in contrast with the cities, where there were too many forces beyond the control of the Communists, the CCP had a chance to develop organizations and administration under planned supervision.

Third, in the freedom of the remote countryside, the Communists were able to carry out many of the social reforms and economic programs they had long been advocating. The efforts to redistribute land, attack various forms of social injustice, and improve the education and social status of the underprivileged masses became a living testimony to the sincerity, commitment, and effectiveness of the CCP, on the one hand, and a powerful challenge to the authority and legitimacy of the KMT, on the other. It was in this period that the image and prestige of the Communists underwent a basic change: they were no longer a force of "destruction," but one of "construction," not saboteurs and criminals, but liberators and builders.

Fourth, the shift to the remote countryside enabled the Party to create an independent political army. The importance of the role the Red Army played in the revolution cannot be overemphasized. As Mao has summed it up: "The seizure of power by armed forces, the settlement of the issue by war, is the central task and the highest form of revolution"; and "political power grows out of the barrel of a gun."[19]

During the revolution, the Red Army was used not only to carry on guerrilla warfare, but also to perform a host of civilian tasks. Far from being simply the military means with which to challenge the government's control and authority, it participated actively in political propaganda, mass mobilization, and economic production.[20] Nevertheless, it was the continued expansion of the military capabilities of the Communists during this stage that laid the necessary groundwork for the Communists to shift in the later years from guerrilla warfare to positional warfare, to move out of the countryside and encircle the cities, and finally to take power.

Fifth, the rural-based operation secured a strong mass base for the Party. Earlier I suggested that the psychological basis of the frustration of the masses tends to be socioeconomic deprivation. In the base areas, the CCP's ability to improve the peasants' economic and social lot in concrete ways clearly enabled it to win and retain their loyalty and develop a solid mass following.[21]

The Communists' success in enlisting the support of the peasantry apparently rested on other variables as well. John W. Lewis, for example, has effectively demonstrated the critical importance of the mass-line technique of leadership developed by the Party—the deployment of Party cadres among the people to learn their problems* and then to lead them by combining the general principles laid down by the central leadership with the specific conditions of the locality.[22] As Mao concluded, the success of leadership was largely determined by how well the "endless spiral" of "from the masses and to the masses" was practiced.[23]

From an institutional perspective, the success of political mobilization in the countryside appears to have been facilitated by the decline of traditional arrangements. As Nathan Leites and Charles Wolf, Jr., hypothesize, the extent to which socioeconomic deprivation leads to systemic frustration and aggression is significantly conditioned by the patterns of sociocultural institutions and their capacity to mediate in the political process.[24] The political stability of traditional rural China, despite the ages-old problems of land hunger and general poverty, was due in large degree to its well-integrated authority structure and strong social and kinship ties (e.g., clan, *pao-chia*, and temple associations). Strong cleavages along these kinship and other parochial lines had the effect of reinforcing the internal solidarity and

---

* Through the practice of the "four togethers," that is, living, eating, working, and studying together.

vertical leadership within each subsystem (group) vis-à-vis a system-wide identity and loyalty based on economic class. In other words, a poor peasant was likely to maintain strong personal ties and commitment, cultural as well as organizational, to his lineage (or some other local unit) rather than identifying with an abstract socioeconomic class beyond his community.[25]

In the 1930's and 1940's, however, as the dislocations of war and industrialization made themselves felt in the villages, this traditional solidarity was weakened, and so also were the sociocultural checks on collective aggression. In consequence, the masses of poor peasants became ever more susceptible to Communist efforts to establish horizontal links among the peasantry based on a new ideology and class consciousness. By the 1930's, the authority of the village gentry and clan heads had so declined that they were powerless to prevent the distressed peasants from accepting the new and compelling concepts of moral legitimacy and political leadership introduced by the Communists.[26]

This emerging pattern of social grouping and loyalty in the countryside was in marked contrast to the situation in the cities in this period. In the urban centers, modernization and industrialization were generating a wide variety of specialized organizations, such as economic enterprises, professional associations, secret societies, and government agencies. As these groups increased in both number and size, so also did their internal regimentation and discipline. Such a development clearly imposed strong constraints on the Communists in competing for organizational leadership and group loyalty among the urban populace.[27] (See Fig. 1.)

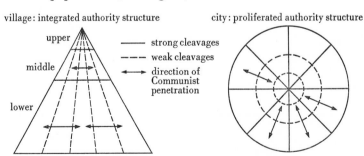

Fig. 1. Patterns of group solidarity and Communist penetration in China in the 1930's. In the village, the horizontal lines indicate the class stratification and the vertical lines the group cleavages. In the city, the circles indicate the class stratification and the straight lines the group cleavages.

*The Disadvantages of the Rural-Based Movement*

Although the benefits of the rural-based stage of the movement, as discussed above, were considerable, the unfavorable consequences of the protracted seclusion from the cities were considerable also. The recruiting and training of Party cadres and leaders was probably the area that suffered most: the peasantry perforce became the main source of manpower for the rank and file of the Party and the Red Army; most cadres received relatively little education and professional training; and the Party and its cadres were largely cut off from the cities and thus from useful contact with modern society. As a result of all this, many cadres failed to develop the skills, attitudes, and outlook required for leadership in the cities in the later years.[28]

The continuous purges of the Communists in the cities, first by the KMT and then by the Japanese and their puppet regime, not only eliminated large numbers of urban cadres, but also effectively prevented their replacement. In the first round of purges by the KMT in 1927, for example, the Party lost 84 per cent of its 57,967 members, the bulk of them from the urban centers. Two years later Chou En-lai reported that whereas the proletariat had supplied 66 per cent of the Party membership in 1926, it had supplied only 10 per cent in July 1928, and by November 1929 the proportion had been further reduced to a mere 3 per cent.[29] Another great loss of urban cadres apparently occurred during the Long March of 1934–35, when more than two-thirds (70 per cent) of the 100,000 participants perished en route.

After these two great blows and the strategic withdrawal into the countryside, the Communists had little alternative but to turn to the rural sector for new blood. Following the Japanese invasion and the formation of the Second United Front in 1937, the Communists did succeed in appealing to the nationalism of some urban students and intellectuals in North China; but the overwhelming majority of the new recruits continued to come from the local peasantry. For example, of the 134 Party members in the Third Township of Yen-ch'uan, Shensi, in the years 1927–39, 97 per cent were local poor and middle peasants or hired laborers.[30] There is little doubt that prior to 1949 the overall "class base" of the Party was the rural peasantry.

Although the proportion of cadres of rural origin in the Party during the guerrilla period was probably always over 90 per cent, such statistical expressions should be kept in proper perspective.[31] In the first place, the Party's categories for the classification of socioeconomic backgrounds were generally broad and ambiguous. The category "peasant background," for instance, did not necessarily mean the person was in fact in agriculture; it could refer merely to the locale of his family residence, or to his childhood experience, or to his father's occupation.

Evidence suggests that though many cadres were indeed raised in villages and were sons of farmers, they were educated in market towns or cities and never pursued agriculture as an occupation. Typically, they worked in the urban areas after schooling or returned to villages as teachers or office clerks. If we add an intermediate category of "mixed rural-urban" for cadres of this background, the patterns of statistical distribution would change considerably. Scattered data suggest that approximately 15 to 20 per cent of the Party members in the early 1940's may fall into this category.[32] A man like Mao would clearly be in this mixed background category, rather than labeled of "peasant background." This group, by virtue of its unique "dual experience," may in fact have played a far more significant role than is generally appreciated. They were equipped not only with the skills and training needed by the movement, but also with the rural socialization experience and social ties essential for an ability to empathize with the peasantry and to lead them effectively.

About a quarter of the Party membership prior to 1945 is estimated to have been in the two categories of "urban" and "mixed background." This means that in the period 1940–45, the Party had roughly 200,000 members with reasonably extensive urban experience, a far from insignificant figure.[33] Representing mainly students and intellectuals recruited in the late 1930's, this group provided much-needed skills, expertise, and leadership from the urban sector. However, those who had never lived in the countryside had to undergo a period of "ruralization," so to speak, in order to adjust themselves to the rural environment—to change their city style of life and learn to lead the peasants through the mass line.

With respect to the relationship between the cadres' socioeducational background and their organizational status and influence, two points are immediately clear. First, as shown diagrammatically in Fig. 2, the higher the level in the leadership hierarchy, the higher the proportion of cadres of urban background; and conversely, the lower the level in the organization, the greater the number of cadres of rural background. Virtually all of the 70-odd Communist leaders

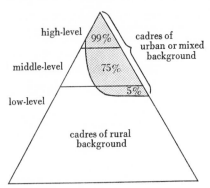

Fig. 2. Organizational hierarchy and social background of Communist cadres prior to 1949. Percentages roughly estimated from the works cited in note 34.

who held membership in the Central Committee prior to 1949, for instance, were of the "urban" or "mixed" categories; and scattered data suggest that probably as many as 75 per cent of the middle-level cadres, from the regional level down to the hsien level, were also from those categories. It is only at the lowest level, villages, that one finds the overwhelming majority of the activists and small-group leaders to have been local peasants who were "strictly rural" both in family origin and in occupation.[34]

Second, as a general rule the powerful and influential in the Party were those who had been extensively educated or trained in the cities. Only positions at the lowest levels of task performance were generally staffed by peasants of local origin. The strong relationship between organizational influence and urban experience was probably most striking at the village and township level. Although cadres with some urban experience at this level were normally few in number (not more than 5 per cent of the total), they often exercised an inordinate amount of power and influence because of their education or administrative experience (or both). Typically, they were Party branch leaders, schoolteachers, organizers of mass campaigns, or propaganda specialists, who were responsible for such indispensable matters as ideology, administration, and communications.[35] Harold D. Lasswell classifies such leaders as "symbol manipulators," "managers of organization," and "men of action." (For Eric Hoffer, they are "men of words," "true believers," and "men of action.")[36] In the Chinese case, cadres of urban and mixed backgrounds virtually monopolized the first two categories. Thus, the severe shortage of educated and trained cadres was greatly compensated for by the strategic role played by the few and the disproportionate influence they exercised in the overall structure of the Communist movement.

## The Return to the Cities, 1946–1949

The protracted period of the rural-based operation in a way prepared the Communists military and politically to evolve from a guerrilla band to a full-fledged revolutionary force. As the Anti-Japanese War moved to its end, the stage was set for a final showdown through direct military confrontation. Mao jubilantly declared in 1949 that the Communist movement in China had entered a new and final stage:

> From 1927 to the present the center of gravity of our work has been in the villages—gathering strength in the villages, using the villages in order to surround the cities and then taking the cities. The period for this method of work has now ended. The period of "from the city to the village" and of the city leading the village has now begun. The center of gravity of the Party's work has shifted from the village to the city.[37]

He tempered his jubilation, however, with words of caution, warning that the Communist forces were still not fully prepared to assume the control and administration of the entire nation, particularly in the cities.[38]

As the momentum of the Civil War surged ahead in 1946 and the Nationalist forces rapidly disintegrated, Mao began taking steps to reorient the rural-based strategy to match the new environments of operation, the cities. Four measures, accompanied by mass campaigns for their implementation, constituted the essence of the new urban strategy he initiated.[39] First, systematic attempts were made to ready cadres for urban work in order "to turn the fighting forces into a working force."[40] Military leaders were instructed to organize crash programs to prepare their troops to work in the cities. In the meantime, large numbers of university students and urban intellectuals were recruited from groups and associations known for their progressiveness and were quickly trained for urban work.

Second, concerted efforts were made to check the so-called guerrilla mentality. Many of the habits, attitudes, and work styles the Communists had adopted during the rural-based guerrilla operation were attacked as incompatible with the new urban environment. It was wrong now for the cadres, for example, "to seize, loot, and abandon cities as if they were still fighting the hit-and-run warfare of the thirties." At the same time, the Communist forces were warned against looking forward to the "pleasures and comfort" of city life, and against calling for an end to "plain living and hard work."[41]

Third, a moderate "new urban policy" was inaugurated to facilitate an orderly takeover and administration of the cities. The new policy stressed three priorities: economic recovery and the development of production; protection for the petty and national bourgeoisie and their enterprises; and cooperation with the intellectuals, professionals, and other progressive elements under the principle of the United Front.[42]

Fourth, the mass movements of "institution-building" and "organizational regularization" were initiated to foster a new set of attitudes and behavioral norms and to develop a new system of rational organization and operation congruent with the urban environment. In order to make the complex and specialized government organizations and economic enterprises function efficiently once the Party was in control, cadres were trained as rapidly as possible in administrative techniques, operational procedures, and organizational discipline.[43]

By mid-1949, when the Communist forces were moving across the Yangtze to take over key urban centers like Shanghai and Wuhan, the mass campaigns to reorient the Party's rural strategy to the new urban environment appear to have achieved their objective. The Communist forces entering the cities at that time were widely reported to have behaved with discipline and purpose; and the military and administrative takeover of the cities was by and large orderly and efficient.[44]

This analysis of the Chinese Communist movement points to three conclusions. First, it is clear that the alternation of the movement between rural and urban orientations holds a significance beyond its obvious historical interest. A study of the sequence, from city to countryside and back (see Table 2), shows a positive functional linkage between the three stages. Each stage fulfilled certain vital functions for the subsequent stage in the movement. The urban-centered stage provided the opportunity for the Party to make Marxism-Leninism viable in China as an intellectual and political force and to organize the first group of dedicated leaders, a group that remained substantially intact as the leadership core throughout the Party's struggle for power. In both respects the contributions of the first stage to the subsequent expansion during the second stage cannot be overemphasized. Without the creation of the "spirit" and "bones" of the

TABLE 2
*Stages of the Chinese Communist Movement, 1919–1949*

| Period | Operational environment | Main sources of recruitment | Central focus | Tactics |
|---|---|---|---|---|
| 1919–27 | Urban | Intellectuals, students, workers | Labor movement | Political (incl. United Front) |
| 1928–45 | Rural | Peasants, students, soldiers | Agrarian movement | Guerrilla warfare (incl. political struggle) |
| 1946–49 | Rural-urban | Students, professionals, soldiers | Military campaign | Positional warfare (with political negotiations) |

movement in the cities, the growth and tempering of the "muscle" in the rural bases would have been highly problematic.

Similarly, the development of the revolutionary bases, of a powerful Red Army, and of a strong peasant following in the countryside in the second stage clearly laid the groundwork for the shift to the final stage of the movement. Without the greatly expanded political and military capabilities developed in the countryside, the seizure of cities in the 1940's would almost certainly have been impossible. The evidence of positive sequential relationship and functional links between the three stages deserves further examination by both the social science theorist and the practitioner of revolution.

Second, it is clear from the process of Communist revolution in China that the insurgency was always faced with the uncertainty of changes in the temporal and structural context of revolution, which in general operated beyond its control. Therefore, one-sided emphasis on either environmental determinism or doctrinal imperatives in the theory of revolution is no useful guide for the revolutionaries. The key to revolution lies in achieving the best possible balance between strategy and environment. It is crucial for the leadership to develop an insight into the decisive variables and processes of revolution in a given situation, and to adjust its strategy constantly and flexibly in accordance with the changing environment at the right time, at the right rate, and in the right sequence.

From the broad perspective of rural-urban differences, it should be noted, the choice between an urban-centered and a rural-based strategy in China's Communist Revolution appears to have been closely related to the legal status that the movement enjoyed at a given time. Generally speaking, when the movement was politically tolerated by

TABLE 3

*Ingredients and Strategy of the Chinese Communist Revolution*

| | Rural-based strategy | | Urban-based strategy | |
|---|---|---|---|---|
| Ingredient | Environmental support | Organizational feasibility | Environmental support | Organizational feasibility |
| Political security | + + | + | − − | — |
| Revolutionary base | + + | + | − − | − − |
| Socioeconomic reforms | + + | + | + | − − |
| Mass base | + + | + | + | − |
| Armed forces | + + | + | + | − |
| Leadership organization | − − | + | + + | + |

NOTE: Plus means favorable; minus means unfavorable.

the government it gravitated toward the city for various reasons, including conventional ideological influences and practical considerations. Conversely, when the movement was declared illegal and repressed, it shifted to the countryside for immediate security and survival and for long-term preparation and development of strength. The long-term approach, however, was taken only under the far-sighted leadership of Mao; the temptation for premature return to the urban centers was always strong.

Third, the Chinese case suggests that six ingredients were crucial to the success of the Communist Revolution in China: a reasonable degree of security from armed repression, an autonomous revolutionary base, a tangible success in socioeconomic reforms, a strong mass base, an independent political army, and a sound leadership organization.[45] As Table 3 shows, the rural-based period proves on balance to have been far more productive of the ingredients required for victory than the urban-based period. The rural environment not only provided a superior array of potential resources, but also provided a more favorable setting for the mobilization of these resources. Although such resources were not totally unavailable in the cities, they were in general far more difficult to organize because of the special structural characteristics of the urban setting. It is only in the area of skilled and educated manpower that the countryside was inferior to the urban environment. Even so, the CCP did not find that an insurmountable problem. By skillfully playing on the themes of nationalism and the United Front to attract urban youth, and by placing their limited resources of skills and talents in strategic positions, the Chinese Communist leaders succeeded to a large extent in overcoming the difficulty.

# Town and Country in Revolution

CHARLES TILLY

In his writings on political conflicts in nineteenth-century Italy, Antonio Gramsci returned repeatedly to the relations of rural and urban populations. He had before him the model of the Jacobins during the French Revolution, "who succeeded in crushing all the Rightist parties, including the Girondins, on the agrarian question, not merely to forestall a rural coalition against Paris, but also to multiply their own supporters in the provinces."[1] The comparison remained at the core of his conception of the *rivoluzione mancata*: the social revolution that could have occurred during the creation of a unified Italian state, but did not.

In pursuing this problem, Gramsci developed two important ideas about rural-urban political relations. The first is a political distinction between industrial and nonindustrial cities. The industrial city, he tells us, is "always more progressive than the countryside, which depends on it organically."[2] Hence a revolutionary movement that sweeps industrial cities draws in their hinterlands as well. The nonindustrial city is different, at least in Italy. "In this type of city there exists," Gramsci writes, "an ideological unity from which even the nuclei that are most modern because of their civic functions ... do not escape: it is hate and disdain for the serf, an implicit united front against the demands of the countryside, which would, if granted, make that type of city impossible."[3] In the North, Gramsci saw the

National Science Foundation Grant GS-2674 supported the research on structural change and political conflict in Europe that lies behind this paper. I am grateful to John Lewis, Louise Tilly, George Totten, and Donald Zagoria for criticism of an earlier draft. Leila Al-Imad provided indispensable research assistance. And Mike Polen gave me a great deal of help in deciding how to revise the earlier draft for publication.

industrial city as already dominant in the nineteenth century; in the South the anti-rural city and the anti-rural sentiment prevailed.

To the distinction between the political orientations of industrial and nonindustrial cities, Gramsci added an idea that was later to occur to Lin Piao: "In the Risorgimento, furthermore, one can already see the embryonic development of the historical relationship of North and South as like the relationship between a great city and a great rural area."[4] The rural-urban relationship Gramsci had in mind here was one of domination and exploitation. Thus the rural-urban division *within* the South and the rural-urban division *between* the South and the North blocked that union of the oppressed which alone could have brought about a social revolution.

In this analysis, Gramsci's idea of rural and urban did not depend on the conventional statistical standards—size and population density. For him, areas in which the basic social relations are built around control of the land qualify as rural; they qualify whether they are large or small, whether everyone is a farmer or not.

More precisely, Gramsci's basic distinctions depend on the relations of production: the *cities* of the South—places like Palermo and Naples—were populated by numbers of gentlemen and merchants who drew their principal incomes from ownership of the soil but took no direct part in its cultivation; in the settlements of the *countryside* were the thousands of landless and land-poor workers who actually planted, tilled, and harvested. The "demands of the countryside, which would, if granted, make that type of city impossible," were demands for redistribution of the land. The rural-urban division Gramsci portrayed was a class division as well. The comparison between the cities of South and North becomes the comparison between "parasitic" and "generative" cities, a comparison that numerous analysts of the non-Western world have made in recent decades. And the treatment of the relationship between North and South as an urban-rural relationship likewise calls attention to its exploitative character.

In these terms, then, Gramsci's analysis of nineteenth-century Italy presents a clear and forceful model of the political relations between town and country. To the extent that the prevailing rural-urban division separates exploited agricultural workers from their exploiters, it tells us, we should expect little collaboration between rural and urban classes and little common action from the necessarily fragmented countryside, despite the probability of widespread conflict on a local scale. A revolutionary movement is likely to bring town and country together only where the town is already serving as a generator of rural activity. And in a predominantly agricultural country the revolution is likely to fail if an effective rural-urban coalition of the exploited classes does not appear.

## *The Gramscian Questions*

The problem of the *rivoluzione mancata* raises a series of questions about town and country in revolution:

1. Do rural and urban populations play characteristically different roles in revolution?

2. What difference to the outcome of a revolution do the extent and character of rural-urban cleavage make?

3. To what extent, and how, does the character of rural-urban division in an area affect the likelihood of revolution in that area?

With some extrapolation, Gramsci's analysis of nineteenth-century Italy yields interesting answers to all three questions.

What does Gramsci say about the first question—the characteristic roles of city and country in revolution? The country struggles over control of the land, the city over control of labor. The interests of the "subaltern classes" of town and country are necessarily different, though they are not necessarily contradictory. The two are likely to act in concert only when united (a) by some linking organization and (b) by a common opposition to the dominant classes and to their instrument, the state.

What difference to the outcome of a revolution do the extent and character of rural-urban cleavage make? That is where Gramsci begins. If rural-urban cleavage is great, a successful revolution is less likely; the cleavage separates the natural revolutionaries, the exploited classes of town and country, from each other. This is, however, quite an extrapolation of Gramsci's analysis, since he was analyzing cases in which both town and country did have important political roles.

Finally, to what extent, and how, does the character of rural-urban division in an area affect the likelihood of revolution in that area? We need another extrapolation: all other things being equal, the more thoroughly the influence of cities pervades the countryside, the more likely is revolution. Revolution, in this case, is the effective transfer of power to a new class. Rebellions of different sorts are quite likely to occur where the working classes of city and country are insulated from each other. But an effective transfer of power requires a union of the two.

Notice that Gramsci avoids two alternative simplifications that have been common in recent analyses of Asian rebellions and revolutionary movements: assuming a one-to-one relationship between the extent of grievance, exploitation, or hardship and the degree of rebelliousness; or treating the involvement in rebellion of any particular population as a measure of the effectiveness of a revolutionary organization (or, for that matter, of a counterrevolutionary organization) in dealing with that population. Either formulation can, of course, become true by definition; all it takes is an appropriate criterion for "grievance" in the one case and for "effectiveness" in the other. But we have had plenty of analyses that go directly from imputed motives to action, on the one hand, and from organizational effectiveness to revolutionary success, on the other, without passing through tautology.

In the case of Vietnam, Edward J. Mitchell's effort to relate insurgency to equality of land distribution (or, more precisely, control by the South Vietnamese regime to inequality, tenancy, previous French ownership, and so on) is an example of the first simplification.[5] As Robert Sansom points out, a more plausible interpretation of the same findings takes into consideration the strategy of the "insurgents," the effects of their land redistribution where they gained control, and the distinction between the grievances of the tenants of an area and the political alliances of its landlords.[6] Gramsci was aware that an elite could persist in the face of mass hostility so long as the mass had no organizational focus and no external allies.

The analysis of Nathan Leites and Charles Wolf, Jr., illustrates the second simplification. (Leites and Wolf wrote *Rebellion and Authority* in an abstract, generalizing style, but with Vietnam very much in mind.) Explicitly challenging the "hearts-and-minds" version of the first simplification, they reach such conclusions as:

> Politically, the capabilities that A must develop and demonstrate involve the capacity to act with speed, consistency, and discrimination. More specifically, A must protect the population; identify desired behavior and reward it by effective programs; and withhold such programs in areas that have failed to perform in desirable ways. A must demonstrate a capacity to act with discrimination and restraint, basing its action on legal and orderly processes that provide a contrast to the putative illegality and disorder of R.[7]

"A" and "R" are, of course, Authorities and Rebels. Leites and Wolf make concessions to the demands of potential rebels, but emphasize the tactical importance of the supply of rewards and punishments. The rewards and punishments are, Leites and Wolf point out, much more elastic than the demands.

Such an organizational argument underestimates the extent to which rebels know where their interests lie and match them with the long-run programs (not just the current tactics) of one side or the other. It also assumes that the national government recognized by outsiders as the government has the advantage of legitimacy, or at least of priority. Gramsci, by contrast, assumes that each class has a vision and a memory: helped by its avant-garde, it is aware of its long-run interests and acts on them when it can, but often lacks the means of effective action. "No mass action is possible," he declares, "if the mass itself is not convinced of the ends to be accomplished and of the means to be applied."[8]

Gramsci worked out most such arguments concretely, with Italian problems in view. One example is his treatment of the position of the Socialists around the turn of the century:

> The insurrection of the Sicilian peasants in 1894 and the rebellion of Milan in 1898 were the crucial experiment for the Italian bourgeoisie. After the bloody decade of 1890–1900, the bourgeoisie had to give up an overly exclusive, overly violent, and overly direct dictatorship: both the southern peasants and the northern workers rebelled against them simultaneously, if not in concert. In the new century the dominant class inaugurated a new policy of class alliance, of class political blocs, that is of bourgeois democracy. It had to choose—either rural democracy, an alliance with the southern peasants, a policy of low tariffs, universal suffrage, administrative decentralization, and low prices for industrial products or a capitalist-worker industrial block without universal suffrage, for protectionism, for the maintenance of state centralization (an expression of bourgeois domination over the peasant, especially in the South and the Islands), and for a reformist policy on wages and unionization. Not by chance, it chose the second solution; Giolitti personified bourgeois domination, and the Socialist Party became the means of Giolittian policy.[9]

Gramsci assumes that the interests and demands of the major classes are known but their political realization is much in doubt. The work of a revolutionary party is to mobilize them, synthesize them, and subordinate them to a general revolutionary program.[10]

Gramsci's analyses have their inconvenient side. Although he has much to say about the objective interests and demands of particular classes, he offers no general formula for calculating them. We cannot move easily from Gramsci's reasoning to generalizations about the revolutionary potential of different kinds of workers or different kinds of peasants. Nor does he have much to say in general about the kinds of countries or the stages of development that are especially favorable to rebellion or revolution. His life and thought centered on strategic questions: most of all, how to build a revolution with the materials provided by different forms and stages of Western capitalism. For the rest, we must go back to Marx or forward to Mao.

In dealing with our three questions, then, Gramsci provides us with a good start, but no more than that. He aims us away from the analysis of short-run fluctuations in hardship, of expectations, of tradition, and toward the analysis of class, power, organization, and communication. The main task of this paper is to present an analysis of town and country in revolution that is Gramscian in tone, if not in detail.

The analysis has three layers. First comes a stark presentation of a general argument, which includes some defining of terms and some elementary model-building. This is followed by a brief discussion of the way the argument applies to the European experience from which it is derived, and then by some suggestions about the possible application of the argument to the collective actions and revolutionary involvements of Asian peasants.

### Europe and Asia

Before the analysis, a warning. I make no claim that the Asian situation today corresponds closely to the European situation at any time in the past. I explicitly reject the idea of standard paths of "political development" that make it possible to anticipate the experience of "backward" countries by scrutinizing the experiences of "advanced" countries.[11] It is possible that the generalizations I propose —however valid they may be for the European past—have no relevance whatsoever to contemporary Asia.

Let us remember what Europe was like. Five hundred years ago, the European population was, compared with the rest of the world, relatively prosperous, predominantly peasant, fairly homogeneous from a cultural point of view. In these respects, Europe as a whole resembled China, and faintly resembled India and Japan. (The comparison of the continent of Europe with the subcontinent of China makes sense, since in 1500 each had something like 100,000,000 people spread over about 4,000,000, square miles.) However, Europe —again, as compared with the rest of the world of 1500—had an extensive network of cities and a series of elites strongly connected by kinship, political alliance, and economic interdependence, yet had rather weak structures of patronage and corporate kinship. Local communities, as such, played an exceptionally significant part in the collective lives of Europeans. That was in part because of the weakness of patronage and corporate kinship, in part because of the historical importance of the parish and the manor as units of settlement, administration, and collective action.

Most of the European territory had, of course, once fallen under the control of a single empire governed from Rome. That empire had left its mark on language, religion, social relations, and communications, but by 1500 the territory had been broken up into hundreds of separate political units. Although the many governments overlapped and depended on one another, at least 500 different rulers exercised some kind of sovereignty somewhere in Europe. Despite the power of the Habsburgs and the pretensions of the Holy Roman Emperor (at that time ordinarily a Habsburg himself), no single political organization outweighed all the rest.

In these respects, Europe differed significantly from China, and from Japan as well; in 1500 it was, perhaps, closer to India. The combination of weak patronage, weak corporate kinship, relatively homogeneous culture, and territorial communities that were prominent as units of solidarity and collective action distinguished Europe from most of Asia. There were, to be sure, similarities in individual items: local communities, for example, appear to have been exceptionally important as units of collective action in Vietnam and (at least from Tokugawa times) in Japan. Any comparison in which one term contains a quarter of the world's population (Europe) and the other term half the world's population (Asia) will suffer many exceptions. Nevertheless, the interesting combination of homogeneity, interdependence, and political fragmentation sets Europe off from most of Asia.

After 1500, a few of the hundreds of governments became the cores of expanding national states. The next three centuries brought a tremendous consolidation, centralization, elaboration, and increase in power of state structures. By the late nineteenth century, the political map of Europe had simplified into a few dozen territories with well-established sovereignty. These national states had grown up in conjunction with capitalism, industrialism, and urbanism. The exact connections of statemaking with these other phenomena remain debatable. Still, it is clear that the states had come to form a *system*: they were tightly interdependent, exercised collective control over each other's claims outside their own territories, monitored entries into and exits from statehood, comprised a well-established hierarchy, warred with each other within constraints set by that hierarchy (but also as a means of adjusting the hierarchy), and depended on a continental division of economic labor. The European states jointly imposed their power on much of the rest of the world. They exported the particular political forms of their state-system into the territories they conquered. The nearly continuous rise of states and of a state-system was therefore the fundamental political fact for Europe over the centuries after 1500, in much the same way that the waxing and waning of successive empires was the fundamental political fact for China until at least the middle of the nineteenth century.

All this means that anyone who wants to generalize from the European political experience to that of Asia will probably do better with China, Japan, or India than with other parts of Asia, but will probably not do very well even there. The generalizations will have to make allowances for the residues of empire in Europe, for the relative strength of local communities, for the relative weakness of patronage and corporate kinship, for the long, thorough concentration of power in national states. My modest hope for relevance hangs on two possibilities: that the sorts of *questions* one can ask fruitfully about the European experience are worth asking in Asia as well; and that some of the general *relationships* suggested by a Gramscian analysis hold widely, even if the concrete sequences, issues, alliances, and outcomes are quite different from the ones Gramsci studied. In pursuing these two possibilities, I will make no attempt to build up an original analysis or a compelling body of evidence. Instead, I will draw freely on other analyses in this volume and on standard treatments of China, Japan, Vietnam, and a few other parts of Asia.

## Concepts and Arguments

Within any arbitrarily defined population, we may identify at least as many possible social categories as there are possible combinations of all the status distinctions made by members of the population. At any given point in time, the members of the population are distinguishing only a small proportion of all those categories from each other. Only a small proportion of those active categories, furthermore, consist of people who are exerting collective control over resources. They are *groups*. We may call an increase in a group's collective control over resources *mobilization* and a decrease demobilization. To the extent that a group applies resources to a common end, it carries on *collective action*. To the extent that it applies those resources to influence governmental action, it is *contending for power*. We have a sort of political continuum: no category—category—group—collective action—contention for power. We will add to the continuum in a moment.

Within the arbitrarily defined population, we can also identify the principal concentrated means of coercion. If there is an organization that controls this concentrated means of coercion, it is a *government*. (If there is no such concentration or no organization controlling it, there is no government; if there is more than one organization controlling it, there is more than one government; to the extent that the organization is centralized, autonomous, and differentiated, and the territory it controls contiguous and bounded, the organization is a state.) Over some arbitrarily defined period of time, we can observe the interactions between the government and the population under its control. As I have said, any group that collectively applies resources to influence the government during that period is a *contender* for power. Some contenders have routine means of making claims on the government that are accepted by other contenders and by agents of the government; collectively, such contenders make up the *polity* related to a particular government; individually, we call them *members* of the polity. Jointly (but usually unequally) the members control the government. Contenders that do not have routine, accepted means of making claims on the government are not members of the polity; they are *challengers*.

Every polity has its own rules of membership—established ways in which challengers become members, and vice versa. How those rules vary and how hard or easy they make changes in membership are among the prime problems of comparative politics. However, the rules of admission operating at any particular time appear to depend heavily on the past history of admissions to the polity. They almost always include the requirement that the challenger demonstrate control over extensive resources, especially manpower. By and large, existing members of a polity resist new admissions; they work to have the rules applied stringently. Yet at times a member forms a coalition with a challenger, the member gaining access to resources under the challenger's control, the challenger gaining a degree of protection from repression and a degree of support in its bid for membership. Members test each other intermittently, and individually resist loss of membership in the polity.

Whatever else they do, then, governments extract resources from the populations under their control, apply the resources to activities favored by the members of the polity, and constrain the collective action of contenders—especially of challengers. To the extent that any governmental activity raises the cost of collective action, it is *repressive*. The quintessential repressive forces are armies, police units, and intelligence networks; they specialize in raising the cost of collective action to one group or another. In some circumstances, bandits, pirates, private armies, secret societies, and other nongovernmental groups controlling substantial means of force align themselves conditionally with governments and become significant repressive forces; those circumstances appear to have occurred more frequently in Asia than in Europe over the last few centuries. Nevertheless, in Europe as well as in Asia, such irregulars have often played crucial roles where governmental authority was weak or divided.

If we wanted to know how repressive a government was in general, we would have to (a) choose some particular contender as our point of reference and assay the net effect of governmental activity on its collective action, or (b) sum over all contenders, making allowances for the variable effects of the same governmental action on different groups. In a situation of competition, for example, raising the cost of collective action to one contender will automatically lower the cost of collective action to at least one other contender.

This dense series of abstractions opens the way to interesting hypotheses about collective violence, and then about revolution. Up to this point the statements have been almost purely definitional. From here on, the frequency of definitions declines, and the pace of generalization rises. As the generalizations begin, I should emphasize again that they come mainly from the European experience since 1500. That is the only experience I have studied seriously in this regard. Nor can I guarantee that they hold up in every particular for Europe itself. They merely sum up my current understanding of what happened there. My suggestions concerning Asia, then, are the reflections of an interested outsider.

*Forms of Collective Action*

In the European experience, three fundamental forms of collective action (each with many variants) have led to violence. The first form we can call *competitive*: members of a group that defines another particular group as an enemy, rival, or competitor act to control the resources of that enemy-rival-competitor. The action may consist of damaging, seizing, asserting a claim to, denying the other's claim to, or blocking access to the resources in question. Thus, armed peasants attack the farms of large landlords; two groups of bandits fight with each other; one carpenters' society interrupts the annual procession of a rival carpenters' society.

The second form is *reactive*. After some group, or its agent, lays claim to a resource currently under control of another group, the members of the second group resist the exercise of that claim. The response of the second group is reactive. Thus, villagers bar the recruiters who have come to claim their young men for the army; members of a national assembly drive out a crowd that has sought to take the assembly's place; a new landlord fences in part of the commons, and the users of the commons tear the fence down. Whereas the competitive forms of collective action have a high probability of producing violence (in the sense of damage or forceful seizure of persons or objects), the reactive forms may well be nonviolent. The resistance may consist of the filing of a legal action or an appeal to friends in power; it may consist of shouts and symbolic acts; it may consist of concealing the resources or withholding information about them. Just so long as a group does these things together, they qualify as collective action.

The third form is *proactive*. It involves an initiative on the part of the acting group. Some group carries out an action that, under the prevailing rules, lays claim to a resource not previously accorded to that group. If collective violence occurs, it characteristically begins when at least one other group intervenes in the action and resists the claim. As a consequence, of two struggling groups, one will often be carrying on a proactive, the other a reactive, form of action. Some examples of proaction: strikers seize possession of a mine; organized squatters move onto vacant land; a junta declares itself the new government.

In all three forms, the "resources" involved cover quite a range:

they include land, people, private spaces, rights to act in certain ways. The competitive, reactive, and proactive forms resemble each other in centering on the sequence: assertion of claim → challenge to claim. But they differ considerably with respect to the current status of that claim and who is making it: Is the claim new? Are the resources already in particular hands?

The characteristic position of authorities is to declare (and perhaps to believe) that competitive action is the predominant source of violence: members of a group that defines another particular group (including the government) as a rival, competitor, or enemy act to control the resources of that rival or enemy. Authorities tend to favor such an interpretation because (a) it is part of the folk conception of violence; (b) it justifies their intervention as guardians of public order; (c) the authorities exclude seizure and damage performed by agents of the government—police, troops, and so on—from the category of "violence"; (d) there is, in fact, a broad division of labor between contenders and government: contenders are somewhat more likely to attack objects, governmental repressive forces to attack persons.

In the European experience since 1500, the reactive and proactive forms of collective action have played a much larger part in the production of violence than has the competitive form. The repressive forces of European states, furthermore, have played an extraordinarily large part in them. To be more precise, the recent European experience falls into three rough phases:

Into the seventeenth century: Local and regional rivalries of various kinds play the major part in collective violence. Competitive action appears as vendetta, competition among groups of craftsmen, religious wars, dynastic struggles, intercommunal rivalries, and so on.

Seventeenth to nineteenth centuries: As the local claims of agents of national states, of large organizations, and of international markets increase, reactive collective action comes to predominate as the context for collective violence. Tax rebellions, food riots, and movements against military conscription become the most typical forms.

Nineteenth and twentieth centuries: Once the predominance of these national and international structures is assured, the focus shifts to proactive forms. Contenders make new claims, and others—especially repressive forces of the state—resist them. Strikes, demonstrations, and coups become characteristic forms of collective action, and characteristic settings for collective violence.

If this summary is correct, governments and their agents are not simply onlookers, arbiters, or cleaners-up in collective violence. They are often major participants in the action. Governments often lay new claims that other parties challenge. Governments often resist the exercise of new claims. In war and elsewhere, governments often play a major part in violence among rivals and enemies—at the extreme arrogating to themselves the sole right to employ force in such encounters.

The three forms are so broad that they might seem, like the definitions laid out earlier, to exhaust the logical possibilities. They do not. All three forms relate mobilized groups to each other. They exclude action by chance crowds, by the general population, and by the disorganized castoffs of routine social life. By the same token, they exclude random, expressive, purely destructive acts.

If my summary of the European experience is adequate, indeed, several drastic conclusions concerning conventional ways of analyzing collective violence follow. First, there is no reason to think that collective violence should co-vary with murder, suicide, theft, family instability, and the other types of behavior that authorities commonly lump together with it under the heading of "disorder." Second, efforts to reason from situations of hardship, relative deprivation, rapid change, or dissolution of social ties to some form of discontent and thence to violence as a form of "protest" are doomed to failure; violence is a by-product of an interaction rather than a direct expression of the propensities of one of the participants in the interaction; furthermore, most of these conditions tend to *demobilize* the social groups they affect. Third, there is an intimate dependency between violent and nonviolent forms of collective action—one is simply a special case of the other—rather than some moral, political, or tactical divide between them. As a corollary, the forms of violent action any particular group carries on bear strong marks of that group's day-to-day organization, instead of falling into a special realm governed by the laws of "collective behavior" or "aggression."

The typology of forms rests on the argument that collective violence results primarily from the interaction of contenders for power (some of them often acting via the government instead of intervening directly in the action) that are engaged in disputes over rights and justice. In that case, a valid theory of collective violence will be a special case of a general theory of collective *action*. In modern Europe, the rules governing that special case have to do mainly with

the ways governments exercise their extractive and repressive powers: mobilization, collective action, and contention for power on the
one side, governmental extraction and repression on the other, the
interplay between the two producing variations in the frequency, intensity, and character of collective violence.

This formulation has some resemblance to Samuel Huntington's.[12]
He treats political "stability" as an outcome of the balance between
popular mobilization and governmental institutionalization. The situations in which governments are multiple, fragmented, or weak relative to other concentrations of coercive power, however, resist that
simple formulation. They are, as it happens, precisely the situations
that are likely to interest the student of nineteenth-century Italy or
of contemporary Asia. They are also, as we shall see, similar in important ways to revolutionary situations. To the extent that governments are multiple, fragmented, or weak relative to other concentrations of coercive power, we may expect them (a) to be involved in
competitive collective action as rivals of other governments and
quasi-governments; (b) to become coalition partners with the exploited contenders in reactive collective action involving rival governments and quasi-governments; and (c) to seek to stabilize and
make exclusive their control over the populations under their immediate jurisdictions by means of stalemates and coalitions holding off
the adjacent concentrations of coercive power.

Under such circumstances, a nice paradox will emerge: since only
a minority of these concentrations of power will receive the conse-
cration of political scientists, historians, or other governments as
genuine governments, a great deal of conflict will involve nominally
*private* violence; yet the governments and quasi-governments will
play an even larger part than usual in the collective violence that
actually occurs. This is, I think, the normal situation where secret
societies, organized bandits, and phenomena like Mafia activity prevail.[13]

The concentration of coercive power is an essential part of the formation of national states. It reduces the importance of competitive
collective action as the matrix of violence within the territory in
question, accelerates reactive collective action as different groups resist the expansion of the state's powers of coercion and extraction,
and eventually produces a transition to proactive collective action.
Competitive collective action producing violence then survives mainly
in the guise of wars *among* states—which is to say that the total
amount of destruction produced by competition may well increase;

that is true despite any implications of my argument that the transition is orderly and benign.

## Revolution

All this is a far cry from conventional analyses of revolution. I hope to show, however, that some of the processes we have been discussing are revolutionary processes. They are revolutionary when they appear in the proper combinations.

To show that, I must continue the conceptualizing a bit longer. Let us refashion Trotsky's useful notion of *dual sovereignty*. A revolution occurs when a government previously under the control of a single, sovereign polity becomes the object of effective, competing, mutually exclusive claims on the part of two or more distinct polities, and ends when a single polity regains control over the government. Most readers will reject that definition simply because it does not correspond to their intuitive notions of revolution. But some will reject it as too broad; they want a genuine transformation of social structure, a massive realignment of social classes, or a movement with a program to have a part in the process. Others will reject it as too narrow; they want to include transfers of power and transformations of social life that occur without any apparent break in the continuity of government. And still others will ask for a sideward displacement of the definition: away from a strongly political conception toward one that emphasizes control over the means of production, states of consciousness, or something else.

The largest disparities in definitions of revolution come from the time spans the definers want to consider. In a short time span, we have definitions that concentrate on a central event: a certain kind of bid for power, a temporary dissolution of government, a transfer of power. In a medium time span, we have definitions that examine the population or government before, during, and after such a crucial event, and ask whether any significant change occurred; a coup d'état that substituted one military faction for another might qualify as a revolution under the short-run definition, but not under the medium-run definition. In a long time span, finally, we have definitions that relate the crucial event and the changes (if any) surrounding it to a reading of broad historical trends—for example, by restricting the name of revolution solely to those transfers of power that produce the durable substitution of one whole class for another.

In general, the longer the time span, the fewer the events that will qualify as revolutions. The long time span, however, does raise the logical possibility of a gradual revolution, or at least of one in which the transformation occurs without violence and without an apparent break in political continuity. As Maurice Meisner suggests elsewhere in this volume, Marxist definitions of revolution refer to long spans of history, even where the crucial transformations are supposed to take place rapidly; Mao's "populist" version of revolution requires a very long time span indeed—and restricts the number of revolutions that have so far occurred to zero or one.

Despite a great interest in the long-run transformations, I choose the short time span, for the political definition of revolution as multiple sovereignty is the closest thing we have to common ground among numerous competing conceptions; permits the creation of all other standard definitions and types by means of further specifications; escapes the more obvious difficulties of common definitions of revolution, e.g., tautology, limitation to *post-factum* explanation, dependence on relatively inaccessible features of the phenomena to be defined; and hooks together neatly the analysis of revolutionary and nonrevolutionary political action.

How can the multiplication of polities occur? There are four main possibilities:

1. The members of one polity seek to subordinate another previously distinct polity; where one of the polities is not somehow subordinate to the other at the outset, this circumstance falls into a gray area between revolution and war.

2. The members of a previously subordinate polity assert sovereignty.

3. Challengers form into a bloc that seizes control over some portion of the governmental apparatus.

4. A polity fragments into two or more blocs, each exercising control over some part of the government.

Anger, revolutionary plans, the broadcast of claims, even widespread collective violence are not enough. In any of these versions, the revolution begins when previously acquiescent people begin taking orders from a new authority. It ends when only that authority, or only one of its rivals, is giving orders that are obeyed. Of course, this way of stating the problem requires us to set some minimum to the number of people, the range of orders, and the degree of obedience. The necessity simply calls attention to the kinship between revolutionary and nonrevolutionary situations.

The analysis so far identifies three conditions as necessary for revolution, and a fourth as strongly facilitating. The necessary conditions are first, the appearance of contenders, or coalitions of contenders, advancing exclusive alternative claims to the control over the government currently exerted by the members of the polity (the contenders in question may consist of, or include, some members of the polity); second, commitment to those claims by a significant segment of the subject population; and third, incapacity or unwillingness of the agents of the government to suppress the alternative coalition or the commitment to its claims. The facilitating condition is the formation of coalitions between members of the polity and the contenders advancing the alternative claims—coalitions that ally the members with the alternative bloc without committing them completely to it.

This statement of proximate conditions for revolution does not contain much analytic news. It is essentially an explication of the definition offered earlier, in terms of the concepts laid out before that. Nevertheless, it orients the search for explanations of revolution. It orients the search away from the assessment of aggregate characteristics of the population—levels of tension, disaffection, deprivation, and the like—toward patterns of mobilization, collective action, and contention for power. That is, I think, an advance.

Every element of this scheme needs refinement, criticism, and confrontation with the facts. This is not, however, the place to undertake a general review of its adequacy.[14] The point is to use it as a means of analyzing the roles of town and country in revolution.

Although that is a big problem, it is far smaller than a general analysis of revolution, or even of the conditions under which peasants or workers join (or make) revolutionary movements. The main thing we are trying to do here is to specify what effect the rural-urban relations prevailing in a population have on the likelihood of a revolution in that population, and on the form and outcome of the revolution, if it occurs.

Let us return, renewed, to the questions we extracted from Gramsci early in the discussion. 1. Do rural and urban populations play characteristically different roles in revolution? 2. What difference to the outcome of a revolution do the extent and character of rural-urban cleavage make? 3. To what extent, and how, does the character of rural-urban division in an area affect the likelihood of revolution in that area? In elaborating new concepts and definitions, I have shifted away from Gramsci's view of revolution as the effective transfer of power from the ruling classes to the "subaltern" classes. But there is no reason why we cannot ask both versions of the basic questions: about revolution as multiple sovereignty and about revolution as an effective transfer of power. Gramsci's question presupposes mine.

Let me offer quick comments on the first two questions, then expand on the third.

## Different Roles for City and Country?

Our initial question has at least two interesting variants. First, over and above the effect of the pre-existing rural-urban division on the character and likelihood of revolution, what difference does it make to the workings of a revolution whether the chief locations of the *action* are rural or urban? Second, given the fact of revolution, do systematically different things happen in urban and rural areas?

A lot depends on how much the instruments of government are concentrated in cities and towns. Throughout most of the world, administrators, repressive forces, and means of government in general concentrate in urban locations. They generate urban locations, for that matter, where they go. Asia is no exception. There, despite the overwhelmingly rural locus of the population, governmental organizations have long based themselves mainly in cities.

In general, the larger governments have dealt with the countryside indirectly, by means of some sort of compact with rural landlords. In Japan, John W. Hall shows us the Tokugawa regime displacing the samurai to castle towns, and cutting them off from effective control of the land.[15] But the overlords then became the pivots of the system. They were the Japanese Junkers: officials from one angle, great landlords from another. The overlords then relied on village headmen to extend their rule into rural areas; the headmen, as chiefs of major lineages, were in effect substantial landlords.[16] In such a system, the individuals at each level down from the top have considerable autonomy within their own spheres, yet control resources and coercion with the backing of those higher up. That puts them in a good position to rebel, and sometimes offers them the incentive to do so. But in this sort system a rebellion whose chief actions take place in towns and cities is likely to be in closer contact with the instruments of government from its inception than one whose actions are primarily rural.

Let us recall the four paths to multiple sovereignty. 1. The members of one polity seek to subordinate another previously distinct polity. 2. The members of a previously subordinate polity assert sovereignty. 3. Challengers form into a bloc that seizes control over some portion of the governmental apparatus. 4. A polity fragments into two or more blocs, each exercising control over some part of the government. The rural or urban locus probably does not affect the likelihood or course of path 1. But it matters to the other three.

Path 2, which is essentially separatist, is a likely path for predominantly rural areas that are already organized into subordinate polities. In Asia those rebellious subordinate polities have often been composed of linguistic and religious minorities that have managed to create or retain their own instruments of government: hill peoples in Vietnam, Chinese in Indonesia and Malaya. The other major Asian form has been the polity controlled by a successful warlord, vassal, or frontier commander, as in the multiple governments that asserted themselves in Japan before the Tokugawa ascendancy.

Path 3 (in which the powerless rise up and take over—a favorite image and a rare occurrence) requires offensive mobilization. It is, I think, likely to occur only in a relatively urban setting, where challengers can use dense, centralized means of communication and organization to establish contact with each other. Donald Zagoria's enumeration elsewhere in this volume of conditions for success of Communist leaders in Asian rural areas (that the leaders have semi-rural origins, establish links with the rural intelligentsia, do their homework, be flexible, give priority to rural problems) is plausible. But those conditions are unlikely to lead to revolution except where such leaders are well linked to urban bases.

The likelihood of the fourth path (one polity fragmenting into two or more) is probably indifferent to the urbanity or rurality of the setting. Yet its exact course does seem to differ along the urban continuum. We can profitably distinguish between center-out and periphery-in revolutions: in the one, the alternative coalition first establishes control at major centers of governmental power and then extends control into the rest of the territory; in the other, the alternative coalition first establishes itself in areas of relatively weak governmental power and then closes in on the power centers. Center-out has been the standard pattern in modern European revolutions. There, the reestablishment of central control over the periphery has often taken a greater effort than the initial seizure of power at the center.

Twentieth-century guerrilla doctrine, however, has called for periphery-in revolutions. Asia has the prime example of China to pull it in this direction. It also has the models of the Huks in the Philippines, the Vietminh in Vietnam, and the Malayan People's Anti-Japanese Army. Although there have been plenty of center-out revolutions in modern Asia—the multiple coups of Afghanistan, Burma, and China being fine examples—on balance Asia has been more hospitable to periphery-in revolutions during the last few centuries than Europe has. No doubt the overwhelmingly rural character of the Asian population has something to do with it. The relative weakness of central governments and the presence of subordinate polities built around common beliefs, languages, and kinship systems, however, probably account more directly for the difference between Asia and Europe.

In highly urban settings, only the center-out pattern has much chance to occur or to succeed. Where rural area and population are extensive, both center-out and periphery-in revolutions occur, depending on the degree to which communications channels, supply lines, means of coercion, and sheer territory are under the control and surveillance of cities; the less effective and centralized the control, the more possible a periphery-in revolution. The bulk of periphery-in revolutions, however, probably follow path 2: a *previously subordinate* polity (for example, the "native" segment of a colonial government) asserts its own sovereignty.

Given the fact of revolution, do systematically different things happen in urban and rural areas? Gramsci gave us the general teaching: the population of the city struggles over control of labor, whereas the population of the country struggles over control of land. That is broadly true in Asia as well as in Europe. Yet it becomes less true in the very cases on which Gramsci pinned his greatest revolutionary hopes: where urban labor markets have penetrated farthest into the countryside. Where wage-labor has become dominant in the country as well as the city, we may find collective drives for collective control of the land, but we should not expect to find collective drives for *individual* control of the land.

Up to this extreme, we should expect to find the people of the countryside, in times of revolution, mobilizing more slowly than the people of town and city—and demobilizing more rapidly than them as well. This, for two reasons: first, because mobilization is intrinsically easier, all other things being equal, at centers of communication than in peripheral locations; second, because demands for control of the land are on the whole more local in scope (hence a less steady ground for a wide coalition) than demands for control of the conditions of labor. Jean Chesneaux sums up the problem for China:

> The peasantry showed itself especially capable of carrying on the mass armed struggle against the national enemy. Nevertheless, peasant intervention remained within geographically limited areas; that is as true of the Boxer movement or of the areas of peasant agitation against the Manchus in southern China before 1911 as of the guerrilla bases of the period 1937–1949. The very nature of technological and economic relations within the peasantry (small-scale cultivation, semi-autarky, weakly developed flows of commodities and information) did not permit it to carry on a unified struggle at the scale of the whole country, with, for example, the range of the great "pan-Chinese" strikes of June 1925. When that level was reached (for example, at the end of the war against Japan) it was because a political apparatus that reached beyond the peasantry gave it direction.[17]

Governments can equalize the rural-urban balance either by concentrating their repression in cities or by attacking whatever local control of the land exists, and thereby increasing the incentives to reactive collective action.

## Rural-Urban Cleavage and Revolutionary Outcomes

What difference to the outcome of a revolution do the extent and character of rural-urban cleavage make? We can distinguish three broad alternative outcomes of multiple sovereignty:

1. The pre-existing polity reappears approximately as before, or minus former members who had joined the alternative polity. Most observers would call this a lost revolution.

2. An alternative polity establishes control of the government and of the population subject to it. Most observers would consider this revolution to have won, though some would want evidence that the new holders of power were going to act in the interests of the population they represented.

3. Some members of the alternative polity that produced the revolutionary situation, with or without members of the pre-existing polity, establish control of the government and of the population subject to it, and others lose their membership as the new regime consolidates its hold. This is the most common revolutionary outcome; it is also the one that incites the angriest debates about whether the revolution has won or lost.

The burden of the earlier Gramscian analysis is that sharp rural-urban cleavage favors the first outcome (a lost revolution); that a coalition involving newly mobilized rural populations and well-organized urban revolutionaries favors the third outcome (a revolution won for some and lost for others); and that the revolutionary rural-urban coalition is likely to continue into power only in an unusual circumstance: when the countryside is durably organized on a large scale. Japanese rebellions illustrate the lost revolution. The Chinese Communist Revolution provides the best example of rural-urban success. And India's drive to independence (despite its rural decor) provides us with an exemplary case of mixed urban success and rural failure.

On the whole, the Gramscian generalizations stand up well to Asian experience. The greatest doubt attaches to the first proposition: that sharp rural-urban cleavage favors lost revolutions. At least one set of conditions appears to be favorable at once to bitter rural-urban conflict, to multiple sovereignty, and to transfer of power: the situation in which an urban-based government faced with a well-organized opposition in its own centers attempts to step up the pace, or change the character, of its demands on solidary rural populations. This situation promotes all the basic conditions of revolution—formation of an alternative polity, commitment to its claims, repressive incapacity of the government, and creation of coalitions between members of the alternative and pre-existing polities.

Again China is the type case—but this time the Revolution of 1911 is the relevant moment. In the Waichow rising of 1911, for instance, Winston Hsieh shows us a coalition of the fighting bands of various clans, local militias, and secret-society troops acting together against the rising Ch'ing pressure for tax revenues, especially the revenues from the salt monopoly.[18] In Hsieh's view, the secret societies (or more precisely, the Triads, which were closely connected with the salt smugglers of the region) played the crucial connective role in the uprising. Furthermore, they carried out the major part of the action in the market towns and the city.

There are, it appears, more paths to the crucial rural-urban coalition than via the city's revolutionary indoctrination of the peasantry. Gramsci does not quite prepare us for the importance of secret societies in Chinese insurrections. Perhaps that is because the bandits and mafiosi of Gramsci's Italy generally played a conservative political game, surviving through the patronage or indulgence of the powers that were. In Asia, one of the paths to rural-urban coalition depends on the prior existence of large networks of bandits or secret societies that are opposed to the government and are well connected in both rural and urban areas. They substitute, to some degree, for a revolutionary party.

A more general condition for rural-urban coalition lies behind both the cases of which Gramsci was aware and the different circumstances of Asia. Under most forms of predominantly agrarian social organization, a single local elite controls the major links between any particular rural area and the national structure of power. Most often it is a landowning elite. So long as the elite is in place and has effective ties to the national structure, no large mobilization of the countryside occurs without the elite's collaboration. That is probably for two related reasons: first, because the rest of the rural population has so much invested in the patronage and goodwill of the elite, and second, because its national ties permit it to call on punishing force to put down opposition.

When the ties of the local elite weaken—however that happens— the costs of independent mobilization go down as its possible benefits rise. The Tokugawa regime deliberately undercut the position of the samurai and thereby facilitated the independent mobilization of the peasants. The French accomplished the same result unintentionally in Vietnam. As Jeffrey Race describes the process elsewhere in this book, French administrative reforms eroded the authority—as well as the repressive and co-optative power—of the village council. Thus the French unwittingly tipped the balance away from the local elite and toward people who could form new structures of collective action. It was at that point, according to Race's analysis, that effective anti-French organization began to link rural communities to cities as well as to each other.

If the Asian experience identifies the dissolution of the national connections of elites as a facilitator of rural-urban coalition, it also identifies a major *obstacle* to coalition. That is the existence of sharp linguistic, religious, and ethnic barriers between the rural and urban populations. The great Asian migrations of the last few centuries have created many situations in which the rural-urban distinction is also largely an ethnic distinction: Malaya, Indonesia, Thailand, and elsewhere. If Michael Stenson's analysis of Malaya is correct, the fact that the vast majority of the rural population was Malay seriously hampered the efforts of the Communists (who were recruited mainly from among the urban Chinese) to organize the countryside. Despite the earlier successes of the Communists in fronts against the Japanese, and to some extent against the British, the urban-Chinese base of the MCP ruined the prospects of its effort, in 1948, to make revolution through guerrilla warfare.

Generally speaking, rural revolutionaries who want to win need urban allies more than urban revolutionaries need them. An independent rural group can initiate multiple sovereignty with relative ease. But how will it end? Coalition with urban allies provides the coordination and communication necessary to transcend the village or the region, making possible a transfer of power at the national level. It facilitates the transition from reactive to proactive movements, to movements that will not dissolve when the first round of demands has been met. It also makes access to armed force easier.

The last point is not incidental. No transfer of power is likely unless the alternative coalition acquires control of substantial armed force early in the revolutionary process.[19] That can happen through organization of a revolutionary army, through the absorption of existing armed irregulars, or through the defection of governmental troops. All three happened in China. None of the three happened in Indonesia. As Rex Mortimer sees it, the Javanese Communists opted for adaptation and short-run success and did well by it; but the adaptation stifled their revolutionary potential. One of the ways it did so was by denying them any strong armed force when a military coup came to dislodge both them and their ally, Sukarno.

These relationships change over the course of urbanization and of state centralization. Urban allies for rural revolutionaries become more probable, but also more indispensable. In a fundamentally urban population, the extent and character of rural-urban cleavage do not much affect the outcome of such revolutions as may occur. In a strongly centralized state, likewise, what happens at the periphery matters little to those who can seize the central apparatus; they may lose some of the periphery, but they will not be dislodged from power. (It probably follows that the more centralized a state, all things being equal, the more liable it is to military coups.) In a fundamentally rural population, by contrast, those towns that do exist carry a large share of the burden of administration, coordination, and communication. Yet they remain highly vulnerable to the withholding of supplies of food, goods, manpower, and information. As the population approaches the rural extreme, then, transfers of power are likely to be fairly easy to accomplish so long as the rural population remains passive. But given the mobilization of the rural population or the involvement of a rural elite retaining effective control over the rest of the population, the winning coalition—whether "revolutionary" or "counterrevolutionary"—will be the one that unites rural and urban contenders.

## Rural-Urban Division and the Likelihood of Revolution

So far, for the most part, we have taken the presence of revolution for granted, and have asked what difference the rural-urban configuration makes to the way a revolution works itself out. Now we must ask whether the rural-urban configuration affects the probability that a revolution will occur at all. Remember that we are entertaining two different definitions of revolution: one as the onset of multiple sovereignty, the other as a durable transfer of power. The conditions for one are not the same as the conditions for the other. Nor is one simply an extrapolation of the other. In fact, they are partly contradictory: many of the circumstances that promote the onset of multiple sovereignty frustrate the durable transfer of power, and vice versa.

Strictly speaking, rural-urban divisions are probably irrelevant to the likelihood of revolution. They become relevant only to the extent that they affect (or at least correlate with) the predominant forms of mobilization, collective action, contention for power, coalition-formation, and repression. The effects and correlations have to do mainly with *changes* in rural-urban divisions rather than with stable configurations.

The most obvious is the increase of urban control over rural political, economic, and demographic life. Eric Wolf's *Peasant Wars of the Twentieth Century* presents a series of studies around that theme.[20] Wolf deals, of course, with peasant populations, not with rural populations in general. He portrays a process that has occurred widely at the leading edge of capitalist expansion: the rising demand from distant markets encourages local capitalists to accumulate control over the land and to shift toward cash-crop production; taxation and monetization draw or drive peasants into the market; patron-client relationships decay; opportunities for wage-labor simultaneously stimulate population increase within the village and increase the proportion of the population that is vulnerable and responsive to fluctuations in the markets for labor and commodities; sooner or later the ability of peasants to meet their major local obligations (which had been guaranteed by what were, in effect, liens on all the factors of production) decline.

These changes may seem subtle and abstract—visible only in retrospect, and then only to the keen eye of an anthropologist. Yet they have some perfectly tangible manifestations. They show up as bourgeois encroachment on common lands, imposition of new taxes that require peasants to sell portions of their crops or of their land, and so on. By the early twentieth century, Wolf tells us, these changes were going on in Mexico, Russia, Vietnam, China, and many other parts of the world. The analyses of Asia in this volume tend to agree. Although Zagoria, for example, emphasizes the current revolutionary propensities of rural tenants and proletarians, what his survey shows is that the process that is creating these revolutionary classes and exacerbating their plight is the same process Wolf describes.

By the end of such a process, peasants are no longer peasants, and communities have lost their collective capacities to resist. That is the dialectic: if the economic, political, and demographic threats to the survival of the community mount faster than its bases of solidarity dissolve, concerted resistance occurs. When a new demand for taxes, a new exclusion of peasants from gleaning, hunting, or gathering on formerly open lands occurs, defensive mobilization begins. The collective action that prevails in these circumstances is the reactive form outlined earlier (claims over already controlled resources—counterclaim). Jeffrey Race shows us just such a sequence occurring in northern Thailand; there government pressure on hill tribes helped align them with the rebels and encouraged them to develop supra-village organization where none had previously existed. By many standards, such reactive movements are conservative, even traditional. Yet, as Wolf and Race demonstrate, they sometimes have revolutionary outcomes. Conservatism, tradition, and revolution are not always so incompatible as conventional wisdom holds.

When might peasant conservatism and revolution converge? The basic conditions for resistance are first, a focused threat to peasant survival, with well-defined agents having visible external connections, occurring simultaneously in a number of localities that are already in communication with each other; and second, a significant local framework for collective action in the form of mutual obligations, communications lines, and justifiable common claims on resources. From Wolf's accounts of twentieth-century peasant wars and from a general survey of modern European experience, it is reasonable to add an important facilitating condition: the availability of urban-based allies in the form of intellectuals, liberal bourgeois, labor leaders, military chiefs, professional politicos, or others.

The "focused threat to peasant survival" appears to lie behind the widespread, reactive peasant rebellions of Tokugawa Japan.[21] The Japanese movements against merchants, tax collectors, and encroaching landlords between 1750 and the Meiji Restoration have many features in common with European rural movements of the seventeenth to nineteenth centuries. Taxes and rents do more than just bite into the peasant household's means of survival; when assessed in money, they drive peasants into the market.[22] Where the terms of trade are unfavorable, where the market mechanisms are ill-developed, or where customary claims on the commodities to be marketed are extensive, the necessity of marketing does more damage to the peasant household than an equivalent loss of resources through theft or natural disaster.

One of Hugh Borton's many relevant accounts of the situation in Tokugawa Japan describes an uprising of 1823 in the province of Kii. "Plotting with two of their fellow officials," Borton tells us,

> two of the *bugyō* decided to store goods for their own profit. Rice exchanges were established throughout the realm, the price of *sake* was forced up, the importation of rice from outside was prohibited, and tickets were required on all rice bags, *sake* tubs and similar articles to prove that they had not come from the neighboring domain of Koyasan. Added to this, the taxation of the land was increased, while taxes were ordered collected not only on new lands, but also on all waste land.[23]

Eventually more than 100,000 farmers marched on Wakayama, "destroying the *sake* and rice shops, pawn shops, and places of the *shōya* and men in charge of the rice exchanges."[24] On the evening of the attack the authorities received the following demands:

1. The fixed taxes be as during the time of Tokugawa Yorinobu. . . .
2. The tax on wet lands . . . be similar to that on dry lands.
3. There be exemption from opening up old waste land.
4. There be omission of *maikuchi*.
5. The storing of goods for profit cease.
6. There be exemption from the repairs of water ditches for irrigation and drainage, and the cutting of the boundary. . . .
7. Inspection be made of the standing crop [to assure a fair tax].[25]

These demands were characteristic of the peasant uprisings of the time. As Barrington Moore says in his review of these same accounts, "The intrusion of commercial relationships into the feudal organization of the countryside was creating increasingly severe problems for

the ruling group. There were three main strands to the peasant violence: opposition to the feudal overlord, to the merchant, and to
emerging landlordism."[26]

Japanese rebellions of the eighteenth and nineteenth centuries also
illustrate the importance of a significant local framework for collective action. As in Europe, the village was both a fiscal unit and the
possessor of collective rights to the land. And it remained a vehicle
of collective action. This appears to set off rural Japan from most of
China. In China, communities *as such* had relatively little collective
life, few common rights, and not much collective action. Kinship
groups and secret societies (the two not being entirely distinct from
each other), by contrast, seem to have played extraordinary roles in
collective action; they cut across individual communities and facilitated actions on a scale larger than the village.

Perhaps I have misstated the contrast. Following G. W. Skinner, it
might be better to distinguish between the bottom-up system of central places, exemplified by the hierarchy of market areas, and the
top-down system of administrative units doing the work of the empire.[27] The Chinese imperial structure did not ordinarily reach down
to the level of the village, however heavy was the indirect weight of
imperial demands. The smaller-scale governments of Europe—and
apparently of Japan and India as well—managed to incorporate villages directly into their structures. They became fiscal, administrative,
and even military units; the administrative pressure enhanced their
importance as vehicles of collective action, ironically fortifying the
resistance to the very extractive processes that built them up.

In China, secret societies and the rebellions associated with them
rarely began with whole communities, but they did rely heavily on
local units. According to Chiang Siang-tseh, the Nien rebels acquired
whole communities under circumstances that fit neatly with the top-
down—bottom-up distinction.[28] After the governmental authorities
organized local militias in Anhwei province against the threat of the
Taiping rebels there—thus extending the central structure downward
to an extraordinary degree—the chiefs of the local militias began to
assume political power within the villages and to exercise it with considerable autonomy. In fact, they frequently took the whole village
over to the Niens. This dialectic, government-promoted local militarization–acquisition of autonomy by military units, has been identified by Philip Kuhn as one of the chief factors in the final crumbling
of the Empire.[29] The Taipings likewise contributed to their own de-

struction by their effort to build a top-down structure rivaling that of the Empire itself; like the Empire, that structure proved incapable of achieving durable control at the village level in the face of local defensive militarization.[30]

The experiences of Japan and China are alike in underscoring the significance of urban-based allies for rural rebellions. Such allies matter because they can make the difference between one more fragmented peasant rebellion and a coordinated revolutionary force. The general pattern of rebellion in Japan and China was outside-in, or bottom-up: first in the periphery or the countryside, only later in the cities. That is unlike the modern European experience, in which most large-scale rebellions had urban bases, regardless of how many peasants they recruited. But in Japan and China successful rebellions had to take over urban centers; control of cities was part of the definition of success, the only means of seizing or supplanting the existing administrative apparatus.

The Revolution of 1911—which was, in its way, successful—provides numerous examples of the advantages of rural-urban alliance. John Lust's description of the insurrection in Kwangtung links republican Canton with People's Armies of "hired agricultural workers, handicraft workmen, discharged troops, local banditti, and militia" around nuclei of "a merger of outlaws, Triads, and peasants" led by "T'ung-meng Hui members, by bandit chiefs who had previously adopted the republican cause, and by veteran Triad leaders."[31] (The description resembles Hsieh's portrait of the nearby Waichow rising.) As the rebels of Kwangtung prevailed, "in Canton, as the result of pressures from the bourgeoisie, and probably also from chiefs of People's Armies, an administration with a strong T'ung-meng Hui representation replaced the compromise regime. In the pungent if patronizing *mot* of the old consul-general, Jamieson, bandit armies had put a compradore government into power."[32] The subsequent effort of the "compradores" to rid themselves of their plebeian allies is also a phase familiar to students of Western revolutions. The personnel and organization of Asian revolutions differ quite a bit from those of Europe, but the broad conditions for revolution in the two continents have something in common.

The basic conditions for rural resistance—a focused threat to peasant survival, a significant local framework for collective action, and the availability of urban-based allies—are *revolutionary* conditions. They are revolutionary because they promote the appearance of coalitions of contenders advancing exclusive alternative claims to control of government in the rural areas, commitment to those claims by a significant segment of the rural population, and incapacity of the agents of the government to suppress both the alternative coalition and the commitment to its claims. The alternative claims of rural rebels are often negative or separatist demands rather than proposals to take over the central government; that does not make them less revolutionary. They are unlikely, however, to lead to a fundamental transfer of power in an entire state unless the negative or separatist contenders fashion coalitions with others at the centers of power, including some who have control of armed force.

Generally speaking, these conditions are more likely to occur where urbanization is rapid, when urbanization is in its early stages, and where the rural population is extensive and dispersed yet predominantly peasant. Such a summary can be only a crude approximation, since the real news is in the relative rates of change of urban-based extraction, urban-based repression, and defensive rural mobilization. If the trend of my argument is correct, Gramsci was only partly right in thinking that the more thoroughly the influence of cities pervades the countryside, the more likely revolution is. Pervasive urban influence makes an effective rural-urban coalition more likely. After a point, however, it also makes reactive mobilization less likely. Gramsci needed a distinction between the necessary conditions for revolution in the sense of multiple sovereignty and the necessary conditions for revolution in the sense of a fundamental transfer of power.

The reactive forms of rural rebellion are only half the matter. In the European experience, they were the larger half: once the peasant revolts of the nineteenth century had faded away, most rural areas stayed quiet. Nevertheless, some European rural populations acted together after peasant revolts (and indeed peasants) became historical memories. Andalusia's rural anarchism, Sicily's Fasci, the Po Valley's socialism all drew their strength from rural proletarians, not from peasants. All had a proactive urge to them that was lacking in the older peasant movements: amid nostalgia for a past that never was and anger about present exploitation, the actors claimed rights and rewards that had never before been theirs.

To avoid confusion, let us remember who peasants are—at least in the present discussion. They are agricultural producers organized in households that yield a surplus to outsiders but have substantial control over the land their members work and raise the bulk of what they consume. By such a definition, agrarian capitalism eventually destroys the peasantry. To the extent that agricultural land, labor, and capital all become responsive to external markets, the cultivators stop being peasants. That can happen through the creation of an agricultural proletariat or through the conversion of everyone who remains in agriculture into a cash-crop farmer.

In looking at reactive peasant movements, then, we were examining only the first phase of the process. Late in the process, something quite different occasionally happens: associations of workers or of producers form, make claims, and act together. Proletarianization occurs through the extension of markets for land, labor, and capital into the countryside, through the stepped-up demand for taxes in cash, through the concentration of land in large holdings. Where this development occurs, it not only creates a rural population polarized into a land-poor mass and a land-controlling elite, but also tends to weaken the political position of the old rural elite. If the government to which the old elite was tied weakens at the same time, the result is the disappearance of one of the great barriers to a large-scale rural revolutionary movement.

Elsewhere in this volume, both Christine White and Jeffrey Race argue that the French promoted this entire process in Vietnam as a consequence of their eagerness for cash revenues from the colony. In Vietnam, by their accounts, it took the Vietnamese Communists to articulate and coordinate the existing rural demands for land reform, control of the food supply, and protection from exploitation by large landlords.

Considering the recency of capitalism's penetration into much of Asia, we should not expect to find many pure examples of proactive rural movements in Asia. The bulk of the many Asian rural rebellions of the last century have been reactive in character: attempts to defend existing rights against encroachment by landlords, tax-collectors, and other exploiters. Even the Chinese Communist Revolution articulated and integrated a great many essentially reactive demands: against the Japanese, against the rich. If that is the case, it becomes idle to search for correlations between radical attitudes and revolutionary actions, and idler still to gauge the revolutionary potential of different segments of the rural population by means of their ideological orientations.

Looking for active grievances comes closer, yet misses nevertheless.

Grievances are fundamental to rebellion as oxygen is fundamental to combustion. But just as fluctuations in the oxygen content of the air are not of major account in the overall distribution of fire in the world, fluctuations in grievances are not a major cause of the presence or absence of rebellion. For that, the political means of acting on grievances that people have at their disposal matter a good deal more. Properly adapted to twentieth-century Asia, Antonio Gramsci's analysis of the political conditions for revolution provides us with an excellent start in determining the place of Asian peasants, and of rural proletarians, in contemporary revolutionary movements.

# Afterword

KATHLEEN J. HARTFORD & JOHN WILSON LEWIS

> Once the insurrection has begun, you must act with the greatest de-
> termination, and by all means, without fail, take the offensive. "The
> defensive is the death of every armed rising." ... You must strive for
> daily successes, even if small (one might say hourly, if it is the case
> of one town), and at all costs retain the "moral ascendancy." ...
> The success of both the Russian and the world revolution depends
> on two or three days of fighting.
> Lenin, October 1917

When we speak of Asian revolutions, we must speak not in terms
of days or even years but in terms of decades. The revolutions we have
studied have operated on a different timetable than Lenin's and the
consequences have been fundamental. Most often revolutionary protractedness is mentioned in passing in the discussion, for example, of
the Chinese or the Vietnamese revolution. Yet the time dimension
deserves a central focus in the study of revolutions in Asia, for it
reflects the peculiar combination of factors that the essays in this book
have sought to assess. It produces in its turn a special form of revolution and of postrevolutionary ethos.

Too often, the protracted nature of Asia's revolutions is attributed
exclusively to near-fatal mistakes made by the revolutionaries. In
many of these revolutions, it is true, the movement has at one time
or another been nearly obliterated because of the leaders' miscalcu-
lation or overreliance on doctrine. The revolutionaries have learned
only slowly and painfully that they must understand their own settings
before changing them.

Yet even a correct calculation at the outset probably would not have
brought the Asian revolutionaries to power much sooner. There was
no center of effective power to seize; rather, most Asian revolutionaries had to create power. The necessity for creating a power system
led them to develop methods for establishing their authority from
the bottom up. In those places where the revolutionaries seem to have
failed, the continued inability of their opponents to create that power
and authority makes us hesitate to pronounce judgment on the final
outcome.

The ten preceding essays provide the reader with specific examples of both the power vacuums and the errors that have prolonged the courses of Asian revolutions. If that prolongation had had no effect on the character of the revolution or on the character of the postrevolutionary regime, it would concern us only as an interesting idiosyncrasy of these revolutions. As we look at the ways in which the Asian revolutionaries discussed in this volume have solved the problems confronting them, however, we are forced to conclude that the problems themselves and their gradual solution over decades of struggle have presented the world with examples of a new and different concept of revolution.

Naturally, the leaders of these revolutions would never have voluntarily chosen the long hard route they took. But the decline of centralized authority throughout most of Asia during the colonial period eliminated the chance for the rapid and effective seizure of power. Most of the national ruling systems, if historically they had existed at all, had already disintegrated. Their power had been dispersed with the rise of strong regional elites or had been grabbed by foreigners. Their eclipse also darkened the legitimacy of the political means by which they had been operating. The techniques that had previously been used to extend the control of the traditional state into the towns and villages by using rural leaders as local agents were discredited, and center-local links snapped. Thus weakened, the state retained only the trappings of mandate and independence, and the old state symbols disappeared or masked the real power, imperialism. Earlier peasant rebellions could aim at overthrowing the emperor or other despot, but who in this new situation could confidently identify a target whose removal could end the grievances and launch a better era? Where a legal government in the capital was deposed, the exploitation of the countryside continued unabated; for exploitation no longer depended so much on national political institutions as on social and economic mechanisms whose operations seemed impervious to quick, direct assault.

The impossibility of winning a fast, decisive victory of course proved a hard lesson to learn. It took the revolutionaries years of costly mistakes before they could grasp the situation that confronted them. Both compromising to buy time and embarking on an insurrectionist path generally proved nearly fatal. In the early stages of revolt, the revolutionaries often realized the slim likelihood of success through insurrection, and considered allying, even if only temporarily, with the noncommunist forces. This was particularly common in anticolonial and nationalist movements, but historically, Communist parties placed themselves at a serious disadvantage in such alliances. In the instances we have seen where Communist parties either ignored the nationalist issue almost completely, as in Burma, or accepted second billing in a nationalist alliance with a stronger party, as in China in the 1920's or Indonesia under Sukarno, the results for the Communist revolution were disastrous. Whoever dominated the nationalist issue was most likely to control the fate of the revolution.

The need for substantial independence from allies can be traced to the central process of Asia's revolutions. Recall that these revolutions have been protracted in the first instance by the diffuseness of political authority in those regions where insurrection has taken root. Revolutionaries in this setting had to be more than rebels; they had in effect to construct their own authority. If a Communist group sought to confirm its own legitimacy by joining with a stronger group in a nationalist alliance, it forfeited its claim to independent authority by confirming the authority of another. The Communists' legitimacy was then granted by the stronger group and, in practice, revocable by it at any time.

The opposite extreme has yielded no more success. Nearly every one of the movements in Asia has tried at least once to win all in a fast game of king-of-the-mountain, and quickly lost. Ironically, it may have been fortunate for the Communists that they were so thoroughly suppressed when they tried to carry out decisive urban insurrections. Had they succeeded, they might have joined the ranks of wrangling warlords and ended up discredited militarists. Instead, in China, Vietnam, and elsewhere, the respective governments pushed the battered Communist organizations into the countryside. Here they attempted to build up the armies that could march on to victory.

It is frequently assumed that the principal advance made by the Asian revolutionaries was the building of these revolutionary armies and the development of new military strategies. This misses the much more basic contrast with previous revolutions. The logic of protractedness under conditions of inferiority keeps forcing the revolutionaries into the total society or far away into splendid isolation. Only the former is revolutionary. Where they relied on military factors alone and shunned involvement in the rural society, as in Burma, the insurrectionists became more bandits than revolutionaries. The protraction of the struggle necessitates a symbiosis between the revo-

lutionaries and their environment that would never have been necessary or possible in the "two or three days of fighting" that Lenin
foresaw. What is learned in a process that is total and perduring is
that war is as much political and social as military. The longer the
revolution goes on the more it must come to terms with the requirements of social support.

Yet once the decision is made to link the revolutionary organs to a
popular base of support—creating "the vast sea in which to drown
the enemy" and in which one must learn to swim—the broader social
circumstances, often rooted historically in peasant rebellion and unrest, become the dominant reality for a Communist leadership. This
new reality must be grasped or else, as Mao put it, "in the end Mr.
Reality will come and pour a bucket of water" over the rebellion. It is
this new reality that makes the revolutionary a student of sociology,
psychology, politics, and economics, as well as someone who can
wield a rifle. It is the prolonged, continuous necessity for adjusting
to reality that has demanded ideological revision and revolutionary
invention.

In forging links with selected sectors of the society, the revolutionaries must retain a wide range of discretion while providing a solid
base of support. This amounts to a great deal more than giving a
group what it wants in return for support or participation. It is clear,
for instance, that relying solely on peasant unrest can cripple the
movement. The peasantry's purposes are limited and short-run, and
often shaped by the memory of ages-old resistance to central authorities. Protracted struggle may necessitate the centralization of authority and the creation of a new order, but the peasants may not perceive
it so. Communist and peasant visions of the preferred outcome of the
upheaval are bound to diverge somewhat, and the gap between them
may grow with the passing of a solid bridging issue such as land reform, or with the campaigns against existing rural social organizations carried out by the Communists after World War II.

If the Communist organization reaches out to bring other sectors
of the populace into the revolutionary movement, a qualitative change
in the character of the movement can occur. The leadership now has
greater long-range flexibility in pursuing its program. The Communist
Party may link villagers and groups with urban roots in a revolutionary coalition and may choose to rely on one or another base of
support depending on the policy it wishes to pursue. At times, the
Party may go much further than that. A coalition implies a union of

diverse groups with standings of general equality for the achievement of agreed-on ends or for action against a common foe. If a Party can go beyond such a coalition and achieve legitimacy in its own right, it can claim a much broader mandate than a coalition. The Party organization, as described in several essays of this volume, becomes more than the sum of its parts. The belief in the Party as a body with a life of its own can approach totality within the membership, where individuals from different classes and geographic areas "forget" their roots in their new allegiance to the Communist organization. Ying-mao Kau has noted this in his discussion of the Party as a microcosm of the urban-rural coalition. The Party elite can count on disciplined support even when the individual members of the organization do not agree on the desirability of a given goal.

This process involves only a fraction of the population more than superficially. Most of the populace are simply aware that a new order is on the rise, and may favor it. Even in times of all-out upheaval— and these are rare—revolution in the full sense of membership in a new hegemony is going on for some, while rebellion or simply dislocation is going on for most. How many are involved fully in the "revolution" is in part a function of the time available to the revolutionaries to allow a natural transformation of loyalties to occur and in part a function of the effort they put into accelerating the transformation through ideological education.

The rise of a new hegemony always triggers a reaction. Its progress forces the counterrevolutionaries to centralize their own power. They normally begin by coalescing around a political or military figure or by turning to foreigners for assistance. But the authority formed in this reaction may be deficient on several counts. Although it is now more centralized, it may not reach any further than previously. It can stop at the formal boundaries of the governmental and military structures, leaving the bulk of the population unimpressed by its claims to legitimacy.

Another feature of the new governmental authority in Asia is that the creation of the counterrevolutionary coalition is usually effected through marriages of convenience of those who could gain from elimination of the Communists. The new government may amass a huge array of supporters, weaponry, and bureaucratic machinery, but find that its interests always take second place to the self-interest of its component parts. It remains less, not more, than the sum of its parts.

The emergence of the counterrevolutionary authority, moreover, has often played a role in legitimizing the revolutionaries. The raison d'être of the Chiang or Diem governments, for example, quickly became the extermination of the Communists. Where the Communist attempts at building effective central authority had preceded those of the counterrevolutionaries, the revolutionaries had already built rural bases and the government's assault inevitably fell most heavily upon the peasantry. This attack on the populace robbed the repressive authority of its legitimacy and strengthened the defensive as well as the order-building appeal of the revolutionary organs. In the past, rebellions had erupted most often in seasons of governmental weakness and subsided with the strengthening of the counterrevolution. With the progress of Communist organization, the rebels went beyond rebellion into revolution; they now aimed at something more than defense, and found a positive weapon, a new hegemony, to oppose the counterrevolutionary regime.

For a long time the revolution and the counterrevolution can create and centralize their authority independently of each other. The contest for power, in the early stages, is not a zero-sum game. Even then, however, the revolutionaries must walk a thin line between concentrating solely on building their own authority and solely opposing the counterrevolutionary authority. If they do the first, they may be isolated and easily smashed; they must capitalize on their opponents' weaknesses when they are themselves in a position of weakness. Neither authority can act in isolation from the other; as one gains, the other to some extent loses. On the other hand, if they concentrate exclusively on their opposition they lose sight of the task that can bring them victory. It is to the Communists' advantage that they are usually the first to remember that the protracted battle is essentially in the society, not with the other side.

Most of the revolutionary movements examined in the preceding essays have not reached the point of successful construction of a strong central authority. They have floundered either in the initial stages of strategic choice, by compromising themselves in nationalist alliances, or in the next stage, by choosing to remain isolated from the rural populace. The argument on protractedness indicates that we should not study their failures in the spirit of reading funeral rites. Rather we should assess to what extent their defeats represent genuine victories for their opponents and to what extent they represent simply another period of stalemate in the race for power.

For those revolutionaries who have won the race, however, the significance of the experience of protracted struggle does not end with the victory proclamation. They have, even before their formal victory, wrought great changes in some sectors of the society. But the long period of symbiosis has brought, as well, great changes in the revolutionaries themselves. Accommodation is a two-way process, wherein the initiators of change must themselves continue to adjust or lose touch. Such adjustments set in motion developments within the revolutionary organization as well as among the general populace. We have noted the relative weakness of social classes in Asia and the critical role played as a consequence by Party intellectuals. Contrary to Lenin's prescriptions and unlike the role played by these intellectuals in the Russian revolution, the successful Asian professional revolutionaries have found a certain amount of "tailism" essential to survival. Over time, that amount accumulated and produced a revolutionary intellectual whom Lenin would not have recognized or perhaps even approved.

Again the protractedness of the struggle has made a profound difference. With revolutions that originated shortly after the Bolshevik revolution—and this is the case for most Asian movements—experiences, lessons, and adaptations have been handed on from one generation to the next. These experiences have led to a movement-wide social vision and the social commitment to it that uniquely stamp the revolutions of Asia. Given the risks in every action, the analyses of the immediate situation and long-term trends and of tactics and the whole process of revolution, have had to be continuously integrated. Each revolutionary experience has been (almost imperceptibly if taken alone) incorporated into the ideology, thereby changing it. An organic relationship between thought and action developed during the protracted struggle, making it all the harder to act in styles not immediately reconcilable with the revolutionary ideology, or to change the ideology fundamentally without repudiating the experiences of millions. The revolutionary vision arising from protracted struggle has wedded ideology and theory to a tradition of mass-based cooperative action and common achievements. In every action the leader is constantly reminded of that vision. It is a vision sweeping enough to match the peasants' traditional utopian outlook, drawing their eyes forward to the creation of something new rather than turning them backward to a grand and shadowy past. There is nothing so profound in the previous "great" revolutions. Their life-spans were too brief. They swept over the participants and quickly faded into faint memories of glory. They disrupted old patterns for a moment; they did not change them for all time.

The persistence of the revolutionary vision in the postrevolutionary era also perpetuates the popularly based drives in which the struggle began. A movement that has won ascendance through the support of the masses cannot so easily forget them when the victory celebration is over, for the ideology, the whole pattern of thinking, forces the new leadership elite to remember the source of its power. Therefore, when the revolutionaries reach the pinnacle, they expect or soon learn to expect any change to occur through the same revolutionary methods as in the past. The vision born of necessity lives on in the commitment to revolutionary style constantly renewed in mass campaigns. Nothing ever quite ends. We have noted that the long-term view of revolutionary conflicts prevents a quick and easy judgment on revolutionary failures. But in the postrevolutionary society, we find that we must exercise the same caution in judging revolutionary success. The takeover is not Armageddon. It simply makes possible yet another qualitative change in the unending process of the revolution.

The complexity of revolutions enmeshed in fundamental social processes, especially those having ages-old histories, leads directly to the planned, continuous wrenching of institutions after the takeover. The goal is not simply the transformation of society, but the transformation of the individual as well, and none realize this so acutely as the revolutionaries who themselves have undergone transformation in furthering the revolution. Continued human transformation becomes the prerequisite and necessary adjunct to any concrete change in society. The choices of policy for the modernization of the nation revolve around reliance on the patterns of popular revolutionary action and on estimates of each policy's effects in strengthening or weakening these patterns.

Such estimates can account for the great reluctance on the part of the Chinese since 1949 to give priority to institution-building. Stable institutions pose an enormous threat to the revolutionary vision and the voluntarist style; they regularize human action and thereby subordinate it to ordered principles. Allowing such a development is tantamount to bringing the protracted struggle to an end.

The relationship between peasant rebellion and Communist revolution in Asia thus can join together a vast array of traditional antagonisms, combative techniques, institutional arrangements, and

visionary drives. The synthesis is usually too complex to work perfectly. When it does work it can generate enormous power and take
on a life of its own that survives both failure and success. Whether it
works or not, the combination highlights the total society, its foundations and its limits, its past and its future, as rebellion or revolution
alone never could do.

*Notes*

# Notes

## Introduction

1. Dankwart Rustow, "The Study of Elites," *World Politics*, 18.4 (July 1966) : 698.

2. For further discussion on the subject of psychological interpretations of revolution, see Isaac Kramnick, "Reflections on Revolution: Definition and Explanation in Recent Scholarship," *History and Theory*, 11.1 (1972).

3. Such scholars provide a social science parallel to Thomas Kuhn's view of scientific revolutions. See Thomas S. Kuhn, *The Structure of Scientific Revolutions* (Chicago: University of Chicago Press, 1962), esp. pp. 91–109. For examples of the approach applied to the study of revolutions, see Paul Schrecker, "Revolution as a Problem in the Philosophy of History," in Carl J. Friedrich, ed., *Revolution* (Nomos VIII) (New York: Atherton Press, 1967), p. 37; and Chalmers Johnson, *Revolutionary Change* (Boston: Little, Brown, 1966), pp. 72–73.

Anthony F. C. Wallace's classic work on revitalization movements makes the birth of a new system a complicated process. He identifies five stages: steady state, period of individual stress, period of cultural distortion (these two necessitating some sort of cultural change), period of revitalization (in which the processes of reformulating cultural principles and building a following for them occur), and new steady state. Wallace, "Revitalization Movements," *American Anthropologist*, 58.2 (Apr. 1956) : 268.

4. Samuel Huntington, *Political Order in Changing Societies* (New Haven, Conn.: Yale University Press, 1968). A useful critique of Huntington's view of revolution is in Charles Tilly, "Does Modernization Breed Revolution?" *Comparative Politics*, 5.3 (Apr. 1973) : 430–36.

5. Huntington, p. 266.

6. Karl Marx, "Preface to *A Contribution to the Critique of Political*

*Economy*" (1859), in Karl Marx and Frederick Engels, *Selected Works* (New York: International Publishers, 1968), pp. 182–83.

7. Marx, "Theses on Feuerbach," *ibid.*, p. 28.

8. For Lenin's classic argument on this issue, see "What Is to Be Done?" in V. I. Lenin, *Collected Works* (Moscow: Foreign Languages Publishing House, 1961), vol. 5. The section "Organisation of Workers and Organisation of Revolutionaries," pp. 451–67, is especially useful in outlining Lenin's view of the role of the revolutionary party.

9. Antonio Gramsci, "The Study of Philosophy and of Historical Materialism," *The Modern Prince and Other Writings* (New York: International Publishers, 1957), pp. 58–75. Tilly's discussion of Gramsci's writings later in this volume emphasizes another side of Gramsci's thought. Here the emphasis is on voluntarism relating to industrial workers, whereas Tilly draws on those writings that are concerned with the conditions necessary for a coalition between workers and peasants.

10. Eric Wolf, *Peasant Wars of the Twentieth Century* (New York: Harper and Row, 1969), pp. 290–92.

11. Hamza Alavi, "Peasants and Revolution," *The Socialist-Register: 1965* (London: Merlin), p. 275.

12. David C. McClelland, "The Two Faces of Power," *Journal of International Affairs*, 24.1 (1970) : 29–47.

13. Konrad Kellen, *Conversations with Enemy Soldiers in Late 1968/ Early 1969: A Study of Motivation and Morale* (Santa Monica, Calif.: RAND, 1970), p. 34.

14. Mao Tse-tung, "The Chinese Revolution and the Chinese Communist Party" (Dec. 1939), in *Selected Works* (Peking: Foreign Languages Press, 1961–65), 2: 308.

15. Mao, "On Some Important Problems of the Party's Present Policy" (Jan. 18, 1948), *ibid.*, 4: 182–83.

16. For a sample of such statements, see *ibid.*, pp. 182, 198, 201.

17. For one attempt to deal with this problem, see John W. Lewis, "The Social Limits of Politically Induced Change," in Chandler Morse, ed., *Modernization by Design* (Ithaca, N.Y.: Cornell University Press, 1969).

*Asian Tenancy Systems and*
*Communist Mobilization of the Peasantry*

1. Arthur Stinchcombe, "Agricultural Enterprise and Rural Class Relations," in Reinhard Bendix and Seymour Martin Lipset, eds., *Class, Status and Power*, 2d ed. (New York: Free Press, 1966).

2. The paragraph above is based on Stinchcombe, *ibid.*

3. Several of the points listed here are based on *ibid.*

4. *Ibid.*

5. Colin Clark and M. R. Haswell, *The Economics of Subsistence Agriculture* (New York: St. Martin's Press, 1967), chap. 6, "Rents and Prices

of Agricultural Land." Clark and Haswell find a strong relationship between rents and agricultural population density in contemporary Italy
and the Philippines, in Chile in 1897, and in 18th-century England. In
France, rents fell as a result of the decline in population during the Hundred Years War and the Great Plagues, but they were rising rapidly in
the late 18th century on the eve of the French Revolution.

6. V. M. Dandekar, "Questions of Economic Analysis and the Consequences of Population Growth," in C. R. Wharton, Jr., ed., *Subsistence
Agriculture and Economic Development* (Chicago: Aldine, 1969), pp.
366–75.

7. Hans Bobek, "The Main Stages in Socio-Economic Evolution from
a Geographical Point of View," in P. C. Wagner and M. W. Mikesell,
*Readings in Cultural Geography* (Chicago: University of Chicago Press,
1962), pp. 218–47; cited in John Duncan Powell, *Political Mobilization
of the Venezuelan Peasant* (Cambridge, Mass.: Harvard University Press,
1971), p. 212.

8. Harry Robinson, *Monsoon Asia: A Geographical Survey* (New
York: Praeger, 1967); R. R. Rawson, *The Monsoon Lands of Asia* (London: Hutchinson Educational, 1963).

9. Karl Pelzer, *Population and Land Utilization* (New York: Institute
of Pacific Relations, 1941), p. 133.

10. Clifford Geertz, *Agricultural Involution* (Berkeley: University of
California Press, 1963).

11. See the discussion in Gunnar Myrdal's *Asian Drama* (New York:
Pantheon, 1968), esp. 1: chap. 10, "Population and the Development of
Resources." For other discussions of "pressure on the land," see Wilbert
E. Moore, *Economic Demography of Eastern and Southern Europe* (New
York: Arno Press, 1972); and Henry Roberts, *Rumania* (Hamden,
Conn.: Archon, 1969).

12. Colin Clark, "Population Growth and Living Standards," in A. N.
Agarwala and S. P. Singh, *The Economics of Underdevelopment* (New
York: Oxford University Press, 1958), p. 37.

13. Roberts.

14. Nicholas Georgescu-Roegen, "The Institutional Aspects of Peasant
Communities: An Analytical View," in Wharton, pp. 61–93.

15. Harry Robinson, *Latin America: A Geographical Survey* (New
York: Praeger, 1964), p. 52.

16. See Table 10-1 in Myrdal, 1: 416.

17. *Ibid.*, p. 430.

18. W. Woytinsky and E. Woytinsky, *World Population and Production* (New York: Twentieth Century Fund, 1953), pp. 463–64.

19. Myrdal, 2: 1056–57.

20. R. H. Tawney, *Land and Labor in China* (Boston: Beacon Press,
1966), p. 64.

21. Karl J. Pelzer, "The Agricultural Foundation," in Ruth T. McVey, ed., *Indonesia* (New Haven, Conn.: Yale University Press, 1963), p. 499.

22. *Ibid.*, p. 162.

23. Erich H. Jacoby, *Agrarian Unrest in Southeast Asia* (London: Asia Publishing House, 1961), pp. 204–5.

24. Tawney, p. 42.

25. Myrdal, 2: 1051.

26. *Ibid.*, p. 1049.

27. *Ibid.*, p. 1050.

28. Robert Sansom, *The Economics of Insurgency in the Mekong Delta* (Cambridge, Mass.: MIT Press, 1970), p. 25.

29. *Ibid.*, p. 18.

30. *Ibid.*, p. 45.

31. H. Wolpe, "Some Problems Concerning Revolutionary Consciousness," *The Socialist Register: 1970* (London: Merlin).

32. *Ibid.*

33. See Karl Marx, *The Eighteenth Brumaire of Louis Napoleon* (New York: International Publishing Co., 1898). I have reviewed Marx's writing on the peasantry's revolutionary potential in an as yet unpublished article titled "Marx and the Agrarian Question."

34. P. Sorokin and C. Zimmerman, *Principles of Rural-Urban Sociology* (New York: Holt, 1929).

35. Donald Zagoria, "A Note on Landlessness, Literacy and Agrarian Communism in India," *European Journal of Sociology*, 13.2 (Winter 1972).

36. *Ibid.*

37. For this and other evidence pointing to the higher politicization of the Kerala Communist voters, half of whom come from the rural poor, see Donald Zagoria, "Kerala and West Bengal," *Problems of Communism*, 20.1 (Jan.-Feb. 1973).

38. See in particular H. Schumann, A. Inkeles, and D. Smith, "Some Psychological Effects and Noneffects of Literacy in a New Nation," *Economic Development and Cultural Change*, 16.1 (Oct. 1967). See also Daniel Lerner, "Toward a Communication Theory of Modernization," in Lucian Pye, ed., *Communications and Political Development* (Princeton, N.J.: Princeton University Press, 1963); and Jack Goody and Ian Watt, "The Consequences of Literacy," *Comparative Studies in Society and History*, 5 (1962–63).

39. Ester Boserup, *The Conditions of Agricultural Growth* (Chicago: Aldine, 1965).

40. *Ibid.*, p. 46.

41. Andre Beteille, "Social Causes of Agrarian Conflict," *The Citizen* (New Delhi), Feb. 14, 1970.

42. For more details, see Donald Zagoria, "The Ecology of Peasant

Communism in India," *American Political Science Review*, 65.1 (Mar. 1971).

43. *Ibid.*

44. Roy Hofheinz, Jr., "The Ecology of Chinese Communist Success: Rural Influence Patterns, 1923–45," in A. Doak Barnett, ed., *Chinese Communist Politics in Action* (Seattle: University of Washington Press, 1969).

45. Roy Hofheinz, Jr., "Peasant Movement and Rural Revolution: Chinese Communists in the Countryside, 1923–1927," unpub. diss., Harvard University, 1966.

46. *Ibid.*, p. 220.

47. Edward J. Mitchell, "Some Econometrics of the Huk Rebellion," *American Political Science Review*, 63.4 (Dec. 1969).

48. Jane Price, "Chinese Communist Land Reform and Peasant Mobilization," paper delivered to the University of Connecticut Symposium on the history of the Chinese Communist movement, 1921–71, p. 8.

49. *Ibid.*

50. Edward J. Mitchell, "The Significance of Land Tenure in the Vietnamese Insurgency," *Asian Survey*, 7.8 (Aug. 1967).

51. Jeffrey Paige, "Inequality and Insurgency in Vietnam: A Re-analysis," *World Politics*, 23.1 (Oct. 1970).

52. *Ibid.*, p. 34.

53. *Ibid.*

54. Juan Linz, "Patterns of Land Tenure and Division of Labor and Politics," unpub. paper, n.d.

55. Henry Landsberger, *The Role of Peasant Movements and Revolts in Development* (Ithaca: New York State School of Industrial and Labor Relations, Cornell University, Reprint Series No. 236, n.d.), p. 23. See also Chalmers Johnson, *Peasant Nationalism and Communist Power: The Emergence of Revolutionary China, 1937–1945* (Stanford, Calif.: Stanford University Press, 1962); and Barrington Moore, Jr., *The Social Origins of Dictatorship and Democracy* (Boston: Beacon, 1967).

56. The above paragraph is taken from a very perceptive article by Marion R. Brown entitled "Don't Blame the Campesino," *Ceres* (Sept.-Oct. 1971).

57. Joseph W. Esherick, "Reform, Revolution and Reaction: The 1911 Revolution in Hunan and Hupeh," unpub. Ph.D. diss., University of Michigan, 1971, pp. 5–6.

58. *Ibid.*, p. 7.

59. See the writings of Kathleen Gough in particular.

60. *Times Literary Supplement*, Sept. 3, 1971, p. 1051.

61. Hugh Seton-Watson, *Neither War Nor Peace* (New York: Praeger, 1966), pp. 129–30.

62. Donald Gillin, review of Chalmers Johnson's *Peasant Nationalism*, *Journal of Asian Studies*, 23.2 (Feb. 1964).

63. On land hunger as a factor weakening the "link" between peasants and "overlords," see Barrington Moore, Jr., *Social Origins of Dictatorship*.

64. George Jackson, *Comintern and Peasant in Eastern Europe, 1919–1930* (New York: Columbia University Press, 1966), p. 38.

65. David Mitrany, *Marx Against the Peasant* (New York: Collier, 1961), *passim*.

66. See Mao's "How to Analyze the Classes," written in 1933.

67. Tso-liang Hsiao, *Land Revolution in China, 1930–34* (Seattle: University of Washington Press, 1969), pp. 254–82.

68. On the crucial 1946–49 period, see Price, "Chinese Communist Land Reform."

69. For an analysis of this law and other interesting insights into the Chinese Communist approach to land reform, see Arthur Dommen's unpub. paper, Sept. 1972, comparing the CCP in Kiangsi and the Indian Communists in Naxalbari.

70. I have found several works very stimulating in organizing my thoughts on the conditions for organization of the peasantry. These include Arthur Stinchcombe, "Social Structure and Organizations," in James G. March, ed., *Handbook of Organizations* (Chicago: Rand McNally, 1965); William H. Overholt, *The Sociology of Political Organization: A Study of Organization, Revolution, and Democracy* (Croton-on-Hudson, N.Y.: Hudson Institute, 1972); and Ralf Dahrendorf, *Class and Class Conflict in Industrial Society* (Glencoe, Ill.: Free Press, 1956).

*The Communist Movement and the Peasants: The Case of Korea*

1. For the causes of the general features of these peasant uprisings, see my unpublished essay for the certificate of the East Asian Institute of Columbia University, "A Study of Korean Peasant Uprisings: 1862–1894," 1970.

2. Tsuboe Senji, *Chōsen minzoku dokuritsu undō hishi* (Secret history of the Korean people's independence movement) (Tokyo: Gannandō, 1959), p. 709.

3. Pak Un-sik, *Chōsen dokuritsu undō no ketshi* (Bloody history of the Korean independence movement), trans. into Japanese by Kang Tŏk-sang (Tokyo: Heibonsha, 1972), 1: 183.

4. Kwŏn Ui-sik, "Chosŏn nodong undong palchŏnesŏ Chosŏn Nodong Kongjehoe wa Chosŏn Nodong Yŏnmaenghoe ka suhaenghan yŏkhware taehayŏ" (The roles of the Korean Labor Mutual Aid Association and the Korean Labor League Association in the development of the Korean labor movement), *Yŏksa kwahak* (Historical science), 3 (1961): 74.

On the nature of the organization, see Kim Chun-yŏp and Kim Ch'ang-
sun, *Han'guk Kongsanjuŭi undong-sa* (History of the Korean Communist
movement), 2 vols. (Seoul: Korea University Press, 1967, 1969), 2:
61–65.

5. For further details, see In Chŏng-sik, *Chosŏn nongŏp kyŏngjeron*
(Agricultural economy of Korea) (Seoul: Pangmun Ch'ulp'ansa, 1949),
pp. 51–52; and Mun Chŏng-ch'ang, *Kun'guk Ilbon Chosŏn kangjŏm
samsip-yung-nyŏn sa.* (The thirty-six-year history of the compulsory
occupation of Korea by the militarist Japan) (Seoul: Paengmundang,
1965), 1: 170–80.

6. Hŏ Chang-man, *Ilch'ŏn-gubaek-isim-nyŏn-dae nongmin undong ŭi
palchŏn* (Development of the peasant movement in the 1920's) (Pyong-
yang: Chosŏn Nodongdang Ch'ulp'ansa, 1963), p. 5. Since Hŏ does not
indicate the source of this figure, there is no way to verify it. However,
considering that the amount of registered arable land almost doubled
between 1910 and 1919, from 2,464,904 chŏngbo to 4,324,679 chŏngbo
(see Chōsen Sōtokufu [Government-General of Korea], *Tōkei nempō*
[Annual statistical report] of 1931, p. 92), the figure is not implausible.
The disorder of the Yi dynasty's land policy accounts for the strikingly
low amount of registered land in 1910.

7. Land prices in both countries varied according to area and quality,
but as a rule Korean land fetched only from a tenth to a thirtieth the
price of Japanese land. Though less productive than the generally fertile
Japanese land, the cheap Korean land was highly attractive to investors,
for it could yield up to four times the profit earned on a similar amount
invested in Japanese land. For further details, see Asada Kyōji, *Nihon
teikokushugi to kyū shokuminchi jinushisei* (Japanese colonialism and
the past colonial landlord system) (Tokyo: Ochanomizu Shobō, 1968),
pp. 73–76.

8. *Ibid.,* p. 78.

9. *Tōkei nempō* (1931), p. 119.

10. Hŏ Chang-man, p. 5.

11. There were only 12 cities with a population of more than 20,000
in 1925. Together they contained a mere 4.36 per cent of the total population of the country. For details, see *Chōsen kokusei chōsa hōkoku, 1930*
(The national census of Korea for 1930) (Seoul: Chōsen Sōtokufu,
1935), 2: 26.

12. Hŏ Chang-man, p. 73.

13. For details of the KCP Incidents, see Dae-Sook Suh, *The Korean
Communist Movement, 1918–1948* (Princeton, N.J.: Princeton University Press, 1967), pp. 68–102.

14. For an English version of the December Theses, see Dae-Sook Suh,
ed., *Documents of Korean Communism, 1918–1948* (Princeton, N.J.:
Princeton University Press, 1970), pp. 243–56.

15. Kim Chŏng-suk, "1934–1937 nyŏn Myŏngch'ŏn nongmindŭl ŭi hyŏngmyŏngjŏk chinch'ul" (The revolutionary progress of the peasants of Myongchon from 1934 to 1937), *Yŏksa kwahak*, 3 (1958) : 29.

16. *Teihei Nōmin Kumiai kenkyo jōkyō* (Details of the capture of the Chongpyong Peasant Union) (Seoul: Chōsen Sōtokufu Keimukyoku, 1931) (hereafter cited as *Teihei nōmin*), p. 9.

17. Kōtō Hōin Kenjikyoku, *Shisō ihō* (Thought reports) (hereafter cited as *Shisō ihō*), 2: 46ff; 11: 256, 265.

18. *Teihei nōmin*, pp. 25–26.

19. *Ibid.*, pp. 36–37.

20. *Shisō ihō*, 11: 146.

21. *Ibid.*, 8: 16–18.

22. *Teihei nōmin*, pp. 7–8, 46–67.

23. *Kōtō keisatsu hō* (High police report) (Seoul: Chōsen Sōtokufu Keimukyoku, 1933 [?]), 2: 72.

24. On the committee's activities, see *Shisō ihō*, 11: 154–69.

25. Kim Chŏng-suk, p. 12. I have changed the total figure from 15,349 to 15,957 to correct errors in arithmetic in the source. The precise breakdown was as follows: landlords, 792; independent peasants, 8,299; semi-tenant peasants, 4,331; tenant peasants, 1,824; and slash-and-burn farmers, 711.

26. For details of the various rates of rent, see *Chōsen ni okeru kosaku ni kansuru hōrei oyobi sankō jikō tekiyō* (Summary of the statutes and references related to tenancy in Korea) (Seoul: Chōsen Sōtokufu Nōrinkyoku, 1933), pp. 69–71.

27. Kim Chun-yŏp and Kim Ch'ang-sun, 1: 30–32.

28. Kang Sŏk-ch'ŏn, "Rit'ŭn pogosŏ wa chae-Man Chosŏnin munje" (The Lytton report and the question of Koreans in Manchuria), *Sindonga* (New East Asia), 3.6 (June 1933) : 11.

29. *Ibid.*, pp. 4, 10, 11.

30. Kim Ki-jŏn and Ch'a Sang-ch'an, "Sŏ-Sŏn kwa nam-Sŏn ŭi sasang sang punya" (Popular thought of western and southern Korea), *Kaebyŏk* (The creation), 59 (Sept. 1925) : 111.

31. Eric R. Wolf, "On Peasant Rebellions," in Teodor Shanin, ed., *Peasants and Peasant Societies* (Harmondsworth, Eng.: Penguin, 1971), pp. 269, 271.

*The Vietnamese Revolutionary Alliance:*
*Intellectuals, Workers, and Peasants*

1. For further discussion of the concept of revolution as used here, see Isaac Kramnick, "Reflections on Revolution: Definition and Explanation in Recent Scholarship," *History and Theory*, 11.1 (1972) : 28–31.

2. Feudal is used here to describe a system characterized by a king and

court at the national level and landlord economic and political domination at the village level. For a discussion of definitions of the term, see: M. M. Postan, Foreward to Marc Bloch, *Feudal Society* (Chicago: University of Chicago Press, 1961).

3. Le Thanh Khoi, *Le Viet-nam* (Paris: Editions de Minuit, 1955), pp. 198–99, 217–18, 232.

4. For a detailed study of the effects of French colonialism on the Vietnamese peasantry, see Ngo Vinh Long, *Before the Revolution: The Vietnamese Peasants Under the French* (Cambridge: MIT Press, 1973).

5. For discussions of this traditional alliance between scholars and peasants against foreign invaders, see Vo Nguyen Giap, "Vietnamese Military Traditions," *Vietnam Courier*, n.s., 1 (June 1972); and Nguyen Khac Vien, "Confucianisme et marxism au Vietnam," *Expériences vietnamiennes* (Paris: Editions Sociales, 1970).

6. David G. Marr, *Vietnamese Anticolonialism, 1885–1925* (Berkeley: University of California Press, 1971), pp. 24–29, 44–76.

7. *Ibid.*, p. 254; *Our President Ho Chi Minh* (Hanoi: Foreign Languages Publishing House, 1970), p. 60.

8. Marr, p. 254; Jean Lacouture, *Ho Chi Minh* (New York: Vintage Books, 1968), pp. 12–14.

9. Russell Stetler, ed., Introduction to Vo Nguyen Giap, *The Military Art of People's War: Selected Writings of General Vo Nguyen Giap* (New York: Monthly Review Press, 1970), p. 13.

10. Jean Lacouture, "Uncle Ho's 'Best Nephew,' " *New York Times Magazine*, May 19, 1968.

11. *Vietnam Youth*, (Mar. 1965); *Vietnam Courier*, 254 (Feb. 2, 1970).

12. Lacouture, *Ho Chi Minh*, p. 15.

13. *Vietnamese Studies*, 24 (1970): 50.

14. This account of Phan Boi Chau, Phan Chu Trinh, the Dong Du and Dong Kinh Nghia Thuc movements, and the 1908 peasant demonstrations is based on Marr, *Vietnamese Anticolonialism*. Doan Viet Hoat, "The Development of Modern Higher Education in Viet Nam: A Focus on Cultural and Socio-Political Forces," unpub. diss., Florida State University, 1971 (Ann Arbor, Mich.: University Microfilms, 71–18, 365), is another excellent source on the modernization movement.

15. Marr, p. 209.

16. *Our President Ho Chi Minh*, p. 61.

17. *Ibid.*, p. 62.

18. *Le President Ho Chi Minh* (Hanoi: Editions en Langues Etrangères, 1961), p. 39.

19. Ho Chi Minh, "The Path Which Led Me to Leninism," in Bernard

B. Fall, ed., *Ho Chi Minh on Revolution: Selected Writings, 1920–1966* (New York: Praeger, 1967), pp. 23–25.

20. *Le President Ho Chi Minh*, p. 41.

21. "Annamese Peasant Conditions" and "French Colonialism on Trial" in Fall, *Ho Chi Minh on Revolution*; Minh Tranh, *Mot so y kien ve nong dan Viet-nam* (Opinions on the Vietnamese peasantry) (Hanoi: Su That, 1961), pp. 49–51.

22. *Our President Ho Chi Minh*, p. 73.

23. Marr, pp. 257–60.

24. *Ibid.*, p. 257.

25. *Ibid.*, pp. 249–74.

26. See excerpt from *The Revolutionary Road* and an account of Ho's course in *Vietnam Courier*, 255 (Feb. 9, 1970).

27. Gouvernement Générale de l'Indochine, Direction des Affaires Politiques et de Sûreté Générale, *Contributions à l'histoire des mouvements politiques de l'Indochine française* (Hanoi: Imprimerie d'Extrême-Orient, 1930–33), 4: 19.

28. Truong Chinh, *President Ho Chi Minh, Beloved Leader of the Vietnamese People* (Hanoi: Foreign Languages Publishing House, 1966), pp. 45–46.

29. *An Outline History of the Viet Nam Workers' Party* (Hanoi: Foreign Languages Publishing House, 1970), p. 12.

30. *Viet Nam* (Nov. 1969): 2.

31. Nguyen Luong Bang, "Brought to Political Maturity Thanks to the People and the Party," in *A Heroic People* (Hanoi: Foreign Languages Publishing House, 1965), pp. 22–23.

32. Le Quang Ba, "Reminiscences of Underground Revolutionary Work," in *Vietnamese Studies*, 15 (1968): 29.

33. André Dumarest, *La formation de classes sociales en pays annamite* (Lyon: Imprimerie P. Ferreol, 1935), pp. 57–60.

34. *Ibid.*, p. 78.

35. Doan Viet Hoat, "Development of Modern Higher Education," p. 38.

36. Tran Van Giau, *Giai cap cong nhan Viet-nam* (The Vietnamese working class) (Hanoi: Su That, 1957), p. 108.

37. Dumarest, p. 63; *Vietnamese Studies*, 24 (1970): 56.

38. Duong Van Giao, *L'Indochine pendant la guerre de 1914–1918* (Paris: Budry, 1925), p. 37.

39. *Ibid.*, p. 115.

40. *Ibid.*, p. 116.

41. *Ibid.*, p. 117.

42. Dumarest, p. 64.

43. *Ibid.*, p. 98; Paul Chassaing, "La naissance du prolétariat en Indochine," *La revue du Pacifique*, 12.4 (Apr. 15, 1933): 211.

44. Biographies of Ton Duc Thang in *Vietnam Advances*, 3.10 (Oct. 1958), and 7.2 (Feb. 1962); and in Tran Van Giau, p. 190.

45. Tran Van Giau, pp. 251–54; Phan Thanh Son, "Le mouvement ouvrier vietnamien de 1920 à 1930," in Jean Chesneaux et al., eds., *Tradition et révolution au Vietnam* (Paris: Racine, 1971), pp. 167–70.

46. *Vietnam Advances*, 3.10 (Oct. 1958).

47. *Ibid.*, 7.5 (May 1962), 8.4 (Apr. 1963), 8.7 (July 1963), Hoang Quoc Viet, "Our People, a Very Heroic People," in *A Heroic People*, pp. 150–53.

48. Tran Van Giau, p. 89.

49. Jean Goudal, *Labour Conditions in Indo-China* (Geneva: International Labour Office, 1938), p. 274.

50. Joseph Buttinger, *Vietnam: A Political History* (New York: Praeger, 1968), p. 171.

51. Charles Robequain, *Economic Development of French Indochina* (London: Oxford University Press, 1941), p. 81.

52. See Tran Huy Lieu, *Les soviets du Nghe-Tinh de 1930–1931 au Viet-nam* (Hanoi: Éditions en Langues Etrangères, 1960), esp. pp. 18–21.

53. Pallu de la Barrière, *Histoire de l'expédition de Cochin-chine en 1861* (Paris: Hachette, 1864), pp. 230–231.

54. Truong Buu Lam, *Patterns of Vietnamese Response to Foreign Intervention, 1858–1900* (New Haven, Conn.: Southeast Asia Studies, Yale University, 1967), pp. 27–28.

55. Pierre Gourou, *The Peasants of the Tonkin Delta* (New Haven, Conn.: Human Relations Area Files, 1955), p. 432. Gourou is the major French source on peasant conditions under colonial rule. Other detailed studies include Ngo Vinh Long, *Before the Revolution*; and Truong Chinh and Vo Nguyen Giap, *The Peasant Question (1937–38)* (Data paper number 94) (Ithaca, N.Y.: Southeast Asia Program, Cornell University, 1974).

56. Marr, *Vietnamese Anticolonialism*, p. 207.

57. Tran Huy Lieu, pp. 25–29; Nguyen Duy Trinh, "A Highlight of the Movement," in *In the Enemy's Net; Memoirs from the Revolution* (Hanoi: Foreign Languages Publishing House, 1962), pp. 14–15.

58. Nguyen Duy Trinh, p. 15.

59. See Tran Huy Lieu, pp. 31–56.

60. *Outline History of the Viet Nam Workers' Party*, p. 20.

61. *Ibid.*, pp. 30–31.

62. See Nguyen Khac Vien, "La leçon de judo," in *Expériences vietnamiennes*, pp. 11–14.

*Traditional Modes and Communist Movements:*
*Change and Protest in Indonesia*

1. Harry J. Benda, "Reflections on Asian Communism," *Yale Review*, 56.1 (Oct. 1966) : 12.

2. *Ibid.*, p. 7.

3. See Clifford Geertz, *Agricultural Involution* (Berkeley: University of California Press, 1963).

4. Donald Zagoria, "The Peasant as a Communist Revolutionary in Asia," paper delivered to the Conference on Asian Peasant Revolutions, Saint Croix, Virgin Islands, Jan. 24–28, 1973, p. 20.

5. Sartono Kartodirdjo, "Agrarian Radicalism in Java: Its Setting and Development," in Claire Holt, ed., *Culture and Politics in Indonesia* (Ithaca, N.Y.: Cornell University Press, 1972), pp. 83–84.

6. Benedict R. O'G. Anderson, "The Idea of Power in Javanese Culture," in *ibid.*, p. 53.

7. *Ibid.*

8. Sartono, p. 75.

9. Anderson, p. 54.

10. *Ibid.*, pp. 54–55.

11. See, for example, Sartono, "Agrarian Radicalism"; Sartono Kartodirdjo, *The Peasants' Revolt of Banten in 1888: Its Conditions, Course, and Sequel* (The Hague: Nijhoff, 1966) ; and Benedict R. O'G. Anderson, *Java in a Time of Revolution: Occupation and Resistance, 1944–1946* (Ithaca, N.Y.: Cornell University Press, 1972). In addition to the instances recorded in these works, other post-independence revolts in which the influence of Islamic religious leaders was critical include the "social revolutions" in Atjeh and east Sumatra in 1945–46, the Darul Islam movement in west Java, and the regional rebellions launched in 1958.

12. Clifford Geertz, *The Social History of an Indonesian Town* (Cambridge: MIT Press, 1965), p. 5.

13. Robert Jay, *Javanese Villagers: Social Relations in Rural Modjokuto* (Cambridge, Mass.: MIT Press, 1969), pp. 188–89.

14. Clifford Geertz, "The Javanese Village," in G. William Skinner, ed., *Local, Ethnic, and National Loyalties in Village Indonesia* (New Haven, Conn.: Southeast Asia Studies, Yale University, 1959), p. 34.

15. See Geertz, "Javanese Village"; Jay; and Koentjaraningrat, "Tjelapar: A Village in South Central Java," in Koentjaraningrat, ed., *Villages in Indonesia* (Ithaca, N.Y.: Cornell University Press, 1967), pp. 262–65.

16. Geertz, *Social History*, esp. pp. 4–9, 145–46; Leslie H. Palmier, *Social Status and Power in Java* (London: Athlone, 1960).

17. Geertz, *Social History*, pp. 31–33.

18. Ruth T. McVey gives a brief but illuminating account of the difficulties experienced by Indonesian nationalist movements in establishing stable organization among these strata in the 1920's in *The Rise of Indonesian Communism* (Ithaca, N.Y.: Cornell University Press, 1965). Note her summary comment that "Indonesian workers of the day tended to be interested in unions only during a crisis" (p. 138).

19. George McT. Kahin, preface to Anderson, *Java in a Time of Revolution*, p. vii.

20. *Ibid.*, pp. 16, 32–33.

21. *Ibid.*, esp. pp. 105–9, 168–70, 332–42.

22. *Ibid.*, *passim*; George McT. Kahin, *Nationalism and Revolution in Indonesia* (Ithaca, N.Y.: Cornell University Press, 1952).

23. B. Schrieke, "The Causes and Effects of Communism on the West Coast of Sumatra," *Indonesian Sociological Studies* (Bandung: Van Hoeve, 1955), Part 1; Harry J. Benda and Ruth T. McVey, *The Communist Uprisings of 1926–1927 in Indonesia: Key Documents* (Ithaca, N.Y.: Modern Indonesia Project, Cornell University, 1960); McVey, *Rise of Indonesian Communism*, chap. 12.

24. See Harry J. Benda, *The Crescent and the Rising Sun: Indonesian Islam Under the Japanese Occupation, 1942–1945* (The Hague: W. van Hoere, 1958); and Anderson, *Java in a Time of Revolution*.

25. Anderson, *Java in a Time of Revolution*, pp. 343–45.

26. *Ibid.*, pp. 345–47.

27. On the background to the Madiun affair, see Kahin, *Nationalism*, pp. 286–303; Ruth T. McVey, *The Soviet View of the Indonesian Revolution* (Ithaca, N.Y.: Modern Indonesia Project, Cornell University, 1957), pp. 58–70; and D. N. Aidit, "We Accuse 'Madiun Affair,'" in *Problems of the Indonesian Revolution* (Bandung: Demos, 1963), pp. 103–36.

28. See Robert Jay, *Religion and Politics in Rural Central Java* (New Haven, Conn.: Southeast Asia Studies, Yale University, 1963), pp. 96–97.

29. These outlines were formalized in the first program of the renewed PKI—*Program PKI* (Djakarta, 1953).

30. Donald Hindley, *The Communist Party of Indonesia, 1951–1963* (Berkeley: University of California Press, 1964), pp. 132–59, 160–76; Rex Mortimer, "Class, Social Cleavage and Indonesian Communism," *Indonesia*, 8 (Oct. 1969): 1–20. For an account of PKI political and organizational techniques in north Sumatra in which this aspect of its approach is stressed, see R. William Liddle, *Ethnicity, Party, and National Integration: An Indonesian Case Study* (New Haven, Conn.: Yale University Press, 1970).

31. See in particular D. N. Aidit, "Indonesian Society and the Indonesian Revolution," in *Problems of the Indonesian Revolution*, pp. 4–62;

*Socialisme Indonesia dan Sjarat 2 Pelaksanaan* (Indonesian socialism and ways of achieving it) (Djakarta: Jajasan Pembaruan, 1962) ; *Revolusi Indonesia, Latarbelakang, Sedjarah dan Haridepannja* (The Indonesian revolution, its background, history, and future) (Djakarta: Jajasan Pembaruan, 1964) ; and *Dengan Sastra dan Seni jang Berkepribadian Nasional Mengabdi Buruh, Tani dan Pradjurit* (With a literature and art national in character serving the workers, peasants, and soldiers) (Djakarta: Jajasan Pembaruan, 1964).

32. Hindley, esp. pp. 154–56.

33. For a regional study of a major manufacturing center where these characteristics are pronounced, see Lance Castles, *Religion, Politics, and Economic Behavior in Java: The Kudus Cigarette Industry* (New Haven, Conn.: Southeast Asia Studies, Yale University, 1967), esp. pp. 74–84.

34. On the August 1951 razzia, see Herbert Feith, *The Decline of Contitutional Democracy in Indonesia* (Ithaca, N.Y.: Cornell University Press, 1962), pp. 187–92.

35. See Hindley, pp. 54–59.

36. On the events leading up to the conclusion of a de facto alliance between the PNI and the PKI, see Feith, pp. 163–78.

37. Jay, *Religion and Politics*, pp. 91–94.

38. For the 1955 general election results, see Herbert Feith, *The Indonesian Elections of 1955* (Ithaca, N.Y.: Modern Indonesia Project, Cornell University, 1957) ; and for figures on the 1957 regional elections, see Daniel S. Lev, *The Transition to Guided Democracy in Indonesia, 1957–1959* (Ithaca, N.Y.: Modern Indonesia Project, Cornell University, 1966), pp. 84–105.

39. See Anderson, "Idea of Power," pp. 22–25.

40. The PKI's emphasis on the "Indonesianization of Marxism-Leninism" also carried a strong implicit suggestion of the uniqueness and intrinsic value of Indonesian ways. See D. N. Aidit, "Lessons from the History of the CPI," in *Problems of the Indonesian Revolution*, pp. 171–86.

41. *Tuntutan untuk bekerdja dikalangan kaum tani* (Demands of work among the peasants) (Djakarta: Departemen Agitprop PKI, 1955).

42. See Ruth T. McVey, introduction to Sukarno, *Nationalism, Islam, and Marxism* (Ithaca, N.Y.: Modern Indonesia Project, Cornell University, 1970), p. 16. For a comment on the ambivalence of relations between the villager and the prijaji in traditional society, see Sartono, "Agrarian Radicalism," p. 85. Jay, *Javanese Villagers*, calls attention to its continued existence in the post-independence period (pp. 363–64).

43. By 1957 class retained only a residual symbolic role in PKI propaganda, as is demonstrated by comparing Aidit's article "Indonesian Society and the Indonesian Revolution," which emphasizes a strict Marxian

class scheme, and the Party's action statements, which stress immediate political tasks and conflicts along a "patriotic" and "unpatriotic" dichotomy.

44. See Anderson, "Idea of Power," pp. 34–37.

45. *Ibid.* See Ann Ruth Willner, "The Neotraditional Accommodation to Independence: The Indonesian Case," in Lucian W. Pye, ed., *Cases in Comparative Politics: Asia* (Boston: Little, Brown, 1970), pp. 248–51.

46. D. N. Aidit, *Ever Forward to Storm Imperialism and Feudalism* (Djakarta: Jajasan Pembaruan, 1961).

47. See D. N. Aidit, "The Form of the Class Struggle in Indonesia at the Present Time . . . Is a Struggle of All the Indonesian People Who Are Revolutionary Against Imperialism (Monopoly and Capitalism) and Feudal Remnants," *Harian rakjat* (People's daily), Aug. 20, 1964.

48. D. N. Aidit, "Untuk Pelaksanaan Jang Lebih Konsekwen dari Manifesto Politik" (For the resolute implementation of the political manifesto), *Bingtang Merah* (Red star), July–Aug. 1960, p. 308; *Revolusi Indonesia*, p. 72.

49. Aidit, *Problems of the Indonesian Revolution*, pp. 314–17. The formula, of course, was taken over from the CCP.

50. Sartono, "Agrarian Radicalism," p. 90.

51. Sartono emphasizes the centrality of these themes in millenarian prophecy. *Ibid.*, p. 94.

52. The offensive was proclaimed in Aidit's report to the Central Committee of the PKI in December 1963. See *Set Afire the Banteng Spirit! Ever Onward! No Retreat!* (Peking: Foreign Languages Press, 1964).

53. An account of the land reform campaign and clashes is contained in Rex Mortimer, *The Indonesian Communist Party and Land Reform, 1959–1965* (Melbourne: Centre of Southeast Asian Studies, Monash University, 1972).

54. *Ibid.*

55. See the article by D. N. Aidit in *Review of Indonesia*, May-June-July 1964, p. 31.

56. Benedict R. Anderson and Ruth T. McVey, "A Preliminary Analysis of the October 1, 1965, Coup in Indonesia," Ithaca, N.Y., Modern Indonesia Project, Cornell University, 1971.

57. All accounts of the Indonesian massacres note the element of communal conflict involved. See in particular the detailed account given in John Hughes, *The End of Sukarno* (London: Angus and Robertson, 1968). I have noted elsewhere the concordance between areas where the most bitter clashes over land took place in 1964 and the areas where the death toll in the massacres was highest. Mortimer, *Indonesian Communist Party*, pp. 63–67.

58. The mobilization of the ex-PKI vote for the government party in

the 1971 elections is documented by Kenneth E. Ward, "The Indonesian Elections of 1971: An East Javanese Perspective," unpub. M.A. Thesis, Monash University, 1972.

59. I am indebted to Mr. Ron Hatley for information regarding the attachment of ex-PKI followers to these movements.

60. Ruth T. McVey, introduction to *Nationalism, Islam, and Marxism*, p. 31.

## *The Ethnic and Urban Bases of Communist Revolt in Malaya*

1. Bibliographical note: I have omitted references where these have been included in my *Industrial Conflict in Malaya: Prelude to the Communist Revolt of 1948* (London: Oxford University Press, 1970).

The most factually accurate account of the MCP's history is contained in C. B. McLane, *Soviet Strategies in Southeast Asia: An Exploration of Eastern Policy Under Lenin and Stalin* (Princeton, N.J.: Princeton University Press, 1966). However, the most comprehensive analysis is G. Z. Hanrahan, *The Communist Struggle in Malaya* (New York: Institute of Pacific Relations, 1954). J. H. Brimmell, *Communism in South East Asia* (London: Oxford University Press, 1959), and V. W. W. Purcell, *Malaya: Communist or Free?* (London: Gollancz, 1954), are other useful sources.

Primary sources are regrettably scanty. I have been able to examine scattered MCP documents, broadsheets, and newspapers, but not a consistent collection. Special Branch files have not been available in recent years, and the official history of the Malayan Emergency, produced by Anthony Short of the University of Aberdeen, has been withheld from publication.

2. Hanrahan is the best source for this period, although V. W. W. Purcell, *The Chinese in Malaya* (London: Oxford University Press, 1948), is also very useful. The available sources are quite inadequate for us to make more precise distinctions regarding the social origins of Communist support. We may assume, however, that the message propagated by Chinese teachers was less specifically Marxist-Leninist than generally anti-imperialist and nationalist in character.

3. Similar relationships have been noted by Paul Mus in Vietnam. Unfortunately, Wilfred L. Blythe's major study, *The Impact of Chinese Secret Societies in Malaya* (London: Oxford University Press, 1970), is far too specific, failing to discuss the precise influence of the secret society tradition on Communist organizational forms. However, some broad similarities in initiation rites may be discerned, and it would appear that MCP Traitor Elimination Corps and similar groups commonly acted in more or less the same fashion as a secret society. That Communism performed a protective role, softening the impact of social change, while at

the same time appealing as a doctrine of revolutionary change cannot be proved on the basis of present evidence. However, the dualistic appeal almost certainly operated in the 1940's, when many joined Communist-front groups in order to obtain security and protection.

4. These trends are best documented in C. A. Blythe, *Methods and Conditions of Employment of Chinese Labour in the Federated Malay States* (Kuala Lumpur: Government Printer, 1938), pp. 2–4. Official restriction of the immigration of Chinese men and encouragement of female Chinese immigration in the 1930's contributed to the marked improvement in the Chinese sex ratio from 225 males : 100 females in 1931 to 144 males : 100 females in 1939.

5. Cooperation with French security authorities enabled the Malayan Security Service to arrest a French Comintern agent, Jacques Ducroux, who had been entrusted with a major task of reorganization. His capture, which led to the arrest of 12 of the Party's top leaders, marked the end of attempts to use European cadres to direct the course of Communism in Malaya. See R. Onraet, *Singapore: A Police Background* (London: Dorothy Crisp, 1947), p. 113.

6. Brimmell, p. 148.

7. See, for example, Lam Swee, *My Accusation* (Kuala Lumpur: Government mimeograph, 1951), p. 2; and Lucian W. Pye, *Guerrilla Communism in Malaya: Its Social and Political Meaning* (Princeton, N.J.: Princeton University Press, 1956), pp. 222–34. Anti-British sentiment was very strong and probably related to deep-seated racial prejudice as much as to dislike of British imperialist policies in China and Malaya.

8. Hanrahan, p. 25. Lai Teck, the Secretary-General, seems to have been sent by the Comintern to reorganize the Party in 1937. His precise antecedents and credentials were apparently as little known to the Party as to the security service.

9. The names of enforcement sections of the AEBUS, such as Hot-Blooded Corps and Dare-to-Die Corps, suggest the influence of the secret society tradition.

10. The Chinese comprised 35.2 per cent of the population of British Malaya in 1931 and 44.7 per cent in 1947. Malays and other Malaysians comprised 48.8 per cent and 43.49 per cent, respectively.

11. Pye and others have overemphasized purely territorial factors. Pye notes that about 75 per cent of the peninsula consisted of dense mountainous jungle and suggests that this was a significant handicap to successful armed revolution (p. 99). In fact, despite the proximity of the interior jungles to the coast and the existence of good lines of communication, they could have provided a secure and convenient refuge in which to build up revolutionary bases and eventually to establish liberated zones.

Limitations on effective utilization of the jungle were less physical than social. In the north of the peninsula the surrounding populace of the Malay States of Perlis, Kedah, Kelantan, and Trengganu was overwhelmingly Malay. In the States of Pahang, Perak, Selangor, Negri Sembilan, and Johore and in south Kedah a total of between 400,000 and 500,000 Chinese squatters provided invaluable links between the predominantly Chinese towns, the narrow strip of agriculturally developed countryside, and the interior jungle refuges. But the squatters never constituted a cohesive geographic unit providing truly secure links with the jungle fringes. Indeed, they were scattered over a wide range of territory, from remnants of jungle near the coast to the very interior. Above all they were intermingled with hostile Malays. Moreover, in contrast to the South Vietnamese, their rural roots were shallow, dating back no earlier than the depression. Lacking title to their land and possessing no strong village institutions, they could be resettled in new villages and isolated from revolutionary contacts in a way that was never possible in South Vietnam.

12. Hanrahan suggests that the guerrillas could and should have seized control of the peninsula, but did not do so because they believed Malaya would be reoccupied by a Chinese army (p. 49). In January 1946 Lai Teck justified the decision in terms of current international Communist strategy and the need to maintain a united anti-fascist and anti-imperialist front. *Ibid.*, p. 52. However, the trend of intra-Party debate is not known.

13. The report of the secret Anglo-Malay constitutional working committee was published in December 1946. Since the MCP was clearly aware of the implications of the discussions, which began formally in July, one is at a complete loss to explain why it held off organizing the AMCJA until just before the report was produced.

14. Official uncertainty about the precise implications and future evolution of government policy contributed to MCP uncertainty, as did differences in policy between Singapore and the Malayan Union. In Singapore the Singapore Federation of Trade Unions was registered in June 1947.

15. Hanrahan, p. 51, and others have emphasized the MCP's retention of an armed capacity. But it is important to appreciate that the capacity was latent and required some time to mobilize in 1948.

16. See "Strategic Problems of the Malayan Revolutionary War," in Hanrahan, p. 102. Any attempt to provide an alternative statistical estimate would be misleading.

17. In 1947 Malays comprised about 17.5 per cent of the Malayan Union industrial labor force.

18. Malay labor played an important role in breaking strikes at Port Swettenham and on the large Socfin estates of Klapa Bali and Lime Blas

in May 1948. Growing official support for the entry of Malays into paid labor led to a scheme whereby the chief ministers of two states recruited Malay workers for the United Planting Association of Malaya in early 1948.

19. See Pye, pp. 207–8.

20. Malayan Union Secretariat, file 7949/46, Arkib Negara Malaysia.

21. Dr. Wu Lien Teh to Tan Cheng Lock, Dec. 5, 1946; Tan Cheng Lock to Dr. Wu, Dec. 6. Tan Cheng Lock papers, Arkib Negara Malaysia.

22. *Monthly Review of Chinese Affairs* (Federation of Malaya), Oct. 26, 1948, App. A; Lam Swee, *My Accusation*, p. 6.

23. Between April 1947 and December 1947 the primacy of the political struggle to obtain a more liberal constitution was constantly emphasized; but between December 1947 and early April 1948 strikes were discouraged more as a matter of indecision on the part of the MCP than anything else.

24. As early as 1936 or 1937 a "left opportunist" faction had denounced the semi-open organization of workers and had advocated the policy of educating the militant workers secretly and striving for the establishment of Soviet power. They denounced the anti-imperialist united front policy of the Party and labeled it the political line of the Social Democrats. Similar sentiments were apparently expressed again in August 1945 and March 1947. See Hanrahan, *Communist Struggle*, pp. 23, 49–50; and Brimmell, *Communism*, pp. 146–47.

25. The "Letter" is printed in full in an appendix to C. Gamba, *The Origins of Trade Unionism in Malaya: A Study in Colonial Labour Unrest* (Singapore: Eastern Universities Press, 1962).

26. Since lawbreakers were threatened with arrest, and with banishment if aliens, the MCP probably felt overexposed, and rightly so. Nine important MCP leaders were deported.

27. The Party later accused Lai Teck, alias Mr. Wright, of being a double British and Japanese agent. He was blamed, for example, for the Japanese massacre of about 100 top MCP and MPAJA leaders on Sept. 1, 1942, a massacre from which he was one of the few to escape. The allegations have never been officially confirmed by the British but are widely rumored to be true.

28. Chin Peng, the son of a bicycle shop owner, was born in the small town of Sitiawan in 1921. He was educated at Chinese and English schools and is widely known for his polished public manner. He was only 26 years old at the time of his appointment as acting Secretary.

29. Had the MCP remained relatively quiescent in 1948, the Federation of Malaya government would have had no excuse to introduce the amended Trade Union Ordinance and could never have enforced a state of emergency. One assumes that there would have been continuing pres-

sure from the British Government for a steady liberalization of policy. There would then have been ample scope for the gradual expansion of open front activities on the lines of those in Singapore in the mid-1950's. As it happened, however, the twin legacies of emergency restrictions and conservative Chinese politicization were to place insuperable obstacles in the way of a large-scale revival of open front activities in the Federation of Malaya.

30. For a discussion of this and subsequent points, see my *The 1948 Communist Revolt in Malaya: A Note on Historical Sources and Interpretation, with a Reply by General de Cruz* (Occasional Paper No. 9) (Singapore: Institute of Southeast Asian Studies, 1971).

31. Stenson, *Industrial Conflict*, pp. 215–24.

32. McLane, *Soviet Strategies*; Brimmell, *Communism*. The full texts of the resolutions are not available.

33. McLane, p. 386.

34. *Ibid.*, p. 387; Brimmell, p. 211.

35. McLane, p. 387.

36. *Ibid.*; Brimmell, p. 211.

37. An editorial in the MCP broadsheet *Voice of the Worker*, May 5, 1948, probably gave a clear indication of MCP assumptions: "Nothing good can come of talking to the British Imperialists, as their laws are flexible. But if you have strength, they will make concessions; if you retract, they will advance further and attack you and will not allow you to exist." The MCP took over complete control of the daily *Min Sheng Pao* and established its English-language *M.C.P. Review* in early June.

38. "Strategic Problems of the Malayan Revolutionary War," included as an appendix in Hanrahan, *Communist Struggle*, is the first known fully formulated revolutionary program. It was not published until December 1948.

39. There are obvious analogies with the position of both the CCP in 1927–28 and the PKI in 1926 and again in 1965.

40. Registration policies and police controls are such that radical Chinese-led unions have been quickly declared illegal and crushed.

41. The Malayan Races Liberation Army was then obliged to fall back on the support and protection of isolated aboriginal groups, which could not conceivably provide it with the means of reestablishing a mass political movement.

42. It would appear that leading British officials had hoped to sponsor a conservative nationalist movement in the shape of the multiracial Independence of Malaya Party in 1951. After the IMP was decisively defeated at the Kuala Lumpur polls by the United Malays National Organization–Malayan Chinese Association electoral alliance, and when the Alliance

Party began pressing in 1954 for early independence, the British continued to favor more conservative groups.

43. *Revolution and the Social System* (Stanford, Calif.: Hoover Institution, 1964).

## Burmese Communist Schisms

1. Most prominently, M. N. Roy, Mao Tse-tung, and Ho Chi Minh, but the list should also include Sneevliet of Indonesia, Kim Il-sung of Korea, and Tokuda Kyiichi of Japan.

2. Premier Le Duan and Vo Nguyen Giap of North Vietnam are now familiar names in this category. The Burmese seem to have been the only Southeast Asians who took the Indian movement seriously, the writers most influenced being Thein Pe Myint and Thakin Ba Tin (Goshal). Prince Souvanavong of Laos and Nai Pridi Phanomyong of Thailand have demonstrated respect for the Chinese achievements but have written little of note.

3. The Irish Free State movement was important to the Burmese as early as 1920. See John Cady, *History of Modern Burma* (Ithaca, N.Y.: Cornell University Press, 1958), p. 211.

4. Thein Pe Myint, *Kyaw Nyein* (Rangoon: Shwe-pyi-dan Press, 1961), pp. 53–57. See also Thakin Tin Mya, *Bone ba-wa-hmar hpyint* (On the causes of our condition) (Rangoon: Pagan Publishing House, 1966), vol. 1.

5. Thakin Tin Mya, 1: 336ff.

6. *Ibid.*, 4: 297–98.

7. See Ruth McVey, *The Calcutta Conference and the Southeast Asian Uprisings* (Ithaca, N.Y.: Modern Indonesia Project, Cornell University, 1958).

8. Thakin Tin Mya, 4: 298.

9. Thein Pe Myint, *Taw-hlan-yei kala naing-ngan-yei Atwei-akyon-mya* (Political events during the revolutionary pre-independence period) (Rangoon: Ramuna Sarpay Publishing House, 1967), pp. 277–87.

10. *Ibid.*, p. 403. Thein Pe himself claims that he resigned from the Party, but Thakin Tin Mya terms it a purge.

11. Yebaw Mya et al., *Thakin than tun ei-nau-son nei-mya* (The last days of Than Tun) (Rangoon: Sarpay Beikman Press, 1970), 2: 655.

12. *Ibid.*, pp. 656–61.        13. *Ibid.*

14. *Ibid.*, 1: 677–82.        15. *Ibid.*

16. *The Burmese Way to Socialism* (Rangoon: Information Department, 1962).

17. Yebaw Mya et al., 2: 6–10.        18. *Ibid.*

19. *Ibid.*, pp. 13–20.

20. *Ibid.*, at pp. 19–20.              21. *Ibid.*
22. *Ibid.*, 1: 53–56.                   23. *Ibid.*
24. *Ibid.*, pp. 60–62.                  25. *Ibid.*, pp. 143–46.
26. *Ibid.*, p. 385.                     27. *Ibid.*, pp. 385–86.

28. Aung San, "Blue Print for Burma," *The Guardian*, Mar. 1955, pp. 33–35; cited in Josef Silverstein, ed., *The Political Legacy of Aung San* (Data Paper No. 86) (Ithaca, N.Y.: Southeast Asia Program, Cornell University, 1973), p. 13.

## Toward an Exchange Theory of Revolution

1. Peter M. Blau, *Exchange and Power in Social Life* (New York: Wiley, 1964), pp. 3–4.

2. Jeffrey Race, *War Comes to Long An: Revolutionary Conflict in a Vietnamese Province* (Berkeley: University of California Press, 1972).

3. Peter M. Blau and W. Richard Scott, *Formal Organizations* (San Francisco: Chandler, 1962).

4. *Ibid.*, p. 237.

5. Blau, *Exchange and Power*, p. 209.

6. Respective references are as follows: George C. Homans, *Human Behavior: Its Elementary Forms* (New York: Harcourt, Brace and World, 1961); Chester I. Barnard, *The Functions of the Executive* (Cambridge, Mass.: Harvard University Press, 1938); Alvin W. Gouldner, "The Norm of Reciprocity: A Preliminary Statement," *American Sociological Review*, 25.2 (Apr. 1960). For economics the literature is summarized in Peter Newman, *The Theory of Exchange* (Englewood Cliffs, N.J.: Prentice-Hall, 1965). On the use of exchange analysis in sociology, see Blau, *Exchange and Power*; Blau's entry under "Social Exchange" in the *International Encyclopedia of the Social Sciences* (New York: Macmillan and Free Press, 1968); and John W. Thibaut and Harold H. Kelley, *The Social Psychology of Groups* (New York: Wiley, 1959). Within political science major citations are Sol Levine and Paul E. White, "Exchange as a Conceptual Framework for the Study of Interorganizational Relationships," *Administrative Science Quarterly*, 5 (1960); R. L. Curry, Jr., and L. L. Wade, *A Theory of Political Exchange: Economic Reasoning in Political Analysis* (Englewood Cliffs, N.J.: Prentice-Hall, 1968); Robert H. Salisbury, "An Exchange Theory of Interest Groups," *Midwest Journal of Political Science*, 13.1 (Feb. 1969); James C. Scott, "Patron-Client Politics and Political Change in Southeast Asia," *American Political Science Review*, 66.1 (Mar. 1972); and Scott, "The Erosion of Patron-Client Bonds and Social Change in Rural Southeast Asia," *Journal of Asian Studies*, 32.1 (Nov. 1972).

7. Blau, *Exchange and Power*, pp. 21–22, 29.

8. Here it seems to me that exchange analysis goes far in clarifying an unexplored insight in the literature: that the amount of power in a system is not fixed but is a significant variable. The discussion in the preceding pages shows power can be "created" through a willingness to enter into exchange relationships. For the development of this insight, see Talcott Parsons, "The Distribution of Power in American Society," *World Politics*, 10.1 (Oct. 1957); Frederick W. Frey, *The Turkish Political Elite* (Cambridge, Mass.: MIT Press, 1965), chap. 13; Frey, "Political Development, Power and Communications in Turkey," in Lucian W. Pye, ed., *Communications and Political Development* (Princeton, N.J.: Princeton University Press, 1963); and Samuel P. Huntington, *Political Order in Changing Societies* (New Haven, Conn.: Yale University Press, 1968), pp. 143–45.

9. Blau, *Exchange and Power*, p. 24.

10. See Blau and Scott, *Formal Organizations*, pp. 100–104, for a discussion of this distinction and an example of a measurement technique to separate the two effects.

11. See Peter M. Blau, *The Dynamics of Bureaucracy* (Chicago: University of Chicago Press, 1955); and Blau and Scott, chap. 5.

12. Robert Sansom, *The Economics of Insurgency in the Mekong Delta* (Cambridge, Mass.: MIT Press, 1970), chap. 2.

13. See Blau and Scott, pp. 121–24, for a sophisticated discussion of this subject and citations of empirical studies.

14. To put all the incentives I have discussed into Etzioni's typology, those regarding wealth and income were remunerative; those regarding power and status were normative; and those regarding protection were coercive. Amitai Etzioni, *A Comparative Analysis of Complex Organizations* (New York: Free Press, 1961), chaps. 2 and 3.

15. For a discussion of this term, see Blau and Scott, *Formal Organizations*, pp. 230–31.

16. Following the Central Committee decision promulgated in the document "The Path of the Revolution in the South." See Race, *War Comes to Long An*, pp. 73–81.

17. *Ibid.*, pp. 184–89, plus the microfilm interview transcript cited there.

18. In *War Comes to Long An* this structure was formulated as "contingent incentives." A subsequent review of the literature reveals that many observers (some apparently independently of others) have concluded that this reward structure has significant motivational consequences. See, for example, Talcott Parsons and Edward A. Shils, eds., *Toward a General Theory of Action* (Cambridge, Mass.: Harvard University Press, 1951), pp. 14–16 ("double contingency"); B. F. Skinner,

*Contingencies of Reinforcement: A Theoretical Analysis* (New York: Appleton, 1969) ; Gouldner, "The Norm of Reciprocity"; and Mancur Olson, *The Logic of Collective Action* (Cambridge, Mass.: Harvard University Press, 1965) ("selective incentives").

19. Talcott Parsons, *Essays in Sociological Theory* (Glencoe, Ill.: Free Press, 1954), pp. 143–47, 239–46. Katz and Kahn have developed a typology of "institutionalization" that would see a stage of "elaboration of structure" at this point. Daniel Katz and Robert L. Kahn, *The Social Psychology of Organizations* (New York: Wiley, 1966), pp. 77–83.

20. See, for example, Charles A. Joiner, "The Organizational Theory of Revolutionary Warfare," *Vietnam Perspectives*, 2.3 (Feb. 1967). Joiner's article is actually an approving review of Douglas Pike's *Viet Cong*, another work advocating the organizational explanation of revolutionary success and the usefulness of administrative measures in counterrevolution.

21. Harold Hotelling, "Stability in Competition," *Economic Journal*, 39.153 (Mar. 1929), treats inelastic demand on a one-dimensional continuum; Arthur Smithies, "Optimum Location in Spatial Competition," *Journal of Political Economy*, 49.3 (June 1941), treats elastic demand on a one-dimensional continuum. A sophisticated formal application to politics is developed by Anthony Downs in *An Economic Theory of Democracy* (New York: Harper, 1957); this analysis is critiqued in Donald E. Stokes et al., *Elections and the Political Order* (New York: Wiley, 1966).

22. John T. McAlister, Jr., *Vietnam: The Origins of Revolution* (Garden City, N.Y.: Doubleday, 1971), p. 330.

23. Robert Scigliano, *South Vietnam: Nation Under Stress* (Boston: Houghton Mifflin, 1964), p. 80. A forthcoming work by John Donnell provides an excellent and more extensive treatment of the problem, especially the chapter entitled "The Government Versus the Nationalist Parties."

24. Scigliano, pp. 40–43, 86, 91–98.

25. Huntington, *Political Order*, p. 78.

26. *Ibid.*, pp. 7, 401, 89, respectively.

27. In "Peasants in Politics," unpub. ms., Dept. of Political Science, Tufts University.

28. Scigliano, pp. 31, 32, 62.

29. This is best formulated in Richard M. Emerson, "Power-Dependence Relations," *American Sociological Review*, 27.1 (Feb. 1962).

30. Huntington, *Political Order*, pp. 21, 79, 85.

31. McAlister, *Vietnam*, pp. 22, 240–42.

32. John T. McAlister, Jr., and Paul Mus, *The Vietnamese and Their Revolution* (New York: Harper, 1970), p. 23.

33. Joseph Buttinger, *The Smaller Dragon* (New York: Praeger, 1968), pp. 279–84.

34. For a discussion of these points, see McAlister and Mus, chap. 1; Gerald C. Hickey, *Village in Vietnam* (New Haven, Conn.: Yale University Press, 1964), chaps. 7 and 8; and Lam Le Trinh, "Village Councils— Yesterday and Today," *Viet My*, 3.2 and 3.3 (June and Sept. 1958).

35. Karl W. Deutsch, "Social Mobilization and Political Development," *American Political Science Review*, 55.3 (Sept. 1961) (reprinted in part in Jason L. Finkle and Richard W. Gable, *Political Development and Social Change* [New York: Wiley, 1971]); Huntington, *Political Order*, chap. 1.

36. Huntington, *Political Order*, chap. 4 *passim*.

37. Gerhard E. Lenski, "Status Crystallization: A Non-Vertical Dimension of Social Status," *American Sociological Review*, 19.4 (Aug. 1954); Irwin W. Goffman, "Status Consistency and Preference for Change in Power Distribution," *American Sociological Review*, 22.3 (June 1957); James A. Geschwender, "Continuities in Theories of Status Consistency and Cognitive Dissonance," *Social Forces*, 46.2 (Dec. 1967); Geschwender, "Explorations in the Theory of Social Movements and Revolutions," *Social Forces*, 47.2 (Dec. 1968). The relationship between inconsistency and action is by no means a simple one, as the studies spell out. Also in point here is Almond and Verba's concept of growing "citizen competence." Gabriel Almond and Sidney Verba, *The Civic Culture* (Boston: Little, Brown, 1965), chap. 7.

38. Powell, "Peasants in Politics."

39. See Barrington Moore, Jr., *Social Origins of Dictatorship and Democracy* (Boston: Beacon Press, 1966), esp. pp. 453–83; Sansom, *Economics of Insurgency*; and Sydel F. Silverman, " 'Exploitation' in Rural Central Italy: Structure and Ideology in Stratification Study," *Comparative Studies in Society and History*, 3.3 (July 1970). See also McAlister and Mus, pp. 33, 81–84.

40. The most comprehensive analysis of this process is in James C. Scott's article "The Erosion of Patron-Client Bonds and Social Change in Rural Southeast Asia." Scott's study is, as far as I know, unique in explicitly applying exchange analysis to these secular changes.

41. Joel Migdal, "Peasants in a Shrinking World," unpub. diss., Harvard University, 1972.

42. *Ibid.*, pp. 293, 313.

43. Scigliano, *South Vietnam*, p. 159.

44. Bernard B. Fall, *Street Without Joy: Indochina at War, 1946–54* (Harrisburg, Pa.: Stackpole, 1961), p. 15.

45. This is the distinction that Etzioni makes between "consensus-spheres" 4 and 5: participation versus performance obligations (*Com-*

*parative Analysis*, pp. 128–30). It should be emphasized also that this discussion refers only to what Etzioni calls "lower participants," not organizational leaders. An empirical study by Paul S. Berman confirms for the Vietnamese revolutionary movement what other studies have shown about organizations in general: that the motivational structure of higher participants differs considerably from that of lower. Berman concludes that higher participants became what he calls "the committed," such that revolutionary activity became part of their identity and to some extent decoupled from individual rewards. Paul S. Berman, "The Liberation Armed Forces of the NLF: Compliance and Cohesion in a Revolutionary Army," unpub. diss., MIT, 1970.

46. Chalmers A. Johnson, *Peasant Nationalism and Communist Power* (Stanford, Calif.: Stanford University Press, 1962), pp. 66–67, and chap. 2 *passim*. Lucien Bianco similarly writes: "In relatively peaceful areas (along the Yangtze, for example, where the pro-Japanese Nanking government offered the peasants relative security), the New Fourth Army made little headway and even resorted to destroying the *pao chia* registers and residence certificates to force peasant villagers to oppose the Japanese." *The Origins of the Chinese Revolution* (Stanford, Calif.: Stanford University Press, 1971), p. 103 n24.

47. Jeffrey Race, "The War in Northern Thailand," *Modern Asian Studies* 8.1 (Jan. 1974).

## Utopian Socialist Themes in Maoism

1. Karl Marx, *Grundrisse*, in Marx, *Pre-Capitalist Economic Formations* (New York: International Publishers, 1965), p. 78.

2. Frederick Engels, "The Origins of the Family, Private Property and the State," in Marx and Engels, *Selected Works* (Moscow: Foreign Languages Publishing House, 1949), 2: 294. Marx's best-known statement on the matter appears in *The German Ideology*: "The greatest division of material and mental labour is the separation of town and country. The antagonism between town and country begins with the transition from barbarism to civilization, from tribe to State, from locality to nation, and runs through the whole history of civilization to the present day." Marx and Engels, *The German Ideology* (New York: International Publishers, 1960), p. 43. However, his most interesting and detailed discussions of the problem are to be found in less well-known writings, esp. the *Grundrisse*.

3. Karl Marx, *Capital*, 1st ed. (Chicago: Kerr, 1906), 1: 387.

4. Marx and Engels, *The German Ideology*, pp. 11–12.

5. *Ibid.*, pp. 43–49.

6. Marx and Engels, "Manifesto," in Marx and Engels, *Selected Works*, 1: 37.

7. Marx and Engels, *The German Ideology*, p. 44.

8. *Ibid.*, p. 22.

9. "Manifesto," p. 51.

10. Engels, "The Peasant Question in France and Germany," in Marx and Engels, *Selected Works*, 2: 384.

11. This possibility is discussed by Marx with reference to French peasant support for the dictatorship and the cult of Napoleon III. See his *The Eighteenth Brumaire of Louis Bonaparte* (Chicago: Kerr, 1919), esp. pp. 144–46.

12. Karl Marx, *The Civil War in France* (New York: Labor News Co., 1965), p. 77.

13. "Manifesto," p. 37.

14. *Ibid.*, p. 50.

15. *Ibid.*, pp. 50–51.

16. Preface, *Capital*, 1: 13.

17. "Die moralisierende Kritik und die kritisierende Moral," in Karl Marx, *Selected Writings in Sociology and Social Philosophy* (London: Watts, 1956), p. 240.

18. Engels, "On Social Relations in Russia," in Marx and Engels, *Selected Works*, 2: 46–47.

19. Marx, "Critique of the Gotha Program," *ibid.*, p. 21.

20. Engels, "Socialism: Utopian and Scientific," *ibid.*, p. 124.

21. George Lichtheim, *The Origins of Socialism* (New York: Praeger, 1969), p. 5. Although Lichtheim's statement is generally true, there are some obvious exceptions, most notably Saint-Simon, the champion of modern industrialism and the "father of technocracy."

22. "Manifesto," pp. 58–59.

23. Babouvism, as Lichtheim notes (p. 21), "enters history as an abortive rising of the nascent urban proletariat against a bourgeois regime. . . . The importance of Babouvism lies in the fact that it foreshadowed the themes of the later communist movement, after an industrial working class had come into being." For a discussion of the relationship between the early socialist and communist theories of the French Revolution and the "utopian socialism" of the early nineteenth century, see Lichtheim, pp. 17–38.

24. Quoted in J. L. Talmon, *The Origins of Totalitarian Democracy* (New York: Praeger, 1965), p. 244.

25. *Ibid.*

26. For Fourier's conception of the phalanstery, see *Selections from the Works of Fourier*, tr. Julia Franklin (London: Swan Sonnenschein, 1901), esp. pp. 137–54. Although Fourier did not totally reject modern industry, it was to occupy a subordinate place to agriculture in a new rural setting. "Factories," he wrote (p. 119), "instead of being, as today, concentrated in cities where swarms of wretched people are huddled to-

gether, will be scattered over all the fields and phalanxes of the globe, in order that man, while applying himself to factory labour, should never deviate from the paths of attraction, which tends to make use of factories as accessories to agriculture and a change from it, not as the chief occupation, either for a district or for any of its individuals."

27. Lichtheim, p. 29.

28. Etienne Cabet, *Voyage en Icarie* (Paris: 1846).

29. The literature by and on Owen is, of course, voluminous. For a succinct survey of his ideas, see G. D. H. Cole, *A History of Socialist Thought* (London: Macmillan, 1953), 1: 86–101.

30. Martin Buber, *Paths in Utopia* (Boston: Beacon Press, 1958), *passim*.

31. Quoted in *ibid.*, p. 27.

32. Quoted in *ibid.*, p. 34.

33. Fourier, as Cole observes (1: 65), "wanted the children to follow their natural bents, and to learn a variety of trades by attaching themselves freely to their elders in a sort of manifold apprenticeship.... He held that the best way to learn was to do, and that the way to make children want to learn was to give them the chance of doing. Given free choice, he said, they would pick up easily enough the kinds of knowledge towards which they had a natural attraction." For Fourier's own words on what he termed "harmonic education," see *Selections from the Works of Fourier*, pp. 67–75.

34. A. Walicki, *The Controversy Over Capitalism: Studies in the Social Philosophy of the Russian Populists* (Oxford: Clarendon Press, 1969), pp. 88–90.

35. For a brief summary of Weitling's ideas, see Cole, 1: 226–28.

36. A. Walicki, "Russia," in Ghita Ionescu and Ernest Gellner, *Populism, Its Meaning and National Characteristics* (London: Weidenfeld and Nicolson, 1969), p. 91.

37. This point is brilliantly elaborated in Walicki, *Controversy Over Capitalism*.

38. See esp. the essay "Our Differences," in George Plekhanov, *Selected Philosophical Works* (Moscow: Foreign Languages Publishing House, n.d.), vol. 1; and V. I. Lenin, *Collected Works* (Moscow: Foreign Languages Publishing House, 1960), vols. 1–3.

39. These notions and views were first put forward by Alexander Herzen in the early 1850's, most notably in his highly influential "The Russian People and Socialism." See his *From the Other Shore* (London: Weidenfeld, 1956), pp. 165–208.

40. *Ibid.*, p. 184.

41. With a wealth of economic data, the argument is pursued at tedious

length in Lenin's 1899 work *The Development of Capitalism in Russia.*
See his *Collected Works*, 3: 23–607.

42. Plekhanov, "Our Differences," p. 326.

43. Lenin, "A Characterisation of Economic Romanticism," in *Collected Works*, 2: 229.

44. Lenin, "The Economic Content of Narodism," *ibid.*, 1: 445.

45. Lenin, "The Heritage We Renounce," *ibid.*, 2: 516.

46. Most notably in the unrevised versions of "Analysis of the Classes in Chinese Society" of 1926 and the "Hunan Report" of early 1927. We shall return to these shortly.

47. Mao Tse-tung, *The Chinese Revolution and the Chinese Communist Party* (1939) (Peking: Foreign Languages Press, 1954).

48. Mao, "Analysis of the Classes in Chinese Society." The official *Selected Works* rendition bears little resemblance to the remarkable original document, and the quotations here are from the extracts from the original translated in Stuart Schram, *Political Thought of Mao Tse-tung* (New York: Praeger, 1969), pp. 210–14.

49. *Ibid.*, p. 214.

50. Mao, *The Chinese Revolution*, p. 22.

51. *Ibid.*, p. 5.

52. *Ibid.*, pp. 11–14.

53. *Ibid.*, p. 13.

54. *Ibid.*, pp. 7, 11.

55. Mao Tse-tung, "On Practice," in *Selected Works* (London: Lawrence and Wishart, 1954), 1: 288–89.

56. This point is noted by Schram in his commentary on the original version of the article, p. 203.

57. Mao, "Hunan Report," in *Selected Works*, 1: 22.

58. Mao, *The Chinese Revolution*, pp. 53–55.

59. Quoted in Franco Venturi, *Roots of Revolution* (New York: Grosset, 1966), p. 35.

60. Buber, *Paths in Utopia*, pp. 46–47.

61. Rhoads Murphey, "City and Countryside as Ideological Issues: India and China," *Comparative Studies in Society and History*, 14.3 (June 1972): 253–54. For a fuller discussion of this strand in traditional Chinese thought, see Murphey, "Man and Nature in China," *Modern Asian Studies*, 1.1 (Jan. 1967): 313–33.

62. On the parasitic relationship of the traditional Chinese city, or "garrison town" (the seat of bureaucratic authority and the residence of wealthy gentry), to the countryside, see Fei Hsiao-t'ung, *China's Gentry* (Chicago: University of Chicago Press, 1953), esp. pp. 91–107. As Fei characterizes traditional urban-rural relations (p. 98): "Economic ac-

tivity in these fortified centers of administration . . . was based not on an exchange of goods between producers but on the purchasing power of consumers who gained their wealth largely from exploitative relationships with the country." Whether Chinese peasants generally perceived the town as parasitic and whether, if they did, this generated any significant anti-urban tradition among them are matters that the literature on traditional China does little to clarify.

63. Frederic Wakeman, *Strangers at the Gate* (Berkeley: University of California Press, 1966), pp. 48–51.

64. Mao, "Hunan Report," *Selected Works*, 1: 56–57.

65. *Ibid.*, pp. 24–25.

66. Mao, "On Contradiction," *ibid.*, p. 336. My emphasis.

67. Walicki, *Controversy Over Capitalism*, p. 143. Walicki here refers specifically to Tkachev and Bakunin, although the notion is a central theme in Russian Populist thought in general, announced by Herzen in the early 1850's, as noted earlier.

68. John Lewis, ed., *The City in Communist China* (Stanford, Calif.: Stanford University Press, 1970), p. 1. See also Lewis, "Political Aspects of Mobility in China's Urban Development," *American Political Science Review*, 60.4 (Dec. 1966) : 899–912.

69. Mao, *The Chinese Revolution*, pp. 30–32.

70. Mao, "Report to the Second Plenary Session of the Seventh Central Committee of the Communist Party of China," in *Selected Works* (Peking: Foreign Languages Press, 1961), 4: 363–64.

71. *Ibid.*, p. 374.

72. Mao, "On the People's Democratic Dictatorship," *ibid.*, pp. 411–24.

73. "Resolution on Questions Concerning People's Communes," 6th plenary session of the 8th Central Committee of the CCP (Dec. 10, 1958). New China News Agency, Peking, Dec. 18, 1958. See *Current Background*, 542: 7–22.

74. This political role of the commune was emphasized by Kuan Feng in "A Brief Discussion on the Great Historical Significance of People's Communes," *Che-hsüeh yen-chiu* (Philosophical research), 5 (1958).

75. Wu Chih-p'u, "On People's Communes," *Chung-kuo ch'ing-nien pao* (China youth news), Sept. 16, 1958, in *Selections from China Mainland Magazines*, 524: 5.

76. "Resolution on Questions Concerning People's Communes," p. 8.

77. For a typical example of this emphasis, see Ch'en Po-ta, "Under the Banner of Comrade Mao Tse-tung," *Hung-ch'i* (Red flag), July 16, 1958, in *Selections from China Mainland Magazines*, 138: 5–17.

78. *Ibid.*, p. 16.

79. Ch'en Cheng-liang, "The People's Commune Is a Necessary Product of China's Political and Economic Development," *Hsin chien-she*

(New construction), Nov. 7, 1959, in *Selections from China Mainland Magazines*, 206: 21, 26, 27.

80. Stuart Schram, *Mao Tse-tung* (New York: Simon and Schuster, 1966), p. 318.

81. "Manifesto," p. 51.

## Urban and Rural Strategies in the Chinese Communist Revolution

1. See, for example, Ted R. Gurr, *Why Men Rebel* (Princeton, N.J.: Princeton University Press, 1970); and Ivo K. Feierabend, Rosalind L. Feierabend, and Betty A. Nesvold, "Social Change and Political Violence," in H. D. Graham and Ted R. Gurr, eds., *Violence in America* (Washington, D.C.: U.S. Government Printing Office, 1969), pp. 498–509.

2. See, for example, Thomas C. Schelling, *The Strategy of Conflict* (Cambridge, Mass.: Harvard University Press, 1960); and John W. Lewis, *Leadership in Communist China* (Ithaca, N.Y.: Cornell University Press, 1963).

3. For various approaches, see Harry Eckstein, ed., *Internal War* (New York: Free Press, 1966); and Ivo K. Feierabend et al., eds., *Anger, Violence, and Politics* (Englewood Cliffs, N.J.: Prentice-Hall, 1972).

4. Ho Kan-chih, *A History of the Modern Chinese Revolution* (Peking: Foreign Languages Press, 1959); Benjamin I. Schwartz, *Chinese Communism and the Rise of Mao* (Cambridge, Mass.: Harvard University Press, 1951).

5. Li Ta-chao, "Bolshevism ti sheng-li" (The victory of Bolshevism), *Hsin ch'ing-nien (La Jeunesse)*, 5.5 (Oct. 5, 1918): 447–49.

6. Hatano Ken'ichi, *Shiryō shūsei Chūgoku Kyōsantō shi* (Collected materials on the history of the Chinese Communist Party) (Tokyo: Jiji tsūshin sha, 1961), 1: 21–41.

7. This section is based on Teng Chung-hsia, *Chung-kuo chih-kung yün-tung shih* (A history of the Chinese labor movement) (Peking: Jenmin ch'u-pan she, 1953), pp. 69, 153; Suzue Gen-ichi, *Chūgoku kaihō tōsō shi* (A history of the Chinese struggle for liberation) Tokyo: Ishizaki shoten, 1953), pp. 361–401; and Nym Wales, *The Chinese Labor Movement* (New York: John Day, 1945), p. 54.

8. Ch'en Ta, *Analysis of Strikes in China* (Peking: Chinese Government Bureau of Economic Information, n.d.), p. 5.

9. Lewis, *Leadership*, pp. 110–11.

10. For particularly good accounts of the purges, see Ho Kan-chih; and Hatano Ken'ichi.

11. Gurr, *Why Men Rebel*; Feierabend et al., *Anger*.

12. Max Weber, *The Theory of Social and Economic Organization* (New York: Free Press, 1964), pp. 339–40.

13. This theme is elaborated on in Ying-mao Kau, "The Interrelation of Environment and Strategy in the Chinese Communist Revolution," unpub. paper presented at the London-Cornell Project Conference, Sainte Adele-en-haut, Canada, Aug. 24–30, 1969.

14. Marion J. Levy, Jr., *Modernization and the Structure of Societies* (Princeton, N.J.: Princeton University Press, 1966).

15. Mao Tse-tung, *Selected Works* (Peking: Foreign Languages Press, 1961–65), 4: 363.

16. *Ibid.*, 1: 179–254.

17. *Ibid.*, 2: 79–112.

18. Liao Kai-lung, *Chung-kuo jen-min chieh-fang chan-cheng chien-shih* (A brief history of the Chinese people's war of liberation) (Shanghai: Hai-yen, 1951), p. 9.

19. Mao, 2: 219, 224.

20. See Ying-mao Kau, ed., *The People's Liberation Army and China's Nation-Building* (White Plains, N.Y.: International Arts and Sciences Press, 1973).

21. Ilpyong J. Kim, "Mass Mobilization Policies and Techniques Developed in the Period of the Chinese Soviet Republic," in A. Doak Barnett, ed., *Chinese Communist Politics in Action* (Seattle: University of Washington Press, 1969), pp. 78–98.

22. Lewis, *Leadership.*

23. Mao, 3: 119.

24. Nathan Leites and Charles Wolf, Jr., *Rebellion and Authority* (Chicago: Markham, 1970).

25. Hsiao Kung-chuan, *Rural China* (Seattle: University of Washington Press, 1960).

26. Ramon H. Myers, *The Chinese Peasant Economy* (Cambridge, Mass.: Harvard University Press, 1970).

27. Richard C. Thornton, *The Comintern and the Chinese Communists, 1928–1931* (Seattle: University of Washington Press, 1969); Harold Isaacs, *The Tragedy of the Chinese Revolution* (Stanford, Calif.: Stanford University Press, 1951).

28. For an elaboration, see Ying-mao Kau, "Patterns of Recruitment and Mobility of Urban Cadres," in John W. Lewis, ed., *The City in Communist China* (Stanford, Calif.: Stanford University Press, 1971), pp. 91–121.

29. Chou En-lai, *Mu-ch'ien kung-ch'an-tang ti tsu-chih wen-t'i* (Organizational problems of the Chinese Communist Party at the present time) (Shanghai: n.p., 1929).

30. Mark Selden, *The Yenan Way in Revolutionary China* (Cambridge, Mass.: Harvard University Press, 1971), pp. 113–14, 150–51.

31. Po I-p'o, "Chia-ch'iang tang tsai nung-ts'un-chung ti cheng-chih

kung-tso" (Strengthen the Party's political work in the countryside), *Hsin-Hua yüeh-pao* (New China Monthly), 4.3 (July 25, 1951): 535–37.

32. See, for example, Ch'en Yün, *Tsen-yang tso i-ko kung-ch'an-tang-yüan* (How to be a Communist Party member; May 30, 1939) (Canton: Hsin-Hua shu-tien, 1950); Robert C. North, *Kuomintang and Chinese Communist Elites* (Stanford, Calif.: Stanford University Press, 1952); Chou En-lai; Selden; and Po I-p'o.

33. See preceding note.

34. The estimate is based on Derek J. Waller, "The Evolution of the Chinese Communist Political Elite, 1931–56," in Robert A. Scalapino, ed., *Elites in the People's Republic of China* (Seattle: University of Washington Press, 1972), pp. 41–66; Selden, *Yenan Way*; Kau, "Patterns of Recruitment and Mobility"; Ch'en Yün; North; Chou En-lai; and Po I-p'o.

35. See preceding note.

36. Harold D. Lasswell, *Power and Personality* (New York: Viking, 1962); Eric Hoffer, *The True Believer* (New York: Harper, 1951).

37. Mao, *Selected Works*, 4: 363.

38. *Ibid.*

39. Lai Chih-yen, ed., *Chieh-kuan ch'eng-shih ti kung-tso ching-yen* (Work experience in the takeover of the cities) (Canton: Jen-min ch'u-pan she, n.d.).

40. Mao, 4: 337–40.

41. Lai Chih-yen.

42. *Hsin min-chu chu-i kung-shang cheng-ts'e* (The new democratic industry and commerce policy) (Hong Kong: Hsin-min-chu ch'u-pan she, 1949); Mao, 4: 157–76.

43. For a fuller treatment, see Kau, "Interrelation of Environment and Strategy."

44. See, for example, A. Doak Barnett, *China on the Eve of Communist Takeover* (New York: Praeger, 1963).

45. For an excellent analytic model, see Tang Tsou and Morton H. Halperin, "Mao Tse-tung's Revolutionary Strategy and Peking's International Behavior," *American Political Science Review*, 59.1 (Mar. 1965): 80–99.

*Town and Country in Revolution*

1. Antonio Gramsci, *Il risorgimento* (Turin: Einaudi, 1949), p. 104.

2. *Ibid.*, p. 95.

3. *Ibid.*, pp. 95–96.

4. *Ibid.*, p. 96.

5. Edward J. Mitchell, "Land Tenure and Rebellion: A Statistical Analysis of Factors Affecting Government Control in South Vietnam"

(Santa Monica: RAND Corporation Memo. RM-5181-ARPA, abridged, June 1967).

6. See Robert L. Sansom, *The Economics of Insurgency in the Mekong Delta of Vietnam* (Cambridge: M.I.T. Press, 1970); and Jeffrey Paige, "Inequality and Insurgency in Vietnam: A Reanalysis," *World Politics,* 23.1 (Oct. 1970): 24–37.

7. Nathan Leites and Charles Wolf, Jr., *Rebellion and Authority: An Analytic Essay on Insurgent Conflicts* (Chicago: Markham, 1970), p. 154.

8. Antonio Gramsci, *La questione meridionale* (Rome: Rinascità, 1951), p. 20.

9. *Ibid.*, p. 22.

10. See John M. Cammett, *Antonio Gramsci and the Origins of Italian Communism* (Stanford, Calif.: Stanford University Press, 1967), pp. 174–76.

11. Charles Tilly, "Postscript: Western Statemaking and Theories of Political Transformation," in Charles Tilly, ed., *The Formation of National States in Western Europe* (Princeton, N.J.: Princeton University Press, forthcoming, Fall 1974).

12. Samuel P. Huntington, *Political Order in Changing Societies* (New Haven, Conn.: Yale University Press, 1968).

13. See Anton Blok, *The Mafia of a Sicilian Village, 1860–1960* (New York: Harper and Row, 1973).

14. For more on this point, see Charles Tilly, "Revolutions and Collective Violence," in Fred I. Greenstein and Nelson Polsby, eds., *Handbook of Political Science* (Reading, Mass.: Addison-Wesley, forthcoming, Spring 1975).

15. Richard K. Beardsley, John W. Hall, and Robert E. Ward, *Village Japan* (Chicago: University of Chicago Press, 1959).

16. Thomas C. Smith, *The Agrarian Origins of Modern Japan* (New York: Atheneum, 1959), p. 59.

17. Jean Chesneaux, "La participation des classes populaires au mouvement national chinois (XIXe-XXe siècles)," in Commission Internationale d'Histoire des Mouvements Sociaux et des Structures Sociales, eds., *Mouvements nationaux d'indépendance et classes populaires aux XIXe et XXe siècles en Occident et en Orient* (Paris: Armand Colin, 1971), 1: 577.

18. Winston Hsieh, "Triads, Salt Smugglers, and Local Uprisings: Observations on the Social and Economic Background of the Waichow Revolution of 1911," in Jean Chesneaux, ed., *Popular Movements and Secret Societies in China, 1840–1950* (Stanford, Calif.: Stanford University Press, 1972).

19. D. E. H. Russell, *Rebellion and Armed Force* (New York: Academic Press, 1974).

20. Eric Wolf, *Peasant Wars of the Twentieth Century* (New York: Harper and Row, 1969).

21. Hugh Borton, *Peasant Uprisings in Japan of the Tokugawa Period*, 2d ed. (New York: Paragon Book Reprint Corporation, 1968). (First published in 1938.)

22. See Gabriel Ardant, *Théorie sociologique de l'impôt* (Paris: SEVPEN, 1965), 2 vols.; and Ardant, *Histoire de l'impôt* (Paris: Fayard, 1971–72), 2 vols.

23. Borton, p. 81.

24. *Ibid.*, p. 82.

25. *Ibid.*

26. Barrington Moore, Jr., *Social Origins of Dictatorship and Democracy* (Boston: Beacon Press, 1966), p. 256.

27. G. William Skinner, "The City in Chinese Society," unpub. paper, Research Conference on Urban Society in Traditional China, Wentworth-by-the-Sea, N.H., 1968.

28. Chiang Siang-tseh, *The Nien Rebellion* (Seattle: University of Washington Press, 1954), pp. 37–38.

29. Philip A. Kuhn, *Rebellion and Its Enemies in Late Imperial China* (Cambridge, Mass.: Harvard University Press, 1970).

30. Franz Michael, *The Taiping Rebellion. History and Documents* (Seattle: University of Washington Press, 1966), 2 vols.

31. John Lust, "Secret Societies, Popular Movements, and the 1911 Revolution," in Chesneaux, *Popular Movements and Secret Societies*, pp. 192–93.

32. *Ibid.*, p. 193.

*Index*

# Index